D1480845

Camping Grounds

Camping Grounds

*Public Nature in American Life from
the Civil War to the Occupy Movement*

PHOEBE S. K. YOUNG

OXFORD
UNIVERSITY PRESS

OXFORD
UNIVERSITY PRESS

Oxford University Press is a department of the University of Oxford. It furthers the University's objective of excellence in research, scholarship, and education by publishing worldwide. Oxford is a registered trade mark of Oxford University Press in the UK and certain other countries.

Published in the United States of America by Oxford University Press
198 Madison Avenue, New York, NY 10016, United States of America.

Library of Congress Cataloging-in-Publication Data
Names: Young, Phoebe S. K. (Phoebe Schroeder Kropp), 1970– author.
Title: Camping grounds : public nature in American life from the Civil War
to the Occupy Movement / Phoebe S.K. Young.
Description: New York : Oxford University Press, [2021] | Includes index.
Identifiers: LCCN 2020045699 (print) | LCCN 2020045700 (ebook) |
ISBN 9780195372410 (hardback) | ISBN 9780190093570 (epub) |
ISBN 9780190093587
Subjects: LCSH: Camps—United States—History. | Camps—United States—
Political aspects. | Nature—Effect of human beings on. |
United States—History—Civil War, 1861–1865. |
Occupy movement—United States—History—21st century.
Classification: LCC GV193.Y68 2021 (print) | LCC GV193 (ebook) |
DDC 796.540973—dc23
LC record available at https://lccn.loc.gov/2020045699
LC ebook record available at https://lccn.loc.gov/2020045700

DOI: 10.1093/oso/9780195372410.001.0001

1 3 5 7 9 8 6 4 2
Printed by Sheridan Books, Inc., United States of America

For Noah

Contents

Acknowledgments

WHEN I STARTED EXPLORATORY research for this book and gave an initial conference presentation about it, I was pregnant with my first child. The book will appear in print as he is poised to graduate high school. Reaching the final stages of completing the manuscript, I wondered whether I should share this openly. I asked a graduate student if she thought the story would appear disheartening, or even slightly ridiculous, to aspiring academics or writers. Her response was not what I expected. To her, the idea that someone might keep at the same project for so long and see it through suggested dedication and tenacity. She was probably too polite to add insanity, but she helped me decide that it was worth going public, though neither as a cautionary tale nor a recommended option. Instead, looking back on this long road, I am struck by the fact that I have been as lucky as I was stubborn. And not alone.

Many people and organizations supported me, and my ability to keep working on this book, over the years, and I'm grateful for the chance to offer my long overdue thanks and recognition. Multiple sources provided me with crucial funding for research and writing. A Mellon Faculty Fellowship from the Penn Humanities Forum at the University of Pennsylvania aided research in the early stages. The ACLS-Oscar Handlin Fellowship from the American Council of Learned Societies supported a full year of focus on the project in 2010, just before Occupy Wall Street arrived to expand the chronology and scramble the analysis. Grants from various units at the University of Colorado Boulder supported new rounds of research, including an Associate Professor Growth Grant from the Leadership Education for Advancement & Promotion program in 2013, a Kayden Research Grant from the College of Arts and Sciences in 2015, and a Travel Grant from the Graduate Committee for the Arts & Humanities in 2018. In addition, a Faculty Fellowship from the Center for Humanities and the Arts, combined with a university-supported semester of sabbatical, allowed major writing progress in 2016–17. Another

Kayden Research Grant defrayed the costs of illustration, and the Department of History helped secure a subvention for the publication. Without any one of these sources of support, the finish line would have been even further away.

I had the great opportunity to present chunks of this project at conferences and invited seminars, all of which prodded my thinking in important ways. I appreciate the responses of commentators and fellow panelists at the American Society for Environmental History, American Studies Association, Organization of American Historians, and Western History Association. In particular, Kathleen Franz, Lawrence Glickman, John Kasson, Kevin Leonard, and Kathryn Morse provided memorable comments that stuck with me as I worked through tough spots. I was grateful also to have the chance to present works-in-progress with different groups of colleagues and students in the United States, Ireland, and Brazil. For these experiences, I want to thank Shane Bergin, Jorge Simoes De Sa Martins, Anne Fuchs, Robert Hoberman, Michelle Jolly, Sarah Krakoff, Margaret Miller, James C. O'Connell, Jed Purdy, Conrad Edick Wright, and others who sponsored and contributed to these productive discussions, from which I emerged with new energy and perspectives on this work.

I appreciate the permission to include in this book revised versions of previously published material. Portions of chapter 3 appeared as "Wilderness Wives and Dishwashing Husbands: Comfort and the Domestic Arts of Camping Out, 1880–1910," in the fall 2009 issue of *Journal of Social History* (vol. 43, no. 1). An essay for a 2010 anthology provided a critical space for me to think about urban camping, the results of which informed several spots throughout the book. It appeared as "Sleeping Outside: The Political Natures of Urban Camping," in *Cities and Nature in the American West*, edited by Char Miller (Reno: University of Nevada Press). Finally, revised portions of an essay on the Occupy movement appear in chapter 6: "Bring Tent: The Occupy Movement and the Politics of Public Nature in America," originally published in *Rendering Nature: Animals, Bodies, Places, Politics*, edited by Marguerite S. Shaffer and Phoebe S. K. Young (Philadelphia: University of Pennsylvania Press, 2015). Many thanks to Bob Lockhart and Penn Press for permission to republish this work, and even more for the support of that volume and the whole Third Nature endeavor.

Archivists, librarians, and staff provided invaluable assistance at multiple stages. I failed to record the names of every individual who helped me, but I remain deeply appreciative of and continually amazed at the work they all do to make the work of historians possible. Special gratitude to Lauren Bissonette at the Forest History Society; Peter Blodgett at the Henry E. Huntington

Library; Frederick Carey, Thea Lindquist, and the whole Interlibrary Loan Department at the University of Colorado Boulder Library; Danielle Castronovo at California Academy of Sciences; Clare Come at Shenandoah National Park; Deborah Dandridge, Kathy Lafferty, and Letha Johnson at the Kenneth Spencer Research Library, University of Kansas; J. Wendel Cox, in the Western History/Genealogy Department of the Denver Public Library; John Gookin, Diane Shoutis, and Shannon Rochelle at the National Outdoor Leadership School headquarters in Lander, Wyoming; Nicole Grady in the Holt-Atherton Special Collections, University of the Pacific; Jo Harmon, Jamie Kingman-Rice, and Nicholas Noyes at the Maine Historical Society; AnnaLee Pauls in Rare Books and Special Collections, Firestone Library, Princeton University; Douglas Remley at the National Museum of African-American History and Culture; and lastly, the dedicated archivists at the National Archives and Records Administration, both in College Park, Maryland, and Denver, Colorado, especially Eric Bittner, Joseph Schwartz, and Cody White.

Undergraduate and graduate students in my environmental, cultural, and US history courses over the years have contributed in significant if sometimes intangible ways to my evolving thinking about the history of camping. Several have made valuable material contributions as well. Leigh Mesler at the University of Pennsylvania helped me compile my original database and copies of early recreational camping articles. At the University of Colorado Boulder, I am sincerely grateful for the assistance of Colin Church with research on the Green Book at the Schomburg Center for Black Culture in the New York Public Library; Rebecca Kennedy de Lorenzini for mining the Barrows' Family Papers at the Houghton Library at Harvard University; Sara Porterfield, for locating and burrowing into the Outward Bound file trailer in Leadville, Colorado; and Michael Weeks with collecting news and commentary on Occupy Wall Street, even as it was unfolding. Lastly, Amelia Brackett Hogstad and Jason Hogstad performed heroic work tracking down image permissions and files, a daunting task at any time, made even more complicated than usual amidst the COVID-19 pandemic.

Scholars of American culture and environment have been superb fellow travelers on this journey, providing inspiration, challenge, and friendship. I appreciate being able to learn from and share ideas with Carl Abbott, Erika Bsumek, Catherine Cocks, Annie Gilbert Coleman, Rachel Gross, John Herron, Sarah Igo, Danika Medak-Saltzman, Susan A. Miller, William Philpott, Sarah Schrank, and Terence Young. Not only has this book benefited greatly from the friendly dialogues and astute questions of these and other remarkable scholars, but they have also made the usual rounds of academic travels a genuine pleasure. I'm profoundly grateful I had the chance to let Hal Rothman know how much I valued his support and unsubtle nudges, and I wish he was still here to tell me what he really thought of the final product.

I was fortunate to find a home at CU Boulder, and even more so to find myself among such smart and generous colleagues. Thomas Andrews, Elizabeth Fenn, Paul Hammer, Martha Hanna, Vilja Hulden, Susan Kent, Patricia Limerick, Daryl Maeda, Kellie Matthews, Natalie Mendoza, Helmut Müller-Sievers, and David Shneer (who left us much too soon) have all contributed to and supported this project in different ways. I'm especially thankful for Paul Sutter and Marcia Yonemoto for long-running historical conversations, steadfast support, professional advice, and genuine comradeship through and beyond academic matters. No matter where I've plied my trade over the decades, Bill Deverell has been in my corner with guidance, empathy, and friendship. A better mentor would be nigh impossible to find in this business, or outside of it.

It has been my great privilege to work with Susan Ferber, Executive Editor at Oxford University Press. Her patience and counsel with this shape-shifting project at every stage of a process that took a dozen years to go from proposal to manuscript alone has been simply extraordinary. The book is so much better for her keen eye and sharp pen. I also owe a great debt to the reviewers for the Press, who gave so generously of their time to offer unusually detailed reports. Their careful readings and specific suggestions proved invaluable in the revision process, and improved key areas throughout the book. Everyone else at OUP provided great support in turning the manuscript into the book, particularly Jeremy Toynbee.

I treasure my Boulder community, with special gratitude to Patricia and Sean, Marc, Jeanette, Jamie, Jill, Jim, John, Heather and Don, Kevin and Anna. You all keep me going and smiling in myriad ways. Tehya and Ken, Theresa, Noelle, and Cari have all done so from afar and going back many years. A host of friends, family, and colleagues pitched in generously during the final scramble and for their contributions, I am grateful to Michael for citation expertise, Jeff for the jacket photo, Mark for the timely sleuthing, Sarah and Sean for the coaching on legal matters, and Angus and Marcia for the skilled wordsmithing.

Were it not for the constant encouragement, prodding, and brilliance of Marguerite Shaffer, this book might not exist in current, or perhaps any, form. Peggy never tired of talking about camping, reminding me to keep plugging away, or showing me how to see bolder implications. Nearly every page bears an imprint of her insights and our discussions, from the gardens at the Huntington to her porch in Maine. I look forward to our continued collaborations and adventures in nature and culture.

My family has been so supportive across the ups and downs and sideways jogs of life and academia. I thank all of you, from across the corners of the country, for your love and support. Along with the whole Young-Auletta-Kropp-Gelles-Finkelstein-Glaros band, I deeply appreciate Edie and Michael for welcoming me and for the fellowship of historians and writers; my dad Al, and Leila, for unswerving faith and support; my sister Chloe, for sharing your courage, wisdom, and laughter, each at the exact right time; and, my mom, Gale, whose humming, clacking Selectric typewriter all those years ago reminds me of the satisfactions and absurdities of being a scholar/professor/ mother, and who is still there to help me through those tricky days.

To my sons, Darby and Marlin, who have only ever had a mom working on a book, I thank you for your patience and your impatience, for all the happy reasons to close the computer and make the book wait just a little bit longer. You are, both and each of you, most wonderful humans.

And finally, I count myself lucky beyond measure to share this journey, and this life, with a marvelous partner. Noah, thank you for reading all the words, talking about all the tents, reciting all the things we *get* to do, sharing all the writer's tears. This is for you, that we may we sit on the stoop watching the sunset, remember back to the time of writing the book, and then amble on together.

Camping Grounds

Introduction

A PUBLIC NATURE

IN JANUARY 2012, Jonathan Jarvis, the director of the National Park Service (NPS), took a seat at the witness table in a packed hearing room on Capitol Hill. He was there to speak on the subject of the inquiry: camping. Specifically, the House Oversight Committee on the District of Columbia wanted to know "who made the decision to allow indefinite camping" in McPherson Square, a park two miles north of where they sat, where 300-some protestors were encamped on National Park land. Jarvis faced the panel wearing the familiar olive-green Park Ranger uniform, his flat-brimmed Smokey Bear hat on the table in front of him. He cleared his throat and began his testimony, declaring that "all 397 of America's national parks, but especially the national parks in Washington, D.C., are places where citizens' rights are guaranteed under our nation's Constitution." His short opening statement explained that both Park Service regulations and US Park Police enforcement approaches to First Amendment demonstrations prioritized this principle, alongside the need "to protect public health and safety." Nowhere did Jarvis mention the word "camping."

Trey Gowdy, House member from South Carolina and chair of the hearing, immediately challenged Jarvis's premise, arguing that Washington enjoyed no special privileges when it came to the Constitution. "There are no more First Amendment rights in this town than there are in any other city, town, hamlet in this country." The question he posed in the very next sentence, however, pressed Jarvis on the camping point: "So define camping for me, because you say it's prohibited. Tell me what it is. . . . What is the definition of camping?"

This seemed like a trick question. Everyone knows what camping is. Pack up the car and hit the road in search of a shady spot in the great outdoors. After wrestling the poles and rain fly into place, unzip the tent and unroll the sleeping bags. As stars peek out in the clear skies above, sit around the campfire with friends or family and roast some marshmallows. Whether or not you like spending your leisure time in this fashion, the scene is instantly recognizable as camping in America. There are, of course, variations on the theme. Through-hikers backpacking the Appalachian Trail or retirees taking the Winnebago out for an adventure on the open road. Kids with flashlights in the backyard or glampers enjoying gourmet meals under canvas. But no matter the type, to camp means to abandon one's indoor home, voluntarily and temporarily, for outdoor recreation. Why do it? Many would say they camp to find respite from the stress and grind of modern life or to enjoy the beauty of nature. Others might camp to connect with people or to seek a thrilling encounter with the wild. Whatever the reason, the definition of camping doesn't seem tricky or controversial. Americans expect the government to provide basic campsite infrastructure—a picnic table, a parking spot for the car, and a place for the fire—for a modest fee in nearly every corner of the country. Why would the head of the National Park Service need to define camping? It seems obvious.

Jarvis, however, did not have the luxury of relying upon this presumptive definition. He found himself on the hot seat in the early days of 2012, well into the nationwide campaign of the Occupy Wall Street movement. Protestors had been occupying McPherson Square for three months by that point. Its dozens of tents formed one of the movement's last and longest standing sites of protest, and they were frustrating Trey Gowdy to no end. While Jarvis had repeatedly called it a demonstration, to several committee members it looked as if protesters were camping. Gowdy insisted on a definition that would explain this situation, because, he said "I need to go back to South Carolina and tell everyone who wants to spend the summer in one of our parks what camping is and what it is not. So, define camping for me, juxtaposed with a 24-hour vigil, because you seem inclined to draw a distinction and I can't draw a distinction."[1] Occupy threw prevailing assumptions about camping into disarray.

Jarvis tried to clarify. Occupy was engaged in a political action for which camping served as a means, as opposed to the recreational pursuit in which camping was the end in itself. Unsatisfied, some representatives pressed him to identify the most fundamental feature of camping, rather than the motivating factor. Jarvis boiled this down to "sleeping or preparing to sleep" outdoors. He might have quoted the National Park Service regulation for Capital Region parks that defined camping as "the use of park land for living accommodation purposes such as sleeping activities, or making preparations to sleep (including the laying down of bedding for the purpose of sleeping) or storing personal belongings, or making any fire, or using any tents or shelter or other structure or vehicle for sleeping or doing any digging or earth breaking."[2] This legalistic description reduces camping to something that seems purely functional, virtually devoid of any of its pleasing qualities. According to this definition, Occupy was in fact camping. Protestors were sleeping, preparing to sleep, and using tents for sleeping, actions that were expressly prohibited at McPherson Square. Jarvis insisted, however, that they were equally engaged in First Amendment expressions through a 24-hour vigil, actions that were explicitly permitted there. For him, protecting these rights superseded prosecuting scofflaw campers.

Occupiers themselves argued vehemently that they were not camping at all, holding tightly to a definition of their action as peaceable assembly to petition the government for redress of grievances. While they framed their protest as the opposite of recreational camping, it was the camping that made Occupy stand out. The tents allowed protestors to take over urban spaces for weeks at a time, driving city, campus, and federal officials to utter distraction. As one reporter described it, what made Occupy Wall Street so memorable and challenging was this sense of "permanence," a grip on space only made possible by the tents and sleeping bags. "These were not drop-in protests, pop-up rallies. These people came, and they came with Coleman camp stoves."[3] Since when did Coleman camp stoves signal serious protest? More typically they conjured pancake breakfasts and temporary recreation, not political discourse and long-term struggle.

Of course, prolonged camping in urban spaces usually implied something else entirely. People experiencing homelessness camp out all the time, without seeking the attention Occupiers hoped to receive. For those without housing, living outdoors is neither a recreational choice nor a political message. Encampments of people without homes to go back to have become familiar features of public spaces and city politics, further complicating any simple definition of camping. Advocates for the unsheltered often focus their efforts on finding ways for people to avoid having to camp. Urban officials and Congressional representatives have worked to shut down both homeless and Occupy encampments. At the same time, state and federal agencies, not to mention the outdoor industry, have consistently encouraged Americans to go on camping vacations and rejuvenate themselves in the great outdoors.

In the heart of the nation's capital rather than out among its natural wonders, Jonathan Jarvis, Trey Gowdy, Occupy protestors, and members of Congress slowly seemed to realize that defining camping in American culture and history was far more complicated than it appeared. What does it mean to camp, and why does it matter? These are the core questions animating this book. By exploring the shifting meanings of camping through the last century and a half, it argues that this activity was (and remains) key to how Americans think about their relationships to nature, the nation, and each other.

WHEN WRITERS AND historians have approached these questions, they have tended to focus on the recreational side of the story, separate from political or functional versions. These narratives locate what it means to camp in the quest for experience in nature, where the desires for "roughing it" reveal Americans' misgivings about modern life or justifications for leisure. They also examine camping as a form of tourism or one among many outdoor pursuits, alongside fishing or hunting, for example. Within this defined category camping developed multiple forms, waxing and waning in popularity over the decades.[4] Accounting for these shifts deepens understandings of the classic picture of recreational camping, yet cannot resolve the conundrums generated at McPherson Square.

Different social contexts can offer alternate perspectives on camping and outdoor recreation. The establishment of conservation-minded regulations in the late nineteenth century, for example, accompanied a first wave of camping enthusiasts. This indicated not just new affinities for nature, but also how those approaches privileged the choices and leisure of white, upper-class urbanites at the expense of nonwhite, lower-class, and rural uses of natural resources.[5] In a different vein, scholars of architecture and design have examined camps as built environments and found consistencies across wide-ranging circumstances. These studies draw provocative, often unsettling links between extremely varied camps not ordinarily found in the same conversation, such as the Guantanamo Bay detention camp and the Burning Man arts festival in Nevada. These experiments use "camp" as a ripe interpretive tool and pose challenging questions about how people "make places and homes in these itinerant times," though they intentionally resist drawing unified conclusions.[6]

If these approaches confirm that a simple definition of camping is no longer possible, a mushrooming list of camps offers little help in connecting such divergent contexts. What do we do with the inescapable realization that camping has run the gamut of possible meanings, never solely representing recreational choice, social marginality, or political expression? How can it be simultaneously a vacation option, a design for unstable futures, and a refuge of last resort? If neither motivation (i.e., recreation) nor appearance (i.e., something one does with tents) resolve what camping means as a whole or why it mattered enough to spark heated Congressional debate, then surely it is necessary to grapple with how these forms developed in relation to each other.

This book employs a pair of concepts that bring a substantial subset of camping practices into greater focus, at least for US history. The first is "public nature," defined as both outdoor spaces and ideas about those spaces as settings where people work out relationships to nature, nation, and each other. Such spaces might range from vast tracts of land identified for possible future settlement and clearly designated national preserves to roadside areas with unclear jurisdiction and small parks amidst crowded cityscapes. This book focuses less on the collection of particular spaces that make up public nature, or their physical characteristics, than on the way Americans have understood the existence and significance of public access to the outdoors. Getting out into nature has often appeared to be a way to escape the central struggles of the nation's history. The labels applied to these spaces put them at a remove: the hinterlands, the backcountry, the wilderness.[7] Yet thinking about the relationship between multiple forms of camping and varied outdoor spaces suggests that public nature serves instead as a critical forum at the center of American culture and politics. Since the middle of the nineteenth century, Americans have laid claim to public nature, often through forms of camping and with assertions of belonging, obligation, identity, and visibility.

These uses of public nature lead to the other useful framework that can shed further light on the meanings of camping: the social contract. Generations of Americans have worked out, and continued to rework, the terms of the nation's social contract—the set of beliefs and structures that establish what citizens and the government owe to each other. Ideas about the social contract were baked into the founding of the United States itself, and from the start public nature was key to those negotiations. English philosopher John Locke outlined the essential contours in the late seventeenth century. For him, as for many of the nation's framers, the social contract revolved around the notion of property.[8] The very purpose of government, or even the reason for forming a community at all, was to ensure that individuals had confidence in the security of their property. Government maintained peaceful order and acted for the public good by protecting a citizen's property from encroachments by others and from government itself.[9]

What Locke and the founders meant by property was somewhat different than it might sound. Neither land alone nor a list of personal items, property emerged when a person took something out of its natural state and applied labor to improve it. If someone cut down a tree for timber to build a house, this action removed the tree from the public reserve of nature and made it private property. When farmers planted seeds in the earth, they mixed their labor with the land and thereby created their own property. This labor turned what had previously been a resource held in common for the whole community into a parcel one individual could call their own. The process of creating agricultural property was fundamental to the Anglo-American vision of this social contract, and the North American continent appeared to contain a great deal of fertile land in the state of nature awaiting the touch of human labor. Locke's formula was enticing: "As much land as a man tills, plants, improves, cultivates, and can use the product of, so much is his property."[10]

Thomas Jefferson understood this framework as central to the political culture of the new United States. In *Notes on the State of Virginia* (1785) he observed that "we have an immensity of land courting" aspiring farmers and hoped all citizens would take up the plow and cultivate it. With a characteristic flourish, he declared that "those who labor in the earth are the chosen people of God," who reaped not just crops but "substantial and genuine virtue."[11] Individuals and government alike sought to acquire and organize land to foster the creation of property with this mission in mind. In this agrarian version of the social contract, citizens held up their end by laboring to create farm property, which contributed to the nation's virtue and economy. The government reciprocated not only by protecting property and but also by fostering access to ever more land. This concept contained several contradictions and consequences. Among others, it sidestepped the glaring fact of the enslavement of a large portion of the agricultural labor force. Moreover, it underwrote the conquest and removal of Indigenous people from their land, claiming eligible sites of public nature to convert to property. Enabled by these mechanisms, the idea of access to land and the ability to work and own it became a bedrock of American identity.[12]

Neither John Locke nor Thomas Jefferson were likely to have gone camping in a way that we might recognize. They probably slept outside at some point, but the activity would not have carried the same meanings that it would for later generations. Nonetheless, the agrarian social contract and concept of public nature that emerged from their era would come to shape how subsequent generations understood camping. From an economic standpoint the early republic never fully realized Jefferson's agrarian dream, abuzz from the start with trade and commodity production alongside farming. The role of government and the character of property would evolve as well, as agriculture could not always guarantee economic stability or civic standing. As early as the Constitutional Convention, James Madison worried about "future times [when] a great majority of the people will not only be without land, but any other sort of property."[13] What was the fate of a social contract based on mixing one's labor with nature, when that effort no longer produced the property necessary to sustain it?

As the growth of industrial capitalism and urban centers began to shift the US economy and population even further away from the farm, the government, land reformers, and agrarian dreamers tried to forestall this fate. The nineteenth century saw waves of agricultural improvement efforts, pushes for westward expansion and conquest, and public land distribution schemes, culminating perhaps in the Homestead Act—an audacious attempt to reconfirm the agrarian basis of the republic in the midst of a Civil War. The 1862 Act kept up the pressure to open up Native lands for agricultural purposes and for non-native settlers to convert it to property by dint of their labor. The government remained in the business of distributing land from its store of public nature for individual enterprise, agrarian or otherwise.[14]

The concept of public nature, however, began to shift amidst calls for going "back to the land," which started as early as the 1840s. Publications in this genre, including Henry David Thoreau's *Walden* (1854), suggested growing unease with the dislocating experiences of urban industrial life. Thoreau's memoir of two years of cabin life outside Concord, Massachusetts, was little noticed at the time, but the back-to-the-land impulse took off before long. As popular New England essayist Donald Grant Mitchell reminded Americans in 1863, "God, and nature, and sunshine, have not gone by; nor yet the trees, and the flowers, or green turf, or a thousand kindred charms, which the humblest farmer has in his keeping" and which remained for all Americans to reclaim.[15]

Back-to-the-land movements peaked in the first decades of the twentieth century, just as the nation became for the first time a majority urban society.[16] Unable to turn back the clock on urban-industrialism, Americans began to seek alternate connections to land and nature. Between 1910 and 1920 agriculture ceased to be the most common occupation for Americans, surpassed for the first time by manufacturing.[17] Despite—or perhaps because of—such demographic trends, beliefs in the importance of rural life persisted, while also evolving alongside the changing nation. The government's interest in securing tracts of public nature endured but expanded beyond the distribution model to include protecting natural resources, particularly forested areas and spectacular landscapes. While this broadening definition of nature's purpose did not slow the process of dispossessing Indigenous inhabitants of their land, farming itself did not keep pace.[18] It seemed the fewer farmers there were, the greater the attachment to rural ideals and the outdoor life became. Only a handful among those harboring dreams of going back to the land pursued full-time rural life. But the idea grew in popularity because it held out a vision of regaining individual control in the volatile new world that industrialism brought into being—cyclical financial panics, economic vulnerability, erosion of independent work. Working one's own land, one's own property, suggested a vision of simplicity and control. While never a practical society-wide response to those national transformations, it continued to hold cultural relevance by proffering a remedy for feelings of disorientation and insecurity.[19]

Many were drawn to the "simple life" and "arts and crafts" movements, where rural life might produce not farm goods but private contentment, with "moral, emotional, and spiritual benefits" for the individual. Time spent in the outdoors, engaged in simple tasks, away from the hurly-burly of urban life, could help recapture a sense of equilibrium and independence of mind, if not of pocketbook. Moreover, those who pursued the simple life could question the new urban industrial order in historically resonant ways, but without forsaking modern life wholesale.[20]

Acknowledging that tilling the soil and owning property were not the only ways to get in "touch with the real and vital things of this life" continued this trend, which would ultimately bring camping into this conversation about public nature. Truman A. DeWeese, a journalist and advertising professional, had little experience in agriculture and less interest in making a serious argument for Americans to return to farming. But his 1913 book *The Bend in the Road* made the case that such rewards were also available by simply spending "a good part of each year in the country." It couldn't be done just by looking at "scenery" by "riding through the country in an automobile," whatever "mental or spiritual elation" that provided. But if "the city man" could "find a place where he can finish well-loved tasks in the deep space of the silent hills," then he would experience all the benefits of rural life—health, happiness, and "rare contentment." While DeWeese wrote of spending his summer on an abandoned farm, camping shared similar characteristics.[21] More than driving through scenery, but less of a commitment to agriculture as a full-time occupation, campers could live simply in the country, if temporarily, and perform some kind of labor in nature, if only symbolically.

As a popular pursuit unto itself, camping arose alongside back-to-the-land movements in the decades after the Civil War. Like DeWeese, campers echoed the appeals of the old agrarian formula, but gave it a modern twist. Rather than mixing labor with land, campers blended leisure with nature, and in that sense they approached the outdoors as consumers, rather than hopeful producers. Much of the story of camping emerges from this long transition toward an urban industrial consumer culture, a significant and well-chronicled transformation in American life. Consumer culture was not an altogether new phenomenon in the late nineteenth century, but attention to its effects intensified. In his influential *Theory of the Leisure Class* (1899), economist Thorstein Veblen coined the term "conspicuous consumption" to explain why people began to flaunt their possessions and leisure time. A person's ability to take a hiatus from labor or to acquire more personal goods became a new way to demonstrate status. This leisure-centered approach contrasted with, and would eventually supplant, labor-based agrarianism, but it did not immediately coalesce into a new social contract. It initially took hold, as Veblen suggested, among a certain elite class before expanding across society.[22] This is true of campers as well, since Americans from the upper classes were among the early adopters of recreational camping.

The gradual shift toward a consumer culture shaped the recreational ethos of camping, with its obvious performance of outdoor leisure.[23] But early recreational camping was different from other forms of consumption like shopping at a department store or from the conspicuous leisure of taking a Grand Tour of Europe. By maintaining some ties to older agrarian ideals, and taking up temporary quarters in the outdoors, campers prototyped a new set of uses for public nature. Access to common land remained important, even in the move away from agriculture. For many Americans who remained suspicious of the newfangled indulgence in leisure and consumption, camping and outdoor recreation seemed to blend these modern practices with time-honored agrarian values. Anxieties about the effects of modernity on American culture thus did not so much drive campers to "rough it" in the woods as allow them to express and assuage those worries in distinctly modern fashion.[24]

At the turn of the twentieth century, worries over the perilous implications of the wholesale embrace of urban industrial consumer culture were amplified by the emerging realization that "nature" was under threat. Modern development encroached upon the nation's vast reserves of natural resources and spectacular landscapes. The establishment of the US Forest Service in 1905 and the National Park Service in 1916 codified what was by then a generation of advocacy on the part of private citizens, like John Muir, and government

efforts, notably led by President Theodore Roosevelt, to forestall private destruction. Conservation of forests, rivers, and wildlife as "public goods," held
in common trust by and for the people, expanded government authority and
national meaning in these spaces.[25] Camping and outdoor recreation weren't
the sole factors driving these endeavors, but they did help to articulate parts
of the justification for preserving these spaces as public nature. Roosevelt, for
example, hoped that these lands could serve as a place for citizens to resist
both the "base spirit of gain" and the appeal of "a life of slothful ease" by
testing their strength and building their character through "natural outdoor
play" and "wisely used leisure."[26]

Though mindful of the critique of commercialism, the National Park
Service understood its purpose in modern terms. Its founding legislation mandated a dual mission: "to promote *and* regulate the use of Federal
areas . . . to provide for the enjoyment" of its landscapes *and* to preserve them
"unimpaired for the enjoyment of future generations." Alongside preservation, early NPS leaders eagerly took up the charge to promote Americans'
enjoyment of the parks, encouraging visitors, and activities like camping,
with advertising techniques drawn directly from new consumer industries.[27]
Herein lay the seeds for a new social contract, with the government starting
to take on responsibilities to provide for citizens' outdoor leisure. The new
recreational ethos of mixing leisure with nature anchored the appeal and
underwrote the steady growth of camping in the decades that followed.

By the 1930s, federally sponsored camping exemplified a new social contract that was coalescing as heir to the faded agrarian one. The New Deal
era solidified a distinctly different relationship between citizens and the
government, and camping showcased the updated role for public nature.
Campground designer and Forest Service plant pathologist Emilio Meinecke
conjured a kind of campers' republic, a social contract wherein citizens had
"a right to a form of recreation" that offers a chance "to live more simply and
closer to nature." Governmental obligations included, on the one hand, "protection of the physical material" and "the essential spirit of the out of doors,"
and on the other, public access, safety, "assured peace" and "enjoyment of the
people." Camping allowed Americans both to be "guests of the nation" and
to claim "part ownership" by establishing a "temporary home" on a "one hundred thirty millionth" share of public nature.[28] Bestowing a sense of "ownership," camping and the outdoor recreational ethos became an implicit right of
citizenship, if not all Americans had equal access to it. Public nature thus continued to serve as grounds for negotiating the nation's social contract, even as
its expected uses, and users, continued to shift.

THIS OVERVIEW ILLUSTRATES how notions of public nature and the social contract can uncover a more complex history of camping. In part, it suggests a way to bring a broader spectrum of campers into the discussion. Whether the tents of Occupy and people experiencing homelessness in this century, or the encampments of tramps and protestors from the last, nonrecreational camping provides a critical context for the rise of the campers' republic and its subsequent fortunes. Accordingly, this book emphasizes the complex interplay of recreational, political, and functional camping. Even with this wider framework, camping remains only one aspect of how Americans have encountered the outdoors, contemplated nature, or expected government service. There are limits to what camping can tell us. Still, looking at camping through these lenses does offer insight into the nation's evolving social contract and the ongoing significance of public nature within it.

The book begins by looking at camping practices amid the disorienting shift from an agrarian society to an urban industrial one. Part One examines the Civil War era and its aftermath, from the 1850s to the 1890s, as the practice of camping began to gain meaning beyond the utilitarian. Chapter 1 considers Union soldiers' and veterans' attempts to make sense of their military camping experiences. Both for individuals, like Maine infantryman John Mead Gould, and for national veterans' organizations, like the Grand Army of the Republic, camping served as an important way to understand the legacy of the war. Soldiers' memories fostered nostalgia and camaraderie, while also providing a platform from which to advocate for a social contract in which veterans became exemplars of the nation. Chapter 2 follows the early travels of John Muir to get a glimpse of the highly mobile landscape of the decades that followed the war, particularly in the South and West. Before he rose to fame as the founder of the Sierra Club, Muir walked the country's roads alongside transient laborers, newly freed African Americans, and Native peoples.[29] He alternately knocked on strangers' doors, slept outside in fear of disease and alligators, and herded sheep in Sierra meadows. These experiences shaped Muir's seminal perspectives on wilderness, which in turn influenced changing views of public nature, including recreational and nonrecreational campers alike in the late nineteenth century.

Part Two traces the birth of the modern recreational ethos between the 1880s and 1940s. Chapter 3 delves into the stories of early leisure camping enthusiasts, largely found among the elite classes, and what they hoped to find by venturing into the outdoors. The numerous stories in proliferating outdoor magazines and guidebooks suggest that rather than being a strictly masculine endeavor, women and families were key to the practice, as campers imagined themselves making temporary homes in the wilderness. They did not have the woods to themselves, however, as the phenomena of tramps, hoboes, and itinerant workers grew during the same era, both in numerical terms and in public alarm about what their seeming rootlessness might portend for the nation. Chapter 4 focuses on how federal agencies responded to the simultaneous growth of recreational camping—popularized among the middle class by the mass production of the automobile in the 1920s—and the challenge of new waves of transients and protestors during the Great Depression. By the 1940s citizens were claiming rights of access to or, in the case of African Americans, protesting exclusion from this public camping landscape.

Part Three assesses the rising dominance of recreational camping, along with its increasing complexity and consequences, in the decades that followed World War II. Chapter 5 looks at how youth who came of age in the 1960s and 1970s shaped new forms of camping to support interests in self-discovery, countercultural values, and environmental awareness. Leaders and participants of the National Outdoor Leadership School, launched in 1965, promoted backcountry styles of camping that fostered younger peoples' critiques of modern society even as they generated new markets for high-tech outdoor gear. Chapter 6 brings the story back to the Occupy movement and its antecedents—particularly a series of political encampments in the nation's capital since the late 1960s. While for many Occupy seemed unprecedented, earlier actions that used camping to protest poverty, racism, the Vietnam War, and homelessness reveal new perspectives on public nature, including some voiced by Supreme Court justices. As Occupy tried to use camping to expand political dialogue, the sharp expansion of unsheltered people camping out in urban spaces, rising to the level of an acute crisis in certain areas, raised the stakes for negotiations over access to public nature and the terms of the social contract.

The epilogue briefly surveys the twenty-first-century landscape of camping—a dizzying continuum encompassing glamping and adventure styles as well as new streams of mobile laborers, from campground hosts to Amazon's CamperForce. Meanwhile, outdoor recreation became key to new claims about human biological needs to spend time enjoying nature. Recreational camping came to promise a good return on private investment in terms of family health and personal well-being, more so than democratic access to public nature. The parallel rise of this justification for leisure camping and the intensifying homeless crisis—both thrown into sharp relief by the COVID-19 pandemic—strongly suggests that the social contract may again be in transition. Public nature, and camping as a method of claiming it, remains a potent forum for these renegotiations.

This book does not attempt to offer an encyclopedic treatment of camping. Trying to include every significant factor even in the history of recreational camping would have been counterproductive, not to mention impossible. That some forms or moments get short shrift here—scouting, sleepaway camps, World War II, RVs and van life, for example—does not mean that they have not been important to the historical development of camping or the experience of individual campers. The selective focus highlights key episodes that provide perspective on how Americans understand access to the outdoors as key to the nation's social contract and that represent significant turning points and figures within it. Further, this book does not attempt to offer a thoroughgoing history of homelessness or protest movements, which are available elsewhere. Instead, it dips into those histories when they collide with the discourse and practice of camping or highlight contests over public nature.

One particular area of exclusion is worth mentioning. Incarceration camps, concentration camps, prison camps, detention camps, and refugee camps are, by and large, not part of this story. While examining these involuntary camps, or why they are called "camps" even when not deploying tents, is worthwhile in its own right, that analysis is not an aim of this book. The campers who appear in these pages include those who resort to sleeping outside under some form of duress, but their practices remain distinct from the powerful coercion or organized violence that spawned those sites. For example, although political factors certainly drove the World War II incarceration of Japanese and Japanese Americans in guarded camp-like outposts scattered across Western states, they were of an entirely different order than the politics that surrounded Occupy Wall Street. The stories of refugees share some commonalities with those who dwell in homeless tent cities, but the camping of tramps, hoboes, and vagrants posed questions about the nation's public nature in the way that refugee camps, perhaps until quite recently, have not. This book does consider several borderline cases, such as Union army camps and "contraband" camps of Black Americans fleeing slavery during the Civil War, in relation to the range of meanings Americans assigned to the act of sleeping outside. However, inasmuch as possible, this book keeps the focus on intentional (or even accidental) camping as opposed to forced camps.

This choice reinforces the book's key questions: What does it mean to camp, and why does it matter? And it serves as a reminder of how the recreational mode of camping represents a particular historical development rather than a universal need to "get back to nature." That Americans have come to prize some forms and places for sleeping outside, while marginalizing and criminalizing others, illustrates how camping embodies certain facets of ongoing national dilemmas. Does sleeping outside promise bodily health or reveal personal weakness? Should tents indicate transience or persistence, leisure or poverty, consumer comfort or political protest? Do encampments warn of social disorder, encourage civic participation, or exemplify the public good? While recreational camping sometimes masquerades as universal, the one form of camping that is without politics, it too arose from a specific outlook and moment in American history. Its development both excluded some Americans and encapsulated a vision of the social contract where citizens could expect their government to provide access to the outdoors for the public good.

To say that recreational camping is a product of history does not mean that people who enjoy it have been duped into falsely believing they are connecting with nature. Many people, myself included, do find genuine connections while camping in the outdoors—to the natural world, to other people, to their inner selves. That capaciousness is in part what gives those outdoor spaces and beliefs about public nature their potency. They hold out the possibility for connectedness beyond our political or economic worlds, even if these places and ideas have been wholly shaped by them. While there's nothing "natural" about the standard issue campsite, with its picnic table, parking spot, and fire ring, it remains a tool for outdoor experience. When we see this set-up as supporting one particular practice among several possibilities for making claims on public nature, camping might complicate our classic mental images. By focusing on that complexity, rather than defining it out, camping can tell us a great deal about the shifting grounds of nature and national belonging in American history.

PART ONE

Outdoor Strategies, 1850s–1890s

I

Comrades and Campfires

THREE DECADES AFTER the Civil War ended, General William Tecumseh Sherman recalled a memorable scene from the Union army's campaign: the evening campfire. "Imagine a group of intelligent soldiers after night—the march done—supper over, and things put away for an early start—a clear sky above and a bright fire beneath, you have the perfection of human comfort and the most perfect incentive to good fellowship." It was a resonant image, a treasured moment removed from the brutality of battle. Yet Sherman, whose earlier *Memoirs* mounted a righteous defense of the "calculated cruelty" required to win the war, was not indulging in any simple nostalgia or sentimentalism. For him, the significance lay in reviving this ritual for modern purposes. He believed it was still important for "the men who 'saved the Union' to . . . meet often at camp-fires; sing their old songs . . . [and] always cultivate the comradeship begotten of war." Younger generations ought to witness and draw wisdom from these "modern 'camp-fires,'" where veterans gathered as "comrades absolutely on equal footing, regardless of former rank, yet subject to self-imposed discipline."[1] While these images bore scant resemblance to the military hierarchy and discipline in actual army camps, the veterans' campfire suggested a symbolic and idealized microcosm for a nation wrestling with new challenges.

The longing for this vision stemmed from the tensions and transformations of the postwar era as much as it reflected any specific experiences of the war. Amid the dislocations that accompanied the enormous growth of American cities, the campfire suggested a simple, rustic outdoor practice, a hallmark of a lost simpler time. Sherman's particular vision, moreover, conjured a sense of equality among citizens, born of an earlier agrarian ideal, when contemporary evidence pointed to growing divides between wealth and poverty. And yet it was not purely backward-looking. This campfire highlighted the emerging figure of "the veteran" as a model citizen, who could in Sherman's words, separate "the true from the false, the brave from the timid, the earnest from the doubtful."[2] The Union veteran embodied the expansion of federal power and continental dominion that followed victory, even while echoing the idealized republic that came before it. Veterans thus came to serve as bellwethers for a nation and a social contract in transformation. It mattered that they did so from camp.

Soldiers, of course, camped as a matter of necessity and obligation. Starting in the Spring of 1861, hundreds of thousands of American men found themselves living in army camps. Neither the numbers nor the experience of sleeping outside made their camping meaningful in the way Sherman was promoting. The Civil War was hardly the first mass camping episode in recent memory. The Overland Trail saw 300,000 people travel west and sleep under the stars for months at a time in the 1830s and 1840s. The California Gold Rush brought thousands more campers to the Sierra Nevada. Moreover, religious "camp meetings" were widespread throughout the early nineteenth century, especially during the Second Great Awakening; the Cane Revival in Kentucky in 1801 drew upward of 20,000 people to its grounds.[3] The significance of Civil War camps lay in what the survivors did when they returned. Veterans shared not only the experience of camping during the war, but importantly, access to a rapidly expanding mass press and a heightened political role to disseminate their memories and imbue them with meaning. While Civil War soldiers made up the biggest wave of mass public camping yet, far more Americans would read and hear about their experiences in the decades that followed.

The reworking of wartime camp experiences in print allowed meaning to emerge from what was, in most cases, an involuntary and regimented endeavor, if not outright drudgery. In the postwar era, veterans went beyond wistful recollections and willingly chose to camp again. Camping became a popular method for reunion, a wholly voluntary practice that fostered veteran identity, fraternal order, national belonging, and political power. In the process, camp became something quite different. Union veterans' organizations and public remembrance privileged certain aspects of camp life as a way of making sense of the war, obscuring both its past unpleasantries and the present problems.

The history of the Grand Army of the Republic (GAR) demonstrates how camp became a key tool for building veteran identity. With 400,000 members by 1890, the GAR was the largest and most powerful organization for Union veterans. While other veterans' groups existed, including societies for officers like the Union League and regimental associations, the GAR recruited veterans on a national level, regardless of rank or unit. Moreover, it sought to blend remembrance with advocacy, particularly for its signature issue of federal veterans' pensions, which candidates for elected office opposed at their peril. The organization used camping to advance this effort on multiple levels, but most notably in its annual gatherings called "National Encampments." These GAR reunions rotated to a different city each year, from Maine to California, from the early 1870s into the 1930s. Not only did the bulk of the veterans camp out in tents during the event, but the public performance of the rituals of camp—the hardtack and coffee, the sitting round the campfire—also became signature activities that evoked the ideal Army camp. Sherman's reverie, in fact, emerged during his attendance at the 1888 National Encampment in Columbus, Ohio. The modern campfires he had in mind were, in fact, the "Camp-Fires of the G.A.R.," as he titled the article. The combined effect of its social and political efforts made the GAR, as one historian has suggested, key to establishing the significance of the "Union veteran in the newly restored Union and, at a deeper level, a story about the new Union itself."[4]

Confederate soldiers slept outside just as much, but they had much less influence in the first few decades after the war. Confederate veterans could not belong to the GAR, and had less access, at least initially, to the claims of ideal citizens or to the media and national politics. The United Confederate Veterans would become an influential veterans' organization in the South, but it emphasized the mythology of the Lost Cause and separateness from the victorious Union more than the egalitarian camaraderie of camp. As the decades went on the GAR would play a vital role in braiding these threads of memory together, in ways that prioritized sectional reconciliation over Union victory and retreated from commitments to Black freedom. The romantic nationalism and revival of militarism of the 1890s began to allow Confederate veterans into a mythology reorganized around the blue-gray brotherhood. Though the Lost Cause captured the nation's imagination by the opening of the twentieth century, capitalizing on the Union's "won cause" remained a major focus in the decades between.[5] The GAR's constant refrain that "they saved the Union" gave northern veterans a special basis on which to claim a meaningful place in an otherwise topsy-turvy postwar nation.

One Union veteran, John Mead Gould (1839–1930), illuminates the ways camping and veteran identity intertwined in life after the war. A bank teller from Portland, Maine, Gould served in three Union army regiments between

April 1861 and March 1866, engaged in multiple battles, including Antietam, and rose to the rank of Major. After a brief interlude as a carpetbagger-entrepreneur, Gould returned to Portland and his job at the bank, where he would work for the rest of his life. His extensive diary detailed many nights spent camping, as soldier and veteran, and with friends and family.[6] He also joined the outpouring of veterans' narratives that appeared in print after the war, publishing both the definitive regimental history of his units, the Maine 1st-10th-29th, and an early recreational camping guidebook: *How to Camp Out: Hints for Camping and Walking* (1877). The camping guidebook was not intended for soldiers or veterans explicitly—they already knew how to camp. Rather, he hoped to pass along the knowledge and meaning of camp to a new generation, for new purposes. It offered a set of social instructions, gleaned from the perspective of a veteran, about how to emulate that "group of intelligent soldiers," gathered around the campfire, as "comrades absolutely on equal footing," in a world where expectations of work, success, and citizenship were shifting under their feet.

While Gould clearly cannot speak for all soldiers or all veterans, his perspectives offer insight into the role of camping, as it moved from an involuntary and functional necessity in the Union army to a symbolic and voluntary activity among veterans in the tumultuous postwar era.[7] Gould and the GAR together offer a glimpse of the development of camping beyond its associations with outdoor recreation or desires for wilderness. Instead, they point to the shared etymological roots of "camp" and "campaign," which both contain military origins. From archaic associations as the field of combat, camp came to indicate the site that soldiers dwelled and defended, before it acquired a more a general meaning. Campaign referenced a series of military operations before its connection with politics. The intertwined nature of camps and campaigns in this story of Union army veterans both echoes the significance of soldiers and warfare to the concept of camping and points toward its evolution as a political vehicle.

Camping thus became a mechanism to make new kinds of claims on the nation through public nature, just as older methods for securing property became less and less reliable. It became increasingly clear in the years after the Civil War that whatever unevenness had characterized the agrarian social contract in the past, it was now fraying badly. While large numbers of Americans still chased the agrarian dream, the goal of a stable family farm often became out of reach amid the economic turmoil of the late nineteenth century. A particular form of camping gained a new purpose by helping to elevate the veteran as a model citizen for the new era and the next generation.

With the nation's social contract undergoing a bumpy transition, modern campfires became a meaningful use for public nature.

"Where Is Our Camp?"

The experience of army camp life was inescapable for the vast majority of soldiers, no matter their background. At their most basic, camps organized space and people, and allowed troops to support their physical needs and defend the site and to move quickly and function efficiently as a group. US Army regulations standardized layouts so that setting up camp would become an easily repeatable task. Soldiers learned to adapt the standard blueprint to any terrain, with regularly spaced, straight avenues of tents, and defined areas for different ranks of men and functions.[8] The organization of camp represented the most orderly space officials could imagine that could also be struck and moved at a moment's notice. That soldiers camped was less remarkable than how they remade that experience after the war, from something that was involuntary, hierarchical, and regimented to an activity pursued by choice to enjoy the camaraderie of presumed equals.

What soldiers did with the basic framework during the war, both physically and socially, lent camp the possibility for meaning beyond military purposes in later years. The common expression "going into camp" implied not only the functional act of pitching tents and but also the social expectation of reconstituting community and routine. Going into camp (or leaving it) bracketed soldiers' experiences and differentiated it from march and battle. Several elements became key: the sense of novelty or initiation into a special social form; battling against the elements of nature and the struggle for physical comfort; navigating the social world of camp and finding camaraderie; and the ambiguity of camp as safe but temporary.

John Mead Gould offers a ground-level view of these experiences of camp, from the day he responded to President Abraham Lincoln's call for volunteers, April 15, 1861.[9] No novice camper, with multiple outings in the woods and islands of Maine as a schoolboy, Gould entered an intense learning phase in how to camp as a soldier. The first thing he realized was that it required a different complement of equipment and clothing than his earlier jaunts. Gould first learned of this from reading "Counsel to Volunteers" from "an old soldier" in the *Boston Daily Journal*. Urging enlistees to remember that "more men die from sickness than by the bullet," the old soldier suggested that men line their blankets with a layer of drilling (a coarsely woven, durable cloth akin to denim or canvas used for work clothes) and to purchase a rubber blanket to lay on the ground or use as a rain poncho.[10] The papers were full of advice to new soldiers about how to insulate themselves from the dangers of life in the outdoors, especially "among troops unacclimated and unaccustomed to the hard routines of camp life," or who were "exceedingly careless," throwing themselves "on the damp ground, often with no covering, and making no camp-fire."[11] Gould vowed to heed these warnings and purchased several rubber blankets and a coat made of oil-cloth (fabric coated with boiled linseed oil to make it water-resistant). He then persuaded his mother to sew cotton drilling into the blankets and his pants.[12]

On May 8, the 1st Maine regiment went into a kind of practice camp near Portland, on what Gould judged a fine prospect on the seashore. "Our camp is in a most charming spot, overlooking the Bay and the country back, the men are jolly at the appearance of things and in high spirits." His company arranged their tents in straight lines and began to settle in, patching up a few leaks after a rain shower and then broiling "beef on the coals," which they ate with "ravenous appetite." Gould evidently enjoyed the camaraderie. "We had a cozy time of it around the blazing fire. The Quarter-Master had ordered us to burn all the wood we wanted to." Several evenings later he reported that "we gathered around the fire and talked and smoked to our hearts content. Fellows of high life and some bordering on rowdyism all mix in with the heartiest good will." Good cheer, however, wasn't automatic, especially after the novelty of the first few days wore off. One night Gould found it "impossible to sleep," as men were "coming and going all night and every man had the idea, that every other man's blanket, haversack, canteen, etc. belonged to himself."[13] What would become central themes of camp life were already notable—battling against the elements, enjoying and begrudging the company of comrades, the tedium and frustration of waiting. Later memories emphasized the naiveté, rather than the novelty, of these early camps, along with the comparatively stable space of the training camp as opposed to life on the front lines.

After his regiment marched to Washington to take up guard duty, Gould wrote less of camp pleasantries and characterized the life of a soldier as "a succession of real hard work, deprivation of sleep, getting wet through, getting mad, etc. . . . You see there is no fun about it at all." Ruing his naïve preconceptions, for example of being able to make astronomical observations during nighttime guard duty, he soon found that battling the elements was a constant chore and that even the best equipment and preparation offered little protection.[14] What to do when it rained and one of his tent-mates had lice: remain in the tent or choose a soaking? He decided on a number of occasions to forgo the canvas shelter, finding convenient spots under baggage wagons, beneath tree boughs, or in an improvised table and wire contraption he rigged up and called his "coop."[15] Sometimes these brought relief, but often he woke wet and cold. Usually he returned to the tent.

Given its centrality, the tent occupied a great deal of discussion. Soldiers constantly complained about the type and state of their tents. The Union army generally used four major types; the most secure and spacious of these was the wall tent, a large square version that could be mounted atop wooden walls. Figure 1.1 shows the other three, in descending order: the Sibley, a modified tipi-style round tent with a tall central pole; the medium-sized A-shaped tent with canvas walls and a steeply-pitched roof; and, lastly, the small and hated shelter tent, which was simply a square of canvas. The shelter tent required no poles, could be hung over ropes or branches, and was parceled out in pieces, where each soldier might carry a half, button it with another man's, and put them up together. The bulkier, larger tents usually had to go in the baggage train, and so were only used for longer encampments. Orders to switch to shelter tents elicited groans; soldiers derided them with the

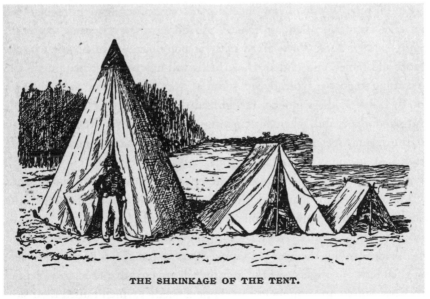

THE SHRINKAGE OF THE TENT.

FIGURE 1.1 This drawing from a soldier's memoir shows three of the main Union army tent types, from left to right: the Sibley, the A-tent, and the shelter or "dog" tent, shown here using two "halves" buttoned together and scrounged branches for poles. "The Shrinkage of the Tent," illustration by George Y. Coffin, in Wilber F. Hinman's *Corporal Si Klegg and his "Pard"* (Cleveland: The Williams Publishing Co., 1887), 577.

nickname "dog tents," since they were so short one had to crawl on all fours to get in or out. Gould called the shelter tent "the greatest improvement on no tent and the greatest sham alongside with another style of tent."[16] Despite these drawbacks, their efficiency led to them being the mainstay of army issue tents through the next century.

Once Gould was promoted, first to the position of Regimental Sergeant Major and then to the rank of First Lieutenant in 1862, he had priority on the better camp amenities. These promotions gained him more regular access to an A-tent. He noted that he now "without any help have always had the neatest tent and the greatest amount of modern improvements inside, while in a Private's tent the earth is thrown up in heaps against the curtain to keep out the cold and with a rickety gun rack and an ammunition box are all the improvements they claim."[17] Having been on both sides of the camp hierarchy, Gould tended to feel empathy for the mass of men: "It is pleasant this evening to be here in my comfortable tent, dry, sheltered and everything cosy [sic] as can be, while 50,000 poor fellows are out in the cold piercing wind and rain storm. . . . My conscience makes me shiver from head to foot to think of it."[18]

Soldiers, however, were inventive in improving upon the standard issue equipment. The landscape itself became a malleable template, as Gould noted late in the war: "We do not lay out camps exactly according to the regulations, but take advantage of circumstances." As soon as the order came to go into camp, soldiers took down fence rails for poles, scrounged boards for tent floors and tables, and raided wheat fields and haymows for bedding.[19] The first thing to go was typically any stand of trees adjacent to camp, cut down for fuel. But soldiers quickly recognized the usefulness of trees for shade and windbreaks and, when anticipating a longer-term stay, they even began to transplant trees and bushes. Gould recorded one memorable episode from 1861, in the sweltering camp outside Washington, DC. He observed a "New York regiment of Germans" who collected "quantities of young trees" and transplanted them around "their tents making it cool and pleasant." The New Yorkers then brought "a fine band . . . and had a lager beer cart going in about an hour after they were encamped." Gould and his tent-mates seized on the idea (minus the beer) and moved several red cedars to provide shade for their tent. A couple of weeks later they discovered that their transplanted trees had wilted and commenced dropping needles which caused their skin to itch. They spent some time replanting young hardwoods, only to have a strong storm knock them all into the tent one night. The days that followed found them trying to devise better methods for securing the trees.[20] Some improvisations worked better than others.

Despite best efforts, struggling with the elements was a battle never permanently won. Cold, rain, wind, snow, or wet ground were constant nemeses. Though Gould was fond of remarking how soldiers could stand cold and heat and wet "better than those who live indoors," he also found himself miserable on plenty of occasions. Pests, particularly fleas and lice had great powers to induce frustration. By 1863 he declared that the camp was "one grand louse trap and a clean man has all he can do to keep clean of the rascals."[21] Gould recounted yet more harrowing encounters with insects in a camp in Culpeper, Virginia during a heat wave that August. Swarms of beetles invaded the camp "as thick as grasshoppers," crawling into the tents and into men's "clothes at night and for some reason or rather they bite me, which they don't do to others. Last night I woke up from a sound sleep perfectly startled by one of the rascals having clutched me by the leg and was gnawing away like a rat."[22]

More often, however, going into camp meant a modicum of comfort, thrown into relief by contrast with the misery outside it. Gould described a hasty, confused retreat from Winchester, Virginia, which required his regiment to abandon a nicely improved camp along with many of their belongings. He mused about the sudden reversals of fortune while sitting under a blanket in a rainstorm:

> What a fool I was to come to war. . . . The whole life of a soldier is one of alternate pleasure and pain. Think of it ye mortals. Step out as you now are in your indoor dress, lie down in the street and let a thunderstorm pass, repass and pass again and you as sleepy as death. Think of it, no shift in the morning, no fire, no house to get into, no hot coffee. Nothing in the shape of fun is this bivouacking.[23]

The next day he was still wet and grumpy. "You may think that a hard pine floor is less comfortable than soft wet earth. To be dry is the greatest blessing a soldier can enjoy. And the loss of our rubber blankets is the greatest loss we shall suffer from our rout of last Sunday." When, ten days later, they were issued new tents, the joy was palpable; dry straw bedding, dry men, and hot fires got everyone "feeling happy at the thought of dry tents and full bellies, [and] were singing and as merry as drunkards." At that moment, he exclaimed, "I wouldn't have exchanged my lot for any mans [*sic*]." From this drier vantage point he reflected, "All good comes by contrast and the contrast between marching in the rain and resting in a tent with the rain pattering on the canvas was so great that the boys could not help being happy." The very next day brought an opportunity to experience that see-saw, as they discovered that the straw with which they had lined their floors was infested with fleas.[24]

The quality of food and digestion varied constantly as well. Rations could be bad or skimpy, alternated with hearty meals made from the produce of nearby farms. Arriving in a Shenandoah Valley camp on a July afternoon in 1863, Gould's regiment enjoyed "a delicious repast of hashed hard bread, pork and onions fried to a crisp. This with hot coffee and a good appetite is as good a meal as any man needs on a cool day." Just a week prior they had been "heated, half starved and sleepless. Miserable enough. Yesterday and today we have been on a regular pic-nic. Everyone is happy. . . . Cherries and blackberries are plenty."[25] Yet diarrhea was a constant menace, whether the eating was good or bad. Gould mentioned diarrhea or a "stomach out of order" no less than forty separate times in the diary. In 1862 he called indigestion a "universal complaint." In 1864, diarrhea was "the prevailing disease of this country."[26]

Gould wrote in the summer of 1864 of the essential connection between misery and comfort: "There is one fine thing about marching all day, getting tired, sleepy, dirty, and impatient, and that is the pleasure you take in camping at night, washing, eating, sitting down before the camp fire and then going to bed, not in linen sheets but in good warm shoddy blankets. And I found it so last night for the thousand and first time."[27] This notion of camp as a return of comforts temporarily missed was one memory that seemed to last. Sitting around a campfire as veterans in after years reminded them more of better days than bad ones.

If surviving the hell of battle together created lasting friendships, camp was where soldiers relished them. Gould's most valued companion was Alpheus Greene, drum major for the 10th Maine and Sergeant Major in the 29th. Greene and Gould became fast friends and tent mates, keeping each other company over the many months of camp life. In 1863, Gould described his comrade: "He believes in cheek and perseverance and in the idea that Greene is just as good a man as any other man. He is a profound lover of good music and we have many pleasant chats." Together they built sturdy winter quarters in Virginia which they named "the Chateau"—a split log structure with an A-tent for a roof, complete with chimney of rocks and mud and a wooden bed frame.[28] On many days Gould reported that he and Greene sat inside reading, writing, and talking the days away and then spooning throughout the cold nights to keep warm. When Greene mustered out in 1864, Gould missed his friend deeply. He found the replacement "a very nice fellow but of course doesn't take the place . . . that an old and intimate friend does."[29]

Gould developed close connections with other soldiers, but he also quarreled with, disapproved of, and complained about many more. The "'secesh,'" as Gould called them, were clearly the enemy, but the Union side was not simply one big happy family. Army camps were full of the social tensions around class, race, and religion that swirled around Northern society as a whole. Even when neighbors served together, camp life threw men of different temperaments and habits together. Navigating these social minefields was a key aspect of camp life.[30] Gould encountered frequent difficulties in navigating differences with men who had different predilections and beliefs. Their behavior frustrated him and he often critiqued them for immaturity or bad habits, such as smoking, gambling, or swearing. He believed they should spend idle days in activities like reading and writing rather than such antics as snowball fights or baseball games.[31] Soldiers' vices were a keen source of consternation for Gould. At one point he moved his tent away from "company lines" because "the shocking profanity of the men is too much for me." He bemoaned that the troops had too much liquor and too little religion, complaining "what a heathenish set this Army of ours is."[32] A lifelong teetotaler, Gould also feared that alcohol was seriously hampering the war effort, particularly calling officers to the carpet for caring "more for liquor than for their country." He fretted about the lasting impact this debauchery would have: "The army will in a measure corrupt the nation when the war is over."[33]

Whether amiable or aggravating, these regimental relationships tended to draw lines between insiders and outsiders, fellow soldiers and everyone else. It was a select group of veterans who could most easily access the claims of camaraderie promoted as symbolic of the nation in later years. Civilians and women clearly sat outside the circle but so too did Black soldiers, who shared many such experiences of army camp life but in segregated regiments. Moreover, the African Americans who lived in camps as cooks and manservants for white soldiers could not gain access to the sense of campfire camaraderie despite their proximity. In fact, the white soldiers able to hire such servants perhaps had more opportunity for such camaraderie, buffered somewhat from the less enjoyable tasks of camp housekeeping.[34]

For his part, Gould was both anti-slavery and held a low opinion of African Americans as people, a not uncommon combination among white New Englanders, though his vision evolved in complexity as the war went on. For example, in 1862 he noted, "I have a profound disgust for the darky as do all soldiers," and frequently referred to them in degrading terms and stereotypes. Early on in the war, Gould hired and then fired a series of Black cooks, reporting for one that "We turned off our nigger cook this morning as he is sick, nasty, lazy, and saucy." As late as mid-1864, he did not seem to object when the regiment, out of boredom, participated in the "ceaseless sport of pelting the negroes as they pass by on mules." The same day, however, he praised "our industrious negro engineers" who were "hard at work making a bridge over Choctaw Bayou." Late in the war he became a careful and considerate observer of slave society, personally interviewing a number of freedpeople about their experiences.[35] Whether viewing African Americans with derision, curiosity, or grudging respect, Gould found little opportunity for a similar sense of comradeship with them, less even than the members of his own regiment whom he found most dissolute.

The precarious nature of camp itself intensified the social relations and emotions it produced. Going into camp brought comfort and relief, but it could never be a permanent haven, for to win, the Union army had to break camp and forge into battle. To stay in camp was to stagnate and soldiers often grew weary with the waiting and the tedium even as they lived in dread of the next march, the next battle. In camp recovering from the bloody ordeal of Antietam in late September 1862, Gould recorded that he sat in "a perfect horror" of the next order to move. He recognized that "the war can never be ended by the Army remaining in camp but as long as the 10th Maine" got to stay in the rear, he was grateful. By November, the regiment was busy settling in to winter quarters near Berlin, Maryland. But on December 9, orders arrived to move the very next day at 3AM to Harper's Ferry, Virginia. "The order went through the camp like flash of lightning and instantly every hammer stopped its pounding and every axe its swinging. A death-like silence reigned and the men moped around with countenances as after a battle." Just like that, a month of work invested in labor to protect themselves from the winter weather was lost. "So we are off in the morning. My heart is in my boots. I never had so little patriotism, enthusiasm, nerve, as now. Awful, awful." Just two days later, Gould chided himself. After an easy march, they pitched camp at sunset, with "haversacks full of good things, the body refreshed by long inaction at Berlin. We were so troubled the day we rec'd orders to march. But to night I felt as jolly as an Irishman after we had got our tent pitched and were eating our supper."[36]

When final victory did arrive, surprising Gould at "how suddenly and unexpectedly this rebellion has ended," the idea of occupation duty left him nonplussed. He had come to loathe the tiresome obligations of being "in camp with nothing to do." Camp without the counterpart of march or battle had lost its purpose. "Once I had an idea that if I could get into the regular army I would not refuse the chance. But peace-soldiering is so contemptible a business that I don't wonder all our truest officers left the army years ago." In the summer of 1865, Gould grudgingly headed south with his regiment first to Georgia and then South Carolina, where he would be appointed a provost judge, arbitrating disputes between Black and white residents.[37]

On the way to his new assignment Gould passed by the prison camp at Florence, South Carolina, which had imprisoned up to 15,000 Union troops, nearly 2,800 of whom died within its confines. He tried to judge from the ruins of the camp what the quarters were like and was at first surprised to find that they did not appear as terrible as he might have expected. But on further reflection, he recognized that he didn't know how many lived within each hut, if they were allowed to make fires for warmth, or what protection they had from rain and mud. Perhaps recalling all his efforts and experiments to make camp livable, he observed that "troops in campaign have so many ways to make themselves comfortable which these prisoners do not have that no comparison can rightly be made between the two. Here is neither shade nor quiet resting place," only space "to starve and starve till the mind could dwell on nothing else but the misery of its lot. Then to crawl out of the damp ground into the cold air to shiver or into the hot sun to melt." It was not camp at all, rather "simply hellishness . . . altogether beyond my comprehension."[38]

If contemplating the singular hell of prison camps provoked shudders, reflecting on army camps intensified the bittersweet feelings soldiers had developed about them. A memorable rendering of this came in a popular war song, "Tenting on the Old Camp-ground," which debuted in 1863. The first stanza recalled camp as a place to share both camaraderie and longing for home: "We're tenting to-night on the old camp-ground,/ Give us a song to cheer,/ Our weary hearts, a song of home,/ And friends we love so dear!" The chorus and later stanzas gave a sense of yearning for war's end, of "weary" hearts and the anxious waiting that accompanied long stretches in camp. The final stanzas emphasized sad truths: "We are tired of war on the old camp-ground:/ Many are dead and gone,/ . . . . Many are in tears!/ . . . Dying to-night, dying to-night,/ Dying on the old camp-ground." Within three months the song sold over 10,000 copies and was a popular campfire tune for soldiers on both sides. After the war it became an emblem for the somber side of war comradeship, remembering the shared hardships of army and camp life.[39]

Walt Whitman's poem "Camps of Green" (1865) extended the metaphor of camp as a beckoning haven, for the living and the dead. The first stanza describes the "camps of white" as inviting refuge: soldiers "pitching the little tents, and the fires lit up begin to sparkle." In the following stanzas, they become "tents of green," the grave mounds where soldiers lie "sleeping under the sunlight, sleeping under the moonlight, content and silent there at last." In closing, Whitman signaled the kinship between the living and the dead: "And of each of us, O soldiers, and of each and all in the ranks we fight,/. . . . O soldiers, we too camp in our place in the bivouac-camps of green."[40]

Whether a place of novelty or weariness, comfort or hardship, safety or precarity, camaraderie or tension, life or death, camp anchored soldiers' experience of war. The memory of going into camp, in turn, would shape veterans' experiences in the decades that followed. In his regimental history written shortly after the war's conclusion, Gould reflected on his use of the word "camp" in his war diaries:

> The words bivouac and camp occur in the diary in the sense in which they were used by the army, or the unlettered portion of it at least. They were nearly synonymous, but the "bivouac" of the dictionary was nonetheless a "camp" in the army. A regimental commander often gave commands like these: "Stack arms!—Bivouac!" but the men were never heard to ask "Where is our bivouac?" but always "Where is our camp?" even if there was not a tent pitched.[41]

Bivouac and camp diverged in the technicalities of length of stay or sleeping apparatus, where bivouacs usually indicated simple overnights without pitching tents. Yet for Gould and his fellow soldiers, they were the camp. The act of reconstituting the community was what mattered. What soldiers made of the involuntary drudgery of Army camp created a template for memory and meaning.

"The Hope of Camping Out"

Sixty percent of northern men born between 1837 and 1845 served in the Union army and survivors emerged at war's end in their twenties. John Gould, born in 1839, was among this cohort. Overall, the 1.8 million veterans of the Civil War comprised 5 percent of the nation's total population in 1870, but how these men might play special roles as veterans was not initially apparent.[42] Previous US wars, which had mobilized narrower slices of the population, bequeathed no clear models for how former soldiers should reintegrate into society, much less influence the nation. If veterans were expected to do anything, it was to resume the course of their lives, as if the war's interruption had not occurred. Yet the expectations they had for their lives in the prewar context often did not apply in the new postwar world, increasingly characterized by industrial cities, new divisions between capital and labor, and shifting understandings of manhood and success.[43]

The Grand Army of the Republic, established in 1866, made one of the first attempts to organize veterans and, in its first decade, it nearly failed. By 1875 it had almost gone defunct, enrolling only 27,000 veterans or 2 percent of its potential membership. If surprising in hindsight, in the immediate aftermath of the war, brandishing one's identity as a veteran promised few material rewards and ran some considerable risks. Civil War veterans found themselves both dealing with the challenges of trauma and confronting public anxieties that correlated their physical debilities with poverty, failure, addiction, and transience.[44] Robert Beath, born the same year as Gould and an early organizer of the GAR, later recalled that the title of veteran provided no obvious benefit for men returning from war to "unsettled" futures, finding "their places . . . filled by others, and . . . compelled to seek new fields for employment." For disabled veterans, "upon whom the hand of adversity has heavily fallen," how could emphasis on a common veteran status overcome the divide between them and the able-bodied?[45] Veterans were reluctant to revisit the bloody details in public or to call attention to their dehumanizing experiences or emotional struggles, even when memories of the chaos and fear of battle could be hard to keep at bay.[46] George Merrill, another GAR leader, later recalled that perhaps the organization should have been able to predict disinterest among homeward bound veterans: "Probably ninety-nine out of a hundred would have responded, 'No; I've had all that I want of soldiering; no more for me.'"[47]

The GAR tried several recruitment strategies before hitting on a formula with wide appeal. In its first incarnation, the GAR attracted a small but dedicated group of veterans as partisan muscle for the Republican Party. This aim, and the high-handed measures to maintain wartime systems of rank and discipline, prevented the fledgling organization from engaging a broader membership.[48] Backing away from strict partisanship and military-style order, the GAR then imported a Masonic grade system to structure the social relations of the group, where members progressed from probation toward seniority. This, too, fell flat.[49] By 1880, when the GAR shifted toward emphasizing what founding member Oliver Wilson called the "ties of war-comradeship" and the tender "memories of camp and march," it began to show signs of life. Veterans began to sign up in order to rekindle "the fellowship of army life . . . formed in the field and trench, in bivouac and battle." The more the GAR strove to serve the simple purpose of reuniting "the 'boys' at a 'camp-fire,'" the more it grew.[50]

Popular writings in the postwar years, by veterans and observers alike, imbued camp life with a sense of romanticism that softened the war's dreadful edges. Pitching tents, eating grub, sitting around the fire, even enduring deprivations, were more approachable ways for remembering the war in public. For veterans, camp supported a focus on the higher purpose of the war and the enduring comrades-in-arms. A preponderance of memoirs by Union soldiers exhibited some combination of continued faith in the cause and the nation and focus on camp and comradeship, more so than those that highlighted the disorienting experiences of combat.[51] As camp became sentimentalized and shorn of its more troublesome experiences, it emerged as a promising basis on which to build veteran identity.

Beyond pure sentimentality, however, camp memories differed from camp experiences in part because they represented a voluntary impulse. Camping by choice, in words or tents, augmented pleasant experiences and obscured drudgery and resentments. These choices allowed camp to become a tool for promoting a sense of equality, individualism, and independence. Gould recognized this even while the war still raged. Home on leave, in the fall of 1861, and again in the summer of 1863, Gould chose to camp out with friends around Maine's Casco Bay. He surprised himself with this desire, reporting that he was "somewhat disgusted with some points of Camping out" and assumed that on leave all he would want was "to get back and hear the piano, to dress in good clothes, to sleep in a good bed, and call on my friends, and so I do, but I ache to get out on a boat, camp-out and be my own master." Camping out by choice seemed an even better remedy for army camp life than the comforts of home, which was a place where a young man remained answerable to his elders. In 1861, as a private in the army and an unmarried twenty-one-year-old, Gould often chafed against military hierarchy and parental control. His parents had disapproved of his initial decision to enlist and constantly harangued him not to re-up. Nor were they pleased with his impulse to ramble "around the woods and old haunts of my school days" with his old chums as soon as he returned home. But Gould was determined. "You can bet high if my wishes are fulfilled that I will enjoy myself and do as I please without asking Captain, Lieutenant, or Colonel. I am getting used to it in a measure but to be a slave and acknowledge a master is the most contemptible of things."[52] These voluntary camps offered direct relief from Army (and other) hierarchies, allowing him a sense of independence and an opportunity for self-reflection, though each time he elected to re-enlist.

Finally returning to Maine for good in 1867, Gould invested in his veteran identity earlier than most. Before long, he started a family and resumed his

career at the bank, and though never wealthy, he became a leading citizen
of Portland's professional class, despite a lingering restlessness and unease. In
the pages of his diary, he continued to wrestle with his wartime experiences,
and how to integrate them into his postwar life. In public, he was an active
leader in veterans' organizations, including the GAR. He helped to establish
the Maine 1st-10th-29th veterans association, serving as its historian, secretary, and treasurer for decades, and quickly got to work writing its official
regimental history. Compiled from his own diaries, research, and extensive
correspondence with other veterans, the well-regarded 1871 publication was a
sales success and elevated Gould as notable authority. The volume focused as
much on camp life as the battlefield, anticipating the broader interest in the
comradeship of soldiers and veterans.[53]

Gould's work sat on the leading edge of an outpouring of published
memoirs about the war. By the 1880s, veterans' access to a rapidly expanding
mass press, and a mushrooming audience of American readers, made these
more than private memories.[54] The GAR began to assemble its own record
of camp memories in the pages of the *National Tribune*, a weekly paper that
operated as its official organ. Beginning publication in 1877, the *Tribune*'s circulation rose swiftly and became largest veterans' newspaper in the nineteenth
century.[55] In its New Year's edition for 1879, the *National Tribune* issued a call
for veterans to submit stories and memories. The editorial specifically invited
memories of "camp, [where] there were ever occurring exciting and humorous
incidents which, put into manuscript form and published in our paper, would
interest and increase subscribers," and thus remind the nation of veterans' service. Veterans used the *Tribune* as a venue to share experiences and debate
narratives of the war, and through its pages, crafted a distinct public identity.[56]

While harrowing or heroic tales of battle certainly appeared in its pages,
the *Tribune* featured many campfire stories with more cheery memories. In
a letter to the editor, one Illinois veteran pushed for even more emphasis on
the lighter side, encouraging his comrades to emphasize "more fun and less
blood ... for camp life was made up of fun as well as misery, and many incidents
might be told that would make the boys forget their aches and pains."[57] The
bouts of despair that found their way into Gould's and others' diaries at the
time had little place in these public memories. While discomforts found
passing mention, they tended to omit the worst aspects and provided helpful
contrast for the more pleasant side of camp life, which veterans recalled in
great detail. Small sacrifices stood in for the larger ones left unspoken and
the ambiguities of camp life were swept away in favor of seeing it as a safe
haven and a defining rite of passage for veterans. Camaraderie seemed to have

flowed naturally, without the social tensions that Gould and others described at the time.[58] Veterans tended to accentuate common experiences and egalitarian feeling, rather than military hierarchy. This vision of camp life, with its emphasis on voluntary camaraderie, formed a mainstay of the GAR's public image.

For all the focus on camaraderie and good times, the GAR did not avoid the issue of death and loss entirely. It promoted establishing national observance of an annual Memorial Day to honor the Union dead.[59] Here too camp proved an evocative metaphor. In the post war years, many spoke of the "eternal campground" as final resting place, both graveyard and heaven. The phrase originated in the words of a veteran of the Mexican American War, eulogizing his fallen comrades in a poem titled "Bivouac of the Dead" (1847): brave men passed over to "fame's eternal camping ground,/ Their silent tents to spread." Inscriptions of the poem came to mark Union cemeteries after the war, including Arlington National Cemetery, and references appeared in GAR Memorial Day tributes to those who have "bivouaced [sic] on fame's eternal camping ground." Near the end of the century, graying veterans were told: "You will soon cross over the river to the eternal camping ground, but your deeds will live forever."[60] For veterans alone was camp a destination for the afterlife.

Before reaching the eternal campground, voluntary camping became a tool for veterans, both as individuals and in organizations, to repurpose memories of the war. Camping evoked the special social bonds of veterans, forged in intense group experience largely shared within a particular generation. In his second book, *How to Camp Out: Hints for Camping and Walking* (1877), Gould promoted the benefits of voluntary camping for nonveterans as well, especially younger generations. The manual advocated camping as a meaningful social endeavor that echoed the lessons and memories of army camp life; it required organization of work, endurance of discomfort, independence of mind, and sociability of equals. Novice campers should look to veterans as models to emulate in attempting to produce campfire camaraderie.

The meanings of camp that emerge in *How to Camp Out* were neither simply war memories nor aligned with other early promoters of camping from the era, such as H. H. "Adirondack" Murray, often considered the father of outdoor recreation and wilderness travel. His *Adventures in the Wilderness: or Camp-life in the Adirondacks* (1869) and *Adirondack Tales* (1877) contended that roughing it in the woods could mend the body and heal the spirit.[61] While Gould did find his spirits lifted in camp, he cautioned that it did not automatically restore health, of body or mind. In fact, careful planning and vigilance were required to avoid the many threats to well-being campers encountered in the outdoors. Nor did he see camping as primarily about wilderness experience. Camping for Gould was all about the people at the campsite, making it a heightened and privileged form of social inter-action. For all the pages the book spends giving instructions for how to sew tents and what kinds of utensils to bring, its purpose revolved around how to create campfire camaraderie.

Accordingly, *How to Camp Out* offered a set of social instructions directed to a specific type of reader. In an April 1875 diary entry, Gould called his work in progress a "manual for students to camp out."[62] Beyond that, Gould left few clues as to what initially prompted him to write this book, though his negotiations with publishers suggested that money was a factor. He eventu-ally came to terms with Scribner & Armstrong.[63] Gould and his publisher agreed that the book was best marketed, as Gould indicated in the Preface to "young men,—for students more especially." Scribner & Armstrong emphasized to booksellers its instructional value for "novices" and suggested that it "should prove especially salable in college towns."[64] This generational marketing highlighted Gould's desire to communicate his experiences as a solider and identity as a veteran, both of which figured strongly into how he conceptualized camping as a recreational endeavor. His model encouraged young men to become properly-equipped and well-behaved campers, using army style bedrolls and dog tents, as Figures 1.2 and 1.3 show. A review in a San Francisco newspaper believed *How to Camp Out* filled a crying need for an ex-plicit and practical camping manual. Anticipating a "grand rush of city folk to the mountains," the editors predicted that many would return home "wearied, disappointed, disgruntled" because they did "not know how to go to work to get the most out of it." Gould's guide filled the gap between serious ambitions and little experience.[65] A review in *The Nation* explicitly highlighted Gould's veteran status as key to the book's usefulness, suggesting that readers, especially "the student class" would benefit from "the author's army experience."[66]

Other clues to Gould's goals for the manual emerge from examining the text in conjunction with his own camping experiences in the 1860s and 1870s. In the preface, he noted that he drew on "the pleasant days when, in my teens, I climbed the mountains of Oxford County, or sailed through Casco Bay," as well as "the diaries of 'the war,' and the recollections of 'the field.'" To this he added more recent experiences, observing and conversing with campers he happened to meet when out on his own journeys and answering "questions about camping, &c., that my young friends asked me."[67] Writing *How to Camp Out* allowed Gould to integrate the different stages and aspects of his

FIGURE 1.2 Illustrated by his good friend Edward Morse, Gould's vision of a properly equipped camper bore a strong resemblance to the Union soldier on the march. Illustration by Edward Morse, in John M. Gould's *How to Camp Out: Hints for Camping and Walking* (New York: Scribner, Armstrong & Co., 1877), 17.

life through camping: memories of boyhood excursions, the involuntary army camp, postwar camping trips with family and friends, and veterans' reunion encampments. Sociability was, for Gould, key to all these forms.

By the mid-1870s, Gould had established an annual summer tradition of moving with his wife and three children for six to eight week stretches out of their house and into tents on the Cape Elizabeth seashore, just down the bay from Portland.[68] Leaving the hot city for cooler climes was a longstanding

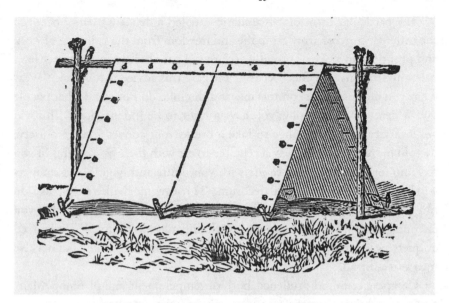

FIGURE 1.3 Surprisingly, Gould recommended the shelter tent as a good option for recreational campers. Illustration by Edward Morse, in John M. Gould's *How to Camp Out: Hints for Camping and Walking* (New York: Scribner, Armstrong & Co., 1877), 70.

tradition on the Eastern seaboard, but for Gould, the motivation was to "go into camp," to seize the opportunity to constitute an outdoor community. It was close enough that Gould could still commute by boat across the Fore River to work on weekdays and return to spend nights and weekends in camp. For him, the open spaces of Cape Elizabeth and his camps were a world away, even as Portland began to cater to crowds of nature-seeking tourists.[69]

Gould invited other like-minded acquaintances to join the annual "Camp St. John." Every spring during this period, he reported his efforts to get friends to commit to camp. In late May 1875 he lamented that his recruiting for "camping out" wasn't going well: "No one wants to go to stay." By late June, he was peeved. "Didn't do much on camping—sort of demoralized. Our company don't accept nor decline & we wait for them."[70] Gould had little interest in going into camp without a congenial group. On the other hand, gathering a large number satisfied him immensely. As he wrote in the summer of 1877, "Have got my self & family in camp since my last & we are enjoying ourselves finely." With two more groups due to arrive the next week, "there'll be sixteen in our family & I'll be proud."[71] Camp St. John was not a rugged solitary outpost, but a site for preferred kind of sociability.

The particular form of camaraderie entailed a delicate balance between the ordered world of army camp life and freedom from the strictures of work and propriety. In 1876, he proudly declared, "I am a barbarian at camp & have worn no stockings for four weeks."[72] He gave this advice in his book: "Wear what you please if it be comfortable and durable: do not mind what people say. When you are camping you have a right to be independent." This was voluntary camping, a chance to take a break from conventional propriety; he told his readers that it was acceptable to eat with their hats on and "if you have no fork, do not mind eating with your knife and fingers." Yet campers still had to observe basic social decorum: "However much liberty you take, do not be rude, coarse, or uncivil: these bad habits grow rapidly in camp if you encourage them, and are broken off with difficulty on return."[73] The relaxed etiquette was conducive to family and social relations, but should not devolve into a free-for-all.

Camping required prudence, both of temperament and planning. Many pages of practical advice in Gould's book cautioned campers not to go overboard in their ambitions, and to focus instead on preventing discomfort. Gould advised readers to avoid self-imposed adversity, like overly heavy backpacks or "all nonsensical waste of strength, and gymnastic feats, before and during the march"—as he continued to call the walk between camps. The "hints for walking" in the book's title became in the text "marching," which added not only to the army connection, but also to the notion of physical effort to be endured, rather than an enjoyable pursuit in and of itself. He recalled that "The most successful marching that I witnessed in the army was done by marching an hour, and resting ten minutes. You need not adhere strictly to this rule: still I would advise you to halt frequently for sight-seeing." The discomforts of the march were an unavoidable initiation. "After you have marched one day in the sun, your face, neck, and hands will be sunburnt, your feet sore, perhaps blistered, your limbs may be chafed." Nothing could prevent these tenderfoot ailments. He promised the second day would be "the most fatiguing. . . . [Y]ou suffer from loss of sleep . . . [Y]ou ache from unaccustomed work, smart from sunburn, and perhaps your stomach has gotten out of order." The only cure was to keep at it, to get accustomed to the exertions and the elements, and thus to gain strength. He suggested that going slowly at first, avoiding over-exertion, and eating healthy would ease the adjustment, and his guide was full of tips for minimizing all the usual discomforts—how to make good beds, prevent blistering, and regulate digestion.[74]

Gould strove to design camping plans that might allow camaraderie to emerge despite these difficulties. For example, he advised prospective campers to rotate group leaders. Especially in larger parties, "there must be a captain,—some one that the others are responsible to, and who commands their respect. . . . [T]he captain must hold each man to a strict performance . . . and allow no shirking." Gould replaced strict military hierarchies with an organized approach to the social cooperation of equals. By way of example, he invented a fictitious party and charted a useful rotation of duties. After a few days some individuals showed themselves to be "Worthless" while others have "Gone home. Sick of camping." This weeding out process then allowed campers to sort out amicably who would take their share of cooking, dishes, care of horses, and other tasks.[75] Fulfilling one's responsibilities was voluntary, but necessary for sociability.

Once work expectations were settled, campers could realize the primary goal of camp: camaraderie. Gould wrote affectionately of his many conversations on the march and storytelling around the campfire. On an 1875 camping expedition to Mt. Carrigain with a group of male friends, Gould wrote, "We enjoyed this walk. . . . Major [Joseph] Sanger's army stories & criticisms were especially pleasing to me. We attempted to go to bed early, but didn't succeed as we had to talk, talk & tell stories." During a particularly difficult 1877 attempt to climb Mt. Mahoosuc, when fog and rain stranded the party high up in their camp, he reported that they nonetheless managed a good time because "Sanger was kept talking & so the trip was enjoyable everyway."[76] As one of the organizers of the White Mountain Club (WMC) in 1873, Gould even helped to define a progenitor of the social-outdoor club. The WMC organized expeditions into northern New Hampshire and western Maine, with the rugged Mahoosuc range a treasured target for peak-baggers.[77] But Gould's most enjoyable WMC activities were likely the in-town meetings, the making of plans for the "summer campaign," and telling stories about camping.[78] The social acts that preceded or followed the expeditions seemed to provide as much if not more of the pleasure than the trips themselves.

Anticipation, remembrance, and sharing with others extended the camping experience. His book opened by describing the delight of preparation: "The hope of camping out that comes over one in early spring, the laying of plans and arranging of details, is, I sometimes think, even more enjoyable than reality itself."[79] His off-season diary entries were filled with notes about group planning and equipment tinkering. He tested his tents by pitching them in the yard, fashioning new tent pins, or worrying that the tents themselves "are growing old & need attention."[80] In April of 1879 he wrote of his obsession with planning a summer WMC trip. "Sat down and read mountain-books, traced maps of two counties; rigged up my . . . kit, made note-books, went up West Promenade to look at the Mts." Two weeks later, he included an update: "As for [the trip to climb Mount] Mahoosuc. We'll go if not prevented. It seems almost too good a thing to think of. But we'll have the fun of anticipation."[81] For Gould it seemed worthwhile to have the anticipation of a trip alone. Recollection was equally key to the experience, particularly the story telling. Gould urged campers to keep diaries and write letters, including ink, paper, envelopes, and postage stamps on his list of recommended provisions. "The act of writing will help you to remember these good times."[82] Narrating the camping experience, whether in club gatherings or written correspondence, furthered the notion of camping as part of a shared social activity.

Gould anticipated the journeys and stories of his readers with equal parts excitement and admonition. He cautioned his young readers to temper their ambitions. Traveling afoot in wild country, he emphasized, "is *very* hard work for a young man to follow daily for any length of time; and, although it sounds romantic, yet let no party of young people think they can find pleasure in it many days."[83] Instead, through reading the book, prospective campers were meant to admire the fortitude and ingenuity of veterans Gould described in his stories of army camp life and to fit their expectations to their novice status. "You have probably read that a soldier carries a musket, cartridges, blanket, overcoat, rations, and other things, weighing forty or fifty pounds. You will therefore say to yourself, 'I can carry twenty.' Take twenty pounds, then, and carry it around for an hour, and see how you like it." Gould softened in remarking that there was no need to attempt the impossible and walk in a soldier's shoes, for this kind of camping was supposed to be pleasurable.[84]

The generational perspective shaped many of Gould's directives. The need for a group leader was especially important for young campers, because their naivete would make them loath to "submit to unaccustomed restraint." Parties of younger folks, Gould warned, were likely to fall into "foolish dissensions when off on a jaunt, unless there is one, whose voice has authority in it, to direct the movements."[85] Because "young people are very apt to forget," Gould offered additional rules for self-discipline:

Play no jokes upon your comrades, that will make their day's work more burdensome. . . . Do not be saucy to the farmers, nor treat them as "country greenhorns." . . . Be social and agreeable to all fellow-travellers you meet. . . . [Y]ou are in duty bound to be friendly to all thrown in your way. . . . Try to remember too, that it is nothing wonderful to camp out or walk; and do not expect any one to think it is. . . . If you will refrain from bragging, you can speak of your short marches without exciting contempt.[86]

If these strictures were heeded, Gould strongly believed that camping trips would be beneficial for the development of youth. Camp offered a form of social preparation, a way of learning how to "Be independent, but not impudent." It could strengthen as well as humble, teach young men how to spend their money and their time wisely. Near the end of the text, he inserted an aside to those of his own generation: "Here I wish to say a word to parents—having been a boy myself, and being now a father. Let your boys go when summer comes; put them to their wits; do not let them be extravagant, nor have money to pay other men for working for them." Camping—planning, enduring, cooperating, wayfinding—was "not bad practice for a young man."[87]

Gould insisted that the benefits only accrued if young men pursue camping in the right way. "I heard once of two fellows, who, to avoid buying and carrying a tent, slept on hay-mows, usually without permission. . . . If you cannot travel honorably, and without begging, I should advise you to stay at home."[88] This was a particularly potent warning when Gould's book appeared in 1877. The ailing US economy produced high unemployment, major wage reductions for workers, and growing tension between industrial workers and employers. Worry about out-of-work tramps taking to the roads and spreading unrest was on the rise. When the great railway strike began in July, followed by violent repression, fear of massive civil unrest spiked. No wonder then that Gould wanted to make clear the difference between "honorable" camping and suspicious tramps who he blamed for causing disorder.[89]

How to Camp Out appeared to be at least a moderate sales success. Scribner's tallied initial figures as coming along "very nicely" and Gould reported in July 1877 that he was "constantly receiving letters from the public concerning my 'How to Camp-out' which I judge is selling well," after three months in print. Still, by the end of 1878 Gould lamented that the book had netted him "scarcely anything the last year" even though "camping out is on the increase hereabouts never so much of it as now."[90] Scribner's continued to promote the book each year, typically in the spring and summer. In 1880 it released a cheaper "Knapsack Edition," which appeared in booklists for the entire decade, though without much fanfare.[91] Even if Gould made less profit than he hoped, his manual highlighted the close connection between camping and veteran identity, if only in his own life. In part through his efforts to promote voluntary camping to the younger generation and along

with other veterans, Gould participated in a broader conversation about the
role of public nature in postwar society. Gould's vision of camping proposed
a social contract in microcosm, one that tried to recreate the fleeting experience of sociable equality elsewhere being lost in the sharp divisions of an
industrializing nation.

"What Purpose Those Encampments, Why Those Campfires?"

In the years after *How to Camp Out* appeared, some Americans began to experiment with various forms of recreational camping in the 1880s and 1890s.
The GAR's expanding vision of voluntary encampments, however, was initially far more noticeable in public life. Nearing its highwater mark of membership and influence, the GAR effectively tailored the generational messages
of camp and veterans' camaraderie as political tools to advance a cause that
was at the heart of the organization's mission. Since its founding, the GAR
ceaselessly lobbied the federal government to provide pensions and a full
complement of benefits for Union veterans and their families. In arguing that
the nation owed veterans a debt, the GAR issued constant reminders that
veterans were both "saviors of the Union" and the "progenitor of the ideal citizen" in the reunited nation.[92] Its leaders employed a wide range of arguments
to press the cause, but the social rituals and remembrance of camp became
particularly compelling vehicles for making the case. In this, the GAR was not
just a reunion organization, but also participated in negotiating a renewed
social contract. Veterans' encampments emerged as a way of making explicit
claims on public nature and postwar society.

At one of the first National Encampments, Commander John Logan fore-
cast a way to link veterans as embodiments of patriotism with the GAR's pension advocacy. He argued that veterans needed to present themselves not "as
relics of a disastrous war, marred and scarred by the enginery of battle, to beg
for alms; not as burdens upon the hands of public charity, but as the survivors
of a glorious and successful struggle on behalf of liberty and independence for
all men." Thus, they should gather annually not as broken-down old soldiers,
but "meet in the strength and integrity of our manhood."[93] Though it took
the GAR some time to recognize, the act of camping itself went a long way
toward demonstrating how veterans remained vigorous men, to whom the
nation owed thanks and awe. In camp, they could again appear as the boys
who went to war and won it. GAR camps thus sought to counter both anxiety

about soldiers' disabilities or maladjustment and skepticism about government pensions.[94]

Decades later, former Army Chaplain John Ireland encapsulated the GAR's message as it had crystallized in the intervening years. In his address to the National Encampment in Buffalo in 1897, Ireland praised veterans for the shining example they set for the nation, earned both "Because you triumphed, and because since the war you have been, one and all, personified patriotism." Ireland highlighted the close connection of patriotism and camp, asking "To what purpose those Encampments, why those campfires, why do the soldiers congregate so often and talk so much over olden times?" The answer he gave spoke directly to a hypothetical mass of hopeful observers: "They do this for the sake of America, they do all this to sanctify and teach patriotism.... Young men, growing up into manhood, having seen you and heard you, will be for their lifetimes better Americans, because they have seen the Grand Army men." Ireland, like the GAR's leaders, downplayed the dissent roiling America and even the diversity within its own ranks, in favor of a mythic image of a nation unified both in law and in spirit. The veterans, who had rescued the Union once, now appeared poised to be its saviors again, by fortifying the patriotism of future generations to combat divisive social struggles.[95] With an emphasis on social order and camaraderie, the GAR's vision of camp life served as an effective stage for this effort.

In the GAR, campfire memories and contemporary mission worked in tandem, as the metaphor of camp proved useful for both organizational and political strategy. Local chapters, called Posts, held regular meetings to manage a variety of business: considering applications for membership, collecting dues and contributions for veterans or widows in need, sharing news of national pension advocacy, and planning social gatherings, called campfires. Though these "campfires" were often held in church basements or lodge halls, their central aim was to rekindle camaraderie: attendees sang songs and told stories, as fellow Post members, visiting veterans, and nonveteran guests listened and drank coffee.[96] Posts reported to state Departments, which in turn were governed by the National Encampment. Post delegates, elected Department leaders and individual veterans traveled to the annual meeting, also called the National Encampment. In the host city, they gathered for an event that was at once soldiers' reunion, urban spectacle, and business meeting. State Departments, as well as groups of posts, often held regional gatherings, which followed a similar organizational pattern to National Encampments on a smaller scale.

Commander Robert Beath promoted GAR gatherings as key opportunities for the younger generation, and Americans as a whole, to watch and learn. He encouraged local posts to invite the public "to attend Camp-fires or open meetings, and that every effort should be made not only to entertain them pleasantly, but to keep fresh in their minds the memory of the services which the veterans rendered in their defense." Though nonveterans could never be members, GAR leaders believed the organization had a duty to bring them into the fold as students. Beath echoed Gould in the belief that without the example that veterans' set, the "new generation . . . growing up" would have "no proper conception of the magnitude of the struggle or the vital importance of the issues involved."[97] The urgency of this need pushed the GAR to continue sharing its narrative about the special role of veterans in society as promoters of patriotism and national unity.

Regional and National Encampments attracted even wider public attention, and in the process, camping gained a host of new meanings that carried political messages. These events were designed to solidify veterans' allegiances by reviving the "incidents of camp and field which inspired the tie that binds [veterans] together more strongly and firmly than the ties of blood."[98] Focus on the everyday sensory experiences of camp provided an important outlet. Savoring the tastes and smells—the fire, the coffee, the hardtack—reinforced a narrative of solidarity. At a Milwaukee encampment, veterans drew "three days' rations and forty rounds. . . . Supper will be served in camp, and will consist of army fare, hardtack, coffee and pork and beans."[99] Full rations, however, were unnecessary. Coffee alone could do the trick. "Every post has its coffee-pot, and he is a rare old soldier indeed who doesn't enjoy his Mocha as he cracks his jokes about the hardtack rations of lang syne."[100]

Reunion camps also created a visual tableau, with peaked white tents arrayed in urban parks by the hundreds. Practically speaking, tents provided inexpensive lodging for veterans. The National Encampment in Columbus, Ohio provided veterans with free accommodations in wall tents with straw bedding. Campers were instructed to bring their own blankets and drinking cups but could either purchase meal tickets for the mess halls or buy food to do their own outdoor cooking. The GAR promoted the appeal of this arrangement, suggesting that veterans "prefer to camp out rather than be camped in halls, armories, and private buildings."[101] The camping was part of the display of vital men, who neither required luxury nor suffered poverty. Civilian tourists visited the camp grounds, and evening campfires were held there for all to attend.

The definition of camping out and campfires could at times be applied quite liberally. Many veterans did in fact opt to stay in the comfort of hotels rather than rough it in tents, and evening campfires also took place inside many grand halls. At one National Encampment, for example, newspapers reported that, "The snowy tents, figuratively speaking, were pitched at the Palmer House"—Chicago's luxurious hotel.[102] Once established as the archetypal form of reunion, any gathering of veterans could then reasonably be called an encampment. In this way it became possible to perform "camp" in a purely symbolic fashion. This extended to the reenactments of military actions, such as shooting contests, mock battles, play-acted courts-martial, and a dress parade, where veterans marched through the host city to throngs of onlookers. These parades reenacted a specific, but highly anomalous event: the Grand Review of all Union regiments held in Washington, DC in May 1865. Less a memory of war than of its first victory celebration, neither the GAR parade nor the Grand Review bore much resemblance to soldiers' common experience of inspections. Staged largely for public viewing, for the GAR's purposes, the dress parade heightened the display of veterans as triumphant victors.

It was no accident that GAR consistently promoted veterans as "Saviors of the Union," or that the *National Tribune* printed a motto on its masthead with the more present-oriented gerund: "Saving the Union." Camp was a visual performance of the narrative of the war as a unique national drama, a singular trial by fire in which Union veterans served as noble saviors.[103] This was nowhere more resonant than in the 1892 Encampment in Washington, DC. With tents pitched in the shadow of the Washington Monument, as Figure 1.4 shows, and the parade retracing portions of the route of the 1865 Grand Review, the memories of victory were potent. As Commander John Palmer put it in his address to the crowd, "Rightly is it named the Grand Army; grand in the justice of the majestic cause for which it fought; grand in the valor, the fortitude and the heroism which shone through. . . . Grand because it saved the Capital of the Nation, KEPT THE COUNTRY UNDIVIDED, the flag unsullied, and assured us a commanding place among the Nations of the earth." He called Americans to witness this gathering of patriotic men, so to "impress upon the minds of the rising generation a profounder and deeper sense of the perils through which we passed to preserve the unity of the Nation." So far removed from war, younger Americans were apt to "forget the sufferings and sacrifices that made us what we are" or to "sneer at the soldier and call him a mendicant."[104] The narrative of Union victory and veteran-saviors was crucial to show that pensions were not charity

FIGURE 1.4 Grounds of the 26th Annual Encampment of the GAR, Washington, DC, 1892. The Washington Monument, finally completed in 1884, elevated the symbolism of this typical arrangement of tents: those in the foreground provided housing for veteran attendees and others in the middle supported public events. "Washington Monument, 555 feet high. Washington, D.C.," photograph by J. F. Jarvis (Underwood & Underwood, 1892). Stereograph Cards, Prints & Photographs Division, Library of Congress, LC-DIG-stereo-1s05973.

for beggars, but a debt owed by the nation and the new generation—a message made more powerful by camping on the nation's capital.

That camp became enmeshed in this narrative of past victory and present obligation made it more than just an exercise of reenactment. GAR encampments established a new form of public nature, where veterans reiterated the significance of the Union victory for the postwar society. Palmer's address also argued that veterans' experience in war made them not just "more mindful of [their] duties as citizens" but also the ideal to which all might aspire: "the progenitor of the successful citizen."[105] Making veterans the prototype of the ideal citizen, embodying patriotic unity and social order, represented a competing model for the agrarian social contract, then under increasing disarray amidst troubling economic crises on farms and in cities alike. As ideal men, veterans were both the "custodians of sacred memories . . . the living history of an immortal past" and "the trustees of that living power of patriotism which looks to a great future for our great Nation. In your hands to-day history, memory, hope—the past, the present and the future unite."[106]

These paeans to veterans both promoted and wrestled with the myth of campfire egalitarianism. In an 1889 speech, Commander William Warner captured this sentiment by reciting an evocative and oft-quoted verse:

> *The rich and the great sit down to dine,*
> *And they quaff to each other in sparkling wine*
> *From glasses of crystal and green.*
> *But I guess in their golden potations they miss*
> *The warmth of regard to be found in this—*
> *We have drunk from the same canteen. . . .*
> *We have shared our blankets and tents together,*
> *And have marched and fought in all kinds of weather,*
> *And hungry and full we have been;*
> *Had days of battle and days of rest;*
> *But this memory I cling to and love the best—*
> *We have drunk from the same canteen.*[107]

It was an egalitarianism borne specifically of camp life, though one that shared ideals common to fraternal orders at the time. Belief in an imagined egalitarianism among white men rose while, outside the lodge, class strife raged and race barriers rose.[108]

That this egalitarian reverie was more imagined than realized was nowhere plainer than when it came to the issue of race. Criteria for GAR membership required only an honorable discharge from Union forces and maintenance of "good character" since. Remarkable for the time, the GAR leadership continued to endorse the organization's original commitment to recognize no distinction of race, color, religion, or nationality, only honorable service to the nation. Yet this commitment sat in tension with the more affective belief in camp camaraderie. When the metaphor for unity was "we have drunk from the same canteen," the racial divides of the postwar era became thornier. In the late 1880s and early 1890s, the GAR nearly came apart over how to address the contradictions. No matter how much respect the US Colored Troops gained from white veterans for enduring common hardships and defeating a common enemy, they had not been allowed to drink from the same canteen.[109] During the war, Black and white units camped separately, and while campfire camaraderie undoubtedly existed within each, they did not sit together, intermingled around the same campfire. Whatever the GAR's commitments, the image of campfire camaraderie and the carefully constructed identity of the veteran as savior of the nation and ideal citizen sat in tension with the increasingly potent racial criteria of the Jim Crow era.

The GAR exhibited a long and noteworthy history of verbal defense of the Black veteran's entitlement to full and equal membership in the organization. Promotion of full pensions and benefits for Black veterans throughout the decades affirmed this commitment.[110] While many GAR posts became segregated in practice, prominent integrated posts did exist, and Black members rose to state and national leadership positions. Moreover, Black veterans worked simultaneously to establish their own fully accredited GAR posts and marched together with other posts at National Encampments and other local celebrations. Black veteran George Washington Williams belonged to the GAR and cited the solidarity he felt there as one inspiration for writing *A History of Negro Troops in the War of the Rebellion* (1888): "I have heard with deep interest, at camp-fires and encampments, many narratives of the heroic conduct of Negro soldiers"—presumably praise offered by white as well as Black veterans.[111] Maps of Encampment grounds did not indicate segregated quarters for Black members or posts. Facilitating regimental reunions did replicate the original segregation of the US Colored Troops in some public areas, but when layouts followed GAR post membership and state of residence, which was most common, the organization's official disavowal of racial divides weighed against formally segregated grounds.[112]

This commitment to egalitarianism was sorely tested when white Union veterans who had relocated to southern states began to advocate for a more official color line. They wanted to bring their GAR affiliation with them but found that integrated organizations were social anathema in their newly adopted states, where Jim Crow laws increasingly came to govern race relations. Southern white GAR delegations came to National Encampments to lobby for formal segregation at the national level, largely on grounds of social propriety. Surprisingly, none made the argument that segregation was the rule and the experience of most soldiers in the Union army. The postwar symbolic unity of camp came to mean more to many veterans than it had during the war itself and led most to oppose official segregation. Both national GAR leaders and rank and file members frequently voiced strong repudiations of segregation and reaffirmed the organization's commitment to an egalitarian campfire camaraderie.[113] These defenses tended to draw upon the mythologies of camp and the unifying "saviors of the Union" label, such that GAR members saw the question of race (at least around veterans' issues) through this lens.

Despite defeating the segregationists at the National Encampment, the GAR never managed to enforce its official egalitarianism and thus ended up tolerating a de facto color line. In 1898 the Commander lamented that "the color line still exists. . . . The race prejudice remains and the chasm seems to be widening, which it seems impossible to overcome, and for which I can only express my extreme regret. What the remedy is, if any, I am unable to suggest." On the one hand, relying on an image of brotherhood from a segregated war failed to provide tools for the GAR to mount broader social or political advocacy on behalf of African Americans, had it been inclined to do so. On the other, the symbols of camp and camaraderie which anchored the GAR's construction of veteran identity permitted a defense of racial equality remarkable for its time and matched by few if any other primarily white organizations in the era. The GAR stood for the hard-won "faith in that law of liberty which respects the manhood in every man, despite all difference of race or color."[114] Defending the "manhood of every man" regardless of race was not a stance taken lightly in this era, and it was the notion of a manhood earned through experience in camp and battle that enabled it in this case.

Despite its organizational shortcomings, the GAR's unrelenting appeal to the special status of veterans, the continuing significance of Union victory, and the myth of campfire egalitarianism allowed it to be a unique voice in favor of racial inclusion during an era otherwise noted for rising anti-Black racism and Northern whites' tendencies toward reconciliation with former rebels. The sentimentalist view of campfire camaraderie that the GAR helped to create certainly contributed to the growth of desires for North-South reconciliation and the decay of Northern commitments to Black freedom. Yet the rise of more explicit visions of Americanism based on whiteness during this era competed with the GAR's repeated insistence on veterans as a unified and special group of Americans.[115]

The late nineteenth century was marked not only by debates around race and class, but also by the forces of national expansion and power—industrialization and urbanization, integrated national markets and improved transportation, continental conquest and imperial adventures. Through the GAR, veterans participated in expanding national tourism and commercial networks, which aligned them with a sense of modern prosperity rather than backward nostalgia. Encampments contained a mélange of activities which reflected these modern developments and linked veterans with these new triumphs, arguing that Union victory provided the basis for the ascendance of national power.[116] Rather than billing National Encampments as old-fashioned glimpses of yesteryear, the GAR collaborated with cities and corporate leaders to showcase the heady advances the nation had achieved in the years following Union victory.

Encampments became major commercial events. Local companies and manufacturing concerns signed on as sponsors, as Figure 1.5 shows. City boosters, especially from western and midwestern states, competed fiercely for the honor of holding the next Encampment. The events gained wide circulation in the national and local press, which was a key factor in the appeal. For example, the St. Louis booster community openly campaigned to be selected as the 1887 National Encampment host. The *St. Louis Globe-Democrat* salivated over the GAR's four hundred thousand members, a subset of whom would come visit their city and, "representing all parts of the Union, they would carry back to the remotest sections the news of our growth and

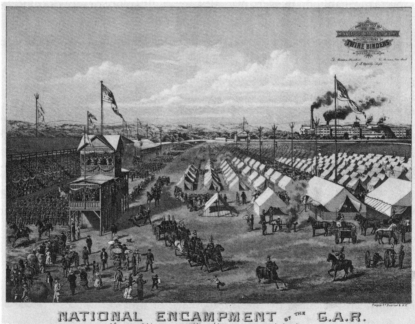

FIGURE 1.5 Advertising broadside for the 1884 National Encampment in Minneapolis, sponsored by a local manufacturer, Minneapolis Harvester Works and Twine Bindery. Here, the encampment is linked visually to a productive factory, setting the tents in a modern, commercial, as well as patriotic context. "National Encampment of the G.A.R., Near the Minneapolis Harvester Works" (Forbes & Co., 1884). Popular Graphic Arts, Library of Congress Prints and Photographs Division, LC-DIG-pga-06746.

prosperity." Once secured, local plans for the program linked events that cel-ebrated Union veterans and victory with those advertising the charms of the city. St. Louis undertook a "grand illumination" to brighten the night-time tent city with 100,000 gas and electric lights.[117] Encampments could thus be as much a celebration of modernity as of nostalgia.

Beyond any one city, the regular round of regimental reunions, state gatherings, battlefield anniversaries, and veterans' events added to the general promotion of national tourism in the postwar era. The national expansion of the GAR both relied on and promoted railroad travel; the organization was adept at negotiating reduced rates for veterans and advertising the routes. By continually moving encampments to different sites and cities, veterans collectively toured a much broader portion of the nation than they likely would have otherwise. This era of tourism played a part in reinventing the postwar nation by turning away from the horrors of the Civil War and to-ward commercial advancement and scenic opportunities. San Franciscans, contemplating hosting the 1886 Encampment, were keenly aware of this dy-namic. "The trip is a long one, but the universal desire in the ranks East of the mountains to visit the Pacific Coast, coupled with the knowledge that the railroad companies are making unprecedented low rates of fare, will certainly assemble in this city a vast army of war veterans." By association, tourism be-came associated with the kind of patriotic, idealized citizenship that veterans were coming to represent.[118]

National Encampments became a way of expressing claims on public nature that adapted camp rituals to modern expectations, in part by con-juring up the archaic vision of the campfire to praise modern life. A *National Tribune* review of the Encampment in Baltimore highlighted this strategy. "As evening approached the camp-fires were kindled and the camp presented much the appearance of a veritable army encamping." And yet "It is such a camp as never fell to the lot of our veterans to tent in twenty years ago, for electric lights have taken the place of the blazing fence-rail as an illuminator." Observers were meant to marvel at the achievements of modern progress, the distance traveled since the rustic life of the army camp. The encampments that followed in the next two decades would grow in visitation and grandi-osity, with ever more spectacular displays of the new. Whether novel or nos-talgic, "the significance of a Grand Army Reunion" was always rooted in the principle that it was "the men, and not the surroundings, that make the camp. So long as a single Post of the Grand Army survives, the spirit of comradeship will shine out like a beacon in the darkest night, and there will be something still to remind us that the age of heroes has not passed."[119] Veterans were to be not just reminders of past glory, but ideal citizens primed for success in the modern world.

In the end, the GAR was quite successful in its pension lobby. While no single comprehensive pension bill ever satisfied the GAR completely, over the years, its work established precedents for the federal responsibility of veterans' care and support. That the GAR's political goal focused somewhat narrowly on veterans' pensions did not prevent it from making expansive claims about the nation and veterans' crucial role in the modern era. As ideal citizens and patriotic saviors, they embodied a masculine and militaristic vision of the nation. As comrades who drank from the same canteen, they projected a nation of harmony and order, without divisions or grievances. As cosmopolitan continental tourists, they inhabited a modern industrial nation with expanding powers and dominion. Camping was a valuable political tool at every level, and National Encampments were stages for the performance of the campfire camaraderie that sat at the core of each. As a result, even when practiced with less pomp or formality, camping gained the capacity to serve political as well as practical purposes. Camp became a key symbol for the GAR's modern political campaign, as much as it had been a necessity for the earlier military one.

WHEN THE NATIONAL Encampment came to Portland in 1885, John Gould was a bit ambivalent. He was a lifelong member of the GAR but found himself a bit uneasy as his city was gradually taken over. "The city is a-stir getting ready for the GAR. Large number of vets already arrived. I keep aloof as much as possible. My heart is not there, somehow." Given his close ties with local Post members and regimental comrades, he surprised himself in not feeling an automatic kinship with veterans from far flung states. Gould appreciated the "magnificence" of the grounds "fairly covered" with tents but lamented the potential for drunken and disorderly men and the sideshow entertainment. His young son was apparently haunted for days after witnessing an amusement where veterans could pay five-cents to hurl a baseball at a small monkey.[120] In the moment, Gould did not recall that he complained just as frequently of similar debaucheries during army camp life. Here, he judged such events a distraction from the kind of camping sociability he developed and promoted in the years after the war.

He elected neither to camp out on the Encampment grounds nor to march in the dress parade, even declining a position of honor because "I wanted to 'keep out of it.'" But at the moment he heard the "old fashioned tunes . . . on fifes and drums," he wrote that, "tears came to my eyes & wife told me to go. So I ran ahead till I found my Post & marched with it." He admitted that, in the end, "I did feel good . . . tramping around town with my old half-unknown comrades."[121] The experience reinforced his connection less to the GAR itself than to his regimental veterans group, the Maine 1st-10th-29th Association, for which he had played a major role in organizing a reunion the prior year.[122] He had planned this event more along the lines of his usual camping excursions than on the GAR's National Encampment model. He made arrangements for many of the men to tent together near his summer family camping grounds on Cape Elizabeth, where he delighted in hosting local friends and visiting comrades alike. Even a few mishaps and outdoor discomforts—"nights of wretchedness from mosquitoes" in particular—failed to dampen his mood. After it was over, he reported that "the funny part of all is that the bed at home I so much coveted was sickly soft after three nights only of camping" with the "boys."[123] For Gould, who would reach the age of 90, camp reminded of his youth as a soldier and reinforced a veteran identity that anchored him throughout his long life.

In his many years as a veteran, Gould continued to draw upon his experience in Union army camps to develop a style of recreational camping focused on sociability. The GAR transfigured memories of Civil War camp life into the form of modern political encampments. This moment hinted at the multiple new meanings camp might contain, as obligatory functional outdoor practices began to diverge from voluntary symbolic modes of camping as political lobby or social recreation.

Sherman's article about "modern camp-fires" employed all three elements—camaraderie, compulsion, and politics—to make its claims on public nature. In the ongoing military campaigns against Indigenous peoples on the plains, the US Army continued to camp on Native lands as part of a project of national expansion. His efforts to pursue and defeat "the Sioux, Kiowas, Arapahos and Cheyennes, who knew that the building of these railroads would result in the[ir] destruction" flowed from his efforts to achieve victory over Southern rebels. "It was, in fact, a continuous warfare, following the close of the great Civil War, and . . . we won [the Indian] war as we had previously the greater, but not more important one."[124] Camp was still a practical means of moving the Army to battle even as it became a potent symbol of a victorious modern nation on a new campaign. The image of soldiers gathered around a campfire

might evoke the ideal of camaraderie of presumed equals even as it accelerated the transformation of the nation's social contract, often built on a series of
conquests and inequalities. Veterans' voluntary camping, whether in search of
sociability or political symbolism, became a newly meaningful way of claiming
public nature amidst the wrenching changes afoot in American life.

2

The Roads Home

THE OPENING LINES of the best-selling book John Muir would publish in his lifetime, *Our National Parks* (1901), included what would become one of his most enduringly popular expressions: "Going to the mountains is going home." Reflecting on the previous decades, the famed naturalist began by applauding signs that Americans had taken this sentiment to heart. "The tendency nowadays to wander in the wildernesses is delightful to see. Thousands of nerve-shaken, over-civilized people are beginning to find out that going to the mountains is going home."[1] Coupling the impulse to wander with the desire to go home proved to be as compelling as it was incongruous, appealing to many outdoor enthusiasts and environmental advocates in the more than one hundred years since it first appeared in print. To find the origins of this influential combination, however, entails looking at a series of experiences Muir had while camping decades earlier, well before he achieved national renown. His journeys wound through the volatile social and political landscape of the 1860s and 1870s, shaping his beliefs about the benefits of wandering and of inhabiting nature's home.

Muir's love of nature was longstanding, but his ability to find himself at home in the outdoors emerged at a particular juncture. He hinted as much in an *Atlantic Monthly* essay published in 1900 which included an earlier version of the famous line: "Going to the woods is going home; for I suppose we came from the woods originally." The next sentence made clear, however, that inborn harmony in nature did not apply everywhere: "But in some of nature's forests the adventurous traveler seems a feeble, unwelcome creature; wild beasts and the weather trying to kill him, the rank tangled vegetation armed with spears and stinging needles ... making life a hard struggle." Not home at all, this nature was distinctly uninviting. Muir's language alluded to unpleasant reminders of his time wandering Southern roads in 1867, though he did not explicitly mention it. Before he ever laid eyes on California, a twenty-nine-year-old Muir had embarked on a "thousand mile walk" that took him from Kentucky to Georgia and then turned southwest toward the Gulf Coast of Florida. While he found much that captivated him, he had many difficult experiences, including a serious bout of malaria that halted his ambitions to continue his exploration of the tropics in South America. Instead, he landed in Yosemite Valley in the summer of 1868, where he found the homelike welcome he now praised in the *Atlantic* article: "Here everything is hospitable and kind, as if planned for your pleasure, ministering to every want of your body and soul."[2]

Both Muir and those who study him have plausibly attributed this shift in mindset to the physical environment itself. Some landscapes appeared simply more hospitable, beautiful, and healthy than others. Many of Muir's contemporaries shared this belief, as nineteenth-century Americans tended to place local environments on a continuum from salubrious to unhealthy based on such factors as elevation, moisture, wind, terrain, and vegetation. On that scale, the sun-drenched hills of California fared better than the humid, marshy lowlands of the South.[3] Before embarking on his excursion through the South, Muir's mother extracted a promise from him: he would avoid camping out in this suspicious nature whenever possible. She echoed similar fears voiced at the onset of the Civil War about the risks to health among Northern boys unaccustomed to either the damp Southern climate or the perils of camp. Evidence of the maladies of camp was everywhere in the nineteenth century. Between the sanitary challenges of military campaigns and the postwar outbreaks of smallpox and other scourges attributed to encampments of varied sorts, camping in the wrong place among the wrong sorts posed bodily threats.[4] Muir himself barely survived his Southern sojourn, and arrived in the Sierra Nevada while still recovering from the ordeal. He then credited the clear mountain air with restoring him to health and began to imagine his wilderness journeys as going home.

The change in scenery alone explains neither Muir's transformation nor the popularity of his pairing of wandering and home. A richer understanding of both comes from giving closer attention to the social context of his early travels and his perspectives on the camps he made and the people he encountered. In short, Muir was not alone out on the road. His distinctive vision and influential role emerged as he moved not only through majestic wild spaces but also among myriad fellow travelers. Experiences he had leading up to and during his expedition to the South, as well as his initial discoveries in

California that followed, were critical in shaping his view of the benefits of outdoor recreation, views that would later come to define many Americans' outdoor desires. They also shed light on the diverse spectrum of travelers, the range of camping practices, and the uses of public nature in the midst of major social transformations.

It is difficult to see Muir as anything other than a prophetic figure in the American environmental tradition, and placing him among the throngs of ordinary travelers begs a question: Did these experiences foster shared sensibilities or emphasize social division? Most have highlighted the universal elements of Muir's visions, even if they went unrecognized at the time. As a recent biographer suggested, the belief that nature could be "a source of liberation, a place offering freedom and equality" based on wits rather than wealth, united diverse users. "Nature offered a home to the political maverick, the rebellious child, the outlaw or runaway slave, the soldier who refused to fight, and by the late nineteenth century the woman who climbed mountains to show her strength and independence."[5] While the idea of nature as holding a potential for liberation had deep roots, the physical world is not inherently liberating.[6] Moreover, not all of the uses mavericks, children, outlaws, slaves, soldiers, and women made of public nature fit easily within either the flagging agrarian ideal of property-owning citizens or the uncertain social contract emerging fitfully in its decay. Comparing Muir's experiences to those he met—especially Southern Blacks who took to the woods to escape forced labor, Indigenous people under pressure to cede their homelands to resource extraction and white tourism, and even Muir's own coworkers with whom he herded sheep in the Sierras—highlighted separation between forms of camping and interacting with the outdoors. Indeed, Muir developed his signature embrace of nature and his promotion of wilderness recreation in part through observing and rejecting the functional and political modes of camping he witnessed on the road.

Muir had not yet honed his perspective when he started out on the long walk south, harboring a general distaste for camping out and fearing its risks to health. During that journey, he slept outside only when left with no other options. By the time he arrived in the high Sierras he reveled in the visceral pleasures of camping, with a pile of tree boughs for a bed and freshly picked flowers in his pillow. It was there that camping became a way of going home. Nowhere along the way did he wander through "untouched" nature. His observations of fellow travelers gradually led him to determine what conditions made camping enjoyable and to define what a home in nature should look like, and who belonged in it. That belief, in turn, contributed to the establishment of new spaces of public nature, like national parks, and the growing belief that their best use was for the legions of "nerve-shaken, over-civilized" Americans seeking refuge in the outdoors.

"I Would Not Lie Out of Doors"

Muir arrived in Savannah, Georgia in October of 1867, about five weeks and 600 miles into his thousand mile walk. He was disappointed that the money he had asked his brother to send him there had not yet arrived. Muir's dwindling pocketbook forced him to seek free lodging while waiting on the funds. Out of options, he considered sleeping in picturesque Bonaventure Cemetery on the outskirts of the city. Like many pastoral cemeteries across the nation in the nineteenth century, Bonaventure served as a type of public outdoor space, if not usually for overnight use.[7] He briefly wrestled with the pledge to his mother, who made him "promise I would not lie out of doors if I could possibly avoid it." The exigent circumstances and the prospect of sleeping amidst Bonaventure's "grand oaks in the moonlight," however, pushed him to make an exception. He even admitted he was "almost glad to find that necessity had furnished me with so good an excuse for doing what I knew my mother would censure." As his drawing in Figure 2.1 shows, Muir slept upon a grave-mound, and when he awoke the next morning, he recorded in his diary that though his "sleep had not been quite so sound as that of the person below, I arose refreshed, and looking about me, the morning sunbeams pouring through the oaks and gardens dripping with dew, the beauty displayed was so glorious and exhilarating that hunger and care seemed only a dream." He decided to hunker down for a few days and built himself a "moss-nest" for shelter from dew, mosquitoes, and prying eyes.[8]

The unique setting seemed to overcome Muir's reluctance to sleep outside on his long southward journey, when he tended to prefer indoor lodging. Yet in other contexts, he had eagerly pursued the chance to camp out. This am-bivalence linked him with many other sorts of travelers in the mid nineteenth century. For a select few, camping offered a means to the notable ends of explo-ration and rejuvenation, while for many others it was a necessity of last resort. Muir straddled this divide throughout his early travels. Driving Muir's ambi-tion to see the American South was his desire to follow in the footsteps of one of those few, German explorer Alexander von Humboldt. First translated into English in the 1840s, Humboldt's entrancing descriptions of his experiences in the tropics captivated the young Muir, as they had Ralph Waldo Emerson, Charles Darwin, Frederic Church, and legions of other less famous readers.[9]

FIGURE 2.1 Muir draws his spontaneous first night in Savannah's Bonaventure Cemetery, sleeping soundly under a live oak tree, October 10, 1867. First Night in Bonaventure, p. 59 in his "thousand- mile walk" journal. John Muir Papers, Holt-Atherton Special Collections and Archives, University of the Pacific Library. ©1984 Muir-Hanna Trust.

Yet Muir's initial journeys more closely, if unknowingly, shadowed American historian Francis Parkman, who had chronicled his youthful travels in the Northeast and West in *The Oregon Trail* (1849) and the novel *Vassal Morton* (1856). While Muir likely never read these books the way he pored over Humboldt's volumes, the two men's early expeditions shared key elements.[10]

Parkman was among an elite group of students at Yale and Harvard who began to experiment with camping excursions early as the 1830s, in part to offset the unhealthy effects of a deskbound college life. A member of Harvard's class of 1844, Parkman took a number of summer excursions throughout his years there. He headed to the White Mountains of New Hampshire following his first year to "have a taste of the half-savage kind of life" and "to see the wilderness where it was yet uninvaded by man."[11] The foray left him craving more. Parkman's journals from the next year show his desire to seek out places where "no trace of a clearing or cabin was visible, and woods, water and rocks had it their own way." His traveling partner was less enthusiastic, complaining that it made no sense to go "tramping up and down through a beastly wilderness just because it *was* a wilderness." This led Parkman to recommend that more men of "a bookish age" ought to go on outdoor adventures. "If all Harvard College were emptied once a year into the backwoods, it would be well for their bodies and their immortal souls."[12] Soon after graduating, Parkman traveled on the Oregon Trail as an adventurer and observer alongside the migrants. It did not prove healthful as he barely made it through alive, and blamed the trip for many subsequent troubles, including heart pangs, headaches, insomnia, rheumatism, and arthritis, some which dogged him throughout his life.[13]

Despite these issues, Parkman's younger classmates followed his lead, taking outdoor excursions to improve health and well-being. In 1857 Harvard student Charles Horton repeated a common refrain that viewed American students as "weak, puny and indisposed to exercise and out-of-door sports." To combat the all-too-frequent encounters with "the 'monster Dyspepsia,'" he recommended a vacation filled with "glorious long rambles, that give us a new lease of health for the coming year." It is against this backdrop of a sedentary, sometimes sickly, academic life that camping travel began to appear more salubrious. Student campers also sought camaraderie with peers and a sense of freedom. For young men on a six-week break from their studies, an unguided excursion with peers provided a chance to experience a "glorious spirit of liberty" that came with blazing new trails into the mountains.[14] They explored, as one student termed it in 1859, "territory unknown to educated man . . . wandering through virgin forest where no traces of human occupation could be seen, making camp and singing Harvard songs where bears had rooted in the moss that very afternoon." Henry Spaulding exulted in their boldness: "Without compass or guide we came, all for the love of adventure and the honour of Old Harvard."[15] Camping out in the wilderness allowed them to combine an educated sensibility with bodily vigor, exuberant camaraderie, and pride as outdoorsmen.

This combination of invigorating and youthful adventure was possible for a specific group of young, elite, educated white men. Rather than pushing into uncharted territory, these students were building upon growing networks for nature-oriented vacations. In this era, the mountains of New England and New York became a crossroads for scenic tourists on multiple types of journeys. Setting out in small groups of friends, students found many folks out on the trail, often their own classmates. Stories of running into classmates on the top of remote peaks or crossing paths with parties from rival institutions in the same valley were neither uncommon nor disappointing. It was a point of pride when Horton asked, "Where don't you meet Cambridge men?"[16] Realized through personal relationships of generation and social class, these experiences began to forge associations between health, freedom, and recreation in nature. In the 1850s, these men began to articulate a kernel of what would later become a primary argument for recreational camping. The Civil War interrupted the development of this line of thinking, when so many from this generation, including Harvard graduate and camping promoter Charles Horton, would experience different types of camping in the army and as veterans.[17] In this sense, the proto-recreational experiences of college campers did not get fully taken up until well after the war.

Unlike Parkman, Muir was no Boston Brahmin, but in the summer of 1863 he too partook in this tradition of camping as a respite from college. Together with two University of Wisconsin classmates, he set out from Madison with a tent, some blankets, and a hatchet. The plan was to reach the headwaters of the Mississippi and then strike north toward the shores of Lake Superior, collecting plants along the way. Though they made it only to Iowa, Muir found the trip delightful both for the time spent in nature, discovering new plant life, and for the sociable experiences of traveling with companions.[18] Despite the similarities with counterparts in New England, this trip would be the last one he would make as a student. Muir's 1863 camping trip came amidst a period of self-questioning and perhaps served as a catalyst in his decision to leave the university for good. Like Parkman, however, it was only prelude to a much bigger journey.

Whatever desires for tropical climes Muir held at the time, he had no interest in marching south in the middle of war. In fact, he was a pacifist and hoped to avoid getting conscripted. He worked for some months on his father's farm, but in March 1864 his worries about the draft overcame him and he fled to Canada to wait out the war.[19] He walked for weeks exploring the landscape, carrying neither blankets nor food, and stopping at houses to ask for lodging and bread, a practice he would continue on his later journey in the South. Eventually he found longer term work at a remote sawmill, and in 1866 he slipped back across the border and took up a position at a wagonwheel factory in Indianapolis.[20] Here, Muir proved to be a successful engineer and found himself torn between applying his talents for the benefit of modern progress and pursuing his love and fascination for nature. Had a workplace accident causing a serious eye injury not interrupted his career, Muir may have put off his journey indefinitely. During the long weeks convalescing in darkness, he determined that if he regained his sight, he would quit his job and take to the road. His eye healed and he finally made definite plans to head south.[21]

When Muir stepped off the train in northern Kentucky in 1867, he sought "the wildest, leafiest, and least trodden way" possible, even as he shared the roads with multitudes of travelers.[22] Many who ranged across the countryside in the years before and after the Civil War had established standard patterns of functional outdoor travel, into which Muir inserted himself. For peddlers, surveyors, naturalists, and migrants, sleeping outside was one of a defined array of travel options, usually less preferable, but unremarkable enough. Camping for most remained a means to other ends—a way of getting to a destination, a platform from which to observe, a temporary form of lodging—rather than an experience in and of itself. And so it was for Muir.

Of his fifty nights on Southern roads in 1867, before the onset of his illness, Muir recorded spending 10 nights outdoors; 10 nights in taverns, hotels, or lodging houses; and 24 nights lodging in private houses. Some of these private lodgings were with distant acquaintances, but most often he sought shelter in the homes of strangers.[23] Typically, near the close of day he would look for an approachable house to embark upon a fairly standard rural exchange—25 cents for supper and a place to sleep on the floor or in the barn or hayloft. With origins in the colonial payments for quartering of soldiers, this exchange proliferated with the travels of peddlers. For example, one German-Jewish peddler who struck out for the Ohio Valley in 1837 found that by knocking upon an unknown door, he could, "for the standard charge of twenty-five cents . . . obtain supper, lodging, and breakfast." That peddlers and other itinerants could generally expect accommodations at farm houses across the country may seem surprising, but goods for sale and news from afar appeared to offer many householders enticement enough to offer strangers a place to sleep, though it was not without its hazards, whether from the elements or malintent.[24]

Amid defeated white Southerners suspicious of wandering Yankees, Muir understood the diplomacy required to gain a safe berth. Approaching one "wealthy planter," Muir asked for "food and lodging for the night[. H]e said, 'No, no, we have no accommodations for travelers.' I said, 'But I am traveling as a botanist and either have to find lodgings when Night overtakes me or lie outdoors, which I often have had to do in my long walk from Indiana.' "[25] Here, Muir framed sleeping outside not as a voluntary choice, but as a necessity imposed upon him. In fact, he went to considerable lengths to avoid camping out, crafting his presentation as a poor unthreatening botanist, as Figure 2.2 hints at, to earn the trust of a potential host.

Evenings when he managed to gain such entry were typically his most enjoyable. In Georgia he recorded a stay "with a very pleasant, intelligent Savannah family, but as usual was admitted only after I had undergone a severe course of questioning." On another occasion in Kentucky, he "inquired my way at a farm-house" and was pleased to be "invited to stay overnight in a

FIGURE 2.2 In this drawing Muir depicts himself as a botanist, holding some greenery in his left hand while talking with a local, perhaps to negotiate for indoor lodging. Untitled, p. 19 in his "thousand-mile walk" journal. John Muir Papers, Holt-Atherton Special Collections and Archives, University of the Pacific Library. ©1984 Muir-Hanna Trust.

rare, hearty, hospitable manner." Here, he enjoyed the company and joining in the "familiar running talk on politics, war times, and theology." He only reported one negative overall experience with this practice, when he was forced to "escape from a heap of uncordial kindness to the generous bosom of the woods."[26] The outdoors could be a place of refuge under social duress but was never his first choice.

His only other indoor option was to lodge in public houses, hotels, or taverns. Along with many nineteenth-century travelers, Muir presumed these accommodations to be dodgy, either because of the human company or the health risks. Beds could be uncomfortable and shared with biting insects.[27] His experience seemed to bear this out; although he found some comfortable hotels, he reported negative impressions about 40 percent of the time, a much higher rate than for private lodgings. Muir's religious convictions and personal reserve made him distinctly uncomfortable in certain arenas of sociability, including a past encounter with boardinghouse exuberance between young men and women he judged crude and improper. Perhaps his reference to "a heap of uncordial kindness" indicated a similar experience with an overly familiar host or unwelcome offers of companionship.[28] Either way, while Muir wished for conversation and intellectual stimulation, he had to navigate several dangers: gaining entry to private homes or risking social discomfort.

Muir preferred to chance "the meanest-looking lodging house" or to approach suspicious and sometimes armed strangers to ask for supper and bed-space than to sleep outside. When he did resort to camping, he had both enjoyable and difficult moments. Alone outdoors at night, he found his feelings of hunger and lonesomeness intensified. He "suffered from cold and was drenched with dew," and worried about being robbed or worse. The sounds of "strange insects and beasts" made him anxious. His thirst once drove him "to drink from slimy pools groped for in the grass, with the fear of alligators before my eyes." Figure 2.3 illustrates the nightmare this caused that night. Muir was willing to endure much to see, experience, and catalogue parts of nature.[29] And yet his words and his drawings often suggest a certain physical vulnerability, of a figure more overwhelmed by nature than striding confidently through it. Sleeping outside, though occasionally refreshing, did not seem to him a particularly worthwhile method by which to appreciate Southern nature. It was always the means to an end.

Naturalist William Bartram preceded Muir's path through Southeastern environments, camping in and studying the region in the early nineteenth century. Ranging over some of the same ground as Muir, he reported far more

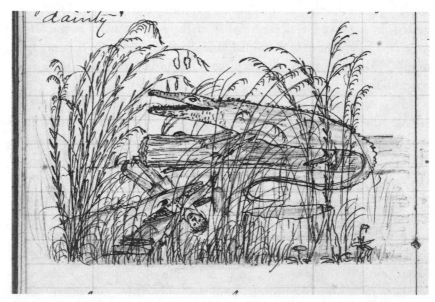

FIGURE 2.3 On one occasion while camping beside a swamp, Muir dreamt that he was consumed by gators, revealing his fears of sleeping outside, though he later wished the "alligator fellows" good fortune. Untitled, p. 99 in his "thousand-mile walk" journal. John Muir Papers, Holt-Atherton Special Collections and Archives, University of the Pacific Library. ©1984 Muir-Hanna Trust.

positive experiences sleeping outside than would Muir some seven decades later. Bartram's *Travels* (1791), describing flora and fauna through a literary combination of personal experience and scientific observation, remained popular, though Muir likely did not consult the book until long after his walk to the gulf.[30] Americans eagerly consumed Bartram's stories of pleasurable traveling alongside his natural history. While he appreciated the "hearty welcome, plain but plentiful board" and conversation while staying at private homes, he wrote much more effusively about the times his party made camp outside. He typically had others to collect firewood, set up camp, and fish for dinner while he wandered off to reconnoiter the area, often finding himself so "seduced by these sublime enchanting scenes of primitive nature" that he would get lost. Returning to camp with the prospect of "having a delicious meal, ready prepared for our hungry stomachs" offered a happy sense of homecoming. The group experience and the hired help buffered him from the fragility of camp life. On his occasional lone camp-outs, Bartram relaxed less and worried more about the dangers presented by having to sleep at the edge of a cliff or next to a swamp filled with mosquitoes and alligators. Bartram's congenial impressions of camp life centered on the group experiences, the evenings around the campfire. "How supremely blessed were our hours at this time! . . . far removed from the seats of strife . . . peaceable, contented, and sociable."[31] With companions, the vagaries of travel and the discomforts of outdoor exposure seemed more bearable.

Muir's aversion to sleeping outside in Southern nature differed from Bartram in more than just the lack of campfire camaraderie. Traveling without a support crew, Muir was subject to the range of factors that were part of the individual traveler's calculus. Deciding one's sleeping arrangements—public or private, indoors or out—was both a common and a risky endeavor. Which was safer? Which jeopardized health? Whether enjoyable or not, for all but the Harvard and Yale crowd, the choice to camp was not about recreation. It was rather a means to an end, and even among those predisposed to appreciate the natural world, like Muir or Bartram, outdoor camps could suggest haven and hazard alike.

"Camping Among the Tombs"

Bonaventure Cemetery was not Muir's first choice of accommodations upon arrival in Savannah. On his first night, feeling "dreadfully lonesome and poor," he elected the cheapest lodging he could find, a "disreputable-looking hotel." The next day, passing the time waiting for his money to arrive, he wandered

around town and after a few miles came upon the graveyard. He found it
a pleasant surprise, after walking through the outskirts of town, passing
"ragged, desolate fields . . . rickety log huts, broken fences, and . . . weedy rice-
stubble." He took delight in the "beds of purple liatris and living wild-wood
trees. You hear the song of birds, cross a small stream, and are with Nature in
the grand old forest graveyard, so beautiful that almost any sensible person
would choose to dwell here with the dead rather than with the lazy, disorderly living."[32] Though sleeping in the cemetery did not immediately occur to
him, Muir admired the cultivated plant life and "noble avenue of live-oaks"
that was the graveyard's "most conspicuous glory" in stark contrast to the neglected and abandoned landscapes he found all around the region.[33]

The devastation the war had wrought was unmistakable. Near the end of his
time in Savannah, Muir remarked that "the traces of war are not only apparent
on the broken fields, burnt fences, mills, and woods ruthlessly slaughtered,
but also on the countenances of the people."[34] In observing the effects of war
on Southern people, their homes and towns, fields and forests, Muir was
hardly alone. A slew of Northerners headed south in the years following the
end of the war, despite irregular transportation and accommodations, to report on conditions, ex-Confederates, and freedpeople—about whom there
was intense curiosity. Initially, most such travelers were Radical Republicans
and journalists who produced an outpouring of newspaper reports and
travelogues.[35] Though Muir did not publish his observations until decades
later, and personal rather than political reasons motivated his journey, again
he had company in his travels.

Among those in whose footsteps Muir walked was *New York Tribune*
editor Whitelaw Reid, a staunch Republican, who spent the better part of
1865 and 1866 "traveling through the late Rebel states," surveying "the chaos
to which the war had reduced one-third of the nation." Reid stayed mostly
in hotels or boarding houses but joined Muir in his suspicion about such
establishments.[36] Muir crossed Reid's previous paths several times, including
at Bonaventure, which Reid judged a melancholy spot. The overgrowing
greenery and toppled marble lent an "impressive gloom" to "the lonely place."
The lush Spanish moss was romantic, but he believed the giant oaks were
"dying in the soft embrace of the parasite that clings and droops, and makes
yet more picturesque and beautiful in decay—dying, even as Georgia was
dying." Reid also hinted that the cemetery harbored a peril more immediate
than metaphor: he reported that the original owners selected the area for a
burying ground because it was an unhealthy "malarious bottom." He saw little
to worry, given that the dead slept without danger.[37]

Following his afternoon visit to the graveyard, Muir considered where he might find a decent "place to sleep" that night that might be free of charge as well as "free from insects and snakes, and above all from my fellow man." He had no desire to return to the lodging house, but the outdoors seemed dicey too; he "feared sickness from the malaria so prevalent here" while rumors that "idle negroes were prowling about everywhere" made him equally "afraid." It was amidst this calculation that Muir "suddenly thought of the graveyard" he had encountered on his walk earlier that day. " 'There,' thought I, 'is an ideal place for a penniless wanderer.' " Fear of ghosts might keep the "superstitious prowling mischief maker" at bay while the canopy of grand oaks offered compensation for, if not protection from, being "exposed to unhealthy vapors." Muir made the best of "Camping Among the Tombs," but there was no mistake that he only considered it due to his temporary poverty.[38] At the graveyard more so than on other parts of his journey, Muir recognized how sleeping outside put him on the margins, in the tumult of displaced white Southerners and freed slaves on the roads. Muir clearly saw less of a sense of kinship with freedpeople than with those who feared the new world in motion. For him, the garden and the tombs offered a slim but important buffer. As Muir's baseless panic about "idle negroes" hinted, he was aware that the mobility of Black folk marked the landscape through which he traveled. This context, and his interpretation of it, would play a key role in his experiences and concept of home, which began to emerge during his memorable cemetery camp out.

For African Americans, traveling and making camp had become both method and symbol of freedom, though it did not come without risk. Enslaved people had begun to trickle and then flood into Union army camps as early as the summer of 1861, fleeing their bondage and forcing the US military and Congress to confront the reality of Black freedom. Absent specific instructions about what to do about these early refugees from slavery, commanders took matters into their own hands. The move to label refugees "contraband of war" not only allowed officers to shelter fugitive slaves from their former masters and put them to work in the Union war effort, but also led to a series of acts that began to unravel slavery well before the Emancipation Proclamation. Enslaved people in large numbers took to the woods and waterways ahead of armed pursuit or walked away from plantations abandoned by fleeing planters until they could reach the Union lines.[39] On the order of 470,000, or a tenth of, enslaved people forged a path of self-emancipation that ran directly through Union camps and posts. Accommodating the growing numbers posed a logistical problem for Army leaders. As General William T. Sherman appraised it, they were "free . . . but freedom don' clothe them, feed them & shelter them."

The problems started at the most elemental level—finding enough tents for initial housing, even after using those that soldiers had discarded as no longer livable.⁴⁰ Eventually, in many places the army established a series of separate camps for contrabands. Figure 2.4 shows a mix of military issue tents with improvised doors and chimneys, but shelters also included deserted houses, makeshift huts, and in some places, cabins the refugees built themselves.⁴¹

Some military leaders went to considerable lengths to figure out workable options, but contraband camps had all the ordinary health and sanitation challenges of army camps, plus more overcrowding and even less reliable medical care. Pneumonia, typhoid, measles, smallpox, and dysentery sickened and killed thousands. In some camps, conditions were so bad that a volunteer aid worker bemoaned the fact that "If the ostensible object was to kill [freedpeople], nothing could be more effective" than contraband

FIGURE 2.4 A contraband camp just over the border into the Union state of West Virginia includes a small grouping of military issue tents with chimneys and doors likely built by escaped slaves seeking self-emancipation there. Photograph by John P. Soule, "Contraband camp—Harper's Ferry, Va.," Harper's Ferry, West Virginia, 1862, Library of Congress Prints and Photographs Division, LC-DIG-stereo-1s04358.

camps.[42] Efforts to make the camps more livable and humane were further undermined by the abuses soldiers, as well as outside employers who leased contraband labor, visited upon the refugees.[43] While some incidents of mal-treatment inspired outrage among Northern civilians, more often contraband camps provoked contempt. Some labeled inhabitants as "idle lazy vagrants" or "camp followers" living on the government dime, blaming freedpeople them-selves for the disease and disorder of the camps.[44]

The widespread problems were not unknown to enslaved people pondering escape. Intelligence networks communicated the risks involved not just in reaching the Union lines, but also the myriad hardships and uncertainties that awaited them upon arrival.[45] Still, Union camps offered at least the possi-bility of achieving freedom rather than waiting to see whether freedom would eventually reach them. As Boston Blackwell explained, the Emancipation Proclamation made no impact on the owner of the Arkansas plantation where he remained enslaved. The months wore on and he decided to try to escape to where the Union army was encamped at Pine Bluff, because, he reasoned, "Iffen you could get to the Yankee's camp you was free right now."[46] Former slaves created both the necessity and significance of contraband camps, where they tested the terms of freedom and suffered a heavy toll.

Contraband camps themselves became important sites for negotiating the permanence and definition of that freedom, which of course remained under debate for some years. Thousands enlisted as soldiers out of the camps, and even more contributed information and labor toward the war effort. In the process, they established expectations about the exchange of service for pro-tection and citizenship—akin to the argument Union veterans would make after the war in lobbying for federal pensions. When the Army tried to recruit former slaves to work in local fields as wage laborers producing food for the troops, however, some initially balked, wanting reassurances that freedoms gained in camp would apply outside it. General Benjamin Butler wrote to President Abraham Lincoln that refugees were "at first a little averse to going back" to work at former plantations, "lest they should lose some rights which would come to them in camp." That Butler had to confirm that they would retain the "same rights as to freedom . . . on the plantation as if they were in camp" suggested how "camp" had become both mechanism and container for a freedom not lightly relinquished.[47] Refugees thus transformed contraband camps into "the first great cultural and political meeting grounds that the war produced," as one scholar observed. Formerly enslaved people gathered and talked, to each other and with Northerners, and engaged in debate over the terms of freedom.[48]

After the war, freedpeople took to the roads and lived outdoors in part to exercise the freedom that victory had granted. As Booker T. Washington remembered, traveling was a kind of test that made freedom real in the minds of former slaves, as many felt "they must leave the plantation for at least a few days or weeks in order that they might feel really sure that they were free."[49] In certain ways, freedom meant the ability to move, without pass or permission. Whitelaw Reid came upon one man who was living in a "patched up ... abandoned tent" in Selma and asked him why he didn't return to northern Alabama where he was from, as he could be "just as free at home as here." The tent, despite its condition, came with some advantages, as the man answered: "But I's want to be free man, cum when I please, and nobody say nuffin to me, nor order me roun.'"[50] Beyond using travel as a test case, freedpeople began to move about the region to reunite families, to seek jobs and Black community in cities, or to return home after wartime displacement in contraband camps, army regiments, or forcible relocation by planters.[51]

Camping or living outdoors was more of a necessity than a symbolic choice, but it remained a material experience of a fragile freedom. Many of the formerly enslaved were "set adrift," "run off," or "kicked out from home" by returning planters. Whitelaw Reid remarked how President Andrew Johnson's decision to restore "confiscated property" to former planters was rendering "many of the freedmen houseless" and "vagrant."[52] In 1865 and 1866, the punitive Black Codes enacted by most Southern states included vagrancy laws that aimed to inhibit the free movement of Black people. Definitions of vagrancy often boiled down to lack of proof of employment or annual contract, and were thus used to break up even relatively settled freedpeople's camps and villages. Punishments often included forced labor on county road gangs or for restored plantation owners who leased convicts from local governments. Though the most overtly discriminatory Black Codes were repealed under pressure from Congress, they were quickly repackaged, remaining substantively similar and enforced only among Black populations.[53] Vagrancy remained a key mechanism by which white Southerners restricted Black movement and made travel a dangerous proposition for freedpeople in the decades that followed. Simply being out on the road, especially after dark, could render one liable to be picked up for vagrancy, rounded up by "citizens' patrols" and beaten, or worse.[54] Despite this, mobility remained one of the few negotiating tactics freedpeople possessed in seeking better wages or work environments. They used it to hold out for greater autonomy, resisting pressure from those, like Reid, who saw Black movement as a problem to be solved.[55]

This was the immediate history into which Muir stepped on the long walk. Struggles over freedpeople's movement and camping were everywhere, and white Southerners circulated sensationalist allegations about their criminality widely.[56] If by 1867 the tumultuous travel of the first year following surrender had settled down somewhat, with labor contracts, land tenancy, and sharecropping beginning to rebind freedpeople to the countryside, there were still many folks on the move. Muir's assessments of this mobile world suggests that he shared common white interpretations and blindspots regarding itinerant freedpeople. He viewed those working on plantations "as of old" as "well-trained, polite, easy-going, and merry," though he attributed this to their being, by nature, "very lazy." His observations led him to believe, for example, that "one energetic white man, working with a will, would easily pick as much cotton as half a dozen sambos and sallies." As for freedpeople on the move, he was more fearful. "Idle negroes . . . prowling about," loose in nature, were problematic figures for Muir.[57]

After five nights in the Bonaventure camp, Muir's money finally came in and he took a steamer to Fernandina, Florida. While cutting westward toward the Gulf Coast, his anxiety about freedpeople increased. One night found him searching "for a dry spot on which to sleep safely hidden from wild, runaway negroes." A few nights later, he found a good spot but "did not dare to make a fire for fear of discovery by robber negroes, who, I was warned, would kill a man for a dollar or two."[58] By contrast, Muir's responses to warnings about roving gangs of unreconstructed white Confederates had been nearly nonchalant. When one Tennessee man informed Muir that the Cumberland Mountains were "far from safe on account of small bands of guerillas who were in hiding along the road," Muir felt sure that most would mistake him for a "poor herb doctor, a common occupation" in the region, and thus leave him alone. "I had no fear . . . very little to lose, and that nobody was likely to think it worth while to rob me; that, anyhow, I always had good luck."[59] By contrast, the mobility of freedpeople rendered them dangerous, "runaway," unmoored to place and therefore "wild," although without Muir's usual admiration for things wild.

Muir's depiction of a Black family living, or at least eating, in the open, exemplified this. Near Gainesville, a desperate thirst drove Muir to follow a light in the woods. Creeping up on the edge of a circle of firelight, "cautiously and noiselessly through the grass to discover whether or not it was a camp of robber negroes, I came suddenly in full view of the best-lighted and most primitive of all the domestic establishments I have yet seen in town or grove." Muir was transfixed at the sight of a man and a woman having dinner by the fire. He continued, "Seen anywhere but in the South, the glossy pair would have been taken for twin devils, but here it was only a negro and his wife at their supper." They returned his astonished gaze and then offered him water and hominy, served to him by a previously unnoticed child, who seemed from Muir's vantage point to have magically "emerged from the black muck of a marsh." To Muir, this denoted his arrival in "the tropics, where the inhabitants wear nothing but their own skins," although in his drawing of the scene, shown in Figure 2.5, they appear clothed. Though fascinated by the "the unsurpassable simplicity of the establishment," he could not bring himself to praise the scene. "It certainly is not quite in harmony with Nature. Birds make nests and nearly all beasts make some kind of bed for their young; but these negroes allow their younglings to lie nestless and naked in the dirt."[60] The personal or economic factors that prompted the campout, the legal duress to which it may have been subject, or the political context in which it sat, seemed to escape Muir's notice.

{Come sonny—eat your hominy}

FIGURE 2.5 Muir's drawing of a Black family living outdoors in northern Florida shows him receiving their offer of water and food, but he criticized the camp as allowing "younglings to lie nestless and naked in the dirt," without considering the broader circumstances. Come sonny—eat your hominy, p. 110 in his "thousand- mile walk" journal. John Muir Papers, Holt-Atherton Special Collections and Archives, University of the Pacific Library. ©1984 Muir-Hanna Trust.

Muir's focus on nesting stands out, especially in light of the shelter in which he had encamped at Bonaventure a few days before, which he referenced several times as his nest. He seemed to view nest-making as the process of creating domestic space in the outdoors, offering protection from the elements whether for bird or human families. He certainly viewed his own nest in more favorable terms than the indefinable outdoor dwelling of the Black Floridian family. What he calls in the text his "moss nest" became in the drawing included as Figure 2.6, "My Bonaventure *home.*" The willing bodily exposure, the seeming refusal to nest, instead suggested to him a noncivilized relationship to nature. As Muir was working out his notion of what it means for humans to be *in nature*, he favored the nest-building as civilized over the unnaturally nest-less.[61]

Neither his Bonaventure moss-nest nor his guise as a poor herb doctor protected him from the advancing malaria. "Weary and hungry" not long after arriving in Florida, he asked at a hut of a white family for dinner. The two dithered but eventually offered Muir some food. He diagnosed the couple as "suffering from malarial fever, and . . . very dirty." He found at least some fault in the dirt itself: "the most diseased and incurable dirt that I ever saw,

FIGURE 2.6 Here Muir labeled his "moss-nest" at the cemetery "My Bonaventure home." He rigged up this small shelter with a "roof to keep off the dew" using scrounged local plant materials. My Bonaventure home, p. 64 in his "thousand-mile walk" journal. John Muir Papers, Holt-Atherton Special Collections and Archives, University of the Pacific Library. ©1984 Muir-Hanna Trust.

evidently desperately chronic and hereditary." This condition seemed endemic and he imagined Southern people accumulating dirt on their bodies like tree rings, in which one could read the age of the wearer and portended sickness. "Dirt and disease are dreadful enough when separate, but combined are inconceivably horrible." Muir's conflation of locality with disease aligned with popular assumptions about the area's low-lying nature. He noted that "All the inhabitants of this region, whether black or white, are liable to be prostrated by the ever-present fever and ague, to say nothing of the plagues of cholera and yellow fever."[62] He, too, would soon be counted among that number.

Social and racial criteria factored into assessments of disease risk as well. Historically, Southern planters had tended to settle their own families on higher ground and relegate enslaved workers to the less healthy, but fertile, "bottom lands." Topographical factors gradually merged with racial ones, and in the aftermath of the Civil War, disease even came to be linked with the arrival of Black freedom.[63] Whitelaw Reid looked for reasons to explain what seemed like a "great disappearance of negroes" from parts of the South. Though a few may have left the region, "disease and privation accounted for the most. Their new-found freedom had soon liberated them, in very many cases from all services on earth." He lamented that diseases like smallpox were ravaging Black communities but assumed that it was because "they had not yet learned to take care of themselves; the emancipation had removed them from the care of their masters, and exposure, neglect and disease were rapidly thinning out the population." Reid chastised Northerners for not helping to address this calamity and condemned white Southerners for pointing to it as proof of inherent Black inferiority. In the end, however, he did not diverge much from the view he quoted disparagingly from a Virginia newspaper that disease was "one of the practical results of negro freedom."[64]

Further, disease became understood as both a result of vagrancy and a justification for controlling vagrants. Many towns used the prevalence or suspicion of disease to break up Black settlements. In Meridian, Mississippi, public health concerns provided cover for officials to burn down a freedpeople's camp and expel its inhabitants from town. In Selma, Alabama, the rumor of a smallpox outbreak prompted a new law prohibiting freedpeople from dwelling in the city unless in possession of written approval from an employer. This rule exposed the fact that associating disease with vagrancy was yet another mechanism to control the mobility of former slaves.[65]

Increasingly, the type of settlement itself—camp—became identified as a problem. The widespread sanitation issues in army camps had already firmly established the link between camp and sickness. During the war, the US Sanitary Commission focused on the camp problem and made advances in controlling the spread of disease, but suspicions lingered that camps were inherently treacherous. "Camp Itch" and "Camp Fever" were common euphemisms for a whole host of diseases from smallpox to malaria. Some of the fears of camp life came not from sanitation challenges, but through the exposure to certain kinds of social dangers. As a function of poverty and certain types of employment, camp indicated a group of people thrown together, unable to choose where or near whom they slept—a dangerous set of conditions for both physical and social bodies. Outbreaks during the postbellum years were often attributed to a marginal or itinerant person whose peripatetic travels entailed exposure to camp environments. The most likely candidates for patient zero were traveling freedpeople, whether they were laborers, performers, preachers, students, or tramps on the road from one place to another.[66] Camp symbolized the hazards of chaotic physical and social mobility.

As African Americans moved between slave and free, plantation and city, South and North, their insistent mobility embodied a massive postwar reshuffling of the social contract. And yet their movement was less an end in itself than a route to freedom and the hope to settle on their own land. Freedpeople's desires for property came just as the prospects for small-scale agrarian ventures had begun to decline in earnest. Largely thwarted in their hopes for property-based independence, freedpeople labored in different sectors of the accelerating industrial economy. They neither had access to public nature in the traditional way, nor a clear place in Muir's emerging vision of nature's benefits. In fact, Muir's racialized reactions clarified for him what he liked and disliked about camp. He wanted camp to feel like a nest, a safe clean orderly home in nature, far removed from the unstable political world of the postwar South.

"You Cannot Feel Yourself Out of Doors"

Muir's travels came to a sudden halt in Cedar Keys, Florida, where he succumbed to a serious case of malaria, most likely contracted during the Bonaventure graveyard campout. He spent three months convalescing there and after a brief but unpleasant stint in Cuba he abandoned the tropics and his plan to head for South America. He retreated to the Northeast where he soon booked passage on a ship to California.[67] The last lines of his manuscript journal suggested a sense of relief as he sailed out of New York harbor in February 1868: "For myself, long burned and fevered, the frost wind was more

delicious . . . than ever was spring-scented breeze." He kept a brief and discon-
nected notebook recording his impressions of crossing the Isthmus of Panama
but did not begin a new journal until well established at a sheep ranch in the
Sierra foothills, nearly a year later. When assembling his unpublished journals
for the posthumous publication of *A Thousand-mile Walk to the Gulf* (1916),
the editor concluded the story instead with this line from reflections in that
later diary about his arrival in San Francisco in April: "I remained there only
one day, before starting for Yosemite Valley."[68]

By the time Muir saw it, Yosemite had been growing in fame for more than
a decade. He had fantasized about visiting the valley during his convalescence
from the eye injury, though put that goal aside in favor of the journey south.[69]
It was only clear in hindsight that Yosemite would redeem his disordered
experiences in the tropics, for Muir initially envisioned California as an interlude. All the time he was discovering the Sierra Nevada those first years
he kept assuming he would soon resume the interrupted journey to South
America, but the longer he stayed the stronger the hold the mountains had
on him.[70] Only in later recollections does the southern walk culminate in the
restorative and home-like nature of California's mountains.

One of the first things Muir noticed upon his arrival was the effect of
California's climate on his bodily health. As he wrote his brother David in
July of 1868, "My health, which suffered such wreck in the South, has been
thoroughly patched and mended in the mountains of California." Writing
more ebulliently to his confidant Jeanne Carr that same month, Muir declared
that "fate and flowers have carried me to California, and I have reveled and
luxuriated amid its plants and mountains nearly four months. I am well
again, I came to life in the cool winds and crystal waters of the mountains."[71]
Identifying California's climate with the restoration of health put Muir in
good company with the state's boosters and the thousands who sought the
balm of its sunshine. Promoters like Charles Nordhoff, who advertised the
benefits of the state's "kindly and healing clime" in *California: For Health,
Pleasure and Residence* (1872), touched off a wave of so-called health-seekers
who came to breathe its curative air.[72] During these years, Muir added his own
items to the list of benefits the state held out for those who took the time to
venture outdoors. While he had admired parts of the Southern environment,
Muir's affinity for full immersion in the wilderness, including sleeping outside, blossomed in the Sierras.

Muir opened his new journal, January 1, 1869, and began by reflecting
on his first months in the state. He now reveled in the liberating experience
of having spent "every day and night of last summer . . . beneath the open

sky." With California's rainy season looming, "a roof became necessary," and he sought means of sheltering and supporting himself. The fall of 1868 found him working on a crew harvesting wheat in the San Joaquin Valley. In December, he took a position shepherding a flock of sheep near Twenty Hill Hollow, a valley north of Merced and not far from Yosemite. When he arrived at the shanty that was to provide his roof for the winter, he found it to be a dubious specimen: "a remarkably dirty and dingy old misshapen box of a place" that gave little protection from rain or wind. There was no obvious bed. Late in the evening, he considered "sleeping on the ground outside, but scattered everywhere there were ashes, old shoes, sheep skeletons . . . etc. And besides these dead evils, a good many wild hogs prowled about, so I had to submit to the perhaps lesser evils of the black cabin. I laid myself very doubtfully down . . . star gazing through the faulty roof, I drifted off into merciful sleep."[73] Despite this inauspicious start, Muir would find contentment with this "simple uncompounded life," though he generally despised the sheep themselves. Regular rain forced him to continue to sleep inside, but he began to think of "the bright green fields" outside the "mean twisted cabin" as his true home. The meadow made him "feel as if I were in a grand building whose walls radiated something that gave sensation of pleasure."[74] The outdoors became for Muir an ideal house.

One of his first published writings, an 1872 article for the California literary magazine *Overland Monthly,* chronicled his transformation at Twenty Hill Hollow: "Never shall I forget my baptism in this font. It happened in January, a resurrection day for many a plant and for me. . . . The Hollow overflowed with light, as a fountain. . . . Truly, said I, is California the Golden State—in metallic gold, in sun gold, and in plant gold. The sunshine for a whole summer seemed condensed into the chambers of that one glowing day."[75] Gone was discussion of the practical inconveniences of traveling in nature that bedeviled him in the South. He urged readers to abandon the beaten path and wander without care. If "traveling for health, play truant to doctors and friends, fill your pocket with biscuits, and hide in the hills of the Hollow, lave in its waters, tan in its golds, bask in its flower-shine, and your baptisms will make you a new creature indeed."[76] As the repeated baptismal metaphor suggested, Muir had undergone a kind of conversion. The invitation to "play truant" and find nature by wandering implied that he had found a greater sense of comfort with the unpredictability of outdoor travel.

By the time spring arrived he was loath to leave his newfound outdoor home and "return to the ordinary modes" of life. When the chance came to keep tending to those wretched sheep that summer, driving them up to the greener highlands, Muir jumped at it.[77] Now he camped enthusiastically, sleeping either in a tent or out in the open, where he could immerse himself in Sierra nature: the "bundle of the Merced's crystal arteries" whose "celestial song" drowned out the bleating of the sheep; the sunset that gave "glorious shafts" of light among "the spruce & pine" that sheltered them; the "small flowery meadow" with a stream flowing with "sublimity & loveliness."[78] This experience generated an increasing attachment to the place and new visions of nature. Four decades later, Muir would reflect on this consequential experience in *My First Summer in the Sierra* (1911), a heavily revised version of the journal he kept in 1869. The narrative established those experiences as the origin of everything he would be known for in later years, founding the Sierra Club, writing books and articles about the glories of nature, becoming a prominent conservationist. While Muir discarded the original journal, the revised narrative combined with his few extant letters provide clues that shed light on the transformative effects of this summer-long camp-out.[79]

Physical experiences played a key role. Sleeping outside in the Sierras brought Muir visceral pleasure. No longer a last resort or a necessary means to the larger end of exploring nature, camping out offered new physical delights. He reveled in making his bed of "plushy, sumptuous, and deliciously fragrant . . . *magnifica* fir plumes, of course, with a variety of sweet flowers in the pillow." Stuffing flowers into his pillow, Muir made sleeping into an immersion experience, nestling within Sierra nature itself. One letter home in August of 1869 began: "We sleep under the open sky upon spruce branches. . . . Dear Sister Sarah Just think of the blessedness of my lot—have been camped here right in the midst of Yo Semite rocks & waters for fifteen days. . . . My foot has pressed no floor but that of the mountains for many a day."[80] He spent but one night during this summer in a hotel, connecting with a visiting friend. He remarked how "it seemed strange to sleep in a paltry hotel chamber after the spacious magnificence and luxury of the starry sky and silver fir grove." He hurried back to his camp the next day, which he credited with improving the quality of his sleep.[81] In June, he recalled, "How deep our sleep last night in the mountain's heart, beneath the trees and stars, hushed by solemn-sounding waterfalls and many small soothing voices in sweet accord whispering peace!" By mid-July he was likening the sleeping experience to rebirth: "How deathlike is sleep in this mountain air, and quick the awakening into newness of life!"[82] This was a markedly different assessment than his distaste for skulking about the swamps of Florida, fearing alligators and freedpeople.

Muir found many sensory rewards in camp, particularly in evening campfires. There was the scented air; the light, especially when the fire was "heaped high . . . [and] blazing like a sunrise"; the glow of warmth which drew him near in the cool nights and worked "enchantment on everything within reach of its rays." Fire also cooked the supper, and he found his appetite "growing keener every day. No lowlander can appreciate the mountain appetite, and the facility with which heavy food called 'grub' is disposed of." In fact, he found that camp repaid for all its efforts: "Eating, walking, resting seem alike delightful, and one feels inclined to shout lustily on rising in the morning like a crowing cock. Sleep and digestion as clear as the air. Fine spicy plush boughs for bedding we shall have tonight, and a glorious lullaby from this cascading creek."[83] These passages conveyed a different, more positive, almost gleeful tone about the mechanics of camp than did his writings from the southern journey.

When his fellow campers and coworkers appeared to neither relish camp as a privileged experience nor notice how it provided access to appreciate the glories of nature, Muir was befuddled. His main coworker over the summer was Billy, the more experienced shepherd of the two. To Muir, California shepherds like Billy led a "degraded" existence. They were "heartily content to 'rough it,' ignoring Nature's fineness as bothersome or unmanly."[84] Muir implored his companion to acknowledge the wonders of the remarkable place, but to Billy Yosemite was nothing but "a lot of rocks—a hole in the ground—a place dangerous about falling into—a d—d good place to keep away from." For Billy, camping remained a matter of necessity, something that came with the occupation. Both he and Muir labored in the western agricultural economy which required residing in camps rather than establishing permanent residence. Though not far removed from seeing camping as a primarily a last resort of necessity, Muir became reluctant to acknowledge its functional purposes, and recoiled from those who still approached it with that calculus. Instead, he sought to exit the growing stream of those who camped out of necessity as a base for labor as quickly as he could. He hoped to become a full-time wanderer, "sauntering and climbing in joyful independence of money or baggage."[85]

Muir's new delight in camping went hand in hand with his association of the mountains as "home." He often wrote about the valleys and meadows of Twenty Hill Hollow and Yosemite as forming a kind of "natural house." Their slopes sheltered an "enclosed, domestic-like nature" where, he suggested, "you cannot feel yourself out of doors; plain, sky, and mountains ray beauty which you feel. You bathe in these spirit-beams, turning round and round, as if warming at a camp-fire. Presently you lose consciousness of your own separate existence: you blend with the landscape, and become part and parcel of nature."[86] Rather than loneliness and exposure, here nature invoked a sense of home-like warmth. His ultimate praise for the outdoors was that it didn't feel outdoors. As Figure 2.7 shows, Muir's sketch of a "Camp on Mt. Hoffman," from the spring of 1869 near the end of his Twenty Hill Hollow journal, depicts a peaceful and domestic scene. The large boulders and both upright and fallen trees encircle Muir and his companion in a protective embrace. All is well in this "natural house": the beds are tidy and one man smokes a pipe while the other tends to supper. At a base camp later that year, under the shade of a hospitable grove of trees near the North Fork of the Merced River, Muir appreciated the familiarity of an established camp, where he had built shelves for dishes and provisions. "Though only a sheep camp, this grand mountain hollow is home, sweet home, every day growing sweeter, and I shall be sorry to leave it."[87] Muir's love of the Sierra grew the more he achieved a sense of domestic harmony in the outdoors.

The particular beauty of the physical environment certainly contributed to Muir's sense of peace and comfort in the California mountains, but his was not necessarily a predictable reaction to it. While tourists were enthralled by the sublime views of Yosemite, they could also find it disconcerting, and

FIGURE 2.7 Muir making himself at home in camp, a "natural house" where "you cannot feel yourself out of doors." Camping on Mt. Hoffman, p. 71 in his "Twenty Hill Hollow" journal. John Muir Papers, Holt-Atherton Special Collections and Archives, University of the Pacific Library. ©1984 Muir-Hanna Trust.

the Sierra Nevada itself was often viewed as danger zone. After revelation of the horrors of the stranded Donner Party two decades before, fear of harsh weather and wildlife lingered. Yet the California landscape had begun to be organized into discrete spaces—some available for development, labor, and resource extraction, and others made safe for leisurely recreation. Muir arrived in a Yosemite Valley tied up in decade-long legal proceedings about land claims of two entrepreneurial white settlers and debate about the fate of the area for development of resources and tourism. The Indigenous occupants of the valley had already suffered several campaigns to force their removal and suppress their land claims well before Congress granted Yosemite to the State of California in 1864.[88] Among the first reserves that would eventually anchor the National Park system, Yosemite was also one in a chain of western spaces where Native people were forced to cede land to the changing priorities of public nature, whether for farms and ranches or for railroads and recreation. Notions that John Muir helped to popularize—preserving pristine wilderness for recreational and spiritual purposes—rested on the prior exclusion of Indigenous people from such spaces and became a rationale for their continued removal. The process that allowed Muir to find comfort and pleasure in sauntering and camping in the Sierra was already underway before he glimpsed its wonders.

"A Rightful Part of the Wilderness"

Long before Muir was moved to call these mountains home, groups of Miwok, Mono, Paiute, Yokut, and other Indigenous peoples had inhabited the region for many centuries. Muir's interpretations of those he met played a key role in his definitions of both comfortable home and pure wilderness, and the relationships between them. These experiences were significant in his evolving approaches to outdoor travel, and thus to those of his devotees who camped and reveled in Yosemite Valley. Muir arrived in California with memories of observing Winnebago people in Wisconsin, who he described as "blackmailing," "pig killing," and "cruel," although he acknowledged that they had been unfairly persecuted. In later years, he would label "Yosemite Indians" a "warlike tribe" that employed "their usual murdering, plundering style" to resist the intrusions of Gold Rush miners.[89] But the stories he told about California Indians in 1869 suggested that he found them a different sort of threat, disruptive to his sense of harmony in a pristine nature.

The Native people Muir encountered represented a small fraction of what had been a large and densely settled population. When the Spanish established permanent settlement in 1769, perhaps 300,000 Indigenous peoples, speaking more than 100 languages, had been living for nearly ten millennia in what would later become California. As many as 100,000 had lived in the Sierra Nevada, on both the California and Nevada sides, using the mountains and meadows for hunting in the summers, collecting acorns in the fall, and holding trade festivals. Spanish missionary incursions made less impact in the Yosemite region than they did on the coast, but disease and other factors contributed to a steep decline in the Indigenous population, approximately cut in half by the eve of US statehood in 1850. The Gold Rush greatly accelerated this decline, and by the time Muir arrived, perhaps only 30,000–50,000 Native Americans people survived across the state. In particular, gold strikes on the Merced and Tuolomne rivers intensified the pressure on Miwok and Yokut peoples.[90]

Miners and other white settlers in the area feared Indian reprisals, and an early act of the first California legislature in 1850 empowered counties to raise their own military force at state expense for the precise reason of pursuing "expeditions against the Indians." It also passed an act denying Native people rights to vote or testify and allowed for certain kinds of forced labor under the guise of "protection" or "adoption." Mariposa County raised a battalion under this law and in 1851 sent it into Yosemite to round up "the remnants of once numerous and powerful tribes." Federal Indian agents dispatched to California that summer pressed for moderation, acknowledging that Indigenous people were the "original owners and occupants of those beautiful valleys and mountain ranges," but at the same time characterizing Indians as "ignorant, lazy and degraded." Given that there was "now *no farther West* to which they *can* be removed," the agents presumed only two possible fates for California Indians: "extermination or domestication."[91] The Mariposa Battalion moved in and began to force groups of Miwok people out of the mountains, in the process "discovering" Yosemite Valley and bringing back the tale of its remarkable natural wonders. The Southern Miwok group known as the Ahwahneechee proved the most resistant to the Mariposa Battalion's pursuit, although they too eventually succumbed and were forcibly relocated. Similar stories of violence and removal echoed across the state.[92]

This transformation of Yosemite not only set in motion the possibility for new uses of public nature for national parks but it also fostered the concept of Indian reservations. The 1850s efforts in California to remove Indigenous groups from their lands in the gold bearing hills and relocate them provided models for this shift. On these proto-reservations called "rancherias," Native people were often coerced into agricultural labor under the guise of instruction and within the framework of industrial production rather than the agrarian ideal. As such, the push to restrict the free movement of Native people and confine them to reservations was not so far removed from the efforts to limit the mobility of Black freedpeople and bind them to plantation labor. In their 1851 statement, the Indian Agents explained the dual advantages of "domestication": not only did it clear spaces for white habitation but it also "secures to the State an element greatly needed in the development of its resources, viz; cheap labor."[93]

Like African Americans, Native people resisted this regime when and how they could, sometimes simply by leaving, often returning to their original lands or neighboring territories in the mountains and foothills. More than a few Miwok and Mono communities reestablished their presence in the Yosemite Valley, joined by Paiute groups from the other side of the range, quietly adapting to the growing tourist industry. Reports of Indian settlements or camps in the Valley and surrounding meadows were nearly continuous throughout the following decades. In 1861 and 1862, tourists recorded an Indian camp at the foot of Yosemite Falls and bark lodges at Clark's Station. In 1867, Native people were working in the tourist trade and delivering the mail. And they were there when John Muir arrived in 1868.[94] Though they did not attempt to expel the increasing number of outsiders, they still understood whites, as one of the Indian agents had recognized, "as trespassers upon their territory, invaders of their country, and seeking to dispose them of their homes." Indigenous people continued to press this view in 1890 in a petition to Congress asking for payment of one million dollars for the theft of their land.[95] So when Muir decided Yosemite was home for him, he stepped into what was both a tentative truce following a brutal battle and an ongoing cold war, as Native Americans continued to assert their rights to this place as home even as their conquerors exerted a tightening hold on it.

The 1850s and 1860s, when Yosemite was gaining fame as a marvel of spectacular nature, were an interlude when the Valley was less inhabited than it was before or would be afterward. The Mariposa Battalion had razed and burned any structures it came across in 1851, and the Ahwahneechee and other groups returned slowly, cautiously, and without fanfare in the years after. In the interim, whites had erected a few cabins and a modest hotel, but Muir and other visitors viewed the region as largely empty before their arrival. Moreover, the accepted history of the white "discovery" of the landscape suggested that the Indigenous inhabitants had used the land not for permanent settlement but only for seasonal forays and had subsequently vanished.[96] Muir seemed largely to share the belief that the valley was an example of untouched nature, virgin wilderness without impactful human history. He occasionally noted that Indians had probably "roamed these woods" for many centuries, "extending far beyond the time that Columbus touched our shores," but saw few traces of their legacy. This vision of wilderness as pristine was built upon the removal and relative absence of Indigenous people from the landscape.[97]

When Muir did encounter Native Americans personally, he tended to imagine them as recent arrivals like himself. Muir's story of a place called "Brown's Flat" illustrates this strange turn. In a long entry for June 6, he recounted the story of "adventurous pioneer David Brown," who established a base camp in the valley. Brown, an Irish immigrant who sold meat and supplies to Gold Rush miners, hunted deer and bear around the place that still bears his name.[98] Muir closed his entry by noting that "Brown had left his mountain home ere we arrived, but a considerable number of Digger Indians still linger in their cedar-bark huts on the edge of the flat. They were attracted *in the first place* by the white hunter whom they had learned to respect, and to whom they looked for guidance and protection against their enemies the Pah Utes."[99] Here, Brown became the original "pioneer" and the Native people the later arrivals. The Indians to whom he refers, using the widespread and derogatory label of "digger," were likely among those that trickled back into the Valley following the 1851 removal.[100] By refusing to recognize them as inhabitants in the first place, Muir rendered Yosemite's Indigenous people interlopers in untouched nature, rather than acknowledging that the Sierras were more deeply their living home than his recent discovery of the region's homelike qualities.

When he occasionally expressed admiration for Native people or sympathy with their plight he did so by likening them to wild nature, rather than human community. Muir characterized one of his coworkers, a Native man helping to drive the sheep from base camp to base camp, as keeping "himself in the background, saying never a word, as if he belonged to another species." Two weeks later, Muir came upon an Indian who had arrived at their camp unobserved, "standing grim and silent within a few steps of me, as motionless and weather-stained as an old tree-stump that had stood there for centuries." He then marveled at the apparently innate "wild Indian power of escaping observation" and their "wonderful way of walking unseen,—making themselves invisible like certain spiders I have been observing here." Because of their wildlife-like qualities, Muir believed that Native people were not as destructive to the landscape as the whites he excoriated for blasting rock, damming streams, and stripping the hillsides. Indians, on the other hand, "walk softly and hurt the landscape hardly more than the birds and squirrels, and their brush and oak huts last hardly longer than those of wood rats." Tree-stumps, spiders, birds, squirrels, and wood rats—to see the value of Indigenous peoples' place on the land he rendered them part of nonhuman nature rather than human community.[101]

While Muir depicted Native impacts as fleeting and their residence as temporary, there was room for another view, even at the time. Eadweard Muybridge, an innovative photographer who visited in 1872 demonstrated how viewers might see Yosemite as home for a community of Indigenous people. In a remarkable series of stereograph views published under the title "Indians of California," Muybridge showed Native Americans not as newcomers in a place heralded for its natural glory but as entirely at home in the Valley. Boys swim in the river, an audience listens to music, families sit outside their encampments, and as Figures 2.8 and 2.9 show, people gather for a meeting and women make bread. The Native people in this series are the central subjects rather than the spectacular scenery, and they reveal interdependent connections with the landscape. Muybridge's images communicate social endurance rather than fleeting otherness.[102] Muir too must have observed some of these activities and noted multiple ways that Native people engaged with nature in the region that summer of 1869. But his interpretation emphasized their strangeness in the landscape, in contrast to his growing feelings of being at home.

In contrast, Muir preferred an ascetic approach. Refusing to rely upon the local landscape for sustenance enhanced his connection with nature. He began to take to the woods with very little food, usually bringing nothing at all on day trips. As he wrote home during his winter in Twenty Hill Hollow, "I can make good bread, and eat good beans. . . . I used to carry a block or two of the bread . . . to the field for dinner, but I have abandoned the practice and make breakfast span the whole distance from morning to night."[103] Lack of bread entirely, however, posed a distinct problem. At one point that summer, he and Billy ran out of flour and had to subsist for a time solely on mutton culled from their flock. Although he claimed that "with just bread and water" he could remain "tethered forever" in the Sierra, going without any bread was a calamity that left him nauseated. A few days into the "bread famine," he awoke "Rather weak and sickish . . . and all about a piece of bread." The craving frustrated him, "as if one couldn't take a few days' saunter in the Godful woods without maintaining a base on a wheat-field and grist-mill." Only after the resupply arrived was he again able to turn his "eyes to the mountains." This ordeal proved to Muir that "no other food of a civilized kind" could sustain his ability to appreciate nature. "Just bread and water and delightful toil is all I need . . . to enjoy life in these brave wilds in full independence of any particular kind of nourishment."[104] It was a specific, "civilized" asceticism, that separated him from the place in which he dwelled.

FIGURES 2.8 AND 2.9 Muybridge captures Indigenous people at home in Yosemite, with these two images in the series showing a group gathering and women grinding acorns to make bread. "Making bread," and "A Summer Campsite," photographs by Eadweard Muybridge, 1868. Eadweard Muybridge Photograph Collection, Department of Special Collections and University Archives, Stanford University Libraries.

Interdependent practices, on the other hand, seemed strange to him. Muir occasionally chastised himself for failing to make use of the biota as the locals might, but he never seriously pursued how to reap nourishment from the land. In his later review of the bread famine, he mused, "Strange we should feel food-poor in so rich a wilderness. The Indians put us to shame, so do the squirrels,—starchy roots and seeds and bark in abundance, yet the failure of the meal sack disturbs our bodily balance, and threatens our best enjoyments." He admonished himself: "We should boil lupine leaves, clover, starchy petioles, and saxifrage rootstocks like the Indians"—but he didn't do

FIGURES 2.8 AND 2.9 Continued

that. Muir held to the ascetic approach as a more civilized path to appreciating nature than the interdependent relationships he observed among Indigenous peoples.[105] In fact, their interdependence was what led him to question their ability make a civilized home in nature.

Muir's ambivalence was apparent in his encounter with a group of Native women harvesting wild rye. Though he guessed that "the bread made from it must be as good as wheat bread," he could not fully praise the harvesting process. "A fine squirrelish employment this wild grain gathering seems, and the women were evidently enjoying it, laughing and chattering and looking almost natural, though most Indians I have seen are not a whit more natural in their lives than we civilized whites." He went on to disparage their "mere brush tents" and "flimsy huts," and to recoil at their eating of buffalo berries, fly larvae, worms and caterpillars. Still, he found pine nuts to be "delicious" and acknowledged that acorns made "good bread and good mush."[106] Unable to characterize Indigenous people as either natural or civilized, their apparent occupation of an indeterminant middle ground left him distinctly uncomfortable.

What kept him from seeing Native Americans as fully natural was what he described as the "strangely dirty and irregular life" they led amidst a "clean wilderness." Even as Muir characterized Indians as more akin to wild creatures than civilized men, he withheld from them the praise he reserved for things truly wild. "The worst thing about them is their uncleanliness. Nothing truly wild is unclean."[107] One Indigenous woman visited the sheep camp on her way to tend "some wild garden, probably for lupine and starchy saxifrage leaves and rootstocks." Skipping over this observation that she was practicing horticulture, he proceeded instead to compare her unfavorably to wildlife.

> Her dress was calico rags, far from clean. In every way she seemed sadly
> unlike Nature's neat well-dressed animals, though living like them on
> the bounty of wilderness. Strange that mankind alone is dirty. Had she
> been clad in fur, or cloth woven of grass or shreddy bark, like the ju-
> niper or libocredus mats, she might have seemed a rightful part of the
> wilderness; like a good wolf at least, or bear.[108]

Again Muir distrusted those he judged as falling somewhere between higher civilization and pure, wild nature and thus forfeiting one's claims to a home in "clean wilderness."

Muir's interpretations evidence his deep misunderstandings about Indigenous lifeways in the Sierra. For example, while "sauntering enchanted, taking no heed of time," admiring the rocky escarpments, he cringed upon encountering a group of Mono people on the same trail. "Just then I was startled by a lot of queer, hairy, muffled creatures coming shuffling, shambling, wallowing toward me, as if they had no bones in their bodies. . . . The dirt on some of the faces seemed almost old enough and thick enough to have a geological significance; some were strangely blurred and divided into sections by seams and wrinkles that looked like cleavage joints." After watching "the gray, grim crowd . . . vanish down the trail," he admonished himself for his "desperate repulsion from one's fellow beings, however degraded. To prefer the society of squirrels and woodchucks to that of our own species must surely be unnatural."[109] Though Muir decided to pray for tolerance, he failed to see that dirt-caked skin was not a sign of negligence, but instead a logical strategy for protection of the body, one he might have found useful. According to the memoir of Ta'a:kai, a Mono man also known as Gaylen Lee, "Grandpa said that covering the body with dirt not only prevents annoying mosquito bites but also protects against sunburn." Ta'a:kai then reinterpreted Muir's trailside encounter with his ancestors. "Muir's observation is actually quite funny. I can imagine him suffering from many mosquito bites while the 'queer, hairy, muffled creatures' protected themselves by covering their exposed skin with dirt."[110]

Though Muir simultaneously recognized and rejected Indigenous peoples' ability to produce a diversified diet from the Sierra ecosystem, he generally failed to appreciate the complex ways they were working the land. Well beyond what is typically called hunting and gathering, Ahwanheeche, Miwok, and Mono people, among others, practiced sophisticated horticulture, anthropogenic fire, and seasonal migration to manage the plant and animal resources within a wide range of territory. Their efforts to produce materials for food, medicine, basketry, tools, and weapons included varied practices of aerating soil, dividing roots, culling plants, weeding, transplanting, and selective harvesting—all of which most white people dismissed under the simplistic and derogatory term "digging." Along with pruning, training, irrigating, and burning, these forms of disturbance increased yields as well as improved the diversity and quality of plant life. While Muir reduced their approach to living like animals "on the bounty of the wilderness," Indigenous people were not simply gathering wild plants. They tended their homeland by intervening in the ecology in ways that made the region more of a managed garden than the untouched nature Muir prized for wandering and camping. It's not unlikely, for example, that many of the meadows he called home were the result of cyclical anthropogenic fire. Yet the effects of these methods were at once so comprehensive and so subtle that white observers missed their significance and mistook the landscape as a pure and virgin wilderness.[111]

Such omissions led Muir to see Indigenous people as unnatural interlopers in a pure wilderness, rather than careful managers and longstanding inhabitants of the place. Instead, Muir advocated for aesthetic and recreational experiences in nature as a salve for mind, body, and spirit. He first invited his friends and family back home to visit the Valley, luring Jeanne Carr to come and " 'camp out'—to alight like birds in beautiful groves of your own choosing . . . among the rocks & waterfalls."[112] Though Muir disparaged the shallow ambitions of the few "glaring tailored tourists we saw that frightened the birds and squirrels" in 1869, he both hoped they might grow from the experience and encouraged many more visitors in the years that followed. As he wrote to Carr a few years later, "I care to live only to entice people to look at

Nature's loveliness." He wanted people to appreciate and enjoy the outdoors, in part that they might advocate to preserve wilderness.[113] The most receptive audience for this message was initially wealthy tourists, for whom nature-oriented sightseeing could be a leisure pursuit. For them, Yosemite could be a spiritual home away from home, where the infrastructure they depended upon was not the Sierra landscapes, but the industrial apparatus that made their journey and their leisure possible.

By the time Muir published "Twenty Hill Hollow" in 1872, one of the first among his many articles extolling the Sierras, tourists had begun to descend on Yosemite in droves, borne along by the newly completed transcontinental railroad. The article implored visitors not to follow the herds "who submissively allow themselves to be packed and brined down in the sweats of a stagecoach . . . hurled into Yosemite by 'favorite routes,'" and rushed through a list of must-see sights on the "touristical see-saw of Yosemite, geysers, and Big Trees." Instead, Muir urged them to model the "the few travelers who are in earnest—true lovers of the truth and beauty of wildness," who had the privilege and foresight to simply wander and soak up the splendor of nature. To them he urged, "cast away your watches and almanacs, and go at once to our garden-wilds—the more planless and ignorant the better." His promotion of the benefits of wandering built in a separation between wanderer and landscape even as he beguiled readers with his description of the Hollow as a home where you "cannot feel yourself out of doors."[114]

Experiences in California and encounters with Native people clarified Muir's preferences for leisured wandering and camping, where his earlier walk through the South seemed to occupy an uncomfortable middle ground. He would continue to elevate contemplative experiences in nature over productive ones. Muir's ideology and prose both inspired many future travelers and reflected the evolving organization of the landscape itself. Yosemite came to embody a new form of public nature, an outdoors developed for recreational use, a respite from productive life rather than the basis of it. As the nation moved away from the agrarian social contract, Muir and others promoted personal inspiration and pleasure as the highest uses of the outdoors. Industrial developments, like transportation networks, tourist markets, and defined leisure time, supported the expansion of the concept of outdoor recreation. While Muir was a prescient advocate for the intricate connections within ecosystems, of the wholeness of nature, he also fostered a particular form of individualized appreciation that worked to separate people from the landscapes through which they traveled. Catering to this recreational impulse, favoring one set of campers discovering an outdoor home over Indigenous inhabitants trying to sustain theirs, influenced how future stewards of Yosemite and other reserves of public nature would organize space and resources.

AS THE SUMMER of 1869 came to a close, Muir resisted leaving the mountains. To stay on through the winter and experience the valley without tourists, he reluctantly took a job helping develop Yosemite's tourist infrastructure. His employer, land claimant and hotel operator James Hutchings, tasked Muir with managing the sawmill and upgrading visitor facilities. Muir worked on and off for Hutchings to support his Yosemite habit and he was still there in May 1871, when Ralph Waldo Emerson arrived. Eager to host the eminent thinker in his beloved Sierras, Muir implored Emerson to extend his stay: "I most cordially protest against your going away so soon," he stated, and proposed the two embark upon "a month's worship with Nature."[115] Years later, in *Our National Parks,* Muir recalled his disappointment that his offer of "an immeasurable camping trip back in the heart of the mountains" was declined. Emerson's entourage scoffed at Muir's "wild plan" and the idea that "Boston people" should need to seek "Sierra manifestations of God at the price of rough camping." Muir lamented that they stuck to "the hotels and trails" for their mere five days in Yosemite but he got another chance when he was invited to accompany the party on their next stop, the Mariposa grove. When Emerson initially agreed to the proposal of a very brief camp out, Muir exulted "that we would have at least one good wild memorable night around a sequoia camp-fire." But this time, health concerns about having "to lie out in the night air" scuttled the plan. Muir protested that "only in homes and hotels were colds caught, and nobody ever was known to take cold camping in these woods," but again he was rebuffed. The two men became friendly correspondents in the ensuing decade, though they had no more opportunities to camp together.[116]

Muir's story of meeting the celebrated Emerson focused largely on his attempt and failure to convince the elder man to go camping. Though the company seemed to find "wondrous contentment" in their visit to the Sierras, for Muir their "ordinary tourist fashion" wasn't nearly enough, especially for a man of Emerson's sensibilities. He had been "so sure" that Emerson, of all people, "would be the quickest to see the mountains and sing them."[117] Even a man like Emerson, Muir seemed to suggest, could not really know nature without camping in it. That this refusal to camp made such a significant impact upon his memory reveals how it had come to be particularly meaningful for Muir as a favored way to engage with wilderness. During his long walk through the South just a few years before, he had not been a fan. Far from privileging camping, he tried to avoid it and its potential for exposure to illness. His experiences on the road led him toward a conception of camping in the wilderness as harmonizing the sense of wandering free with the appeal of going home.

Muir's own practices of sleeping outside, and the meanings he attached them, shifted as he came into contact with varied sorts of travelers—students and freedpeople, sheep and shepherds, Native peoples and tourists. To read Muir's later works, the desire to camp out appears so natural it begged little explanation. His earlier travels reveal the sometimes fitful journey he took toward his signature vision. His was just one of many possible interpretations Americans made of outdoor travels during these tumultuous years, and it was built in part upon his own inabilities to acknowledge the complexity of those whose paths he intersected—African Americans looking to exercise freedom or find work, Indigenous people working to sustain their own homes and lands. Muir's reading of his experience as both the most natural and the most civilized, however, affected more than just his own outlook. His luminous praise for the Sierra Nevada and tireless advocacy on behalf of wilderness would inspire generations of "nerve-shaken, over-civilized people" to embrace the mantra that "going to the mountains is going home." In doing so, they relied upon wrenching social transformations of the industrial age that made that new conception of public nature possible.

PART TWO

Outdoor Promises, 1880s–1940s

3

Tramps and Tramp Style

IN 1884 SAMUEL JUNE BARROWS, a Unitarian clergyman and reformer from Boston, chronicled his experiences camping with his family on a lake that straddled the Vermont–Quebec border. Serialized in a new outdoor magazine, Barrows's stories of "The Shaybacks in Camp" suggested that the best mechanism for partaking in nature's "wild, luxurious freedom" was "through the medium of camp-life." Barrows's view of camping as a medium to experience the freedom of the outdoors would become an increasingly common interpretation. His rationale for camping also emphasized that his family sought "a happy medium between the enervating luxuries of highly-wrought civilization and the rude asperities of savage life."[1] In aiming for the space between those two poles, Barrows advocated neither John Muir's ascetic wandering nor John Mead Gould's veteran outlook. His vision, however, built upon the growing divide between recreational and functional forms of camping and included a desire to find both home and sociability in the outdoors.

In *The Shaybacks in Camp: Ten Summers Under Canvas* (1887), June and his wife Isabel Chapin Barrows addressed their volume to the "American business and professional" classes puzzling over what to do with their annual vacation. "Camping out," they proclaimed, offered a "practical solution," providing a real "summer rest" from the pressures of urban life. The search for relaxation was not the only problem for which camping supplied a solution. June and Isabel were then in the middle of a fifteen-year stint coediting *The Christian Register,* a national Unitarian weekly and they pursued a great many Progressive causes, from women's suffrage to prison reform. Their advocacy of recreational camping intersected with these endeavors in occasionally surprising ways.[2] Both as mechanism and middle ground, the Shayback camping formula guided many Americans in their enjoyment of the outdoors and their changing estimation of its social purposes.

One thing did give June Barrows pause. At the start of one of their first summer forays, the family arrived on a train platform with piles of baggage. He recalled a sudden feeling of discomfort with the "motley array of bedding, boxes, bags, and bundles" that might lead some to mistake them for something other than vacationing travelers. Rather than the sheer amount of luggage, what raised "suspicions of vagrancy" was the messy appearance: "the roll of bedding tied up in a piece of old carpet, . . . the oat-bag filled with tent-pins, or . . . the shapeless bundle, a little out at the elbows." Observers might reasonably assume "that the owner has just graduated from the poor-house, and has embarked for some new domain of pauperism."[3] Barrows, along with other recreational campers, recoiled from such associations and the surface similarities caused no small measure of anxiety among those extolling the benefits of outdoor leisure.

Though he did not employ the word, Barrows conjured the figure campers hoped to avoid resembling: the tramp. Before the 1880s, the word tramp simply meant a long walk, a strenuous hike, or a tiring march—the road traveled, not the traveler. This usage was soon eclipsed by a more charged definition of tramps as itinerant travelers, men on the move, without homes. John McCook, a social investigator who would become known for his studies of tramps in the 1890s, listed their presumed attributes: "aimless wandering, no visible means of support, capacity to labor along with fixed aversion to labor, begging from door to door, camping on property of others without their consent."[4] What came to be called the "tramp problem" signaled discomfort with the presence of a persistently itinerant, perhaps intentionally rootless section of the population. Homeless tramps, traveling hoboes, and migratory workers appeared to engage in a kind of "casual lodging" that ran counter to growing middle-class beliefs in the symbolic importance of "the home" as an anchor for social order.[5] Beneath stereotypes about tramps as lazy freeloading con artists lay condemnation for their apparent rejection of the pursuit of property. Tramps fit neither in the fading agrarian ideal nor in the focus on the home as the central form of property in the social contract that was emerging during the industrial age.

Recreational camping and the "tramp problem" developed in tandem. The rapid advance of industrialization and urbanization between the 1880s and the 1910s both created new forms of itinerancy and underwrote camping as a leisure pursuit. On the one hand, dramatic economic shifts left many

Americans adrift, with neither the skillset required in new white-collar sectors nor dependable wage labor. They roamed from one city to another seeking better options in factories, they followed the expanding rail network to the West to find work in resource extraction, they alternated job-seeking with hoboing, and they endured forced migration or expulsion for vagrancy. All of these necessitated functional camping of one sort or another. As one scholar evocatively suggested about this era, "The United States was not just a nation of farms, small towns, and industrial cities. For the country's poorest working people, America was a vast archipelago of camps."[6]

On the other hand, the urban industrial economy expanded the opportunity for outdoor recreation. More white-collar office workers gained the ability to take periodic vacations and access to new transportation networks. Infrastructure for travel, such as roads and railroads, smoothed their path to a new array of outdoor spaces like national parks and state preserves. Commercial outfitters and gear providers began to cater to a consumer market. The expansion of the periodical press particularly helped to define the benefits of outdoor leisure and spread the popularity of camping. Barrrows's Shaybacks stories, for example, appeared in *Outing* magazine, established in 1882 amidst a new crop of outdoor-oriented publications. Owned and edited by a series of well-known and well-off outdoorsmen, *Outing* became one of the fastest growing mass-market monthlies of all types, with a circulation of more than 100,000 by 1905. During its four-decade lifespan the magazine cultivated a readership among white, native-born city-dwellers from the upper and middle classes. The expanding publishing industry encompassed a spate of similar outdoor-focused periodicals, national and regional magazines, guidebooks and travelogues. Together, they assembled a recreational ethos that linked outdoor adventure with enlightened modern mindsets.[7]

If the simple impulse to enjoy the outdoors was part of what drove interest in leisure camping in the late nineteenth and early twentieth century, the proliferating accounts and descriptions of camping themselves became a medium for broader social conversations, even for those who did not physically go to the woods. To talk about camping was to contemplate rising class tensions, changing gender roles, and shifting racial dynamics. Where did servants, Native people, or mobile workers fit in this new camping landscape, or in the nation? Discussion on these points shaped new uses for public nature in a volatile era from which was emerging a social contract that prized a novel combination of home, work, and leisure.

"The Most Comfort Consistent with
the Most Freedom"

For camping to become both a "practical solution" and a "happy medium," as the Barrowses envisioned, it had first to become a pursuit unto itself. Early issues of *Outing* tended to feature camping primarily as support for other activities, such as hunting, hiking, climbing, boating, fishing, cycling, adventure travel, and nature study.[8] Before long camping earned a discrete subsection, within which enthusiasts began to work out specific formats and rationales. Most framed it as a temporary escape, built upon the eventuality of returning to a real home. Recreational camping thus aligned with the developing context for vacations.

Over the course of the nineteenth century, the vacation grew from a luxury practice reserved for a small set of elite Americans to something of an annual expectation among a broader swath of the middle or professional classes. It would not come within the reach of the mass of laborers until a few decades into the twentieth century, when unions began to make greater headway in securing vacation benefits. Before then, the ability to take a regular vacation was one of the markers of middle-class status, as well as of broader shifts toward industrial, clock time and away from agricultural, seasonal schedules. Many destinations relied upon the attraction of the outdoors, especially mountains, woods, lakeshores, and beaches. Federal and state agencies began to set particular landscapes aside for recreational development, with new tourist amenities to attract vacationing Americans—from the Adirondacks to Yellowstone, the Glaciers to the Grand Canyon.[9] Alongside specific places, promoters began to extol the benefits of taking a deliberate respite from work and the city.

Summer resorts, scattered on the shores and foothills of the Eastern seaboard, catered to the longstanding instinct to leave the city and lowlands during the hot, humid, and buggy months and promoted outdoor pursuits, like ocean swimming, hot springs bathing, and nature walks. Yet as they grew, these resorts also became places to experience high society. Guests expected dress balls and haute cuisine, and their sojourns appeared in city newspaper society columns. Facilities turned up in all regions of the country, advertising themselves simultaneously as nature retreats, social events, and health resorts.[10] Social expectations could become so formalized that some began to see the strictures and schedules of resort life as too closely mimicking urban patterns.

Those disaffected with resorts were among the early adopters of camping. In multiple national publications, these advocates compared rustic camping favorably to luxury resorts. As early as 1875, an article appearing in the "Home and Society" section of *Scribner's Monthly* imagined some city folk looking to escape the coming "miasma and heat and dust of August" but fretting about conforming to onerous etiquette and fashion requirements and suffering "more anxious swarming crowds than those left behind." Instead, the article suggested a practice "rapidly growing in favor with many cultured people who really wish rest in the summer, and go out of town to find health and nature. . . . We mean camping out." The article offered a quick overview of camp needs and possible destinations, painting an enticing picture of relaxation and abundance. "The men of the party can furnish trout, sea-fish, venison, etc., etc., and the women can cook them. . . . People who are above conventionality, and who have a lucky drop of vagabond blood in their veins, will, of course, find the keenest enjoyment in this mode of passing the summer, but everybody will find it healthful."[11]

The Barrows family established their regular camp on the Canadian side of Lake Memphremagog. Though in close proximity to summer hotels in the region, they argued fervently for the benefits of camping over resort living. June predicted that once learning how to camp, readers would "be loath to turn again to the tame insipidity of hotel or boarding-house life." Peppered throughout their book were comparisons between camp and hotel, and camp always came out on top. "In good weather we cook and eat out-of-doors, and then we would not change dining-rooms with any hotel in the country."[12] *Camping and Camp Outfits*, an 1890 guidebook, concurred. "More people are learning every year that the fashionable summer resorts . . . are not the best places to rest, but that perfect rest can only be had in their own little tent." The opportunity "to wear what is most comfortable, to come and go when they will, to eat and sleep and wake as they will" was more conducive to "perfect happiness" than "velvet carpets, richly upholstered furniture, cut-glass, and china plate." The author, George Oliver Shields, a major promoter of sport-hunting and the editor of *Recreation* magazine, urged his readers to "take up their abode for a season in tents in the woods, in the mountains, by the lake-side, or on the river bank" where they could expect genuine relief.[13]

The improvement of mental and bodily health emerged as a key benefit of camping in these narratives. Relatively new to the promotion of camping, this line of reasoning built on a particular strand of outdoor writing. In *Adventures in the Wilderness* (1869), for example, H. H. "Adirondack" Murray popularized a way of writing about wilderness vacationing as a remedy for common physical and mental ailments, as well as spiritual and social malaise. Some followed his lead—not only into the Adirondacks, but also into writing about nature and camping with a similar formula.[14] An *Outing* writer in 1886 was typical: compensation for "a vacation spent at the lakes" was "the health of mind and body due to an out-door life in the cool, fragrant air." Another wrote that just the act of sleeping outside, in "a wide, high, crystal-aired chamber of sleep," could relieve any number of health conditions and "nervous catastrophies [*sic*]" and refresh body and soul.[15]

Renovating the soul and spirit had a long camp tradition of its own. Since the late eighteenth century, multiple Protestant denominations sponsored camp meetings in various parts of the country which served social and recreational purposes alongside religious revival. They were usually weeklong affairs, moving from town to town to reach more potential adherents. Over the course of the nineteenth century some grew to resemble permanent, if rustic, resorts, complete with cottages and assembly halls, to which participants might return annually. The sociability of camp meetings related more closely to Civil War veterans' reunions or to the educational focus of the Chautauqua movement, than the vacation escape that recreational campers emphasized.[16] June and Isabel Barrows, for all their religious sensibilities, found such a camp meeting unsatisfying. In their first foray into family camping in 1877, the Barrowses had accepted an acquaintance's invitation to join a Methodist camp meeting in Penobscot, Maine. After a few days they felt overwhelmed by the hubbub, so picked up and left. As June recalled, they "longed for more rest and solitude" and found it in a camp site just four miles down the road. Pitching their tents on a quiet peninsula, they were glad to be "far from the noise and the bustle of the world."[17]

They found greater opportunity for spiritual communion in their new secluded camp than in the camp meeting. In describing their own Sunday services, Barrows echoed John Muir in seeing Nature as a cathedral: "No priest could ask a finer temple than that which God has built for us." In this church, Barrows prayed by going fishing and the chance it brought to notice and contemplate the passage of the day. Even when the fish failed to bite, he was pleased to catch "the charm of the sunrise . . . the inspiration of the infinite blue above us . . . the glorified span of the rainbow and the poem of the sunset." Better than a full creel were "grateful emotions" as well as "muscle of body and beautiful pictures for the mind."[18] Many camping writers would adopt a similarly inspirational tone.

The *Outing* editor praised the Shayback pieces for showcasing the "practical and prosaic details of camp life, as well as its poetry and romance."[19] And there were many practical details to address. The Barrowses' writings, like many such camping guides, offered a wealth of specifics, recommendations, and how-to lessons. Lists of provisions and recipes, tent blueprints, clothing advice, and social do's and don'ts filled many pages, along with first aid primers and chapters on related pursuits, such as fishing or hunting. The effort and expense camping required in this era was significant, whether campers hauled their outfit by the wagonload, on pack animals, or on their backs. Upon arrival, they had to locate and clear suitable sites, find water sources, chop wood, and then make camp from scratch, often improvising from the landscape for everything from seats and tables to bedding. Barrows didn't disguise the fact that camping entailed a great deal of work, though he tried to put a good spin on it: "In the work of settling there are no spectators.... The first day is usually a hard one. The muscles are unused to exertion, but they are quickened by an active and unflagging enthusiasm."[20] No matter how inviting the stories made it seem, the work it took to produce a camp was surely daunting.

Published stories of camping made miserable by work and conditions were relatively rare, and they never appeared in *Outing*. Those that were published often appeared under a pseudonym, suggesting the risks of revealing that camping wasn't always as simple or as pleasant as promoters made it seem. One woman painted a disagreeable picture of the experience in 1880: "We made our camp in a snowstorm, and the wood was wet and would not burn, and our tent was damp and would not dry." When the weather warmed up they had to battle bugs: "The black flies made the days unendurable and the mosquitoes made the night as well as the day a wasting misery." Far from finding bodily health and repose, she reported, "My nose was peeled by sun and cold. My lips were decorated by three large cold sores. My hands bled constantly." She admitted that "The scenery *is* lovely, but one cannot enjoy it.... It is hard work." Unsurprisingly, she did not recommend the experience to others. "No, don't camp out unless you can make up your mind beforehand to every kind of discomfort and inconvenience to mar all that is beautiful and all that is pleasing."[21] Camping promoters often wrote off such complaints as the result of bad luck, poor preparation, or spineless campers. But they didn't try to dodge the fact that camping entailed work.

The question remained: Why go to all the trouble? Were campers working hard in order to atone for seeming to indulge in idle leisure? Perhaps some were, but most camping stories spent surprisingly little time justifying the concept of leisure itself. More typically they offered thoroughgoing encouragements for people to enjoy vacation time: "Remember that you are out for a good time, and not to test your endurance."[22] Camping writers tended to present physical labor as a chance to escape sedentary urban lives and an experience to relish. As a newspaper report of the Barrowses' camp noted, "Everybody in camp has his or her allotted round of duty, and, while it is not in any sense drudgery, it is plain that life with the 'Shaybacks' is calculated to invigorate both mind and body."[23] Outdoor recreation promoters may have been assuaging some feelings of guilt in emphasizing the benefits of camp work, but these appeared less as a hedge against indolence and more as a mechanism to produce the happy medium between self-indulgence and self-denial.

Campers directed their labors toward creating the ideal outdoor experience, avoiding both resort-style amenities and harsh discomforts. On the one hand, Charles Greene believed that true campers must "scorn wooden floors to a tent, despise sheets on their beds, scoff at china plates and glassware, and frown at all superfluities of baggage." On the other hand, he and other writers disparaged the idea that "hardships [should be] sought for their own sake" or that the "best camper" is the one "who can endure most misery and discomfort." The "charm of camp life" had to be made in the space between misery and luxury.[24] Barrows agreed, suggesting that "'roughing it,'" while full of its own "novelties, exhilarations and discomforts," was itself kind of self-indulgence, a "luxurious state of privation." Drawing on his own experiences as a journalist camping with army and surveying expeditions in the West in the 1870s, he saw no reason to seek deprivation voluntarily. Only the "proud heroism of the boy-camper" would spurn "comforts which are within his reach." Instead, comfort emerged as a way to locate an appropriate middle ground, neither too decadent nor too austere. Accordingly, Barrows declared, "The Shaybacks have long since passed by the heroic stage of camp-life. . . . The object is to get the most comfort consistent with the most freedom."[25] "Comfort" itself came to signify a middle ground between luxury and austerity, whether in camp or otherwise. For members of the rising middle class, comfort suggested material security, personal well-being, and respectable taste.[26]

The ideal balance between comfort and freedom proved to be the subject of ongoing debate. As recreational campers triangulated their practices between resort luxuries and rough adventures, they could not help but rely upon modern developments in cities, travel, and tourism which generated escalating expectations. Camping writers pondered when, whether, and how many new campsite amenities they could adopt and still call it camping. How much distance from the height of urban comfort should they maintain? While campers never entirely agreed on the answer, the shared goal of finding that perfect medium allowed each writer to assert a position on the question. The details varied, but, taken together, the material items, social organizations, and cultural expectations created a recognizable picture of what camping was supposed to look like. Their work to locate a comfortable middle ground supported an emergent recreational ethos that most clearly divided campers from those who slept outside for other reasons.

"A Temporary Home in the Wilds"

For all the effort to locate a middle ground, at the end of the day camping was a temporary pursuit that reinforced vacationers' real homes. Many camping stories concluded with the joys of returning home after a satisfying outdoor excursion. Writer Frank Stockton closed his account by noting that, while it was "hard for us to break up our camp . . . our place was at home." The temporary hiatus even made home seemed "all the fresher and brighter and more delightful. . . . We went from room to room and seemed to appreciate, better than ever, what a charming home we had."[27] Recreational forms of camping out, like so many other late-nineteenth-century desires for the simple life, were therapeutic interludes.[28] Outdoor leisure became a natural complement to home and returning there a necessary stage in defining the vacation. It was what made camping fully recreational.

Camping without a home to which to return was an altogether different proposition. The budding form of recreational camping coincided with economic dislocations that set many Americans adrift and made such itinerants suspicious in new ways. Concern about travelers of ill repute has a long history, but between the 1870s and the end of the century, they sparked social fears on a newly expanded scale. Whether more people were on the move than previous generations is difficult to discern. What is clear is that many middle-class Americans became increasingly alarmed by the "tramp problem," unemployed men lacking permanent homes and oscillating between seeking work and living off some combination of begging, stealing, and charity, and what it portended for the nation.[29]

No single cause appeared to explain this growing group of marginalized men, although several theories arose. The initial focus centered on Civil War veterans who had somehow been corrupted by the "lazy habits of camp-life" during their time as soldiers. Methods of outdoor living learned in the Army appeared repurposed to avoid regular work once mustered out. None other than Allan Pinkerton, who would establish the fearsome private police force often used in enforcing corporate discipline, advanced this theory in 1878. While it is difficult to imagine how one might characterize army camp life as "lazy," many Union veterans did have difficulties readjusting in postwar society, whether for physical, financial, or psychological reasons. Still, the

aftermath of war alone could not have fostered the enduring tramp population or the prolonged panic about it.[30]

The volatile economy that accompanied the postwar acceleration of industrial capitalism was a major factor in the persistence of itinerant populations.
Subject to great economic fluctuations, boom periods alternating with dev-
astating "panics," these decades produced cyclically high unemployment
and stubbornly low wages, as well as escalating tension between employers
and employees. Pinkerton acknowledged that the unpredictable and "unprecedented hard times" put many in desperate straits, but he and others
presumed that tramps came from the ranks of working-class malcontents.
Throughout this era, massive strikes followed by violent reprisals focused
public attention on rising social conflict and civil unrest. Out-of-work and
disaffected men taking to the roads incited acute fears of social disorder.[31]
Between 1876 and 1898, all but four state legislatures enacted laws designed
to undermine the means and motives for tramping and contain the spread
of the threat it supposedly posed. Statutes shifted from prior emphases on
begging and disorderly behavior to policing the act of wandering without
regular work, with especially repressive effects for African Americans in the
Jim Crow South.[32]

Beyond the legal proscriptions, tramps were villainized in the press, understood as pests or diseases to be eradicated, armies and menaces to be
defeated. *Outing* contributed to the popular belief that tramps were con artists and thieves, reprinting jokes at their expense and including stories that
featured tramps as criminals or dangerous characters. More compassionate
treatments hinged on mistaken identity, where tramps were dramatically revealed as long-lost relatives or honorable men trapped by unlucky circumstance. In both views, the tramp embodied many of the fears and struggles
that accompanied the transformation to an urban-industrial society, even
among the middle and upper class Americans reaping its benefits.[33]

The image of unemployed men making camp wherever they pleased struck
terror into the hearts of many American commentators, well out of propor-
tion to tramps' numerical strength. Henry George wrote in 1883 that the
tramp was "more menacing to the Republic" than military attacks from rival
nations. The threat came from both the potential for violent unrest in the ongoing struggle between capital and labor and what seemed like the corrosive
descent of the honest workingman into "a vagabond and an outcast—a poi-
sonous pariah." Whether the road turned men into barbarians or individuals'
barbaric nature inclined them toward vagabond life made little difference to
George. Either way, their mobility made them newly suspicious and marked

them as deviant and potentially dangerous. The context for mobility had clearly changed since George, as a young man in the 1850s and by his own admission "pretty damn hard up," lit out for the West in search of adventure and riches.[34] By the 1880s, similar actions by impoverished men carried more ominous undertones. In this new context, tramps' uses of the outdoors came to represent the antithesis of ambition and honest labor rather than a traditional strategy to achieve property and success.[35]

Tramps, nonetheless, were crucial to the fitful emergence of the industrial economy. Despite common assumptions that tramps were unwilling to perform honest labor, many if not most had gone on the road in order to seek jobs of one sort or another. Indeed, the expanding industrial system and the fluctuating business cycles demanded workers without settled residence and tramps joined the ranks of a mobile, fluid labor supply. As migratory farm workers following the seasonal demands of different crops, or factory operatives responding to cyclical labor needs, tramps were both outsiders to various communities and fixtures within them, socially marginal and economically essential.[36] The West's expanding resource extraction economy relied heavily on migratory labor. Lumber camps, for example, were composed largely of "tramp lumberjacks" who adapted to the volatility of the timber trade. Tramp laborers moved from camp to camp or town to town, promised good wages one week and let go the next, and then picked up for vagrancy, cast out from a community for the very reason they had been welcomed in the first place.[37]

The willingness to live without an established home, even if the nature of work required it, caused public consternation. Press coverage often sensationalized tramps' outdoor "jungles," group encampments on the outskirts of cities and towns. Pinkerton included harrowing descriptions of what he characterized as the "grotesque company" of tramp communities. For example, he depicted one group this way: encamped in a good position to raid nearby farms, they were nonchalantly "cooking their supper at the edge of the timber," roasting "foraged" chickens, potatoes, and green corn, while the light of the moon "fell across the camp, giving its inmates a weird, witch-like appearance." Most of this "tired, dreary, wretched lot ... [had] fallen upon the ground for rest and in all sorts of sluggish positions were dozing in a stupid sodden way that told of brutish instincts and experiences." Another group of tramps, shown in Figure 3.1, engaged in equally disreputable activities in their evening encampment. While the tramps seemed "contented and satisfied" without the usual domestic comforts, Pinkerton doubted that it was "possible for these outcasts to really enjoy their degrading experiences." He hoped that

FIGURE 3.1 While this scene looks pleasant enough, for readers of Allan Pinkerton's 1878 tract, the men's tattered clothes and appearance, their card game, and sleeping on the ground added up to suspicious behavior. "Night encampment of tramps near the Boston and Albany Railroad," in Allan Pinkerton, *Strikers, Communists, Tramps and Detectives* (New York: G. W. Carleton & Co., Publishers, 1878), 38.

when "brighter days return to our industries" tramps would happily leave this shameful life and return to work, homes, and respectable manhood.[38]

Pinkerton spoke to public fears, but his portrait was incomplete. These camps provided both inexpensive places to dwell and communities of mutual support, which reduced the need for continuous paychecks. Tramps lived in the open, cooking, eating, and drinking, washing their clothes and their bodies, alternately enjoying friendships and fighting with each other, and collaborating to ward off external threats, whether thieves or police. Though outside observers characterized tramps as "let loose from all the habits of domestic life, wandering about without aim or home," they in fact shared domestic activities and responsibilities in improvised semicooperative settings. If hardship and strife remained constants, tramps could still find some measure of comfort and pleasure in camp life.[39]

Living outside could have its rewards. William "Roving Bill" Aspinwall corresponded with the investigator John McCook over several years and often touched on the pleasant side of tramp life.[40] Aspinwall, a Union army veteran, wrote in 1893 about his delight one "lovely Sabbath morning and how Happy I feel with Nature adorned in her lovely Summer Robes all around me; everything so quite except the Rusling of the Breeze through the Butiful foliage and the sweet singing and the warbling of Birds." Nor did he appreciate all this on an empty stomach. After snacking on some ripe strawberries collected from a nearby patch, he assembled "a quart of good, strong Coffee, Bred, Cheese, and some cooked Beef & Onions; and there I sat on the grass . . . and I ate a harty Breakfast and I enjoyed it." Afterward he smoked his pipe and reveled in the day: "I would rather sit close to this Butiful sheet of watter and write than to be in the most luxurious drawing Room in this land. . . . Surely God has blessed me!"[41] It is possible that Aspinwall embellished the scene, but he wasn't in the habit of romanticizing tramp life. Other letters revealed moments of despair and discomfort and acknowledged that the jungle had its drawbacks. Still, he reasoned that the shared efforts to gain food, the pleasant outdoor surroundings, and the moments of camaraderie outweighed his other options.[42]

The social exposés that brought Aspinwall's stories to the public contained, for some, a seductive glimpse of a free and unconventional life. Jack London experienced tramping in the 1890s and wrote widely-popular stories about tramps that were, in a way, precursors to his bestselling wilderness adventures like *Call of the Wild* (1903). Literary fascination for tramping hinted at an incipient dissatisfaction with the regimes of modern middle-class urban life. From some angles, tramps appeared to retain a sense of independence that was eroding in the shift to industrial systems of work and time.[43] Even Alan Pinkerton recognized the appeal of tramping as a form of escape: "No person can ever get a taste of the genuine pleasure of the road and not feel in some reckless way . . . that he would like to become some sort of tramp."[44]

A popular travel book even advised prospective tourists to play the tramp. Lee Meriwether's *A Tramp Trip, or Europe on Fifty Cents a Day* (1886) argued that traveling as a tramp brought authentic freedom. "As a tramp, with a modest bag on your back, you will be taken for an itinerant journeyman or peddler, and as such can fraternize and live with the peasants and people." Otherwise one might be "looked on as a *tourist* and will be treated accordingly."[45] The appeal of "tramp" as an aesthetic label for travel began to make its way into *Outing*, such that in 1893 one writer reported his intentions to "rough it in the most approved 'tramp' style—to abjure boiled shirts and feather beds and dainty food, and even good grammar."[46] Going in "tramp style" and becoming an actual tramp were entirely different undertakings—the quotation marks suggesting the distance between them. Men like Meriwether could go tramping about Europe and mingling with vagrants in America in pursuit of aesthetic liberation without finding themselves judged as irresponsible and subject to surveillance, discrimination, and arrest.[47]

Secure in their assumption of a return home, recreational campers felt free to enjoy the novelties of tramp style. Dan O'Hara, author of a recurring column on camp cookery in *Outing* in the 1880s, praised the serendipity of camping. "As to breakfast, dinner, and supper, all are unknown quantities. There is no bill of fare. We don't know what we shall have; we only hope it will be enough! There is no finer sauce than unexpectedness."[48] Romanticizing temporary hunger and uncertainty was only possible for those confident in eventually resuming regular meals. In this context, the discovery of hunger became enjoyable. In camp, many reported delighting in meals and habits they would have found intolerable at home. One writer assured readers that "even if the pine needles drop into the coffee and the chops are burnt, you are so hungry that the meal will taste good just the same." The informality and the plain foods, the sheer physical sensations of eating, offered some a refreshing break from the intricate menus and manners common to upper-class American dining during this era.[49] That camp life was a temporary adventure rather than a permanent existence lent these experiences their appeal, and emphasized the separation between tramps and tramp style.

Despite the divided destinies, recreational campers and tramps alike could appreciate similar outdoor pleasures like nature's beauty, a good meal, and sociable gathering. Aspinwall's streamside breakfast rhapsody and Barrows's praise for outdoor dining echoed each other more than one might expect. They both seemed to scorn excessive luxury and strict social protocols. Both groups drew from a seemingly similar demographic profile: native-born white Americans, city dwellers, Civil War veterans. Class status did divide the groups, but the tramp population contained individuals who in other moments or turns in their lives might have just as easily become recreational campers. When Pinkerton noted that "a man may be eminent to-day and to-morrow a tramp," he may have exaggerated social and economic instability, but not by much.[50] When tramps like Aspinwall recommended that city folk would "enjoy better health and live longer" if they lived "a more nomadic life," enjoying "fresh air" and "good wholesome exercise," the comparison may have been too close for comfort.[51]

Recreational campers took notice of the uncomfortable resemblance and sought to distance themselves and their camping practices from tramps. June Barrows, perhaps reacting to his own discomfort with the slippage between tramp style and tramp life, asserted that the Shaybacks always went "well heeled" and inhabited a "de luxe" tent, as Figure 3.2 shows. His descriptions of their careful preparation and abundant equipment drew an implicit contrast with tramps and their meager possessions. He further advised campers

INTERIOR DE LUXE.

FIGURE 3.2 June Barrows insisted that the Shaybacks always went "well-heeled," and thus drew an explicit contrast to Pinkerton's portrayal of a tramp encampment. "Interior De Luxe" in S. J. Barrows, "The Shaybacks in Camp—Part II," *Outing* 4, no. 6 (September 1884): 443.

to arrange for annual storage of all this bulky gear, near the destination if possible, to support the appearance of more stately travel. Properly equipped leisure camping, if less expensive than fashionable resorts, was rarely promoted in this era for its affordability. It required a "necessary outlay" of no small funds, "as a tenter's kit to be complete for an enjoyable camping time costs considerable."[52] When campers described their campsites as comfortable homes, talked about equipment and clothing in painstaking detail, or insisted on making a point of paying fair prices, the implied costs bolstered a notion of respectable recreational camping against the tramp menace.

Outfit and behavior were key to achieving proper presentation. As early as 1877, John Gould had suggested that one dress for camping "sufficiently in fashion to indicate that you are a traveller or camper" rather than risk being misidentified as a down-and-out tramp.[53] Two men preparing for a canoe-camping expedition feared their casual attire would give mistaken impressions and hoped "the canoe would explain our tramp-like appearance" and confirm their recreational intentions.[54] In other instances, comportment held the key. One *Outing* writer in 1892 instructed campers in the delicate task of approaching farm wives to purchase bread, vegetables, and dairy products. Campers must never accept any item for "free ... , nor higgle about prices" but should instead "state ... politely what you want, and that you want to buy, not beg it." He cautioned readers to remember that "a sportsman in shooting gear is frequently suggestive of some new type of tramp to the unsophisticated mind. Tramps are dangerous customers for a lone woman to open her door to, hence a brief explanation of your temporary occupation will help to reassure."[55] Emphasis on the "temporary" nature of the outdoor travel served to further distance what had been a relatively ordinary mode of travel that John Muir, for example, had slipped into two decades before.

What did persist for some time was the assumption that temporary campers had tacit permission to camp on open land, even private property. Outdoor recreation enthusiasts, however, began to recommend that travelers seek explicit approval from the owner. One advised that "permission ought always to be obtained of the owner or lessee of the land, of course, but any objection is rare, where the farmer has no reason to suppose you will damage his property by stealing firewood from his fences or carelessly setting fire to his woods."[56] Stealing farm goods and starting accidental fires were crimes often blamed on tramps, and thus campers worked to stay above suspicion on those fronts. While Aspinwall and other tramps did admit to "liberating" produce from farmers' fields, McCook believed the charges of arson were misplaced. "Careful inquiry satisfies me that tramps are extremely intolerant of the slightest carelessness in the use of fire in their sleeping places. They have no fancy for being roasted alive."[57] More than tramps themselves, who in certain ways represented older travel patterns, the tramp scare altered the social landscape.

When tramps made an overt and organized political challenge in 1894, it further drove a wedge between recreational and functional camping practices, between tramp style and tramp life. Reeling from the cataclysmic 1893 depression, unemployed men by the thousands set out from all corners of the country to serve a "petition in boots" to the nation's leaders. They marched on Washington to pressure Congress to institute public works programs and put the unemployed on the federal payroll. Initially proposed by Jacob Coxey, an eccentric businessman and monetary reformer, these were radical ideas at the time. Beyond this purpose, the movement of "Coxey's Army" and the specter of tramps, roused from their supposed aimless wandering to a focused and resolute mission, provoked escalating fears of a newly militant version of the tramp menace.[58]

As marchers hopped trains, walked, and camped their way toward the Capitol, living on begged and donated food, they commanded national media attention (if not always sympathy) for weeks. One paper dismissed them as a "motley aggregation of homeless wanderers." For their part, marchers tried to present themselves as citizens with standing to petition their government— "honest workingmen," family earners, and Civil War veterans. Though fewer than half arrived, weeded out by hunger, travel difficulties, local police, and railroad security, at least 8,000 people encamped in late April in a park just north of Washington, DC, with several thousand local spectators on hand to watch. On the first of May, a detachment marched toward the Capitol, with a crowd of onlookers that grew to nearly 30,000. Though Coxey was not allowed to speak, and police dispersed the marchers with batons, the attempt made a claim to the Capitol grounds as rightful "property of the people." Coxey's Army, progenitor of the "march on Washington," also built on the political forms of camping established by the Grand Army of the Republic. Participants of both armies made claims on public nature to appeal to the government and renegotiate the terms of the social contract.[59]

Recreational campers occasionally expressed sympathy for tramps but made no common cause with those who camped with Coxey. A difficult night lost outdoors, "tired, and cold, and hungry," gave one camper an appreciation for what it meant "to have no roof over one's head." She was moved to declare, "I believe I shall never turn a tramp away again."[60] Her newfound compassion, however, derived from the fact that she had returned to the safety of her roof and her position as benefactor to tramps. Camping stories thus emphasized social order and hierarchy rather than shared experiences. Where tramps seemed to be permanently drifting, recreational campers focused on creating temporary respectable homes. Adorning the campsite with homelike comforts was key to this effort, as an *Outing* article proclaimed in 1898: "There is, to most men, if they would only realize it, a real pleasure to be found in the very act of making a temporary home in the wilds comfortable and attractive."[61] This action—a man supporting a decent outdoor home— drew a stark contrast with tramps' apparent willful abandonment of home, work, and their responsibilities as men.

In fact, campers felt compelled to defend their temporary homes and the tramp style against the encroachments of tramp life. Site your camp, one writer instructed, "where the casual pedestrian will be least likely to discover it. The great American tramp, the hobo, prowleth the face of the earth during camping weather. . . . [Y]ou do not wish him to find your temporary home any more than you yourself wish to find your future" place among his number.[62]

Recreational campers' claims to respectability rested upon their use of public nature to establish temporary homes, a distinctly different strategy than previous generations had pursued to achieve the agrarian dream.

"We Were at Last Really Keeping House"

The concept of camping as a temporary home relied upon expectations of the elite home at the turn of the century, often geared toward displaying class status. Yet its family models of domesticity as well as standards for housekeeping and roles for servants were all in flux during the era. Many saw camping as a chance to create little islands of civilization in the wilderness, where they both replicated and contemplated the habits of home life. June Barrows once described making a campsite on an island in Lake Memphremagog as akin to forming a new social contract out of the state of nature: "We had wrested an uninhabited island from the dominion of its own solitude; we had established law and order; instituted republican government; introduced the Christian religion; reorganized society on a cooperative basis; effected a reform in labor; secured the rights of woman; founded a free public library of a dozen volumes, and opened a school of practical philosophy."[63] The Barrowses' inclinations to imagine camp as utopian experiment was perhaps more radical than most but the impulse to see camping as the opportunity to make home and society anew was common.

Campers marveled at their own abilities to establish replicas of their homes in remote spots. In "A Family Camp in the Rockies," published in *Outing* in 1893, Charlotte Conover took readers through her initial, disorienting experiences and her efforts to remedy them by producing comfort and familiarity in wilderness. "What to do first? The magnitude of our undertaking dawned upon us. Here we were, a family of nine, set down among the rocks and sand and pines, to *begin living*! Nothing to sit on, sleep on, eat on, or cook on; no place to lay a thing down or hang it up; two miles from an egg and six miles from a safety-pin." She began to feel more at ease as they set up camp. As the men worked at building tables and chairs, "Alice and I arranged our part of the household—put up curtains, tacked on table-covers, and 'read up' in the cook-book. . . . When we had a jar of dried bread crumbs and a dish of cold boiled potatoes on the pantry shelf it seemed as though we were at last really keeping house."[64] For many, the experience of keeping house was an important element of camping satisfaction.

Conover had specific expectations in mind. Recounting the group's deliberations on what to bring, she advocated "from the standpoint of a well-stocked house." Her bachelor brother-in-law, conversely, suggested a more rudimentary approach which to her seemed suspiciously uncivilized, uncouth, and perhaps even tramp-like.

> A skillet and camp-kettle seemed to him ample provision for any culinary necessities. "Do you mean," said I, aghast, "to boil the ham and the towels in the same kettle?" "To be sure," he answered with the nonchalance of an experienced camper; "only you needn't put them both in at the same time." This was too much. I made a valiant stand for my prerogatives, and secured a stew-pan.[65]

Though Conover seemed to find the humor in the situation, maintaining standards remained crucial to her experience. Her ability to keep a respectable house allowed her to enjoy the beautiful setting.

This labor of domestic transformation became a meaningful part of recreational camping and a new iteration of the agrarian ideal. Conover mixed labor with the land, not to cultivate farm products, but to establish a respectable temporary home. Campers spent a good deal of time and devoted many pages to their efforts at fashioning tables, chairs, beds, and a semblance of home out of the landscape itself. They defined areas of the campsite as they would rooms in houses, often set off in their texts by quotation marks. As Conover noted, "it became our nightly custom to assemble in our 'parlor,' as we called the hammock-encircled spot before the tents, and enjoy the warmth" of the campfire. The Barrowses advocated pitching a tent for each specific purpose—bedroom, parlor, kitchen, dining room. Campers then proceeded to embellish their "rooms" with appropriate decorative schemes. One writer instructed her readers to purchase brightly colored rugs, blankets, and pillows, because, she insisted, "a camp can be made just as gay and attractive as a drawing-room, and ought to be."[66] By constructing these comfortable temporary homes, campers turned public nature into a new sort of symbolic property.

This vision of camp as domestic idyll seems far removed from the stereotypical masculine image of roughing it in the wilderness. That too gained renown in the era, popularized by men like Theodore Roosevelt, with his Western adventures and advocacy of the strenuous life. Some writers did envision camping as a manly endeavor and a test of resilience for both body and mind. And yet even among the sportsmen with whom Roosevelt established such male domains as the Boone & Crockett Club, the promotion of civilized comforts and behaviors was a top priority. Moreover, in the pages of outdoor magazines, appeals to the home-like camp and stories by and about women in camp ran right alongside those detailing manly adventures in the wild.[67] Volume 26 of *Outing*, covering April through September of 1895, included five major feature articles on camping, two of which presumed the masculine model and the other three of which promoted the family camp. Emily Palmer opened her entry in this group with this invocation: "Happy the home where father, mother and children can gather together their needful belongings, betake themselves to the shores of some lake or stream, and raising their temporary home of white tents, find their best pleasure in being together and leaving behind them the care of conventional life."[68] Women's presence in the camping landscape did not prevent it from promoting a sense of manhood. Rather, seeing camp as a novel and harmonious setting for a recognizably middle-class family life reinforced the notion of men as heads of household. This served as another mechanism by which to demonstrate that campers maintained responsibilities of work and home that tramps seemingly abandoned.

June Barrows made clear his belief in the significance of family camping. "The Shaybacks have long since accepted the ideal of Genesis. They have chosen an Eden for their camp-ground, and have always maintained that every Adamic member should be neutralized by an Eve. Little Cain and Abel are taken along too, on condition that they will not club each other." If "Adam was the first camper-out," he discovered "as many a modern camper has done, that it is not good to live alone, even in Eden. . . . Eve was essential to the completeness of the Edenic camp. It was the serpent that was superfluous."[69] Isabel eschewed the biblical metaphors but agreed with the principle. Rowdy men who left a trail of "broken bottles and cigar stumps" behind them should not "go off by themselves for a rough good time," perhaps too closely mimicking tramp life. Instead, having women in camp helped "to refine and elevate . . . the moral tone and increase the social amenities which make the charm of existence." Men and women thus served as necessary complements in creating a respectable camp. To achieve this goal, campers had to create an "attractive" and comfortable place of rest, where simple "decorations are not forgotten." Elevating this particular domestic order as "natural," the Barrowses insisted that the family model was the ideal way to camp and, furthermore, that camping enabled "the ideal life for the family."[70]

The Barrowses so firmly advocated for the "equal division of labor" among all campers—women, men, and children—that they railed against the temptation to bring servants or hired help into camp. Accordingly, the Shaybacks regarded servants "as a necessary evil of city life" and a severe disruption of the family ideals of camping. "The presence, therefore, of any person who is in any sense considered an inferior has never been tolerated in this little republic of campers."[71] June and Isabel thus weighed in on the potent servant question, a matter of no little debate during this era.

The emergence of leisure camping coincided with major shifts in the context for hired domestic labor. Employing servants, especially those who "lived in," had been one of the clearest ways of defining middle-class status in the nineteenth century. By 1870, between a fifth and a third of families in the major urban areas of Boston, New York, San Francisco, Philadelphia, and Chicago had at least one live-in servant to light stoves and fireplaces, prepare meals, make beds, diaper babies, sweep, launder, and iron. With the turn of the twentieth century came a notable shift in the economy and expectations of domestic service. The increase in alternate employment for working-class women after 1900 accompanied a drastic decline in the availability of servants; by some estimates, the years between 1890 and 1920 saw the ratio of domestic servants to the general population fall by half and shifted from white immigrant live-ins to nonwhite day workers. The "servant problem" proved vexing for middle-class households struggling to redefine the tasks of keeping house, leading them to express perpetual dissatisfaction with their hired help and ponder the meaning of a home without servants.[72]

Camping provided another venue to explore this question. For some campers, hiring help freed them up to enjoy the scenery. Having someone else do the most disagreeable chores meant that "there was nothing to mar the pleasure of the nightly home-coming" into the campsite. One woman exhorted readers to hire a cook: "Don't attempt to do the cooking yourself. You'll regret it if you do, for it is one of the duties that is never at an end, and there are so many other things you want to be doing when you get into the woods and find yourself in the thrall of nature."[73] For others, servants diminished the wilderness experience and camping relieved the burden of managing them. One writer linked the hiatus from "conforming to regular hours in the matter of meals [and] the conventionalities of dress" with the refreshing opportunity to "escape from the tyranny of servants." For her, servants embodied those strictures of city life she hoped to escape temporarily. As a vacation from servants, camping redefined certain tasks as part of the making of a comfortable home, rather than as menial chore one could pay others to perform.[74] Most campers advocated leaving city help at home but dithered over whether to hire outdoor staff or to aspire to the self-sufficiency of the Shaybacks' "little republic of campers."

For some, servants added unique elements to the camping experience, incorporating certain ethnic types as stock characters in their accounts. One writer correlated destinations by ethnicity: in the Canadian Rockies "you get the real broncho [*sic*] busters for guides, Indian ponies to ride, and a Chinaman for a cook, and you sleep in Indian tepee tents," while in Maine "you can get Indian, Yankee, or Canuck guides." Camping writers typically featured such guides speaking in dialect and possessing quirky talents and superior flap-jack skills. One woman described their head guide as "a Scotch half-breed, with a sturdy name and quaint accent," ably assisted by a "merry, handsome" French-Canadian and a retinue of "dusky mates." Labeling the latter as "our Indians," this canoe-camper enjoyed the end of the day where "we could lie down in a shaded place and watch the now picturesque Indians carrying and loading."[75] Whether the enjoyment came from having the laborious task of portaging and making camp done by others or done specifically by "pictur-esque" others was difficult to disentangle. Other campers were less enamored of such arrangements. In her journal of a 1908 canoe trip, Caroline Turner recorded a dispute in their party on this question. Her husband Fred insisted on Indian guides who were most "familiar with river & rapids." She complained that they were "very dirty"; another woman refused entirely "to be in canoe with an Indian." In the end, the party decided to make a change, and Caroline was pleased that their new guide was "a Canadian boy & nice fellow."[76]

Employee relations could be tricky. Camping advocate and country club executive Herbert Jillson advised *Outing* readers in 1901 to mind the class divisions between campers and guides with care and respect. Maine guides, he asserted, lived plainly but honestly, and gave of their experience and strength with willing humility. "With scarcely an exception, they know their place and keep it, seldom mistaking kindness for familiarity. . . . They only ask to be treated like men, nothing more. . . . Treat that guide 'white,' and there will be no trouble." Jillson outlined the "sportsman-guide" relationship as one that cohered to a particular pattern of deference, where common whiteness and manhood as well as social hierarchy was respected.[77] This contrasted with the hand-wringing around the servant question in the city. As Jillson and others hinted, perhaps the outdoors provided a temporary answer, as an ideal servant might be one of the rewards of a camping vacation.

Establishing domestic order in the wilds became a carefully calibrated ex-ercise for this generation of recreational campers. Make the campsite com-fortable and attractive but not too plush or fancy. Get outdoors in tramp style to enjoy the freedom of nature but avoid being mistaken for tramps who neglected the responsibilities of work and home. Hire only the right sort of help, picturesque and deferent. Keep a respectable temporary home on the family plan but depart from conventional city life. No wonder camping writers spent so many pages sorting it all out. Campers elevated this recreational ethos as a fitting claim on public nature, superseding older agrarian models and devaluing new functional forms. This extended beyond the tramp scare to marginalize campers who found themselves outside of the increasingly dominant nature-seeking family camping paradigm.

"Beyond the Ken and the Means of Wage-Earners"

Elite recreational campers knew they weren't alone in sleeping outside. Moreover, they knew that there was a spectrum of camping practices and practitioners that filled the gulf between them and the vilified tramps. One camping writer told a revealing story in *Outing* in 1905 that spoke to subtler class tensions. "The Fallacies of 'Roughing It,'" by Robert Dunn, a Harvard graduate, explorer, and journalist, recounted a conversation between himself and some friends on a train. Spying a cluster of lakeside shacks from the window, the men scoffed at the lower-class vacationers who presumably rented these cabins because they were afraid to "live in tents and do the real out-door thing." One man proposed teaching these families authentic camping, but another retorted: if you let "that class of beings" into the wilderness, then "it's good-bye to all sportsmen like us."[78] Dunn hinted at the tensions between "sportsmen," as the *Outing* set thought of themselves, and so-called pot hunters—those who hunted, fished, or scavenged from the land for subsistence or market purposes. A similar debate over the merits of recreational and functional hunting was occurring in parallel, and management of public nature, whether land or game, increasingly favored leisure users.[79]

The story jumped ahead a few years, when one of the more skeptical of the men came across a family camping in the woods who confessed to having rented one of the lakeside shacks on a previous vacation. Though the elite observer found them "the queerest party," he admitted, with great surprise, that they were doing a tolerable job at camping. "They weren't bad company. The father—he was a letter carrier in Boston—was no fisherman, but he had a sense of humor, and the right idea about the state's preserving the woods from lumbermen. His wife could turn pancakes and nurse the baby at the same time." The praise struck a patronizing tone, but lauded them nonetheless for renouncing their "foolish summers" spent in the cottages and for endorsing conservation. He begrudgingly conceded that "they behave themselves.

They're careful about starting fires, and can't fish the streams out. Every one's going to the woods these days, all classes. You can't stop it."[80]

Dunn used this story to chastise those of his own class for not sharing knowledge about proper sorts of camping more widely. "Customs of going to the woods aright have been very badly fostered; have appealed to class, but never to the people." He faulted most camping guidebooks for discouraging people of lesser means: "Their condescending tone, exorbitant detail, often false imagination, have made folk hesitate" to give the outdoors a try. These books, and by implication the articles in *Outing* as well, made camping seem "a fad beyond the ken and the means of wage-earners."[81] Though he hoped to create a more welcoming attitude, in the end, Dunn relied on many of the same tropes as his colleagues, emphasizing one's status back home, as did the caption for an illustration in his article, shown in Figure 3.3. Roaming the woods for leisure had become the rightful reason and reward for camping. Conversely, laboring in the wilderness out of necessity no longer created property and virtue but indicated personal and social failure.

Still, many people continued to camp for functional purposes—as a base to hunt for food, fish for supper, gather firewood, and make shelter for living—in similar spaces as recreational campers made their temporary homes for leisure purposes. Families like that of Alphonso Reeves did all of those things, employing camping as part of a complex subsistence strategy. Between 1900 and 1906, Mrs. Reeves kept a diary that recorded what at first glance seemed to be an unusual family life. Born in 1876 in Nebraska and married at twenty, Mrs. Reeves spent a chunk of her early family life rotating regularly between house living and tent-camping. They would take lodging in small Wyoming, South Dakota, and Montana towns, and when work or welcome ran out, they would encamp outdoors for months at a time in search of new opportunities. Sometimes they lived and traveled with another couple, pooling resources and labor. The family included several small children, some born during these years.[82]

Mrs. Reeves recorded all of this as part and parcel of their normal existence. They tended to move indoors when the cold weather set in and head out again in the springtime. She did appreciate a nice cozy house, recording one Thanksgiving Day: "Well I think tonight that I have very much to be thankful for. That we have a good comfortable home for the winter." And yet she greeted the recurring move-outs matter-of-factly, with little complaint or emotion. As she put it one April, "Well we have started away again but I guess we will not go very far this time." Typically, they camped within reach of a town, to retrieve mail, purchase supplies, and have a social life. July 4, 1901

FIGURE 3.3 While the author believed that recreational camping was accessible for all, his article still emphasized the professional class of most leisure campers. "A slight transformation—the city lawyer becomes camp cook," in Robert Dunn, "The Fallacies of 'Roughing It'," *Outing* 46, no. 6 (September 1905): 651.

found them encamped outside of Newcastle, Wyoming. They headed into town that afternoon for speeches and a baseball game, and then they danced late into the evening, before returning to camp.[83] Camping was an ordinary phase within daily life, rather than a vacation from it.

The diary frequently mentioned enjoyable experiences in nature. The family occasionally paused to admire a beautiful view or take photographs. She enjoyed side trips to bathe in crystalline lakes or hot springs, though omitted the flowery descriptions and self-congratulations common to *Outing* writers. As Mrs. Reeves observed following an afternoon ride through a canyon, "We saw some nice scenery. Waterfalls, Rocks and Hills. Fall River is a lovely river." She clearly appreciated pretty places and moments like these and had her fair share of grumbles, particularly about mosquitoes. The domestic duties of camp took up a great deal of her time, with days spent cooking and baking in her Dutch oven. Their situation made this work more than symbolic and largely contiguous with home living, such as the day she hauled out the sewing machine to do some mending in camp. Occasionally they crossed paths with leisure campers, including a group traveling "clear from Minnesota and are going to Yellowstone park."[84] If Mrs. Reeves thought they were crazy to be doing that just for fun, she didn't say. That they camped alongside one another for a few nights suggests the still fluid landscape of camping.

For Alphonso, camping supported a series of employment and subsistence opportunities. He learned to trap wolves and coyotes for bounties and hunted grouse, deer, rabbits, and antelope for food. When offered, he played the other side, working as a game warden and forest preserve ranger. He assisted the military detachment patrolling Yellowstone, arresting poachers who were illegally taking elk and beaver, and instructing locals where they were allowed to cut timber. He also guided tourists on hunting and camping excursions. He did a short stint as a miner and occasionally pursued in-town jobs as a manual laborer or played his violin for dances, whether he was living indoors or outdoors at the time. The family tried living in larger cities, like Denver, and at one point moved back to Nebraska to work a homestead claim. But they could not make it pay and before long returned to Montana, believing "we can do better here than we can there" and headed back out to "hunt coyote dens" and take up camp life again.[85]

If this living strategy appears odd, much evidence points to it being quite typical for this era in this part of the West. The variety of jobs that Alphonso worked would not have been unusual at the time, some requiring outdoor residence, others assuming travel between worksites. Mobility was a reasonable approach to lack of suitable employment or to try and get ahead. The Reeveses weren't wealthy but they weren't entirely broke either; they owned horses and personal property. More likely they were working to accumulate enough to establish themselves securely, and camping was both a tool to help them get there and a fall back plan.[86] Busting out on a homestead claim was a common fate, for by 1900, claimable acreage remaining was often ill suited for small-scale family-based agriculture. Agriculture, along with the extractive industries of the West like mining, logging, and ranching, tended to be organized on a large-scale basis that needed wageworkers, not small owner-operators. It was, moreover, an economy that prized a worker's willingness to move locations frequently and have a wide range of job skills.[87] The Reeves family responded to these complex conditions, using camping instrumentally as they sought the promises of the West.

The West was full of mobile workers, many dubbed "bindlestiffs," after the rolled-up blanket, or bindle, they carried with them. Bindlestiffs expected to sleep outside as they traveled, often widely, between jobs and during stints in outdoor labor, like logging. Railroad expansion had opened up new areas to cultivation and extraction and brought workers in to harvest the crops and dig the ore. The line between tramps and bindlestiffs was porous. They both hopped trains and camped along the road to jobs in agriculture, construction, or forest industries. Bindlestiffs marched with Coxey in 1894 and would subsequently participate in union agitation. In one such action two decades later, loggers demanded the company provide them beds, rather than relying on workers themselves to tote their bedrolls around with them. When they succeeded in this demand, the victorious loggers ceremoniously burned their bindles and sougans (early sleeping-bags) in giant bonfires.[88] This didn't put an end to mobile labor in the West, but it suggested that some workers attempted to resist a system which kept them constantly on the move. For wage-earners like bindlestiffs, as for the Reeves family, camping was not about means or interest, but part of regular work patterns.

Even when required for labor, camping without a home to return to could still provoke alarm over the apparent lack of commitment to household responsibilities. One group rendered especially suspect in this regard were Native communities, who became the target of a series of coercive federal campaigns against camp life. This program was part of a wide-ranging assimilationist program pursued by both government agencies and Christian organizations. June Barrows was among those who supported the push for assimilation that escalated in the 1880s, which included partitioning reservation lands into individual allotments, forcible removal of Native children from their families to reside in boarding schools, and moralistic lessons about the superiority of white middle-class house-living. White Americans identified Indian camp life as the antithesis of the civilized American home and a major obstacle to assimilation. In the words of one former Commissioner of Indian Affairs in 1892, camp encouraged "habits of idleness ... [and] bloodshed" and perpetuated "life without meaning and labor without system."[89] Evoking the fearful side of freedpeople's camps and hobo jungles as incubators of disease, crime, disorder, and rootlessness, camp in this context also connoted primitive barbarity. Symbolically and linguistically, camp sat at the heart of white fears about the tramp problem, freedpeople's labor, and Indian nonconformity.

The contrast between a dismal picture of camp and a clean and proper home became part of the rationale for removal of Native children to boarding schools, which enforced total immersion in white culture. Indian Affairs administrators believed that a few short hours in school would not be enough to induce Indian children to appreciate "the comforts of the white man's civilization" and "home-life" or to acquire "a distaste for the camp-fire" and "barbarous life." By contrast, boarding schools removed children from "the perverting environments of the Indian camp and are put at once under the influence of the methods of civilized life," learning to sleep on a bed, "to sit on a chair . . . to eat at table."[90]

This logic also undergirded an adult education project in the 1910s, officially aimed at reducing the incidence of disease, particularly tuberculosis, on reservations. A medical director in the Office of Indian Affairs developed a slide lecture demonstrating the importance and criteria of home hygiene and presented it to Native people in more than a dozen states. The argument hinged on the essential move from outdoors to indoors, camp to house. The series of before-and-after photographs linked camp life with unsanitary conditions of eating, sleeping, and washing, as well as dysfunctional family structures and morbid outcomes. By contrast, Indian families dwelling in multiroom frame houses, with wallpapered and well-furnished rooms, showcased health and a peaceful domestic scene.[91]

Overlooked in the public narrative, negative factors attributed to Indigenous lifeways were in fact a result of the poverty that followed conquest, dispossession of lands, and forced sedentism. The lack of opportunities for wage work on reservations and federal negligence in providing essential supplies as stipulated in treaty agreements exacerbated the situation. Many Indigenous groups had once practiced seasonal mobility as part of broader subsistence strategies within a defined structure of territory, culture, and social rules, which US seizure of territory disrupted. Ascribing camp problems to Indian culture did more than obscure that history. It both justified a host of oppressive policies toward Native people and aligned with the marginalization of mobile, apparently rootless people.[92] Far from solidifying house life, federal Indian policies led to an exodus of Native men from their reservation homes to seek wage work in the West's mobile labor force. They worked as ranch hands and loggers, cut hay and hauled freight, constructed irrigation works, and toiled in underground mines, though there were never enough employment opportunities.[93] The comfortable house-living the slide lectures pushed was less of a lifestyle choice than an unrealistic standard, another demonstration of the primacy of home and the distance between good and bad campers.

When publications like *Outing* praised the same features of family camping that Native Americans were instructed to abandon, it suggested that the issue lay not with how to camp, but who camped. For example, Native audiences learned that the only way to prevent consumption was to give up camp life and move indoors. Recreational campers read that exposure to fresh air and sunlight could prevent or even cure the malady. One camping guidebook detailed a recent experiment where afflicted people who convalesced in tents recovered more rapidly and with less loss of life than those who remained in their own homes. A *Sunset* magazine article quoted a physician who declared unequivocally, "Houses cause consumption." Conversely, those that "camp in tents in the woods" resisted the disease and improved "in color, appetite, energy."[94] Native attendees at the tuberculosis prevention talks heard the opposite message: tents caused disease and houses protected the family from physical and social ailment.

None of this prevented recreational campers from occasionally using Indian as a metaphor for both healthy outdoor living and the feeling of freedom and escape they associated with camping. One camping writer who brought his wife and baby on a canoe vacation declared that "the out-door life" made the child "as hearty as an Indian papoose, and much the same color." Campers also participated in a longstanding white American tradition of "playing Indian" in various guises and organized youth camping movements, such as the Boy Scouts and Campfire Girls, which often placed romanticized native themes at the core of their mythology.[95] For white camping writers, invoking Indianness or labels used as close cognates—savage, primitive, nomad—granted license to take temporary leave of civilization. An *Outing* contributor, whose byline indicated his profession as a medical doctor, described it this way: "Every year when the month of June arrives, . . . I am seized with an irresistible desire to flee from the haunts of men and take up and live the life of a savage in all of its most primitive simplicity and naturalness."[96] For some, camping thus possessed the latent ability to awaken dormant desires for wild freedom. Along with "tramp style," "Indian" became one name for this impulse, but only if properly pursued as a temporary hiatus from one's respectable, professional existence.

Still, recreational campers tended to couch primitive instincts in the domestic frame. Among those who harmonized these sentiments most compellingly was Horace Kephart, whose prolific writings on outdoor recreation in the early twentieth century made him an oft-cited expert. He described rugged forms of camping as a chance to recapture the primeval satisfactions of self-reliance. For Kephart, the outdoors allowed a man to "hunt, capture, and cook his own meat, erect his own shelter, do his chores."[97] He called to campers: "Let us sometimes broil our venison on a sharpened stick and serve it on a sheet of bark. It tastes better. It gets us closer to nature, and closer to the good old times." In this context, the sharpened stick was a deliberate style choice, here wielded to raise doubts about the creeping "overcivilization" of urban society in comparison to days of yore. As would others, Kephart invoked pioneer history to protest against the rise of camping luxuries. "Fancy Boone reclining on an air mattress, or Carson pottering over a sheet-iron stove!"[98] Another guidebook writer suggested that campers "must unlearn" modern methods and relearn the skills of their "forefathers." He reasoned that "men were campers before they were house-dwellers; but, hemmed in by brick, stone, or wooden walls for generations past, their hand has forgotten its cunning in the matter of out-door homemaking." The "woodcraft" and domestic work of recreational campers kindled these pioneer fantasies and reenacted a process that had, not incidentally, contributed to the conquest of Indigenous lands, later to be claimed as public nature.[99]

Though Kephart's vision of self-reliance might seem antithetical to domestic comfort, the two were closer than they appeared. They each produced a feeling of independence, whether through achieving outdoor dominion or supporting individual freedoms. In one edition of *Camping and Woodcraft*, his most popular tome, Kephart summed up the rewards: "The charm of nomadic life is its freedom from care, its unrestrained liberty of action, and the proud self-reliance of one who is absolutely his own master. . . . Carrying with him, as he does, in a few small bundles, all that he needs to provide food and shelter in any land, habited or uninhabited, the camper is lord of himself and his surroundings."[100] To be lord of yourself and all you surveyed was a pretty heady feeling to attribute to camp. It harmonized seemingly incompatible characteristics: the joys of camping chores, a family domestic idyll, and rugged self-reliance. The combination embodied nothing less than a sense of command, as campers took temporary ownership of their outdoor surroundings.

The functional camps of tramps, bindlestiffs, and Native people, however, offered no such rewards. Using public nature for necessity now precluded access to narratives of self-reliance. But how to account for the existence of a family like the Reeveses in the first years of the twentieth century? They fit in neither categorization. For them, camping did not appear to provide a route to either virtual or actual property-ownership, though not for lack of trying.

They had one foot in the fading agrarian ideal, and the other in the new economic realities of mobile labor, with little access to the recreational ethos, which promised the feeling but not the substance of independence.

"What a Relief It Is to Travel in the Woods without a Skirt"

The symbolic sense of ownership that recreational campers enjoyed gave them another mechanism for exploring social issues. That camping was temporary allowed campers to try out new outlooks and behaviors they might not have attempted in their real home. That the campsite was understood as a home made it particularly ripe for experimentation around domestic arrangements, family relations, and gender roles. At the turn of the twentieth century, what place women should hold in the modern family and public life remained a pivotal, open question. Indeed, this was the era when families were having fewer children, more women were becoming both paid workers and public reformers, and the movement for women's suffrage was gathering steam, as well as opposition. Camping provided a forum to wrestle with these and other matters in the modern urban world, though it did not resolve them.

Where men's presence and duties as outdoorsmen were generally assumed, camping writers spotlighted women's appearance and functions in the campsite. Women were regular participants in recreational camping throughout the period, but narratives and guidebooks often treated them as perennial novelties. Apprentices rather than "natural born campers," they had to learn that fine line between knowing they would not "find a drawing room in the woods" and reproducing a campsite version of a drawing room.[101] Male writers emphasized the special contributions women could make as enjoyable companions and attentive homemakers. Bring "along a sister or two, and a pretty girl or two, and a chaperon, who, when she is not busy chaperoning, can and will cook. There are days when fish will not bite and when bait is elusive, and there are days when it rains. . . . At such times a pretty jolly girl is more than ever a joy." While this hardly represented an invitation for women to partake in the same way as men, the gender arrangement bolstered the campaign to showcase outdoor recreation as a respectable pursuit.[102]

Women employed similar themes in their camping stories, though sometimes to different effects. In a story for *Ladies' Home Journal*, a medical professional in Philadelphia explained how arriving in camp made her promptly forget "that she was a doctor." Instead she "became very domestic, . . . gathered fruit and berries, and then turned out the most delicious pies and puddings, rice cakes with honey, and fried chicken done to a turn." Her camp, however, included only "two young, independent professional women" who "had very little use for men" and "yearned to . . . try camping out by themselves."[103] Grace Gallatin Seton-Thompson adopted the stance of an apprentice. Her oft-quoted *A Woman Tenderfoot* (1900) traced her learning curve from novice to knowledgeable, fear to confidence. Her tutor was her husband, Ernest Thompson Seton, a well-known outdoorsman and one of the founders of the Boy Scouts of America. Grace opened the book admitting that the "number of things I had to learn appalled me," and ended it with this observation: "Though I am still a woman and may be tender, I am a Woman Tenderfoot no longer." Indeed, she would go on to become a well-known outdoor writer in her own right, and a prominent suffragist. Her camping story both echoed the belief that women were outdoor novices and, with her closing affirmation, challenged it.[104]

Isabel Barrows bypassed the apprentice metaphor and yet she too relied upon the appearance of more traditional domestic arrangements. The Barrowses' book, for example, specifically mentioned that Isabel, not June, wrote the chapter on camp cookery which portrayed her as thrilled to take on the duties of the kitchen. Anticipating readers' doubts about "who does the cooking" and "how long" it really takes "to do the domestic work of camp," she answered breezily that "it does itself." Isabel thus relied on the axiom that the domestic work of camp was enjoyable and worked to assure potential "skeptics . . . that one of the pleasantest ways to spend a vacation is to go into the woods and cook for ten or a dozen people for a month." For her, the "delights in cooking" offered a change of pace from the rest of the year where her hands were never "free from pen, pencil, or editorial scissors." There is evidence, however, that she continued this work in camp. One report suggested that both June Barrows and "his accomplished wife keep up their literary work with almost as much regularity as when at home. . . . The typewriter clicks merrily in the little tent set apart for office work, while Mr. Barrows is out upon the lake or tramping over the green hills."[105] Perhaps Isabel spent more time in the typewriter tent and did less of the cooking than she let on.

While cloaked, these departures from the dominant narrative suggested how some women were approaching the gender question in camp. Some were more explicit than others. Suffrage leader Alice Blackwell was a regular visitor to the Memphremagog camp, and featured Isabel Barrows's camping roles as evidence of women's capabilities and equality in articles for the suffragist newspaper *The Woman's Journal*. Barrows, she proclaimed, could "do anything from taking down a German oration in shorthand and writing it out in English in time for the next morning's paper, to concocting unparalleled soups and chowders." Blackwell used her observations of women in the Memphremagog camp as support for the key suffrage argument that women need not sacrifice femininity to show their fitness as citizens. For her, Isabel's adept management of the camp was both "disproof that a woman is incapable of exercising government" and shattered the delusion that "women would lose their influence if they took to wearing divided skirts."[106]

What women should wear to camp was not a trivial subject. Both male and female camping writers urged women to choose comfort and utility over fashion, and at the very least to abandon their corsets. As early as 1889, Margaret Bisland wrote succinctly in *Outing*: "Corsets are out of the question." George Shields concurred: "Women are becoming too practical to much longer tolerate such an impractical nonsensical piece of furniture as a corset." As late as 1910, Sara Stokes Baxter still had to remind women not to take their corsets into camp. She further suggested that "conventional clothing is in every particular unsuitable for life in the woods, so much so that no compromise may be made and one cannot start from the city properly dressed for both." She suggested making the change between proper attire to camping clothes and back again in a gateway town, far from the city.[107] This reinforced the idea of the campsite as a place apart, where one might try out novel ways of being.

In these experiments, women insisted that wearing practical clothing should not require abandoning fashion or femininity. They desired, as one woman put it, "a costume both sensible and becoming." Another cautioned, "do not be persuaded that anything will do to wear: it will not; a great deal of your pleasure depends on having comfortable and pretty clothing, nay, even stylish, for the camping-out dress has a style and grace that can be very effective and becoming." Grace Seton-Thompson insisted women need not settle for ill-fitting, cast-off menswear but could have suitable and stylish clothes with ample decorative touches. "One can do a wonderful amount of smartening up with tulle, hat pins, belts and fancy neck ribbons, all of which comparatively take up no room and add no weight."[108] Vermont writer and Smith College graduate Zephine Humphrey followed Seton-Thompson's instructions in preparing for a three-week camping expedition in the Canadian Rockies. She was especially pleased with the recommendation for a short full skirt, made for riding astride, but was less satisfied with "Mrs. Seton's advice to her sisters to take tulle bows and fancy hatpins into the wilderness. . . . A tulle bow on a flannel shirtwaist? Perish the thought of such a combination." Moreover, the

fresh ribbons she brought were lost or torn within the first few days of outdoor travel and thus were as pointless as they were mismatched.[109]

Humphrey had agreed with the "spirit" of embellishment, even though
she found it impractical. Men were more skeptical of the idea itself. In 1906
Kephart asserted that "properly dressed for the woods, and not overburdened,
the average woman can keep up anywhere with the average office man." But he
worried that desires for typical attire would hamper them: "In a tight or draggy
skirt she is simply hopeless." Other male writers fretted that women would
use irrational logic to dismiss advice on things like sturdy footwear: "Women
don't like to make their feet look big, and sometimes are afraid their costumes
are not going to be becoming."[110] Seton-Thompson offered a rebuttal. When
men wondered, "'Why take a hat pin,'" she replied that they could not reasonably expect to deprive a woman "of all her gewgaws and still have her filled
with the proper desire to be pleasing to your eyes."[111] Finding the right balance of sensible and becoming entailed some delicate negotiations.

Rena Phillips's 1904 contribution to *Outing* illustrated these sartorial
dilemmas. Improper clothing made her first outdoor trip the "most miserable day" she ever spent: "Of course I wore a long skirt, a shirt waist, straw
hat and veil, kid gloves and low shoes, and was as uncomfortable as it was
possible for a woman to be." After several dreadful forays, Phillips decided
to pursue a more suitable outfit. Her husband's answer to the problem was
simple; she should purchase "a boy's suit of corduroy knickerbockers." Phillips
was appalled: "I objected vehemently and told him it positively would not
do; that I would not make a monkey of myself by appearing in public dressed
in boy's clothes."[112] She wanted freedom from conventional dress, but still
imagined nature as enough of a public arena to require appropriately feminine attire.

Phillips surveyed outdoor outfitters and dress shops and found none that
sold ready-made clothes for women in the outdoors. As had Seton-Thompson,
she concluded that she would need to customize. Her finished ensemble included "a short skirt, an ordinary canvas hunting coat, a soft felt hat, a double
breasted woolen shirt converted into a blouse waist, a pair of trousers that
were neither bloomers nor knickerbockers, cotton stockings with woolen bi-
cycle stockings over them, and a pair of ordinary heavy shoes with sensible
heels." Several items required specific alterations. For example, she wanted
the boy's hunting coat she purchased to "fit less like a bag," so she "went to
work with the scissors and needle on the side seams and took out enough to
give it a little shape at the waist." The finished version satisfied her in terms
of its appearance, utility, and comfort, and she delighted in the large number

of pockets uncommon in women's coats. Phillips found the whole fiasco ultimately liberating and encouraged others to follow her lead. "I very frequently, after going to the woods, take off the skirt and put it in the big back pocket of my coat so it will not be a source of annoyance on the trail. This leaves me as free in my movements as a man, and I slip the skirt on again before coming back to civilization. No woman knows, until she tries it, what a relief it is to travel in the woods without a skirt."[113]

In their camping stories, women remarked again and again upon their joyful discoveries of the freedom of bodily movement. Bisland found that after three glorious weeks in the woods, "coming back to civilization was a disagreeable wretch. Not since I was a child in short frocks did I appreciate" what it felt like to "leap from stone to stone in the brook without having to reach for the tail of my gown." In camp, she came "as nearly as woman can ever hope to experiencing the pleasurable sensation of bodily ease and comfort that is [our] brother's right from his youth up."[114] Seton-Thompson savored the chance to use her "muscles . . . , to run where walking would do, to jump an obstacle instead of going around it, to return, physically at least, to your pinafore days when you played with your brother." She invited women to "Come with me and learn how to be vulgarly robust," to feel the "glorious freedom, the quick rushing blood, the bounding motion, of the wild life."[115] Instead of giving women pause, these camping writers presented the rare chance to shake off restrictive dress as an incentive to try camping.

On the one hand, women's discovery of bodily ease and vigor had the potential to destabilize certain gender norms, and a secluded campsite, or even an outdoor magazine, offered a protected venue to give it a try. On the other hand, the assumption that the hiatus from civilization was temporary, along with the accompanying unorthodoxy, necessarily limited the possibilities for seeing camp as a form of cultural critique. To wear pants in camp could emphasize their inappropriateness "back home" as much as the feeling of freedom they allowed in the woods. Nonetheless, recreational camping did allow protected experimentation with modern ideas.[116]

The repeated emphasis on camp as a temporary home shined a spotlight on domestic relationships. Phillips confronted this in the matter of washing dishes, among her least favorite camp chores. As Figure 3.4 illustrates, she decided to

turn this job over to my husband, who takes the dirty, greasy frying-pans and other cooking utensils down to the creek, . . . and there, with his pipe a-light, he sits complacently down on a convenient rock and

FIGURE 3.4 Rena Phillips, in her short skirt and customized hunting coat, observed her husband's creekside dishwashing technique. "Begins by throwing a handful of mud into the frying pan," photograph by J. S. Phillips, in Rena A. Phillips, "The Woman in the Woods," *Outing* 46, no. 4 (July 1905): 472.

begins by throwing a handful of mud into the frying-pan. Then he dips up a little bit of water and with a handful of moss proceeds to scour and rinse alternately on every dirty dish until the camp culinary furniture shines like a brand new pin.

His technique, and perhaps his cavalier attitude, took a while to win her over. She admitted that she "used to be skeptical of this process," but could not argue with the results. Ultimately, she realized that "men do not really object to dish-washing in camp" as long as they could do it in this fashion.[117] The creek and the mud gave the task a different, perhaps more manly, effect. Phillips seemed to suggest that the context of an outdoor vacation enabled the male willingness to cook and scrub, a factor that potentially blunted the lasting impacts of the inversion.

Whether the dishwashing husband was replacing his wife or his servants, camp highlighted gender issues at the heart of the usually masked labor of housework. The self-conscious pose, and its publication in a popular magazine, exposed the role-reversal and hinted at how marital relationships were shifting. By the first decades of the twentieth century, women and men appeared to be auditioning in camp what would become known in the 1920s as "companionate marriage." A social label for new relational expectations and economic functions of families, companionate marriage prioritized sexual and emotional intimacy between husband and wife, privacy and freedom from parental control, more democratic family organization, and delayed child-rearing with fewer births. The early years of marriage gained significance as a period of companionable partnership for the young couple. Companionate marriage accommodated new opportunities for women within otherwise traditional middle-class marriage structures.[118]

Camping writers foreshadowed much of this discussion, often writing about outdoor adventures taken as honeymoons or before children arrived. Seton-Thompson camped and published her book before her only daughter was born, dating her first trip afield to "the year after our marriage." When her husband announced, "he must go West and take up the trail for his holiday," she cited the maxim of the "Quaker wife, . . . 'Whither thou goest, I go,'" and shelved her plans for a summer resort or European tour. In her book, she deliberately and repeatedly referenced her reader as "the woman-who-goes-hunting-with-her-husband," essentially assuming the relation of companion within the camping enterprise.[119] Phillips appeared to be experimenting with her relationship during this period as well. She described the motivation to take up camping was to join her husband who was always coming home late from the woods. She soon shared in his enthusiasm, "for now we go together. We have tramped and camped together up and down the land. . . . We have learned to camp comfortably and to live in the woods for a week on what my husband can carry in his pack sack and we enjoy every minute of the time."[120]

Camp provided a kind of laboratory to test these new relational waters. In a 1905 piece titled "Camping for Two," Charles Greene even suggested that camp could provide a useful lens through which to evaluate potential partners. He instructed his readers, "If you are going to choose a wife with the idea of making a camping comrade of her, you must be more than usually careful in your selection." Beyond this, Greene continued, "If you choose the best camper from a bevy of maidens as your life partner, you can hardly make a mistake. She will be an active, healthy, courageous, and merry companion, not easily disheartened, and ready to take the good of life with whatever hardship it may bring."[121] Camp might thus serve as a tool for forming this modern family.

The Barrowses portrayed themselves as a model democratic family on the companionate plan: they had only one child, Isabel had a professional identity outside the home (though she did not work for pay after her child was born), they advocated women's equality in education and public life, shared some household labors, and enjoyed an intellectual partnership. Camp demonstrated the balancing act this required, at which Isabel Barrows was an acknowledged expert. As June wrote in admiration: "The facility with which Mrs. Shayback will use a saw and hammer, a screw-driver, . . . and other useful tools, is only equaled by the ease and promptness with which she can get a meal for a dozen hungry campers."[122] When guidebook writer Emerson Hough characterized a woman with this combination of talents in 1915 as a "thoroughbred," he revealed the less progressive version of Barrows's praise. To be a thoroughbred implied "sincerity and a readiness to be of use to others." The way "to walk into the heart of all the men about the camp," he suggested to his female readers, was to "make a fresh camp dish once in a while" and never allow themselves "to be regarded as a burden." And, he concluded, "If I had to give only one word of advice to the woman going into camp, I would say, 'Smile.'"[123] Hough's characterization of women as useful ornaments hinted at persistent imbalances underneath modern companionate ideals.

The temporary camp-home became a unique platform on which to audition forms of modernity, like the servantless household, the corsetless woman, and companionate marriage. This made sleeping outside a very different proposition three decades after the Shaybacks had made their debut in *Outing*. In 1890, Shields could still pitch his guide both to "those who camp merely for rest and recreation" and to "the thousands who must depend on it, for at least a portion of the time, while pursuing their regular vocation": the "Loggers, raftsmen, surveyors, cow-boys, prospectors, miners, timber estimators, and many others" who pursued camp life "either from choice or from force of circumstances." By 1915, Hough had no such need to address his handbook to a wide audience. The title of the first chapter of his *Out of Doors* made this underlying assumption overt: "Your Vacation." The opening line queried readers: "How and where shall one spend the summer vacation?"[124] Not only had camping become a definable leisure practice, separated from functional experiences of tramps and laborers, but it also came to host the possibility for generating new outlooks on modern life. Making camp into a temporary home allowed recreational campers both privileged access to new forms of public nature and a medium for engaging key questions of the age.

JUNE BARROWS ADDED one more Shayback camping story to the collection in 1894. The camp at Lake Memphremagog again served as the main setting, this time for a play titled "The Beacon Street Tramp." He framed it as a tale of two tramps: Dennis Want, a poor and suspicious-looking Irish transient, and Harry Dudeson, a wealthy bachelor from fashionable Beacon

Street looking for a cure for his dissolute wandering and frivolous lifestyle. Sent to camp with the Shaybacks, both come to repent their anti-social ways and find contentment and respectability. There are multiple subplots and a complex story of hidden class identities, where the Shaybacks don't know that Dudeson is rich, and Want turns out to be an honorable man. But the main driver of the plot is that camping provides a valuable, perhaps unique, social curative.

The plot is set in motion when the Rev. Mr. Shayback writes a social investigator requesting she identify a "representative Boston tramp" and send him to Memphremagog. In a Henry Higgins-like proposal, he wagered that "In the course of six weeks . . . he will be entirely cured of any aversion to labor and will be capable of earning his living and willing to do so." She was already aware that Shayback had assembled "an Indian, a Negro, a Chinaman, a Greek, a Turk, and an Armenian" in camp, and with the help of their usual extended family of white campers, Helen, Daphne, Gilbert and others, was teaching them to "live together peaceably in a sort of happy family." He wanted to demonstrate how "all social problems can best be solved together," and by adding the tramp, he could cure "pauperism and crime" along with "the race question".[125] Not only did camp appear to be the ideal venue for inculcating white middle-class models of work and family, but recreational camping—tramp style—now proffered a cure for tramp life itself.

The work of the recreational camp, in mixing leisure with nature appropriately, provided a new route to proving one's worth. In a scene titled "Domesticating the Tramp," Helen and the Indian girl, "Pokie," by then an experienced camper, teach Dudeson the correct way to do various camp chores. He is skeptical that "a wild Indian . . . can teach a man to be domestic," but the efforts of the two women transform him. Dudeson learns to chop wood, peel potatoes, assist with dinner, and wash dishes, all while maintaining an appropriately cheerful attitude. The particular combination of camp housekeeping encouraged Dudeson, and presumably any tramp or Indian, to realize the value of responsibility and a commitment to home life. Barrows concludes the play with Shayback declaring his experiments a success. "I undertook to convert a poor tramp; I've succeeded in the far more difficult task of converting a rich one. The rich and the poor have struck hands in fraternal helpfulness," while "the Indian and the white . . . are beautifully reconciled."[126]

Staged in Boston on May 12, 1894, a scant two weeks after Coxey's Army had entered Washington, DC, "The Beacon Street Tramp" held out a rosy solution to the wrenching social tensions of the moment. Barrows was sympathetic to the down-and-out Irishman in his play, who he characterized as wanting "to earn an honest livin' but . . . niver learned to do honest work." But his portrayal implied no endorsement of the tramp life, as Want is chastised for the "flimsy excuse" of putting "the responsibility of your misfortunes upon other people's shoulders. . . . Straighten yourself up like a man and bear your own burdens. Don't be a curse to yourself and a curse to society." Nor does Dudeson escape an analogous criticism for "leading a life of self gratification, . . . never giving himself to any cause, principle or service for the benefit of humanity."[127] Recreational camping served as a medium between Dudeson and Want, between the wealthy sloth and the degenerate rabble which Barrows framed as equally problematic. It also provided a method for their joint rehabilitation. Whether this morality tale contributed to June Barrows's 1896 election to Congress or not, the Shayback stories epitomized the development of a recreational ethos that made camping not just a happy medium for leisure but mechanism for envisioning a harmonious social order.

Campers and writers like June and Isabel Barrows, Robert Dunn, Charlotte Conover, Horace Kephart, Grace Seton-Thompson, Rena Phillips, and all their fellow travelers made recreational camping into a distinctly meaningful and definitively modern practice. The temporary home embodied competing aspirations: the desire to go wild and the comforts of keeping house, the exhilaration of feeling free as a man and the ability to remain feminine in a feral environment, the excitement of escape and the assurance of coming home. Inhabiting the outdoors as a symbolic platform rather than a set of resources, campers developed a discrete set of practices that remade the outdoors for a self-defined public: Americans seeking to mix their leisure with the land. More and more, this premise would shape the emerging social contract. Those who camped to capture the feeling of independence pushed to the margins those who sought more material rewards from public nature. This divide would only widen as the twentieth century progressed.

4

Establishing the Campers' Republic

EMILIO MEINECKE WAS not the Lorax, but he did try to speak for the trees. A California-born, German-educated botanist, Meinecke worked as a plant pathologist for the US Forest Service (USFS) and other state and federal agencies, including contract work for the National Park Service (NPS) from 1910 until the mid-1940s. His 1914 manual *Forest Tree Diseases* advanced the field by focusing on forest stands rather than individual trees. He was active in academic and public conversations about land use issues, but of all his scientific studies and recommendations, arguably what left the most significant imprint upon the land was his design of the "loop campground."[1] Instantly recognizable to campers today, the loop drive, interspersed with automobile turnouts pointing to individual campsites, still owes its essential contours to Meinecke. His plan originated in the discovery that heavily used campsites caused major damage to tree roots and aimed to minimize the trampling effect of campers' vehicles, boots, and tents on the forest floor. It also constituted an elegant and easily reproducible design principle that fostered a vast expansion of camping facilities and accommodations for the automobile in parks and forests. Ironically, the "Meinecke plan," as it became known among federal and state planners in the 1930s, enabled so many more campers to visit the woods that they were likely to overwhelm its protective purposes, loop or no loop.

Meinecke was fully aware that he was unleashing a plan that would facilitate greater access to the outdoors. He intended the loop simultaneously to protect trees from the camping masses and to foster positive experiences on public lands. "Visitors to the outdoors are the guests of the nation," he wrote in 1935. By encouraging people to camp, "governments are rendering immediate and intrinsically friendly service . . . to the individual in the quest for a legitimate satisfaction of fine and clean desires."[2] Meinecke believed that camping on public land, in specially designed experiences, strengthened the bonds between government and citizen. In taking up the Meinecke plan not only did the state protect forests and standardize camping expectations, but it also adopted a new conception of public nature. The loop campground modeled an emerging social contract based on leisure and consumption rather than labor and production. Over the course of a single decade the federal government vastly expanded the public camping landscape and promoted recreational camping as a civic good.

It is not coincidental that leisure campers gained state endorsement at a time when other kinds of campers—Bonus Army marchers or Dust Bowl migrants, for example—caused public alarm. Divisions between functional and recreational camping continued to widen as the tents of unemployed and uprooted Americans raised concerns about social disorder and economic tragedy in the 1930s. This broader spectrum of sleeping outside continued to shape the meanings vacationers, and now the state, made of camping. Debates about the responsibilities of the government, and the relationship between nation and citizens swirled throughout the Depression era. These discussions became particularly vexed by examples of Americans who had fallen through the cracks, such as impoverished veterans, unemployed transients, and drought refugees whose disheveled encampments were a last resort. They also seemed to suggest the final failure of the agrarian ideal for most Americans, though different government agencies persisted in trying to keep some version of it alive.

Meinecke's vision of campers as "guests of the nation" in clean, orderly, well-regulated public camps instead showcased a new paradigm for public nature, where the government supported the ability of citizens to mix their leisure with land. Americans demonstrated their fitness not by working productive property, but through virtuous recreation and consumption.[3] Recreational camping became embedded in multiple New Deal efforts—public works, jobs programs, economic stimulus, land conservation, scenic patriotism, cultural recovery, and social development. Inside the loop, the outdoor setting solidified the bonds between citizen, state, and nation; beyond the loop, sleeping outside suggested an alienation from the national community. With Meinecke's blueprints and federal investment, campgrounds entrenched the outdoor recreational ethos in American landscapes and values. They both embodied and helped to establish the terms of the new social contract organized around consumer citizens and leisure experiences.

"The Clamor for More"

Meinecke's loop, and the federal enthusiasm to build it in the 1930s, partly came in response to the ways recreational camping had changed in the previous two decades. A fashionable pursuit among the upper classes, camping might have remained a niche pursuit for the well-off if not for the arrival and mass-production of the automobile. At the turn of the century, automobiles were largely playthings for a small cadre of elites, with approximately 100,000 machines in the country by 1906. After Henry Ford introduced the inexpensive, factory-made Model T in 1913, car ownership became a mass phenomenon, with 10 million automobiles on the road in 1922 and 23 million in 1929—one for every five Americans. Using cars for vacation travel and camping became common, especially as leisure time increased for select groups of workers. In the late 1920s, over ten million Americans took off on auto-camping journeys every year, perhaps as high as 15 percent of the total population. Many lobbied for an expanded national road infrastructure to accommodate the automobile, in part to foster recreational travel.[4] The remarkable popularity of recreational uses of the automobile set in motion three major changes to camping practices by the mid-1920s. More people overall, and more from the middle and lower-middle classes, were camping. They brought more and different gear with them, giving rise to new markets, industries, and cultures built around outdoor equipment and gadgets. And they demanded more infrastructure, such as good roads, ready-made campgrounds, and on-site amenities. Together these significantly shifted the standard practice of recreational camping in a short time.

Writers in the *Outing* tradition initially incorporated the automobile into the elite presumptions of camping. As an expensive experimental novelty, early automobiles largely served to enhance campers' membership in an exclusive group and their feelings of independence. A 1905 article in *Outing* emphasized how automobile camping required both mechanical know-how and traditional outdoorsmanship. Campers marveled at the prospect of "modern man brought back to Nature on the latest vehicle of civilization . . . free to roam, to camp, and to change your ground at will, to surmount the obstacles of the open country."[5] These campers soon found themselves outnumbered by a wave of "Tin Can Tourists," who drove less expensive Model Ts and dined cheaply from canned foods, sometimes heated on the car engine. Auto-camping narratives highlighted affordability and convenience, the ease rather than the effort of creating a temporary outdoor home. A 1921 *Vanity Fair* article reviewing the "Fast Growing Sport of Motor

Camping" highlighted its reasonable costs and varied options; auto-campers could choose either to "get away from people" and go to "secluded woodland nooks," or to "rub elbows with your fellow men with a degree of democracy possible in no other ways." Exaggerated or no, celebrating camping as a great equalizer was a new impulse.[6] When *Outing* ceased publication in 1923, it was a bellwether for the declining relevance of many of its elite pretensions around sports, amateurism, and outdoor life.

The newly democratic spirit of camping was not without its contradictions. In the early 1920s municipal authorities began to construct free auto-camps, with city leaders banking on the increase in tourist dollars to outweigh the expense. Fairly soon, these municipal camps instituted modest charges, in part to select for particular campers and "shut out undesirables." A *Sunset* magazine article in 1925 argued that while this could lead to a decrease in the number of campers, it elevated "the class of tourists." The better auto-camps made "every effort . . . to discourage the use of the camp by the so-called 'tin-can' tourist" as well as semipermanent nomads "who spent the entire year on the road, working for two or three days" before moving on to the next stop.[7] Over time, rifts between poor and wealthy recreational campers declined, and the division widened between those who camped for functional purposes and recreational campers no matter their class.

Wherever they were headed, auto-campers toted trunks full of new kinds of equipment along with them. As one promoter suggested, when you "use your automobile," you can bring "equipment unthought of by the old-timer with his horse-drawn outdoor home." The car allowed campers to "deprive themselves of nothing of comfort and convenience" and enjoy even "more of the luxuries and niceties of home living." Drivers could get very creative with expanding their storage space, lashing boxes to running boards and bumpers. Modern "special equipment, made to nest, telescope," or fold compactly, allowed them to cram more stuff into the car. Campers quickly warmed to these newfangled products. While writers continued to caution that proper outfitting still entailed balance, the happy medium moved definitively toward greater technology and comfort.[8]

New industries sprang up to respond to the demand for specialized equipment. Coleman, for example, got its start just after the turn of the century manufacturing gasoline lamps sold primarily to farmers. The company realized that the new portable all-weather lantern its engineers devised in 1914 had major appeal for campers as well. It started to advertise the same "Quick-Lite" lantern with different messages, one for farm families and another for recreational campers. It also began to develop new products specifically for camping needs, including a gasoline stove introduced in 1923. Promoted as "The Smooth Way to Rough It" (as shown in Figure 4.1), Coleman quickly made the stove seem essential. Why cook over old-fashioned, dangerous, hot and smoky fires when "two minutes will set your inexpensive little

FIGURE 4.1 The Coleman Camp Stove, along with the Quick-Lite Lantern, became "Two Best Pals of Every Camper" and the new must-haves for auto-campers seeking "The Smooth Way To Rough It." "Dealers; Advertising Cut Service" (Coleman Lamp Co., 1926), box 3, folder 1, Coleman Company advertising records, Kenneth Spencer Research Library, University of Kansas.

gasoline camp stove to work as efficiently as your gas range at home and as clean—no soot to blacken your pots and pans?" Connections between home and camp remained important, with modern equipment smoothing out the differences. With cutting-edge advertising techniques, Coleman soon acquired a nationwide customer base for its products.[9] It hired guide-book author F. E. Brimmer to write a *Coleman Motor Campers Manual* in 1926. Brimmer wrapped his own advice and techniques for auto-camping around the indispensability of Coleman products. "Nothing is more typical of motor camping than the gasoline stove. . . . With a COLEMAN on the job, the cook has time to enjoy the scenery as well as take care of lusty appetites."[10] Whole new types of equipment—air mattresses and folding tables, miniature phonographs and portable heated showers—entered lists of recommended camp provisions. In a short time, it became hard to imagine camping without these conveniences.

Many campers began to tinker and invent new possibilities. Articles on auto-camping began to appear in magazines like *Industrial Arts Monthly* and *Popular Mechanics*, offering do-it-yourself guides for creating custom camping gadgets. By the mid-1920s, *Popular Mechanics* had become a widely read monthly that aimed to disseminate knowledge about technological developments and skills to a general readership. It encouraged consumers to take innovation into their own hands, and auto-camping was a prime candidate for creative tinkering.[11] *Popular Mechanics* frequently printed instructions and blueprints to make your own equipment, reader-submitted ideas for new products, and nearly countless ways of modifying one's car. From attaching tents to the body and converting the interior into sleeping areas to the eyebrow-raising idea to use the exhaust pipe to power a stove, auto-camping tinkerers imagined a vast landscape of custom gear.[12] When they ran out of room in or on the car itself, campers developed specialized camping trailers and motor homes, which also became popular. Options ran the gamut from a basic model designed to make "Camping Easy," which included simple step-by-step diagrams, to a luxurious twenty-two-foot "Elaborate House on Wheels." Such uninhibited experimentation became a defining aspect of the camping experience during the 1920s.[13] Campers reveled in the ability to bring the latest modern technology into the outdoors through the practice of camping.[14]

For all their customized vehicles and portable gadgets, campers began to desire—and then demand—a more ready-made welcome, with on-site amenities, convenience for their cars, and connections to the modern, urban, consumer world. The pop-up auto-camps run by municipal authorities, as

well as private entrepreneurs, played a major role in escalating campers' expectations. Municipal auto-camps advertised their proximity to town, accessibility to the road, indoor plumbing, and functional kitchens. Los Angeles
opened an auto-camp in Griffith Park in 1920 with the enticement that "forty
machine parties may park their cars, pitch their tents, and enjoy practically
every privilege of a modern hotel." Facilities included "running hot and cold
water, shower baths, a laundry, and gas stoves and a wash rack where the
camper may wash the stain of travel from his car." Campers jumped at the
city's invitation, and prompted the city to open an even larger camp two years
later. Denver's camp put most others to shame, hosting up to 1,500 cars in
Overland Park by 1923. For fifty cents a day, carloads of campers had access to
electric lights, laundries, indoor restrooms, and an on-site grocery store, res-
taurant, gas station, and auto repair shop. Campers could receive daily mail
service and department store delivery, as well as visit the camp playground or
barber shop. What travelers did not have to deal with were hotel reservations,
meal schedules, workers looking for a tip, or lack of parking spaces. In many
ways auto-camps were an alternative to hotels more than they were an ana-
logue of wilderness camping, but they changed what campers expected at all
campgrounds.[15]

At national parks and forests, as well as at state and public reserves,
campers began arriving in droves and expecting a certain level of amenities.
Officials at all levels had to decide whether to admit automobiles, but once
they did, visitation mushroomed. While the national parks often charged fees
for automobile entry, camping itself was free, with "fire wood, electric lights,
facilities for washing clothes, garbage collection and showers" often included.
Traveling around the West in 1925, one couple noted, "We were agreeably surprised with the accommodations found at the national parks." These campers
had been particularly worried about "the bathing problem" but were pleased
to report "no difficulty in locating camps with shower baths." That one could
camp across the West and have no trouble finding a hot shower soon became
as ordinary as it had been novel only a short time before. Others hinted that
federal agencies were having trouble keeping up with demand and suggested
that campers bring a "folding table and chairs" to make up for the "scanty
provisions" of camps built by "your efficient but sadly overworked National
Park Service." What NPS campgrounds provided came to seem "scanty" in
comparison to what auto-camps were leading travelers to expect. This article
predicted that the federal government would continue to improve its facilities
to keep up with campers' expectations. "Uncle Samuel is rapidly building the
most perfect system of auto-camps extant, both in the National Parks and

in the National Forests—wonderful playgrounds!—but he will always have trouble in meeting the clamor for more."[16]

The clamor for more only grew louder over the course of the 1920s. With their cars and gadgets, campers overran the scenic wonders of the nation. They got in each other's way, complained about overcrowding, demanded more amenities, and provoked concern among park managers. Fear of the effects of automobile tourism would spur new enthusiasm for wilderness preservation, but park managers faced immediate practical challenges in attempting to contain the damage of tremendously expanded visitor numbers.[17] The first Director of the National Park Service, Stephen Mather, felt this dilemma keenly and personally. He watched as the very success of the promotional campaign he had initiated to popularize the Parks began to undermine the basis of their appeal.

Mather, having first lobbied for the creation of the NPS itself in 1916, embarked on a widespread and memorable effort to entice Americans to visit the parks. Building on his effective marketing campaign for a brand of detergent, "20 Mule Team Borax," Mather applied similar advertising techniques to raise the profile of the parks. He also capitalized on the ongoing "See America First" campaign, started a few years earlier by railroad companies and regional boosters to encourage tourists to visit the nation's many nature-oriented sites, such as the recently established Glacier National Park. The slogan gained even greater currency during World War I, when travel to Europe was curtailed. Mather extended the patriotic allusions of "See America First" and oversaw the design and construction of expanded visitor facilities and ready-made tourist experiences at many parks. Landscape architects remade the topography to choreograph visitors' activities and frame their visual perception. Altogether, the promotion and visitation of national parks in the 1920s was far more aligned with the consumer zeitgeist of the time than a wilderness-oriented antidote to the modern world.[18]

Camping was central to the purpose of the national park visitor experience in the Mather era. A 1918 memo from Secretary of the Interior Franklin Lane to Mather established this principle. Equally as important as preserving the unique nature in the parks, Lane asserted, was the speedy and thorough development of a "national playground system." Free or "low-priced camps" should be built in each park and "equipped with adequate water and sanitation facilities." Modern camping facilities were part and parcel of the larger assumption that the NPS should give visitors quality accommodations "in the manner that best satisfies the individual taste." This meant permitting "automobiles and motorcycles . . . in all of the national parks" and ensuring that "the parks will be kept accessible by any means practicable."[19]

Plans for developing parklands for automobiles and for campers were closely tied to each other. Mather lobbied for funds to expand roads within parks as well as between them, but automobile entrance fees, though "very unpopular," served as the "principal source of revenue" for these efforts. Mather explained to Congress in 1926 that campgrounds helped to address this issue. "As rapidly as conditions would allow we established these public camps on a better and better scale, with more and more facilities . . . , and we felt then that we were giving a much better service and were in a much better position to defend these charges."[20] The more cars that arrived, the more and better campgrounds could be constructed; larger modern campgrounds enticed even more automobile campers, who in turn paid for yet more roads and camping facilities.

Visitor numbers at national parks jumped fivefold in the 1910s, reaching one million in attendance in 1920. Over the course of the decade that followed, visitation continued to increase, more than three times by 1930, far outpacing the growth of the US population, as Table 4.1 shows. So many more visitors over such a short time began to overwhelm the Park Service's ability to respond and to fulfill the other half of its mission: "conserve the scenery" and leave it "unimpaired for the enjoyment of future generations." With increased

Table 4.1 National Parks and Monuments Visitor Counts, 1910–1930

Year	Number of Visitors	Growth over previous 5 years	Growth since 1910	US Population	Growth of US Population since 1910	Visitors as % of US pop.
1910	198,606	1.4	—	92,228,496	—	0.2%
1915	335,299	1.7	1.7	—	—	—
1920	1,058,455	3.2	5.3	106,021,537	1.1	1.0%
1925	2,054,562	1.9	10.3	—	—	—
1930	3,246,655	1.6	16.3	123,202,624	1.3	2.6%

Source: U.S. Department of the Interior, National Park Service, "Public Use of the National Parks: A Statistical Report, 1904–1940," (1968), i, 1. Growth numbers appear as a multiple of the previous relevant figure. Year begins October 1 and ends September 30. NPS statistics for this era only report total visitation, and do not disaggregate overnight guests, campers, or types of camping. While there were many campers among these visitors, it is very difficult to estimate camping numbers, given the difference in types of parks, lodging options, and uneven campground development. The increase in visitors who camped likely paralleled the rate of increase in visitors overall, but this is conjectural.

campers came increased sewage and garbage, polluted streams, foraging for firewood, and other sorts of depredations by careless or negligent visitors. Public health challenges arose particularly where visitors concentrated in large numbers. Yellowstone, Mount Rainier, and Rocky Mountain National Park were each hosting over 200,000 visitors annually in the late 1920s, and Yosemite over 400,000 in 1927.[21]

This was nowhere more evident than in California, where crowds congregated in the popular Sequoia and Yosemite National Parks and in several state Redwood parks. The grandeur of the state's "Big Trees" and spectacular valleys, promoted so memorably by John Muir and others, attracted a wealth of visitors. The ancient groves of Giant Sequoia and Redwood trees began to decline sharply amidst the onslaught. It was this problem that prompted the call in 1927 for the services of Emilio Meinecke. What good was it, Meinecke would ask, to save forests from the axe of industry only to have them fall victim "to slow but fatal changes . . . brought about by excessive tourist travel"?[22] He succinctly described a dilemma park administrators would come to know all too well: How could they prevent parks from being loved to death? By the late 1920s, recreational camping was an entirely different proposition than it had been at the turn of the century. Campers traveled around the country en masse with new kinds of equipment and expectations. Private entrepreneurs and public agencies all scrambled to keep pace with the demands of the vast numbers of tourists. Meinecke aimed to strike a sustainable balance between the new habits of auto-campers and the natural integrity of the forest.

"Visitors to the Outdoors Are the Guests of the Nation"

The rapid deterioration of the Sequoias and Redwoods caused great alarm. Park administrators knew that if the trees were lost, their parks would lose their defining feature. Barring visitors might protect the trees, but a park without visitors contradicted the agency's mandate. Unable to explain what precisely was interfering with the trees' ability to regenerate, the NPS commissioned Meinecke, a respected expert at the Office of Forest Pathology, to locate the culprit. In his initial studies of Sequoia (1926) and the Redwood parks (1928), Meinecke declared the repeated trampling by automobile and foot traffic as the cause of injury to redwoods' shallow root systems. Sheer visitor numbers were a problem, but they were magnified by the system of camping itself or, rather, the lack of system. During this era, designating a campground typically meant providing a few common facilities (water pumps, trash receptacles, latrines, and showers) within a large open area but few or no internal divisions between sites, as the example in Figure 4.2 shows. Defining perimeters contained the damage, but intensified it. Meinecke determined that "the packing of the ground over a very large part, if not over the whole, of the root spread, such as is found in camping grounds" far outweighed other impacts. Campers parked haphazardly upon meadows and pitched their tents at the base of tree trunks. Criss-crossing the site in "unconsciously formulated traffic" patterns, they clambered on exposed tree roots, denuded the undergrowth, and compacted the soil, adding up to severe localized effects.[23]

Meinecke took a Forest Service perspective on this problem and argued that many of the Park Service's troubles arose from its "irreconcilable" mandates: to preserve "the physical unit in its natural state" and to offer it "to the enjoyment of the public." The paradox meant that every improvement or accommodation for visitors entailed "destruction of some of the wild plant life." Though Meinecke acknowledged the need for compromise, he urged the NPS "to endeavor to hold this destruction down to a minimum."[24] This assessment was indicative of a bureaucratic rivalry between the two agencies. While the Park Service began using tools from the emergent consumer age, marketing outdoor recreation and scenic grandeur to a broad audience of potential visitors, the Forest Service retained its Progressive-era commitment

FIGURE 4.2 In this campground at Mount Rainier, cars and tents are scattered about willy-nilly, causing damage to trees and ground cover. Postcard by Ranapar Studio, ca. 1925. Author's personal collection.

to scientific expertise and resource management. Meinecke advised the NPS to heed the lessons of the older, wiser USFS, which had longer experience in protecting trees from being overrun by human desires.[25]

Yet in the 1920s, the Forest Service was even less prepared for the onslaught of visitors. It had never been oriented toward recreation and had built few campgrounds or facilities. Before 1919, those that existed were extremely basic—a few latrines and fire pits to reduce the risk of water pollution and wildfires. That year, the Denver regional office of the USFS hired landscape architect Arthur Carhart as a "recreation engineer" to develop potential strategies. He designed a prototype for an integrated visitor complex that included campgrounds, picnic areas, hiking trails, community pavilions, and scenic roads. Cobbling together funds to build this model outdoor recreation facility in the San Isabel National Forest, just twenty-six miles west of Pueblo, Colorado, he pushed the agency to build more such "municipal playgrounds" especially for those in the working class. Carhart maintained that the USFS was better equipped than the NPS to offer a truly democratic form of outdoor recreation.[26]

Internal skepticism within the USFS about venturing into the recreation business, as well as pushback from Mather and the NPS, killed Carhart's plans. When Congress declined to grant the agency modest appropriation requests for recreation development in 1921 and again in 1922, he angrily resigned. With a parting shot, he assailed the agency's shortsightedness. Recreation was "a permanent fundamental human need" that "citizens are going to get" one way or the other, so the USFS might as well start thinking about it as a legitimate resource to conserve. It belonged in the agency's multiple use portfolio; along with timber, watersheds, and grazing lands, recreation "is one of the most worthwhile services the forest can give to people." Carhart had predicted, earlier than most, the rapidly rising demand, writing in 1920 that "more and more people will become gypsies of the auto highways, and there must be camps to accommodate visitors. These camps are needed many places now and the coming few years will witness a greatly increased need."[27] By the end of the decade, multiple agencies were scrambling to address this exact predicament.

Meinecke's recommendations prioritized protecting trees from mindless campers. He felt a keen responsibility to defend a forest that represented "one of the greatest wonders in existence" against overenthusiastic hordes. In the face of the threat visitors posed, the state had a responsibility to "see to it that the life of the individuals"—by which he meant individual trees—"is not shortened through yielding to the demands of a well-meaning but not equally well-informed part of the public." He prescribed a swift and decisive remedy. In severely threatened areas and valuable groves, structures and campers should be immediately removed. "The fine old Redwoods are the last place where the pleasures and functions of daily life, playing, cooking and sleeping should be concentrated." Relocating existing campgrounds and gradual construction of new ones in peripheral areas should proceed with careful regulations. All of this should be done in conjunction with an active, scientifically controlled program of reforestation—which, he cautioned, would not succeed without the other elements of restraint.[28]

Meinecke insisted on the urgency of this plan, anticipating that visitor needs would only expand and thus compound the damage. "The public is going to demand more buildings, more playgrounds, more conveniences," until the "wilderness, the natural setting for the Redwoods . . . must recede until nothing is left but a man-made recreation area in all its dreariness." In their endless needs, visitors represented the primary menace: "Of all enemies of the parks none is more to be feared and less amenable to control than man for whom the Parks were created."[29] While he wistfully posited that "the ideal redwood forest is without doubt one on which man has left no mark," he admitted this was no longer possible. A founding member of the Wilderness Society, Meinecke viewed the automobile as "an incongruous invasion of the wild," yet he nonetheless accepted it as "an indispensable necessity" which called for pragmatic regulation.[30]

In response to his recommendations, Sequoia superintendents did close down some camping areas and limit cars in the groves. But without a clear blueprint that balanced trees and campers in space, park designers and visitors remained unsure what to do next.[31] Suspecting that speaking only "in the interest of trees" might not be enough to convince NPS planners, Meinecke decided to try his hand at a new layout. By 1932, he had worked out a novel campground design. First prepared for a conference of Park Superintendents and issued soon thereafter as a USFS pamphlet, Meinecke's *Camp Ground Policy* laid out his concerns and solutions in practical steps. He followed this up in 1934 with *Camp Planning and Camp Reconstruction*, which explained the philosophical approach that underlay his design. Where his earlier reports generated interest but only modest action, these manifestos became something of a bureaucratic sensation. Two factors prompted this changed response: his directives offered both an easily adaptable blueprint and a rationale grounded in social as much as ecological purposes. Harmonizing the social with the ecological, Meinecke's plan aligned with New Deal administration priorities and spoke to park planners in ways in which strictly conservationist (or consumerist) approaches had not.

In *Camp Ground Policy*, tourists were no longer the enemy. Meinecke still geared many recommendations toward mitigating their destructive potential, yet his argument now identified park policies as "the chief element in the deterioration." When parks left the selection and use of individual sites to "the whim of the visitor" as they generally did, the result would be a "slow but steady destruction" until a whole area would be "rendered undesirable for the more appreciative class of tourists" due its loss of vegetation and disordered and "dirty appearance." For example, in one Sierra camping ground, campers constantly chose new spots to build the "evening fire . . . because it is unpleasant to cook while standing in the scattered ashes of an old one." As a result, he found a single quarter-acre to contain "no less than 43 ash heaps, 4-5' in diameter."[32] He bemoaned the effect, but inquired what this might say about campers' legitimate needs.

To begin with, Meinecke admitted frankly that visitors approached a campground in exactly the ways they had been encouraged to do: "The public has been invited to make itself at home in parks and forests." Making one's self at home in the woods was among the foremost prospects animating recreational camping for decades. Campers assumed that they could, and should, fashion their site into a temporary home, whether out of the woods themselves or from ready-made amenities in their trunk. Meinecke even defended these preferences as central to the home-making instinct. "Level ground, shade, pleasing vegetation, the proximity of fresh water, accessibility, in short all the factors that make a given locality suitable for camping are the same factors that have attracted men for the purpose of settling and making a home." Therefore, once "given the privilege to camp," a tourist "undoubtedly has the right to expect that the site he is to occupy will be large enough to accommodate his car and belongings and that it offers at least some privacy."[33]

Thinking of a campsite as a "temporary home" led Meinecke to explain his design principles in particular ways. Designs could still goad oblivious tourists into right practices, but he attempted to meet campers on their terms. Park planning should rest "on a clear and sympathetic understanding of the ultimate objective, namely the creation of green and shady camps where the American lover of the out-doors can feel happy and at home." Making campers feel comfortable and at home meant that planning should "not end with the setting aside of a campground" but go on to designate "individual campsites of legitimate sizes, each one offering approximately as much privacy, shade, and other advantages as the other." When each camper had an equitable allotment of space, trees, and fixtures, arranged logically, campers would more willingly stay within their sites and not be tempted to stray out of bounds, where they might do damage.[34] Arriving at a campsite prepared for them as a temporary home, they would be more inclined to preserve it.

Meinecke proposed two design strategies to encourage this outlook. The first was the road and parking system. A one-lane, one-way road that looped around to each campsite required a narrower roadbed and obviated the need for drivers to veer into the vegetation to pass other cars. His diagram for this system appears in Figure 4.3. Arriving at the site, cars should then remain "fixed at the entrance to the camp site and not be permitted to enter" the central space. He called this feature the "garage-spur." Essentially a short driveway and parking space dedicated to each site, it diverged slightly from the main road, defining the entry point and marking the endpoint with large boulders or logs. Every site, Meinecke wrote, should have its own "definite garage in

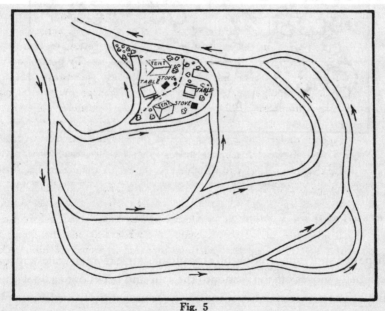

Fig. 5

Proposed layout of a camping ground under regulation, with system of one-way roads. Only one section is developed to show proposed car parking (garage spurs), tables, fireplaces and tents.

FIGURES 4.3 AND 4.4 Meinecke's diagrams of the one-way loop road system, "garage spurs," and campsites envisioned as "roofless cabins," complete with tables, fire-pit stoves, and tent areas, to minimize the damage of cars. "Proposed layout of a camping ground" and "Proposed layout of a regulated development," figures 5 and 6 in E. P. Meinecke's *A Camp Ground Policy* (US Forest Service, 1932). Forest History Society, Durham, NC.

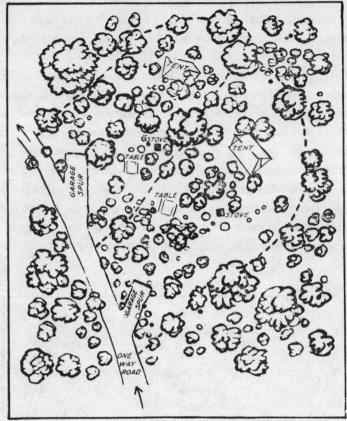

Fig. 6

Proposed plan of regulated development on a newly laid out camp ground. It shows the system of garage spurs for car parking, sites for tables, stoves and tents. The chart represents identically the same unit of land as Fig. 4 with which it should be compared. There are two camp sites instead of one, and a minimum of timber is removed.

FIGURES 4.3 AND 4.4 Continued

the shape of a short spur leading off at a suitable angle from the one-way road. The car easily moves off the road into the spur and backs out again without turning."[35] The garage-spur kept the car in close proximity, to retrieve supplies and to use camping equipment attached to the car, while minimizing collateral damage to the site.

The second strategy involved site preparation. Making sites physically ready for the camper entailed, counterintuitively, clearing the ground rather than preserving the natural state as much as possible. Meinecke reasoned, "It is better to remove, beforehand, the shrubs and trees that could reasonably be regarded as being in the way or annoying to the tourist than to leave the choice to him." When campers had to clear their own site, it unwittingly encouraged a general tendency to trample everything in their path. Alternately, by establishing obvious differences between the cleared ground for camping and the natural surroundings, campers were more likely to respect the boundaries. "The aim should rather be to set up a reaction of contentment in the camper's mind and to foster a respect for the plant growth that makes his camp site a livable and pleasant place."[36] Creating private spaces in which campers had some temporary investment created a new dynamic. Campers would not attempt to alter campsites that appeared "comfortable and convenient," easily recognizable as a ready-made unit, by both a system of numbering (i.e., Site no. A-14), and the presence of necessary elements, as shown in Figure 4.4. The idea, Meinecke would note in a later publication, was to invite visitors to stay in "a roofless cabin, in which the essential commodities are the garage, the kitchen stove, the dining table and the sleeping quarters, with enough space to move around without inconvenience."[37]

Campers' new preferences for ready-made amenities became part of the strategy. Meinecke believed that if provided convenient facilities like permanent fire pits, cooking grates, and picnic tables, campers would use them. Not only would fixed fireplaces mitigate danger to trees and the potential for a disordered mess of ashes, but they would also lend the campsite-home a familiar, and familial, focal point. Indeed, his design for a tall, stone camp stove echoed a rustic hearth.[38] As more and more campers brought portable gasoline stoves, the fire became less necessary for cooking and more an occasion for sociable gathering. The fireplace, he reasoned, "determines the physical arrangement of the outdoor home. The camp table will always find its place nearby, and the tent will not be far removed. . . . So long as . . . the ground plan of the temporary home is logical and practical the camper will have no incentive for a rearrangement to suit his needs."[39] In a notable shift from his earlier approaches, Meinecke attempted to induce campers' contentment rather than mere compliance.

Camp Planning and Camp Reconstruction, Meinecke's 1934 manual, buttressed the ecological and practical assessments with a philosophical architecture about the social good of supporting campers in these ways. Why did Americans go camping? "To spend some time in the open, away from cities and towns, in forest and woodland." To seek "release from the restrictions of town and city life." To experience "a certain amount of freedom." Moreover, he believed that "When people go camping they want nature as unspoiled as possible . . . the illusion of wilderness." Campers' desire for personal freedom combined with the wilderness setting, however, tended to overwhelm their usual respect for "legitimate regulation." Viewing campground life as a "primitive community," Meinecke insisted that campers had to temper their "ideal of absolute liberty." Individual freedoms, he argued, should be limited "by the respect for the rights of others, including those of the Government, which in turn, is obligated to protect the interests of all and insure the permanence of the camps for the use of coming generations." And yet in his version of the social contract, he hoped that restrictions might "encroach as little as possible upon that legitimate degree of personal liberty which the camper has a right to enjoy." Heavy-handed tactics to suppress camping freedoms not only ran counter to its benefits but also prompted the kind of rule-breaking that damaged the trees. The goals should be "to introduce just that degree of order which is necessary" while maintaining a sense of being in "unspoiled nature."[40]

Meinecke leaned on the good-fences-make-good-neighbors principle to help park visitors respect the needs of fellow and future campers. To imagine their sites as temporary homes, campers needed a buffer from the larger group. Meinecke proposed that "each camp should have the advantages of shade and more or less privacy against adjacent campsites. This seclusion is provided for by a neutral zone left between adjoining sites." Beyond creating privacy, leaving a few unused "open spaces covered with a tangle of vegetation . . . or picturesque outcrops of rock" were like "pictures on the wall." They simultaneously provided a "decorative element" for the outdoor home and added "to the feeling of living in the woods, away from the restrictions of civilization."[41] Feeling protected in their private spaces, campers could practice the joys of outdoor domesticity with a better understanding of their neighborly responsibilities. Opportunities for sociability also furthered this goal. Given that campers tended "to gather around the campfire when the sun goes down," Meinecke suggested each campground incorporate a central community campfire area in addition to the hearths at individual sites. This balance of private comfort and public community reminded Meinecke more and more of a hotel where "a kind of community life develops, though the guests may be changing daily."[42]

Thinking of forests as hotels, however, might lead to a surfeit of modern amenities, so Meinecke refined the concept in his 1935 treatise, "Human Aspects of Conservation." He started by chastising the Park Service, the Forest Service, and the Bureau of Reclamation for assuming that more visitation, more conservation, or more irrigation was always better. Instead, government agencies ought to think more about their responsibility to provide for human happiness. Treating "visitors to the outdoors" as "guests of the nation" would help to fulfill that charge. Meinecke believed the government should organize public nature in ways that supported this recreational ethos, allowing citizens to realize their "quest for a legitimate satisfaction of fine and clean desires." To be clear, he did not mean that campers should get everything they asked for: rather only what conduced to "the simple life in the open" and not, for example, "expensive plumbing with porcelain baths, tile floors and chrome fixtures and the like for the use of the millions who cannot afford any of these luxuries in their own homes."[43] The campground, he hinted, could still embody an idealized medium between poverty and excess.

Meinecke's theory and method convinced national park administrators at many levels, if evidenced only by the ubiquity of the loop at campgrounds today. NPS records further reveal the swiftness with which Meinecke's advice became standard policy. Not long after his initial paper circulated at the Spring 1932 Park Superintendents' conference, administrators shared mimeograph copies. Once *Camp Ground Policy* was published, Park Superintendents told the new NPS Director, Horace Albright, they found it a "valuable, . . . splendid guide." Albright ordered more than 250 copies to send to planners across the agency, urging them in an accompanying memo to consult it straightaway. "This subject is one of the most important of our national park problems. . . . [G]ive this paper your careful study and attention." Arno Cammerer, who took over for Albright in 1933, had a personal, signed copy of *Camp Ground Policy*.[44] By late 1934, NPS superintendents passed a resolution thanking the USFS for lending Meinecke, whose expertise had already proved of "immense value and benefit" and which would "undoubtedly continue to be much in demand."[45]

Meinecke's plan gained enthusiastic acceptance on the ground as well. After the NPS approved the "Meinecke system" for service-wide use and implementation in 1935, Park landscape architects readily adopted the design.[46] Soon, Parks were "Meineckizing" their campgrounds as fast as funds allowed. With construction underway, the NPS employed Meinecke on several inspection tours of campgrounds in Parks and Monuments across the West. Superintendents beseeched the central administration to put their parks on his itinerary to get customized advice. Those granted an audience found it "a real treat to accompany Dr. Meinecke in the field and discuss the various problems pertaining to vegetation, campground plans and protection" and were grateful for his suggestions.[47]

Meinecke's reports to NPS leadership pulled no punches. Some parks were doing well in their campground design projects, while others were failing, either through inaction or misdirected efforts. Visiting Glacier in 1934, for example, he judged "some work pretty good, in other places quite bad. The cooking places are hideous and quite useless. No one could cook even an egg on them. Many were placed wrong . . . far too close to living trees. . . . Of course, they will have to come out." Meinecke attributed much of the problem to "the fact that none of the men on the ground had a copy of *Camp Planning*."[48] Other parks were doing better. Although he found the landscaping at Crater Lake, "too elaborate and 'gardened,'" the work was generally "creditable" and the "cooking places are the best I have seen on this trip." NPS administrators, from the head of the forestry division to the local superintendents, took Meinecke's opinions seriously though they did not always follow his suggestions, particularly when it came to aesthetics or matters not directly related to his "own bailiwick, namely, forestry."[49] Despite residual bureaucratic rivalry between the Park Service and the Forest Service, the ongoing relationship indicated the widespread acceptance of the Meinecke system, as did the rapid construction and use of the new campgrounds, shown in Figure 4.5.

FIGURE 4.5 Whether or not Meinecke would have found this tightly packed organization of cars and campers up to his aesthetic standards, this "Meineckized" campground represented a shift from the earlier, chaotic and damaging practices he witnessed at Sequoia. "Campground Congestion Labor Day," Lodgepole, Sequoia National Park, California, photograph by Howard Stagner, 1951. National Park Service, Asset ID: 98ec5c5a-87cd-4bcf-a559-5d29b86dda31.

Meinecke's theories of the government's role in supporting the outdoor recreational ethos contributed significantly to the acceptance of his designs. He continued to develop these ideas in the late 1930s, in collaboration with forester and wilderness advocate Bob Marshall. These efforts examined such issues as the affordability of "forest recreation" and social needs for nonurban recreation. He specifically elevated camping as a "freer form of recreation in the country" than most, and one that was "peculiarly American." More broadly, in reconsidering the "host–guest relationship," he concluded that the state had an obligation to provide recreational opportunities that "give the public the opportunity to live in safety, order, and decency, under simplest conditions."[50] Despite his earlier portrait of visitors as menacing dolts, Meinecke imagined outdoor recreation as upholding the nation's social contract, a message that resonated deeply amidst the effects of the relentless Depression.

One key difference between Meinecke's first proposals, issued in the late 1920s, and his more fully formed designs of the early 1930s was the emergence of the New Deal which stimulated national recovery in part through massive public works programs. Building campgrounds was a logical field in which to pursue this strategy. Campground construction provided an opportunity for the state to extend its reach and influence in beneficial ways. Infrastructure development was a common strategy to address issues of employment and morale, and demonstrate the efficacy of government itself. The more "guests of the nation" enjoyed their fire rings and picnic tables on public lands, as did the family shown in Figure 4.6, the more they might appreciate the services government provided.

Meinecke took the notion of a temporary home and amplified it. He convincingly argued that the outdoors allowed Americans to discover and solidify their connections not just to nature and family, but also to their fellow citizens and to the country. Camping on public lands thus fostered "the pleasure of finding (establishing) one's temporary home on ground which one has a right of part ownership, even if only one hundred thirty millionth."[51] He elevated the feeling of independence through private claims to a share in the public good. Mixing leisure with public nature bequeathed a new kind of property for a social contract where the government was obligated to support outdoor recreation for all.

"If Something Breaks We Camp Right Here"

Meinecke's vision of campers as "guests of the nation" in orderly, well-regulated public camps provided a notable counterpoint to the troubles of the 1930s.

FIGURE 4.6 Nearly three decades later, this scene suggests the success of Meinecke's social proposition as well as his campground designs. "Guests of the nation," this family established a temporary home, complete with standard amenities and nature's beauty, finding their "right of part ownership" by mixing leisure with public nature. "Camping, Sierra National Forest, California," photograph by Leland Prater, 1963. US Forest Service photo courtesy of the Forest History Society, Durham, NC.

Among the most visible effects of the Great Depression involved poverty-driven transience and functional camping. Hooverville shantytown dwellers, Bonus Army marchers, and Dust Bowl refugees became prime examples of the depth of the crisis. While camping continued to be a response of last resort for economic troubles and a potent vehicle for political pressure, it also became for many observers a worrisome indicator of social tragedy and disorder. While government agencies moved quickly to solidify the physical and social infrastructure for recreational camping, federal solutions for transients and migrants tended to reinforce the instability or marginality of these functional camps. Federally-sponsored leisure camping thus emerged within a landscape marked by both the travels of functional campers and public response to them.

    Like many industries, travel and tourism took a major hit in the first years of the Depression. Hotel visitation fell way off, and nearly two-thirds of the establishments across the country entered receivership. Americans still hoping to travel looked for economical ways to do so.[52] Tent camping, auto-camps, and roadside cabins—a relative newcomer to the casual lodging world—gained new attention for their low costs. Articles on camping emphasized cost-consciousness but continued to prize respectability. A 1931 article in *Sunset* about the Grand Canyon told readers there were "accommodations . . . for rich and poor—from fifty cents a day for camping to $7 or more a day at Hotel El Tovar." In between these extremes, "there is a splendid motor camp with over fifty cabins, each equipped with beds, stove, and sink, for $1.50 a day."[53] While this may still have been out of the reach of many families, camping could permit a vacation with little expense, even without having to forego modern conveniences. As one observer noted that same year, "Tourists are a bit weary of pitching and breaking camp" but if the work of camping could be reduced by amenities provided at the site, their travels might bring feelings of being "at home and . . . at ease," as opposed to cheap hotels, which made those of modest means "feel like a bum."[54]

Bearing any resemblance to a bum was, for many, no small concern. Camping could put vacationers uncomfortably close to the increasing numbers of those who slept outside not by choice, but under duress. Early in the spring of 1933, researcher Nels Anderson conducted a one-day census of the homeless population, producing a conservative estimate that 1.5 million Americans spent the night in public shelters or slept outdoors.[55] With so many of the down-and-out sleeping outside, the divide between camping as a form of recreation and camping as a function of poverty became a contentious space. Camps of Depression-driven transients often figured in the reports of observers, whether sympathetic or not, as portents for the downfall of home, nation, and social order.[56] Concern revolved around two major streams of transients: the unemployed who congregated in Hoovervilles, old hobo jungles, and notably in the Bonus Army encampment, and rural refugees from the Dust Bowl who migrated through auto-camps, impromptu roadside squats, and shantytowns in search of agricultural labor.

Well before President Franklin D. Roosevelt's inauguration in 1933, many thousands had already taken up residence outdoors and lack of reliable housing would remain a persistent problem. As he observed in his second inaugural address, the Depression had produced "one-third of a nation ill-housed, ill-clad, ill-nourished." Turned away from overwhelmed municipal and charity organizations for temporary shelter, transients operated in a new context but bore some resemblance to earlier tramps and revived associated fears. Despite continuing suspicions about social deviance, transients could still find semblances of community, and more than a few expressed a preference for the independence of outdoor lodgings to the social regimentation of the limited number of public facilities, even though the choice was forced upon them by circumstance.[57] If Hoovervilles represented a rational response to unemployment, this fact was often lost amidst the focus on transience as a worrisome symbol of deeper national perils.

While Hoovervilles embodied the latent potential for social unrest, one highly visible event produced a palpable force. As the economic crisis deepened during President Herbert Hoover's term, veterans from the First World War began to urge the federal government to pay out their service bonuses immediately, rather than the original scheduled date in 1945. Calling themselves the "Bonus Expeditionary Force," thousands of veterans loaded up the family car or hoboed their way to Washington, DC in the spring of 1932. They had decided to make camp in the capital to pressure Congress to pass the "Bonus Bill," granting full and immediate payment. As Figure 4.7 shows,

FIGURE 4.7 The "Bonus Army" makes camp in Washington, DC to pressure the federal government. "Encampment built by veterans in the Bonus Expeditionary Force in Washington, D.C," photograph by Theodor Horydczak, 1932. Library of Congress, Prints & Photographs Division, Theodor Horydczak Collection, LC-DIG-ppmsca-05577.

they pitched tents and assembled makeshift dwellings along Pennsylvania Avenue in view of the Capitol, in Anacostia Flats near the Potomac River, and in several other locations around the city.[58] The nation's many unemployed had so far remained relatively quiescent and few had organized politically to protest their situation. In fact, many of these men had likely already joined other transient streams before turning east to encamp with the Bonus Army. Nels Anderson had noted that in this earlier mode of " 'bumming' their way . . . singly or in small groups[,] their moving caused no alarm." When they changed course to camp en masse, for a common cause, they prompted fears of rising social disorder.[59]

The Bonus Army extended the logic of earlier forms of camping as a political vehicle. Occupying the Capitol grounds and other public spaces in Washington, marchers echoed Coxey's Army four decades earlier. They used the symbolic location and the visual effect of camp to increase the pressure their movement could exert on Hoover, Congressional representatives, and the nation at large. By bringing army-style order to camp life and emphasizing their status as veterans, the group tried to summon the patriotic respect offered Grand Army of the Republic (GAR) reunions. Emulating this veteran tradition helped to counter negative portrayals of the group as an assemblage of unemployed malcontents, radical agitators, and degenerate tramps. As Figure 4.8 depicts, veterans posed for photographs showing themselves maintaining neat, ordered families within canvas houses and peddled the prints in the street to generate income and allies. In advance of the House vote on the Bonus Bill, more than five thousand veterans, in true GAR fashion, paraded from the White House to the Capitol. These tactics worked to some extent, and the House passed the bill, but they did not entirely alleviate public suspicions. To many observers the camps looked less like an army reunion and more like "an immense hobo jungle." Figures such as retired Marine Corps General Smedley Butler condemned those who now called the veterans "tramps" and noted the irony that "they didn't call you that in '17 and '18." Butler praised the marchers as "fine soldiers" to whom the nation owed its thanks, and the bonus encampment "the greatest demonstration of Americanism ever seen."[60]

On June 17, ten days after the march and three weeks after the encampment had begun, the Bonus Bill was resoundingly defeated in the Senate. The veterans dug in for the long haul, with more arriving to join the demonstration, but as the weeks went by, conditions deteriorated. The Hoover administration's unsuccessful attempts to induce marchers to leave voluntarily and rumors of radicals circulating in the camps set the stage for a more

FIGURE 4.8 Veterans in the Bonus Army represented themselves as upstanding citizens and echoed the sense of order and patriotism of Grand Army of the Republic
encampments. "Frank Tracy of Pittsburgh, Pa., and his six children, photographed in
front of their tent shelter in one of the bonus expeditionary force's encampments around
Washington, D.C., June 19, 1932." AP Photo.

concerted eviction. By the end of July Hoover had grown impatient, and ordered the US Army to clear out the camps. Troops under the command of
Douglas MacArthur entered the camps with bayonets drawn, launched tear
gas canisters, and then "applied the torch to the shacks in which the veterans
lived." Veterans tried to hold their positions with improvised weapons, but as
the *New York Times* reported, "the disordered camp" quickly became "a mass
of flames."[61]

Hoover tried to defend the repressive action by falsely blaming Communists
and criminals. His rationalization backfired and the violent destruction of
the encampment became a public relations nightmare that only confirmed
Hoover's inability to manage the multiplying effects of the Depression and
further imperiled his reelection chances. While the Bonus Army did not
achieve its immediate objective, the episode demonstrated the effectiveness
of camping as a vehicle for political protest. The incoming Roosevelt administration learned from the events and tended to take a more tolerant view of
protests both by veterans and in the public space of the capital. In mounting

its encamped protest, the Bonus Army combined elements of GAR methods and Coxey's march into a long-remembered model for citizens to petition the government.[62]

Among the relief efforts included in Roosevelt's initial New Deal legislation was the Federal Transient Program (FTP), which aimed in part to forestall potential unrest in such self-formed transient communities. Serving perhaps 300,000 individuals at its height, the FTP established government camps for itinerants who paid for their lodging through work for local public agencies. Inhabitants had mixed reactions to the camps, which often required adherence to strict disciplinary regimes and were located far from cities and potential jobs. Shut down by 1935, the FTP never served more than a small fraction of the need and failed to gain robust support among local residents. In Los Angeles, where the idea had initially been welcomed, protests arose over an FTP camp in Elysian Park. Transients and their "problems of public health" belonged in "more outlying areas near railroad tracks" or in "the old auto camp," which despite its disrepair was "plenty good enough for transients." Suspicions lingered that those who entered the FTP were not sincere jobseekers but, as one camp manager alleged, "a motley group of fugitives, misfits, handicapped, bums, hoboes, and tramps." Federal officials came to believe that FTP camps had unintentionally created more comfortable versions of the hobo jungle that discouraged residents from returning to "normal" social life. The FTP heightened awareness of the transience issue, but failed to establish effective solutions.[63]

The transient problem only deepened in the latter half of the decade. Without federal relief targeted to transience, many localities simply tried to keep unemployed itinerants moving down the road.[64] The issue became even more complex when refugees from the drought-stricken farms of the Dust Bowl took to the highways en masse in the late 1930s. Unable to produce crops or incomes from their lands, perhaps two million tenant farmers and sharecroppers from Oklahoma, Kansas, Texas, Colorado, and other plains states sold their tools and possessions, loaded up their cars with what was left, and headed out in hopes of work and a fresh start. California alone drew nearly half a million migrants. Those who made it that far found not the promised land but low-wage labor in the state's factory farms, continuing migration between harvests, and a prolonged and challenging camp life.

The Okie exodus prompted troubling questions for many Americans. Were these desperate migrants tragic but inevitable casualties of the crisis? Or the descendants of the hardy pioneers, thwarted by maltreatment? Did their motley camps suggest loss or perseverance? John Steinbeck's *The Grapes of*

Wrath (1939) posed these questions through the fictional travels and travails of Tom Joad and his family. Having spent time in 1936 as a newspaper correspondent reporting on migrant camps in California, Steinbeck drew upon first-hand observations of living conditions and daily dilemmas, as well the journeys refugees had survived. In aging trucks, crammed with possessions and people, they had set out on the highways. Route 66, funded by national road improvement efforts amid the enthusiasm for the modern freedoms of auto travel, now became "the path of a people in flight." Drivers worried about "leaky radiators," "loose connecting rods," and long stretches of empty roads. "It is a terror between towns. If something breaks—well, if something breaks we camp right here while Jim walks to town and gets a part and walks back and—how much food we got?"[65] Where auto-camping guidebooks celebrated the spontaneities of the road, for migrants, uncertainty was something to fear.

While the last thing migrants wanted was to be camping in this vulnerable way, the impromptu roadside camp was a typical strategy for finding a place to rest for the night. Travelers tended to gather around spots that offered some protection from the road, level ground, shade, wood, and water. As Steinbeck described the process, "one family camped near a spring, and another camped for the spring and for company, and a third because two families had pioneered the place and found it good"—after which followed neighborly conversation and the pleasant "sounds of camp-making, wood chopping, and the rattle of pans."[66] Other observers remarked upon this unexpected ethos of community under the difficult circumstances. Prominent journalist and activist Carleton Beals marveled at it in a national magazine in 1938: "Though many a tragedy is locked in the mystery of this strange twentieth-century migration of folk, it is surprising on the whole to observe their unfailing optimism, religious faith, and spirit of mutual aid."[67] Steinbeck viewed these roadside clusters as complete, if temporary, societies: "Every night relationships that make a world, established," made anew each time migrants pulled off "the highways, made them with their tents and their hearts and their brains." It remained a perpetually unstable community, however, as every morning these worlds had to be "torn down like a circus" and moved along the road.[68]

Alternately, migrants could overnight at private or municipal auto-camps, the same ones that had been avidly catering to tourists since the early 1920s. Nearly all, by this time, charged fees. By 1936, more than 11,000 businesses operated some form of tourist camp across the country, ranging from cabin courts and full-service campgrounds to filling stations with a few basic campsites attached. More than 40 percent were located in eleven states within the Dust Bowl region or along typical migrant routes.[69] The Joads once reluctantly chose to pay for an auto-camp: "Got shade an' got water in pipes. Costs half a dollar a day to stay there. But ever'body's so goddamn tired an' wore out an' mis'able." Though the fee was steep, it offered a brief hiatus from the exposure of the road. Yet the idea of having to pay rankled: "Pa's all mad about it costs fifty cents jus' to camp under a tree."[70] Given the historical assumptions of tacit permission to pitch a tent for the night, on public or private land, resistance to the principle of charging for the privilege of sleeping outside was understandable.

While the roadside might still appear free for the taking, it had become a more constrained landscape. Local law enforcement often harassed migrants and forced them to move on. When Tom declared a preference to "sleep in the ditch right beside the road, an' it won't cost nothing,' " the auto-camp proprietor threatened as much: "Deputy sheriff comes on by in the night. Might make it tough for ya. Got a law against sleepin' out in this State. Got a law about vagrants." Tom's response signaled the precarious divide between recreational campers and functional transients: "If I pay you a half a dollar I ain't a vagrant, huh?"[71] As this debate highlighted, migrants had to tread an increasingly narrow line between these two mutually reinforcing landscapes, one that catered to the paying tourist and the other that policed the impoverished vagrant. Pitting two uses of public nature against each other, recreational assumptions prevailed and functional campers had to play by their rules.

Arrival in the Golden State did little to alleviate camp conditions or the risks of vagrancy. Beals explained the predicament that awaited migrants in California's fields: like mobile workers of an earlier era they were recruited by growers when the crop needed tending, but after the harvest, "they are railroaded from county to county, jailed for vagrancy." This situation suggested a new form of permanent transience. "The only life they can lead is a gypsy life. . . . Once they were farmers; now they are nomads."[72] The agrarian ideal had become an agrarian disaster, and farmers refugees from the failure of its social contact. Though the Joads had been warned about the surplus labor, intermittent jobs, low wages, and poor housing prospects, when they finally made it to California they were distressed to find fellow refugees living in dirty, disordered camps, with tents that were ragged and torn and shanties made from materials scavenged from the local dump.[73] The prospect of escape to better quarters seemed bleak, particularly as growers conspired with local law enforcement to drive down wages and forestall a more settled labor force. Organized attempts to resist this system, when combined with their vagrant camp life, exposed migrants to charges of being a "red" and a "troublemaker."

The fear of political awakening among unemployed transients ran as high in California as had the Bonus Army's incipient threat. When migrants tried to settle in one place and hold their ground, even while still camped in tents and shanties, municipalities often responded by trying to keep them moving, vulnerable as vagrants, with few resources and little recourse.[74]

Migrants who refused to move on risked having their camp demolished by another longstanding tactic—being declared a public health menace. Health conditions in migrant camps were far from ideal. The same auto-camps described for tourists as modern and homelike acquired an unsavory cast when populated by migrants. According to a 1937 report of Labor Secretary Frances Perkins, the "living conditions for most migrants are deplorable. . . . At night they sleep by the road-side, in squatter camps, or crowd into one- or two–room cabins in low-priced tourist camps," which were often "inadequately equipped, and unsanitary." Under these circumstances "exposure in camp life" took on a different cast than it might for recreational campers. Beals's survey agreed with Perkins's conclusion. All throughout the West he came upon "transient labor camps a step above the Hooverville jungles but almost equally deplorable with regard to health and broken lives."[75] Migrants knew that improvised long-term outdoor living held many hazards for health and well-being, but had few alternatives. Their camps were functional responses to necessity, but even more so than the tramps and bindlestiffs of the previous generation, they hoped it would prove temporary.

The federal government had been slow to accept the idea of building decent migrant camp facilities but by 1938, as public health concerns escalated, it began to act. Steinbeck referenced one of the earliest ones in Grapes of Wrath—Weedpatch Camp, built in 1936 in Arvin, California. Ma Joad learned from a fellow migrant that not only was the government camp "a nice place to live" with "toilets an' baths, . . . good drinkin' water . . . a place for kids to play," and protection from the sheriff, but also that it operated on a cooperative system, where residents exchanged a few hours of labor for the weekly fee. As a fellow migrant reckoned, at Weedpatch they "Treat ya like a man 'stead of a dog. . . . This here's United States, not California." Highlighting the positive aspects of the camp, in the novel and in earlier newspaper reports, Steinbeck aimed to generate public support for accelerating the building process.[76]

The overwhelming focus of the several New Deal agencies working to address rural displacement, however, was to keep farmers on their land and rehabilitate acreage rather than assist those that abandoned it. The Farm Security Administration (FSA), the leading federal agency in a position to address the migrant emergency, struggled to recognize its implications. Descriptions of camp-building plans did not appear in its annual report for 1937; in 1938 the report only listed the migrant issue in a section titled "Unsolved Problems." As tenant farmers became "migrant farm laborers," the report lamented that "the problems of this group, precipitated down the agricultural ladder by circumstance, have not as yet found a satisfactory answer." In fact, the FSA had only recently recognized migratory labor as a problem, as California's harvest labor force was previously made up largely of immigrants from Mexico and the Philippines whose working and living conditions drew little attention until displaced white farmers arrived to take their places in the fields. Even as the FSA recognized a need for more relief camps, it refused to see camp construction as a primary strategy.[77] In some sense, it was still trying to preserve a remnant of the promise of stability—if not property—for some Americans who mixed their labor with the land.

The FSA did build additional camps along the lines of Weedpatch: simple plywood platforms on which migrants could set up their own tents and cooking facilities; sanitary units, with showers, flush toilets, and laundry areas; community buildings and a medical clinic. The 1939 report led off a section on "Camps for migrant farm workers" by asserting that "the need for such camps has increased rapidly and the camp program was expanded to meet it."[78] In 1940, the FSA reported that 56 camps had either been completed or were under construction in seven states. When built, they could accommodate a total of 13,205 families at any one time in 11,476 shelters and tent platforms. Despite the stepped up effort, it admitted this was "nothing like a full answer to the difficulties of some 350,000 families which follow the harvests." Though the camps were "highly effective in relieving misery and in protecting the migrants and the communities through which they pass," the FSA was providing camp facilities for less than 4 percent and continued to insist that they should not be a "real solution." This was evident in the budget allocation for migrant camps. Prioritizing the attempt to check new migration at the source over camp building, the 1940 report noted that "for every dollar spent to aid migrants in California during the past 5 years, $20 was spent in the chief States of origin."[79] The FSA could have spent and built more, but chose to allow government camps to be the exception rather than the rule.

In this way, the federal approach to migrants and transients revealed a basic apprehension about making them too reputable, comfortable, or normal. Officials in the Federal Transient Program had worried that the relief camp might become "a glorified jungle where a great many men accustomed to travel at no expense to themselves were invited to settle down for a spell at the expense of the Government." Rather than encouraging those who found themselves homeless to get back on their feet and into mainstream communities, FTP leaders feared that the camps instead fostered positive associations with hobo life. One camp manager attributed the program's shut down to the fact that, rather than resolving the problem, it "tended to make a cult out of transiency." In his postmortem, Harry Hopkins blamed FTP camp occupants for being lazy, but also recognized the appeal for those struggling to hold onto settled lives. Hopkins, a leading official in Roosevelt's administration, admitted that transients appeared "a cross between a carefree gypsy and a fugitive from justice," and thus might be modeling a feasible and attractive method of dealing with economic woes.[80] While agricultural migrants desperately hoped their camp life would be temporary, the resistance to addressing their needs suggested desires to hold onto a remnant of the agrarian model of public nature. Government agencies, ironically, displayed strong preferences for building recreational campgrounds to host vacationers over functional solutions for transients and migrants. As options for outdoor leisure multiplied, they dwindled for those sleeping outside by force of circumstance.

"A Sharp Line May Be Drawn"

By and large, government agencies attempted to establish a clear separation between the types of camping it hoped to encourage and discourage amid a broad spectrum of camping practices during the 1930s. This was no simple task. As Hopkins had hinted, an escape fantasy lurked within the combination of the seemingly endless Great Depression and the romantic strain of hobo mythology. Novelist John Dos Passos's trilogy *U.S.A.*, published between 1930 and 1936, featured the hobo as a heroic radical because of his very marginalization and freedom from standard civic expectations—which were increasingly difficult to uphold in the ongoing economic crisis. The 1936 film *Modern Times* contained a strident, though hilarious, critique of industrial society and the physical and mental toll it took on workers; the movie's happy ending had Charlie Chaplin's lovable tramp simply walk away from the factory and head out on the road to greener pastures hand-in-hand with Paulette Goddard.[81] More wistful longings than reflections of social reality, government agencies still worked to combat the image of the happy hobo.

Documentary photographers for the Farm Security Association often endeavored to represent Dust Bowl refugees in the tradition of the independent yeoman farmer rather than as tramps or hoboes. There is perhaps no more iconic image of the Depression than Dorothea Lange's 1936 photograph of migrant Florence Thompson known as "Migrant Mother." Shown in Figure 4.9, Lange's photograph became a high symbol of both tragedy and perseverance. The close-up did not seem to be about camping at all, but it confirmed that migrants were not leading a carefree life. Migrant Mother challenged viewers to confront her fate, whether it was fit for Americans and what were they going to do about it.[82]

Lange's famous image, however, did not capture the particulars of Thompson's circumstance as well as the series of photographs she took before capturing the definitive one. The makeshift tent in a muddy squatter's camp, the empty pie tin, the tattered shirt sleeve—these details in Figures 4.10 and 4.11 testify to the material struggles that accompanied the functional camping that migrants had little choice but to pursue under great strain. The tenuous

FIGURE 4.9 The iconic photograph known as "Migrant Mother," representing the displaced farm family as symbol of American perseverance and tragedy. "Destitute pea pickers in California. Mother of seven children. Age thirty-two. Nipomo, California," photograph by Dorothea Lange for the Farm Security Administration, 1936. Library of Congress, Prints & Photographs Division, FSA/OWI Collection, LC-DIG-fsa-8b29516.

FIGURES 4.10 AND 4.11 Lange's preliminary images of Florence Thompson and her family in a pea-pickers camp in Nipomo, California, showed the particulars of their camp but remained unpublished at the time. "Migrant agricultural worker's family . . . Nipomo, California," photographs by Dorothea Lange for the Farm Security Administration, 1936. Library of Congress, Prints & Photographs Division, FSA/OWI Collection, LC-USF34-9095 and and LC-USZ62-58355.

nature of the camp life revealed in these photographs hinted at the longer history of suspicion about tramps and functional campers. They also spoke to growing fears that the American experiment was going to fail. If the agrarian social contract had reached its end, what would replace it? Lange's preparatory images remained unpublished until decades later, perhaps because they suggested neither the agrarian resilience of Migrant Mother nor the kind of camping that supported a modern social contract rooted in consumerism and recreation.

Migrants and vacationers could sometimes find themselves in close quarters. Sorting out these encounters became increasingly important to recreational campers, who had long cultivated a self-presentation differentiating themselves from tramps. One California woman described the constraints which shaped her 1934 camping trip: "The medical profession might disapprove of a camping trip for a baby. But upon finding themselves with a vacation sans salary, a six months' old son, a dilapidated coupe, and almost exactly no money, what is a young couple to do?" Little in this description might have separated this family from functional campers—low on cash and possessing a run-down car—except, of course for the concept of "vacation" and writing about it for *Sunset Magazine*.[83] This story celebrated thrifty camping, while elsewhere migrants or Bonus marchers appeared as social tragedies or threats even if they managed a clean and orderly camp life. Key points of contact, and possible confusion, between recreational and nonrecreational campers emerged most pointedly at auto-camps and about trailers.

Echoes of the early praise for auto-camps as cross-class utopias could still be heard in the early 1930s. A *New York Times* article proclaimed that Americans of "all kinds and conditions," driving "all sorts of cars," took refuge under the "democratic shelter" of the "tourist camp." While one "portly tenant . . . has the look of a banker," the "undernourished chap next door appears to be a drought-stricken farmhand." Despite this divide, the author claimed they shared a natural American "friendship" and "social life." Examples of such commingling could certainly be found, but democratic good feelings were not universal.[84] As one woman recalled about a camping trip to Florida in 1935, traveling amid migrant laborers became a moment not to make common cause but to caution against their fate. Migrants' plight served as "a warning to our sons to have ambition and industry so that they would not end in similar circumstances."[85] Auto-camps could both exemplify a vision of democracy and a deep gulf between experiences.

For leisure campers with an increasing focus on "how to motor camp without hoboism," owning equipment designed only for use in occasional recreation made a notable impression. A *Sunset Magazine* writer advised readers that "camping with the family is less work than living at home, less expensive even," but implored them to "make your camp comfortable and your meals lavish."[86] The burgeoning camping equipment industry continued to cater to this desire by expanding the array of products. A 1937 *New York Times* article remarked that "during the past year many novel and useful additions have been made to the long lists of gadgets and devices already available for those lovers of the outdoors." A *Popular Mechanics* contributor warned readers of the dangers of buying too little: "Don't make the mistake of cutting down on too much equipment."[87]

Camping trailers contained similar contradictions. Trailers increased in popularity in the early 1930s, with cost-conscious models promoted as paying for themselves in "savings made from rent." This logic also appealed to migrants and transients as viable option for inexpensive mobile living. Beals noted how both Dust Bowl refugees and Hooverville residents used "elaborate homemade trailers" for transport and innovative housing.[88] *Fortune* magazine noted in 1937 that trailers, originally intended as "a handier and cheaper means of making a vacation camping trip," were becoming employed as mobile, "prefabricated shelter" and an inexpensive alternative to the costs of settled housing. With "no rent, no taxes—the life of Riley"—some alarmists worried it might encourage people to abandon responsibilities at home. How would the temptation of trailer life affect home life? How would the nation account for these wanderers, "living briefly here and there as squatters, rootless as air plants, paying no taxes, creating a new kind of motor slums?" Manufacturers insisted that trailers were designed "to be a vehicle, not a permanent address.... [W]hat we're mostly trying to sell is a vacation." That they saw the need to rebut the charge that their product was breeding national rootlessness testified to the concern.[89]

Auto-camps and trailer parks also had to combat negative images of harboring not just itinerants and migrants, but radicals and criminals. Hotel operators tended to view low-cost tourist camps as unfair competition for lodging and attempted to paint them as disreputable. A New Jersey hotelier impugned such establishments as an "assortment of dime dance halls, beer joints, disorderly houses and 'criminal hangouts.'"[90] As part of the fast growing "roadside market" that catered to tourist desires for convenient stopping places rather than downtown establishments, camps were often located on the outskirts of town, at somewhat of a remove from local law enforcement. Critics feared this gave freer rein to scam artists who aimed to fleece travelers or safe haven to those with illicit intentions. Though auto-camps were generally subject to similar sanitary regulations, inspections, and requirements for public records as hotels, sensationalized depictions circulated widely in popular media. As one hotel owner claimed, "A man who will hesitate to take a girl to a hotel knows that he can go to an auto camp."[91]

Among the most sensationalized accounts of tourist camps appeared in a national magazine in 1940 coauthored by J. Edgar Hoover, director of the FBI, with the melodramatic title, "Camps of Crime." "Behind many alluring roadside signs are dens of vice and corruption. . . . Hundreds of unsupervised tourist camps" were providing "hideaways for public enemies" and "bases of operations from which gangs of desperados prey upon the surrounding territory." The lengthy article related salacious details about bank robbers, drug traffickers, gamblers, prostitutes, kidnappers, and murderers who patronized tourist camps. Hoover believed that there was a "place for the well-conducted, clean, wholesome type of camp which can offer a quiet night's rest to decent people" at reasonable rates. But public safety demanded that law enforcement and legitimate camp operators work together to "outlaw the renegade tourist camp." One way "honest" camp owners could draw a clearer line between the two was by changing their brand from camps to "courts, as the better type of proprietors often prefer that their places be called." The camps Hoover wrote about were largely what had come to be known as "cabin camps," with few or no sites for tent camping at all. As the 1935 Census of Business and other observers attested, rustic cabins and "small wayside bungalows" were quickly replacing campsites in these establishments.[92] In Hoover's hands, "camp" was a label that bestowed a nefarious illegitimacy where a "court" implied something more settled and respectable.

As the word "camp" reanimated older fears and came under new suspicion, tourist and trailer camp operators catering to recreational travelers worked to establish themselves firmly on the safe side of the divide. *Fortune* made a convincing case for trailer camps as orderly and appealing establishments. One illustration of a camp in Clearwater Beach, Florida showed trailers and palm trees on the sand, as tourists played volleyball on a sunny day. The caption noted that it was "filled mostly with midwestern families with their grandmothers, children, and dogs, none obviously rich." The article admitted that trailers did not transform people into saints: "Occasionally some get drunk or noisy and couples break up." But it denied the allegation that they were "dens of vice" that harbored fugitives. As the manager of a luxurious Miami tourist camp quipped, "If people wanted to raise hell, they wouldn't go to a trailer camp."[93]

Public parks and forests also worked to emphasize the right over the wrong kind of camping. Emilio Meinecke again played an influential role. In his tours of national park and forest campgrounds, he took note of areas that were failing to live up to the new standards of an ordered and pleasant community. At one Forest Service site, he lamented the lack of a defined road system where "cars and trailers mill around wherever they like and the whole camp ground has that 'used,' second-hand look that everywhere goes with a lack of regulation." His language in this internal report alluded to the other side of campers as "guests of the nation":

> Rapidly it is taking on the characteristics of the slums-like camps in the Yosemite, a thing that we hoped could be kept out of the National Forests. Some people, evidently camped for a long time, put up canvas and blanket fences, just as in the Yosemite. This formation of slums at their worst is bound to increase, and since they are right on the highway, in plain sight, the campground is spoiled for all the many decent people who are not slum-minded.[94]

Drawing a line between "decent people" and the "slum-minded" became central to the federal approach to public campground policy.

What Meinecke—and indeed many of these responses—failed to account for was the frequent overlap between the categories of migrant, transient, and vacationer. Beyond sharing spaces, individuals and families could cycle among or blur the boundaries between these labels, occupying any number of intermediate spaces on a recreational-to-transient continuum. Echoes of the Reeves family abounded, where a man might seek migratory labor to support a settled family, or seasonal transience could alternate with both temporary housing and occasional camp outs for respite. One man in Washington state went in on a venture with his neighbor to cut timber for the summer, in order to sell it at the end of the season. To support this labor, they established a camp in the woods and brought their families along. With a summer off from teaching, one of the mothers did the domestic labor and minded the children, one of whom recalled it as a magical vacation—"swimming and catching snakes and sleeping out." When a forest fire swept through the area near the end of summer, the two men volunteered to help battle the blaze, but the family had to flee the camp and their entire cut was lost.[95] Family stories like this one, the intermingling of labor and leisure, delight and misfortune, resonate across the Depression, challenging those who tried to police the boundaries between them.

NPS and USFS campgrounds began to define campers by regulating behavior. They prohibited the "erection or use of unsightly and inappropriate structures or appurtenances," such as "shacktowns" or the "blanket fence" campers used to create a circle of privacy and sense of semipermanence around their site. The agencies also began to impose limits on length of stay, typically fourteen consecutive days, to free up sites for more visitors and discourage long-term camping. Campgrounds established a maximum number of occupants and cars per site to prevent the formation of more sprawling group settlements. Such regulations were clearly designed to prevent the kinds of camps that Depression refugees had made and to create a clear divide between leisure campers and homeless itinerants. Codes of behavior dictated that occupants keep their campsites in "neat, clean and sanitary condition," respect posted quiet hours, and not use nearby streams to "wash clothing or cooking utensils." Violating any of the regulations could result in removal.[96] These regulations enforced specific social expectations and class-based assumptions about the purpose of camping.

Meinecke also worked to address this problem as it involved trailers, a contraption he found nearly intolerable for several reasons. He certainly shared the suspicion that trailers encouraged rootlessness. "In its least objectionable aspects trailer life is the expression of a revolt against the organized camp. In its extreme forms this nomadic life tends to run into a gipsy type of existence." Reminiscent of the preference of tramp style over tramp life, he worried that when the trailer becomes "the only home the family possesses," it leads to "shifting and unstable settlements of suburban slum character." He also bemoaned the "the introduction of the roving home into the recreational domain [which] interferes seriously with the enjoyment of those who seek pleasure and rest away from city influences."[97] Here, he wanted to protect the recreational ethos from encroachment by functional forms of camping.

In a 1935 memo, "The Trailer Menace," Meinecke outlined additional objections. Trailers both multiplied the environmental damage caused by regular car campers and offended his vision of authentic outdoor recreation. Visitors who went "to the wilds as campers, satisfied with the simplest life and glad for the opportunity to live it," were those who "conform[ed] most closely to the ideal for which both Parks and Forests are created." Meinecke would have preferred to ban trailers altogether, but developed a compromise. "On this basis a sharp line may be drawn between genuine campers and those who prefer city comforts. For the latter there is ample provision made in hotels, resorts and privately owned auto camps." In public areas designed for the former, "an automobile with a trailer which contains merely accessories for camping would be admitted. The trailer in this case will never be unduly large. Trailers and units actually used for living and not for camping would be excluded."[98] The characteristics he mentioned were hardly crystal clear. He wanted to divine intention and character, use a subjective measurement of size, and determine the difference between using equipment for living versus camping. If the Great Depression had shown anything about camping, it was that a wide and messy spectrum of sleeping outside made such determinations difficult.

That the government aggressively built campgrounds according to Meinecke's design and philosophy at the same time it was breaking up Hoovervilles, evicting the Bonus Army encampment, resisting the construction of migrant camps, and marginalizing tourist "camps of crime" seemed ironic. But by doing so, it was investing in one vision for the use of public nature over others. While auto-camps, trailer parks, and cabin courts near the highway had become generally private and fee-based, the government was expanding the number of free campsites available in the Parks and Forests. For those who could least afford to pay, the fee-based camps were the most accessible, as free federal campgrounds tended to be in more remote locations and sought tighter control over campers' recreational intentions. Free options for homeless folk and drought refugees, near roadside culverts, behind highway billboards, and in marginal public spaces on the edges of towns or the banks of rivers, were risky. The emergence of a publicly sponsored, carefully regulated landscape for recreational camping served to highlight and isolate those who fell on the other side of that line.

"No Government Can Keep Any of Its Citizens Out of Forests and Parks"

In the late 1930s, Meinecke reflected on the remarkable growth of recreational camping. "What a short quarter of a century ago was barely growing into a desirable need of the American people has now become a necessity for millions." What had once been a private leisure fad had become a government-sponsored public good. Federal agencies during the New Deal combined to produce a recreational camping landscape meant to serve myriad social goals. Individuals came to insist upon campground access as a right of citizenship and hold the government accountable when it fell short. Providing for the general welfare came to include ensuring that citizens had reasonable access to well-equipped campsites. Meinecke argued that "No government can keep any of its citizens out of forests and parks. All people have the same rights of occupancy, contingent only upon behavior during occupancy."[99] In seeing recreational access to public nature as both individual right and social pre-scriptive, Meinecke shared intellectual approaches with other New Dealers. Having relegated to the social margins forms of camping that represented a disordered retreat of last resort, they promoted the idea that recreational camping, carefully designed and regulated, could be restorative for citizens and the civic body alike.

The rapid implementation of the Meinecke plan would not have been pos-sible without a large infusion of funds into the National Park system through various New Deal agencies, starting in 1933. NPS director Horace Albright was quick to act on this potential, which more than doubled the agency's budget by the end of the 1930s. He welcomed programs like the Civilian Conservation Corps (CCC), approved in Roosevelt's first hundred days, which put hundreds of thousands of men to work in the parks and forests on recreational and conservation projects. Building and rehabilitating camping facilities was a priority, and CCC crews constructed or renovated some 90,000 acres of campgrounds; about half were new and almost all were on some version of the Meinecke system. The CCC enrolled nearly three million men before it was shut down in 1942 because of the heightened need for war-time labor and left a vast new infrastructure in place.[100]

The New Deal ideology that animated this work further cemented the idea of camping as a public good. Federal agencies designed programs to remedy several crises at once, and so, in addition to building recreational facilities, the CCC employed young out-of-work men, injected cash into the economy (by requiring workers to remit most of their pay home to families), and conserved the nation's threatened soil and landscapes. Moreover, the outdoor experience was meant to restore the health and vigor of the men themselves. Initially, some local communities were apprehensive about the federal government bringing these men to their areas. They worried that the camps would be more like hobo jungles filled with "street-slum foreigners" and "bums." Operating more like army camps, however, CCC camp life called for the "healthful" and "vigorous outdoor work" that made "muscles strong and hard." With a slogan of "We Can Take It," physical labor and outdoor life was supposed to restore manly strength to demoralized youths: "Our purpose is not only to rebuild forests and lands, but to build men." Veterans of the World War, including those who had participated in the bonus marches, became prime candidates. While CCC enrollment was otherwise restricted to those between seventeen and twenty-eight, up to 25,000 veterans were allowed to enroll in the Corps regardless of age.[101] Again, one kind of camping provided a cure for another, as the CCC blended the recreational ethos with the older concept of mixing labor with the land to produce virtuous citizenship.

The Corps' own camps, and the ones it built following Meinecke's design and philosophy, contributed to a sense of national regeneration. Public outdoor recreational facilities came to be seen as important resources for securing a social contract in which Americans could expect economic security and consumer happiness. CCC work transformed the Park Service itself to some extent, as the agency began to view its own mission as evolving beyond preserving spectacular landscapes for visitation to providing multiple public goods. As one NPS official who supervised CCC work reflected, "We are probably going to see much more tent camping than in past years," and he urged the agency to anticipate this need by not just clearing sites, but offering "every social service and as much of it as possible."[102]

That the NPS accepted CCC labor to carry out plans already associated with its mission is perhaps unsurprising. That Park leaders endorsed social goals that fell outside the agency's central mission, such as reducing unemployment, spurring local economic recovery, and conserving public health, made strategic sense, as it expanded NPS budgets and profile within the federal government. However, that it also signed on to a Resettlement Administration plan to develop Recreational Demonstration Areas (RDAs) on sites that bore very little resemblance to national parks suggests the depth to which NPS leaders were committed to the social goals of the New Deal and to the significance of outdoor recreation in national life. The NPS supervised the development of nearly four dozen RDAs, totaling nearly 400,000 acres, in the hopes of expanding opportunities for outdoor recreation in regions and for people far from most national parks. Beyond the "public relations value," the RDA project embodied the philosophy of New Deal social planning that the NPS came to embrace.[103] As much as the physical construction of campgrounds, it was these social policies that embedded recreational camping in the fabric of the nation and shifted the ideal of public nature toward recreational space.

The RDA plan, like the CCC, addressed several Depression problems in one program and even more clearly embodied the shift toward a new social contract. In the words of the director of the Federal Emergency Relief Administration's Land Program, which coordinated the project, RDAs could 1) provide "recreational facilities necessary to the promotion of better health and morale, and a greater appreciation of nature"; 2) induce "wiser use of land" by converting "submarginal agricultural land" to "more constructive" purposes; 3) provide for "the rehabilitation and resettlement of thousands of indigent farm families"; and 4) allow for "the employment of hundreds of thousands of persons . . . on developments which will result in far-reaching permanent social benefits." The RDA idea emerged in 1934 as an outgrowth of broader strategies to address agricultural problems and populations. But rather than trying to salvage some version of the agrarian ideal, RDAs repurposed depleted agricultural land for the "permanent social benefits" of recreation and marked a transition to a new conception of public nature. The same federal agencies confronting the prospect of whether to build camps for migrant laborers first participated in a plan to build recreational campgrounds.[104]

Camping, in conjunction with other active outdoor activities, increasingly appeared an important lever for social improvement in New Deal approaches to the problems of the Great Depression. For example, it addressed implicit fears about the prospect of unemployed people with extra time on their hands and few opportunities for inexpensive, wholesome leisure. Worries about the dangers of idleness, the corrupting influences of cheap urban entertainment, and the possibilities of lawlessness drove the desire to expand outlets for forms of recreation, like camping, believed to be more beneficial. As one NPS administrator involved in the RDA project suggested, the nation was in "dire need" of facilities for "camping, hiking, and swimming for adults and families" to counter the lure of debased "commercialized" leisure and "haunts that breed crime." Efforts to address this shortfall of public recreation, particularly outdoor activities, were widespread, as federal relief programs pumped money not only into campgrounds but urban playgrounds, parks, parkways, zoos, botanical gardens, swimming pools, and public beaches. RDAs contributed unique and important features to this portfolio by "encouraging vacations in natural surroundings and by placing such vacations within the means of every person."[105]

Achieving the multiple goals of the RDA would require the NPS to depart significantly from its usual focus on enticing visitors to spectacular landscapes. With RDAs, the Park Service was tasked with bringing recreation to larger masses of people with little regard for the unique scenic qualities of the land itself. Two key criteria for selecting an RDA site suggested the new priorities. First, RDAs should be well-distributed across the country and "within 50 miles" of population centers, so that citizens could easily reach and "advantageously utilize" them, even using public transportation. They ought especially seek to serve "underprivileged people," which required the site-selection team to investigate not just the location, "topography and physical features" of the proposed site itself, "but also the social and economic conditions of the entire region which a proposed area is to serve."[106] The NPS was not accustomed to taking such criteria into account, but in doing so embraced one set of New Deal social goals.

Second, RDAs emphasized the practice of camping over the nature in which it was set. As one policy document explained, "The proposed recreational area need not necessarily conform to [usual NPS] standards as to scenic quality." It was more important to foreground "considerations usually borne in mind in selecting camp sites." Instead of choosing potential national park locations first for their unique and magnificent landscapes and then finding suitable campground locations in or near them, RDA sites should be chosen primarily for what would make the best potential camping areas, and then the landscape modified to accomplish that purpose. Far from preserving the landscape, the NPS embarked on massive construction projects. In addition to laying out campsites, workers planted thousands of trees and built dozens of artificial lakes, remaking eroded farmlands into ecologically questionable but pleasant and shady oases. RDA designers identified swimming as an important active outdoor pursuit, and so where there was no body of water, the crews created one. A swimming area need be neither aesthetically pleasing nor natural to the region; it need only contain water. Trees need be neither native species nor impressive examples; they need only provide shade for campsites. The goal was to create space for the cooperative outdoor recreation, exemplified by the Meinecke campground, that New Deal planners believed would lead to a more cohesive and democratic society.[107]

Such heavy-handed alterations of the landscape generated minor opposition to what was becoming an outdoor recreation juggernaut. In Meinecke's own backyard, for example, preservationist minded activists of the Save-the-Redwoods League feared overdevelopment and remained unsympathetic to the goal of democratizing access to the outdoors. In 1938, the League opposed the creation of a new national park in the redwoods, having come to believe the NPS had lost sight of its mission to teach and inspire visitors through nature, rather than create playgrounds.[108] While echoing the longstanding tension between protection and visitors, these viewpoints were drowned out by the growing enthusiasm for outdoor recreation, for the moment at least. The 1937 *Encyclopaedia of the Social Sciences* recognized that camping had risen to the level of a "national habit, . . . markedly woven into the pattern of social life" in the United States. With the support of "government promotion," "standardization," and "regulations," this "temporary but periodic retreat to the out of doors as a form of recreation" had become nothing less than a "folkway of an urban civilization."[109]

Americans flocked to RDAs as soon as they opened to the public, with many campgrounds filled to capacity. The agency's *Invitation to New Play Areas,* a Spring 1938 brochure describing available RDA facilities, highlighted camping opportunities. "Means for nearly every type of camping are provided on these Federal recreation areas. There are public campgrounds for family tents and trailers. For the hiker with his pack there are trailside campsites." The *Invitation* underscored the social imperative in a paired photo montage that proposed, "Every person needs recreation." The first page asked "Shall it be this? . . . " and pictured urban kids up to no good, playing in the street and sitting in a movie theater. The facing page offered an alternative: " . . . or this?"—young people camping, swimming, and fishing. It was a heavy-handed appeal, but apparently a popular one. One camper wrote to the NPS in praise of RDAs for the social good they created: "The beauty about camping and recreation is that they are so concrete and easily grasped by the public. . . . As a camping person, as a sociologist, as one keenly interested in community organization not to mention my role as a citizen, I wish to express my very genuine appreciation . . . of so well conceived a program."[110] More than a popular recreational pursuit, the multipronged New Deal policies turned camping into a valuable social tool and an implicit individual right.

The Forest Service stepped up its efforts to develop campgrounds for similar social reasons in the early 1930s, as officials began to realize that forest lands could "play a vital part in meeting today's recreational needs." With more than 150 reserves in 37 states, the USFS already had a greater distribution of potential recreation areas than the Park Service, even with the addition of RDAs, but had done little recreational planning. Now moving quickly, the agency boasted more than 3,000 such campgrounds by 1935, all free to the public and readily available "to that overwhelming majority of people which prefers—or for economic reasons must find—inexpensive, 'come-as-you-please' recreational opportunities."[111] The NPS bristled at this initiative, complaining that the Forest Service had "over stepped" its mandate and encroached on the Park Service's claim "to be recognized as the recreational agency of the Federal Government."[112] That campgrounds had become spaces in which to claim bureaucratic worth suggests how New Deal social goals had elevated camping as a civic good.

NPS bureaucrats should not have feared losing campers, since their sites were being inundated by visitors. If the growth in the teens and twenties had been significant, the increasing crowds of visitors arriving at national parks and monuments in the 1930s dwarfed the earlier numbers, as Table 4.2 demonstrates. Between 1935 and 1940 alone visitation doubled, from just

Table 4.2 National Parks, Monuments, and Recreation Areas Visitor
Counts, 1930–1940

Year	Number of Visitors	Growth over previous 5 years	Growth since 1930	US Population	Growth of US Population since 1930	US Visitors as of US pop.
1930	3,246,655	1.6	—	123,202,624	—	2.6%
1935	5,338,583	1.6	1.6	—	—	—
1940	10,830,912	2.0	3.3	132,164,569	1.1	8.2%

Source: U.S. Department of the Interior, National Park Service, "Public Use of the National Parks: A Statistical Report, 1904–1940," (1968), i, 1 Growth numbers appear as a multiple of the previous relevant figure. Year begins October 1 and ends September 30. The NPS statistics for this era only report total visitation, and do not disaggregate overnight guests, campers, or types of camping. While there were many campers among these visitors, it is very difficult to estimate camping numbers, given the difference in types of parks, lodging options, and uneven campground development. The increase in visitors who camped likely paralleled the rate of increase in visitors overall, but this is conjectural. Starting in 1935, figures exclude visitors to recently designated National Historic Areas (which were less likely to include camping facilities, and had considerable visitation). They do, however, include visitors to National Recreation Areas which also included some RDAs. These area types contributed 655,910 visitors to the 1940 total.

over five million to nearly eleven million, a figure that represented over 8 percent of the total population and more than fifty times the attendance from 1910. The NPS had become a much larger agency during the era, so it was in some ways better equipped to handle the onslaught, but until the war years, when visitation temporarily dipped, pressures from increasing demand never ceased.

Americans were voting with their feet—or rather their tires and their tents—for public outdoor recreation, and they did not much care which agency provided the picnic tables, fire rings, and driveways. The massive expansion of available public campsites achieved by the combined efforts of federal and state agencies, along with the rhetoric by which they promoted the practice, led Americans to see such accommodations as a right of citizenship. One camper repeatedly credited the federal government with sponsoring her positive experience: "This trip has changed me into an enthusiastic camper. Thanks to the U.S.F.S. we enjoyed many comforts we did not expect." She also appreciated the low cost of the vacation: "We hiked, camped, fished, and saw the wonders of the Sierra National Forest for almost nothing. It was an inexpensive vacation, but the most enjoyable one we ever had."[113] Those who had traditionally filled the ranks of both camping writers and their readers—white and middle-class Americans—heartily endorsed the efforts of federal agencies to expand their access and meet their expectations.

In the ensuing decades, many wrote to the National Park Service to advocate for even more camping services. They articulated their sense of entitlement to this landscape by asking to stay longer, to have more campgrounds to choose from, and to find a greater supply of on-site provisions. The language they used in making their very specific demands suggested they had assumed ownership of this landscape—a notion Meinecke had promoted. For example, two California women wrote on behalf of a retired couple to protest the "injustice" of the fifteen-day camping limit in King's Canyon National Park. "Surely an exception could be made" for "elderly people who have been worthy citizens in this community for many years." The assistant director replied, noting that despite NPS efforts to expand "campground facilities as fast as possible . . . the needs far exceed available supply." Given this situation, he explained that "we have the responsibility for providing equal opportunity for all visitors to the area."[114] That the agency and its users communicated in the language of "worthy citizens" and "equal opportunity" suggests the ways in which the public camping landscape had expanded in both size and significance. Making good on the promise that all citizens in search of recreation had, as Meinecke suggested, "the same rights of occupancy" in the campers' republic, however, proved more difficult.

"An Inexcusable Violation of the Letter and Spirit of Democracy"

That some claimed rights of access and ownership made it newly noticeable for those who were shut out. The vast expansion of the public camping landscape highlighted, or even exacerbated, the imbalance in facilities available for whites and for African Americans. Black camping enthusiasts wrote to press for faster construction of accessible facilities. In 1933, a group of outdoorsmen from Tennessee wrote the NPS to request the construction of local campgrounds available to the Black community. Individuals and advocacy groups, like the National Urban League and the NAACP, argued that the national parks and the RDAs needed to create more "camping facilities for Negroes." In a June 1935 letter, T. Arnold Hill of the Urban League wrote Secretary of the Interior Harold Ickes to protest the dearth of recreational facilities for African Americans in the South, where local and state parks were typically whites-only. Hill urged the agency to establish facilities that would "definitely take care of the needs of Negroes," and "offer camping, hiking and picknicking sites."[115] The tone and context for these letters differed from those who demanded expanded services in places to which they already felt entitled. For African Americans, access to public campgrounds necessitated a push for equal rights.

African-American newspaper *The Chicago Defender* evidenced Black interests in the outdoors since the early fad for auto-camping in the teens and twenties. In 1914, for example, Dr. A. Wilberforce Williams used his recurring column on health to extol the benefits of camping as a "preventative measure" against urban ailments. He recommended readers "get in the habit of camping out" and take a week or more to "treat yourself and your family to a delightful summer outing in a camp." He noted the increasing popularity of the pastime and, for novices, included practical advice and an equipment list. An editorial later that summer suggested that "the atmosphere of camp life ... brings out the best things in our nature."[116] With similar rhetoric about its restorative benefits, notices of parties heading out on camping adventures appeared in the *Defender* society section throughout the twenties. Outdoor resorts catering to African Americans emerged to provide protected private retreats.[117] In the 1930s, Black organizations also worked toward expanding camping facilities. As the *Defender* reported in 1937, the Mississippi Federation of Colored Women developed a campground on land the organization owned near the town of Clinton—the first and only camping area known to be available to "members of the Race" in the state.[118] That this discussion appeared more or less consistently in such a major public forum suggests that African Americans numbered among camping enthusiasts.

Tracing a history of Black recreational camping, however, does not reveal the whole story. Plenty of evidence suggests that many African Americans associated sleeping outside with unfavorable experiences. Outdoor camping often resulted from the denial of indoor accommodations. As the *Defender* warned in 1924, "Colored acts playing Carbondale, Pa., had better take a camping outfit along with them," as a touring group reported being unable to "find sleeping accommodations in the town it was booked for performances." In this context, the reference to camping gear was sardonic, meant to call out discrimination. The lack of reliable accommodations at inns or hotels, tourist camps or cabin courts, whose operators often refused to accommodate African Americans, made long-distance travel a risky proposition. Failing to find lodgings might mean driving all night, sleeping in cars, fields, or barns— all of which could leave them vulnerable to being harassed by local sheriffs, thrown out from "sundown towns," or accosted by the KKK, which was experiencing a national resurgence in the 1920s.[119]

While the automobile spurred interest in recreational travel in part because it offered some relief from the Jim Crow regime on the railroad, it still subjected African Americans to roadside discrimination and vulnerability. In his 1933 account of auto-touring, well-known journalist and New Deal advisor Alfred Smith detailed the difficulties. At a bare minimum, the uncertainties took "the joy out of gypsying." While he received some pleasant welcomes at tourist camps, "every time a camp manager announced his camp full for the night," he had to wonder, "Is he doing this because I am a Negro?" Smith generously acknowledged the possibility that he might have "imagined slights where none were intended," and yet his experiences suggest the chilling effect the lack of a robust choice or reception could have on Black travelers.[120]

In 1936, Victor H. Green, a mail carrier for the US Postal Service, began publishing a guide intended to help navigate these difficulties. Geared toward middle-class African Americans, *The Negro Motorists' Green Book* provided simple white-pages style listings of accomodations by state and town and advertisements that indicated lodging and dining establishments where Black travelers would find a friendly welcome. The thirty-year publication run suggested how the *Green Book* became a uniquely valued aid throughout the Jim Crow era. Beyond the practical benefits, it simultaneously rebuked segregation (if not overtly challenging it), fostered strategies of Black capitalism, and promoted the already popular faith in the automobile as a tool of individual freedom.[121]

Green's guide aimed far more at helping African Americans get indoors safely for the night than in promoting camping as a form of recreation. As such, private lodgings run by other African Americans greatly outnumbered public outdoor choices, with very few listings for public campgrounds, tourist camps, or trailer courts. The 1937 edition indicated that some New York state parks offered a "lovely place for family gatherings and camping" and provided campsites at reasonable rates.[122] Subsequent editions dropped this listing and provided no information on state or national parks. Summer resorts and a few organized group camps appeared scattered throughout, but camping was neither highlighted nor promoted as a distinct activity in listings, advertisements, or descriptive articles. To the contrary, on isolated routes with sparse listings, especially in the West, having to camp might be an unfortunate, functional necessity.[123] The absence of camping discourse in such a significant travel publication as the *Green Book* suggests the lack of any basic assumption that the emergent public camping landscape provided a welcome option for Black travelers.

The NPS bore responsibility for this sense of exclusion, having historically undermined broader Black participation. At a 1922 conference, Park superintendents voiced their discomfort with the sometimes "awkward" presence of Black visitors. "One of the objections to colored people is that if they come in large groups they will be conspicuous, and will not only be objected to by other visitors, but will cause trouble among the hotel and camp help, and it will be impossible to serve them." That African Americans could be visitors, requiring service by white staff in lodging and camping facilities, confounded the presumption that Park tourists would always be white and middle-class. The resolution of this quandary was an unofficial policy of discouragement: "While we can not openly discriminate against them, they should be told that the parks have no facilities for taking care of them."[124] Suggesting that parks misrepresent available supply, at the very least, suppressed potential demand. More broadly, it contributed to a longstanding lack of welcome that pushed African Americans to look elsewhere for their travel needs and outdoor interests.

This, of course, rested on a longer history. Freedpeople sleeping outside were criminalized as vagrants wherever they set up camp, while white travelers could assume permission to camp on public or private land. Assumptions about who belonged in outdoor spaces often shaped how park rangers, law enforcement, and camp managers approached Black presence in the recreational landscape. Meinecke said little that bore directly on racial issues, but appeared to conceive of outdoor recreation and wilderness preservation as white by definition: "The one great and truly American contribution to the culture of the white race is the deliberate saving and setting aside" portions of the landscape that allowed for the "appreciation of beauty in nature" and periodic "return to nature and her gifts" through activities like recreational camping. This, he argued, was "one of the most powerful means of keeping the nation's soul sound and sane." No wonder, then, that African Americans felt less of a sense of belonging or ownership in the new public camping landscape.[125]

Given the cumulative effect of such stances and actions, it is unsurprising that African Americans might visit national parks in disproportionately low numbers. NPS leaders tended to interpret this data in ways that failed to account for the longer history and thus seemed to confirm internal assumptions that there was little demand for campgrounds from Black communities. By the late 1930s, some NPS employees were pushing to reverse the historic campaign of dissuasion and spur increased Black participation, but Director Cammerer balked. Before authorizing construction of new facilities, he wanted direct evidence of African Americans demonstrating greater demand, presumably by showing up at campgrounds at which they would be refused admittance. The construction-follows-demand premise allowed Cammerer to stonewall plans for accommodating Black visitors.[126] The establishment of two new national parks in the Southeast, Shenandoah in Virginia and Great Smoky Mountains on the North Carolina-Kentucky border, brought matters to a head.

Created from a patchwork of purchased private holdings consolidated in 1926, these lands had no existing public facilities. As late as 1933, a Great Smoky brochure informed potential visitors that "as yet no camp grounds for motorists have been prepared," but promised that "adequate camping places with pure water and other necessities will be provided" soon. The NPS proceeded to deploy CCC labor to construct roads, trails, and campgrounds in both parks. When it came to the question of how these new facilities would accommodate Black visitors, the NPS elected to bow to "local custom" and establish segregated protocols at Shenandoah, Great Smoky, and the southern RDAs.[127] Like many New Deal agencies, it was officially nondiscriminatory but permitted a divergence between national policy and local practice. The CCC, for example, made a similar choice, operating segregated units for most of the 300,000-plus African American enrollees. Black Corps members were also subject to quota limitations, and pressure from localities to move Black camps out of their vicinity.[128] Loath to ruffle feathers among white Southern Democrats, Roosevelt extended more services to the region to cultivate their support. The NPS, accordingly, was reluctant "to set up 'jurisdictional islands'" of integration within otherwise segregated states that might stir up discontent among white communities.[129]

Frustrated Black citizens wrote to protest segregated camp and picnic grounds, as well as comfort stations and dining establishments, exemplified by Shenandoah's Lewis Mountain "Negro Area," CCC-built facilities that opened in 1940. The idea of segregation on federal land, announced with the prominent sign shown in Figure 4.12, and in a campground otherwise promoted as an example of ideal democracy, rankled—as did official attempts at obfuscation. The assistant director insisted that NPS did not consider "separate facilities as any evidence of or intention toward race separation in the park," but rather the need "to conform with the generally accepted customs long established in Virginia." African Americans objected to the federal government introducing segregation into national parks, which had previously supported equal access in principle, if not always in practice. NAACP director

FIGURE 4.12 A sign of segregation that occasioned protest for access. Shenandoah National Park, ca. 1940. Courtesy of Shenandoah National Park Archives.

Walter White wrote Secretary Ickes in 1937 for clarification about the "establishment of a Jim-crow project on Federal territory." White wanted to "go on record as most vigorously protesting against the inauguration of such a policy." Due to the federal imprimatur, segregated parks set an ominous precedent, and the campgrounds of Shenandoah and Great Smoky Mountains became key sites at which to claim not just opportunity for outdoor recreation but also rights to equal federal benefits.[130]

Gaining access to campgrounds acquired new significance in the context of the growing federal commitment to provide Americans with a nearby, low-cost, well-equipped campsite. The NPS might have been reluctant to create jurisdictional islands, but if African Americans could pressure it to desegregate, they might instead create a jurisdictional wedge to advance other civil rights efforts in the region. One visitor wrote the NPS excoriating the segregated accommodations at Shenandoah as "an inexcusable violation of the letter and spirit of democracy." Another argued that "this is a National Park and should show no race separation at all." Fisk University sociologist Charles S. Johnson wrote Cammerer in 1937 arguing that it was incumbent upon the agency to include "the participation of all elements of the population" in planning campgrounds and picnic areas. The NPS dragged its feet, but could not entirely escape the logic that promoting camping for all citizens entailed a greater degree of inclusivity.[131]

Pressure on the NPS also came from within the Department of Interior. In 1939, the Department's adviser on Negro affairs, William Trent Jr., implored Secretary Ickes to address the issue of the "participation of negro citizens in all of the benefits of the national Park Program . . . fully and frankly." Trent argued that the NPS should operate on the "fundamental" principle that "citizens regardless of color shall participate in all of the benefits . . . of any governmental program." He presented his case directly to Park superintendents at their conference that year, maintaining the agency's responsibility to serve all citizens, white or Black, rich or poor. He could already point to one victory; informed of African Americans' exclusion from RDA campgrounds, Ickes forthrightly reversed the policy. Trent hoped this would inspire park superintendents to disavow their unofficial mechanisms of "subterfuge." He insisted that opening campgrounds to all comers was the only feasible way Black Americans could demonstrate their camping desires to NPS officials, who continued to insist on a show of demand before construction. As Trent put it, to do otherwise—to prevent some citizens from full and equal access to this important social practice of outdoor recreation—was to create "a contradiction in democratic government."[132]

In response to Trent's continued pressure, Ickes decided to designate one picnic ground at Shenandoah for integrated use, to serve as a demonstration of good faith (or an experiment that might be easily reversed). He also instructed Cammerer to build ample and equally equipped facilities for African Americans at least commensurate with current visitation levels and without regard to assumptions about "demand." Another opening came in 1940, when a federal auto-camp on the outskirts of Washington, DC ended its whites-only policy. The *Chicago Defender* reported that the policy shift was a direct result of "repeated protests to the National Park Service" by various Black organizations. According to the *Defender*, Ickes's order "opening the camp to all tourists regardless of race on the basis of first come first served" represented "a signal victory for civil rights." By 1941, the new NPS Director Newton Drury proved more open to persuasion to expand the so-far quietly successful experiment in integration to all of Shenandoah's facilities, and the next year, Ickes followed suit and directed the NPS to end segregation in all Southern park lands.[133]

In June 1942 Southern park superintendents received a memo from Drury that directed them in no uncertain terms "to make certain that the policy of the Department on the nonsegregation of Negroes is carried out in the Southern areas by the National Park Service." Trent had been instrumental in bringing this policy change about, and must have welcomed the resolution. And yet it was just one in a list of recommendations he had prepared outlining a broader, multipronged approach that began, but did not end, with desegregation. He argued that the federal government had a "responsibility" not just to take down signs, but also to work actively to "destroy racial barriers." He argued for a more proactive approach to increasing the participation of African Americans, as both employees and visitors. The NPS and Interior needed to mount a targeted promotional campaign to explicitly welcome African Americans, advertise available facilities and opportunities to get outdoors, go camping, and visit the parks. He suggested the NPS might hold events in Black communities, appear at conferences of Black organizations, hire more Black park rangers, and publicize in the Black press. For Trent, it was incumbent upon the Park Service to do more than respond to demand, but to cultivate it among African Americans, similar to how Mather had vigorously promoted the Parks in the 1920s.[134]

Trent's suggestions largely fell by the wayside. Later studies would identify that a "lack of marketing efforts towards minority communities" was among the chief constraints to nonwhite participation in national parks and camping-type activities. Collective memories of discrimination, fear of traveling through "hostile white terrain," and violence visited upon African Americans in the woods all contributed to lingering apprehensions that national parks were places where Black people would be neither welcome nor safe.[135] Drury later recalled that the NPS stood fast on the commitment to nondiscrimination, even against complaints of US Senators. But in his tours of the southern parks he still saw legible traces of segregation: "I found that originally there had been facilities with this same distinction ['white' and 'colored'] marked on them. The order of course had gone out from Washington to eradicate them and the workmen, who evidently were Southerners, had covered this lettering over, but the paint was not quite opaque and they still were distinguishable."[136] In the thin coats of paint, the remnants of discrimination persisted in the NPS. The agency's failure to follow through on efforts to invite Black participation in a proactive way, as Trent had outlined, certainly contributed to this persistent divide.

In its popularity and complexity, camping had become embedded in government policy, federal lands, and public mindsets by the mid-1940s. The vast physical expansion of campground acreage matched the intensified rhetoric around the social benefit and national purpose of camping. As a result, Americans came to understand camping as a right of citizenship, demonstrated on the one hand by stated expectations of access and services as well as a sense of ownership and belonging, and on the other by protests for equal access. Meinecke's notion of treating campers as "guests of the nation" not only envisioned campgrounds as models of democracy in action, but also generated mechanisms for saving and improving the nation itself, even in ways he might not have imagined. The camper's republic elevated the recreational vision for public nature and embodied a new social contract.

IN 1944, EMILIO Meinecke consulted on the design for a new campground in Yosemite National Park. Among the most overcrowded parks, Yosemite was still struggling to keep up with camper demand and mitigate damage. The NPS planned to build a series of large modern campgrounds to address these issues. The superintendent made a specific request for greater privacy within each site, in part so campers would not resort to erecting artificial barriers, like blanket fences. Instructions also called for "distinctive names, significant of the locality" to enhance numerical designations for loops and sites in order "distinguish them from the still unregulated campgrounds." Moreover, it might induce a greater sense of individual ownership and neighborly community among the occupants of the 212 campsites. Meinecke's design for the prototype, Camp Merced, included subtle changes and embellishments to the standard loop: evocative street names, curvilinear road system, more clearly demarcated site boundaries. As a whole, the resulting plan shown in Figure 4.13 seems to resemble an organic tree-like structure. But the proposed map for the campground also offers a striking visual foreshadowing of a suburban housing development, a blueprint that in a few short years would subdivide thousands of acres of rural land into new home sites. This suburbia in the Sierras suggests the powerful legacy of the loop and the connections between homeownership and outdoor recreation embedded in the new social contract.[137]

That same year, President Roosevelt proposed a "second Bill of Rights" in the radio broadcast of his State of the Union address. He asked Americans to look ahead after World War II was won, and to move toward "a new basis of security and prosperity . . . for all—regardless of station, or race or creed." He enumerated key basic economic protections, such as entitlement to "adequate medical care" and a "good education," "the right to earn enough to provide adequate food and clothing and recreation" and "the right of every family to a decent home." While this second Bill of Rights was never formally adopted as part of the Constitution, many pieces of Roosevelt's vision would find

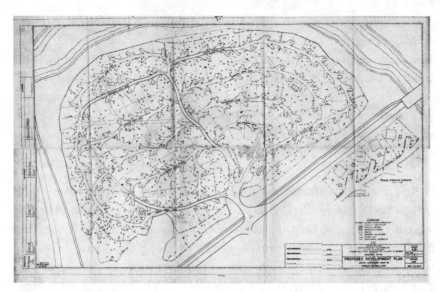

FIGURE 4.13 Suburbia in the Sierras? Meinecke's design for Camp Merced. "Proposed Development Plan, Merced Campground (Camp 15), Yosemite National Park," for the Branch of Plans and Designs, Forestry Division of the National Park Service, 1944. © California Academy of Sciences.

expression in government policy and cultural mindsets. The provision for a "decent home," for example, built on several New Deal programs intended to stimulate residential construction, homeownership, and home-related consumption.[138] With modest effects during the Depression, these efforts increased the cultural importance of the home while largely failing to address the needs of transients and migrants without homes. In the postwar period, federal investment sparked rising homeownership rates and the expectation of a decent home became a bedrock component of the American Dream.

That recreation might number among these new rights may at first seem surprising, though citizens had already begun to assert their rights to leisure in public nature. Three years prior to Roosevelt's proposal, the Department of the Interior issued a comprehensive *Recreational Land Plan for the United States* that recognized governmental obligations to support outdoor leisure. The report asserted that "every element and all types of population need areas for outdoor recreation" and called for the "coordinated efforts of all agencies, at all levels of government" to bring "an outdoor vacation experience ... within easy reach of the whole population." It recommended expanding "public ownership of lands" to support "camping, hiking" and other outdoor activities that offered a "sense of freedom," especially for those of "limited means." The right to recreation, paired with the right to a decent home, exemplified what had evolved into a new social contract. Federal sponsorship of opportunities for mixing lesiure with public nature now contributed to achieving the broad "new goals of human happiness and well-being" that Roosevelt envisioned.[139]

In practice, these goals continued to be undercut by unequal distribution. Two decades before, intellectual and activist W. E. B. Du Bois had lamented the extreme difficulties African Americans faced in accessing this vital experience of freedom. He asserted in *Darkwater* (1920), "I believe in Liberty for all men: the space to stretch their arms and their souls, the right to breathe and the right to vote, the freedom to choose their friends, enjoy the sunshine, and ride on the railroads, uncursed by color; thinking, dreaming, working as they will in a kingdom of beauty and love." He recounted profound experiences at places like Acadia National Park and the Grand Canyon, where the grandeur allowed him to glimpse the possibilities of true freedom, perhaps, he believed, an especially crucial opportunity for Black Americans: "Why do not those who are scarred in the world's battle and hurt by its hardness travel to these places of beauty and drown themselves in the utter joy or life?" He concluded that hazardous travel and segregated, unwelcoming conditions, which persisted throughout the Jim Crow era, deterred many from seeking such experiences.[140] The lack of NPS follow-through was but one component of ongoing exclusion, as other cornerstones of Roosevelt's postwar vision, notably federal housing programs, in fact served to extend segregration and inequality into new suburbs across the country.[141] For long after Du Bois's assessment, African Americans, among others, had to fight for access to significant markers of the new social contract, as both homeownership and outdoor recreation continued to contain mechanisms of discrimination.

The campers' republic enacted in parks and forests across the country incorporated key elements—and blind spots—of the new social contract embodied in the second Bill of Rights. Meinecke's Camp Merced hinted at the close connections between camp design and suburban prototype, where camping in the woods came to suggest a model for home and neighborhood rather than an escape from them. Homeownership went hand-in-hand with the sense of a "130-millionth" part-ownership of public nature. Mass expectations of recreational camping on public land, begun in the 1930s and growing exponentially in the 1950s, rose in synchrony with massive postwar suburban development. This campers' republic modeled the new social contract, which had now definitively shifted from an agrarian ideal to a consumer and recreational ethos, where mixing leisure with nature became a potent way for citizens to demonstrate national belonging.

PART THREE

Outdoor Challenges, 1950s–2010s

5

The Back-to-Nature Crowd

ON TUESDAY EVENING, January 20, 1970, American television viewers were getting ready for the start of the NBA All-Star Game. Those who tuned in to their local ABC station one hour early would have come across "Thirty Days to Survival," the first documentary in a series of prime-time specials produced by *Life* magazine for *The Alcoa Hour*. In the days before the broadcast, local newspapers highlighted it in their entertainment sections. An Ohio paper promoted it as an "Adventure Special" that followed "a group of teen age youngsters at the National Outdoor Leadership School (NOLS) in Wyoming, headed by legendary mountain climber Paul Petzoldt, who are being trained to live in the wilderness for 30 days, and then turned loose 70 miles from base camp with no food." A Wisconsin daily heightened the drama: "A group of young people pit themselves against cold, hunger and nature in a five-day endurance test." Further drumming up viewership, Petzoldt had appeared the week before as a featured guest on the popular interview program *The David Frost Show*.[1]

A month earlier, *Life* had profiled Petzoldt and NOLS under the title, "Last Mountain Man? Not if He Can Help It." His program, it explained, included "no weaving of lanyards, no compulsory singing of jolly songs around the campfire," as kids might do in traditional summer camps. Instead, the teens carried 40-pound backpacks, "eat what they carry and find and catch, sleep in tents, and read topographical maps" to make their way through the "rugged Wind River Mountain Range, some of which has never been accurately mapped." They emerged from the month-long trek having discovered "astonishing reserves of strength" and a new sense of "self-reliance." Wyoming Senator Gale McGee spoke of this effort on the Senate floor, alerting his colleagues to the continuing "need for the true men of the outdoors" and endorsing NOLS' focus on "outdoor life, conservation, and survival." On McGee's request, the *Congressional Record* included the entire text of the article, though it omitted the teaser about the upcoming *Alcoa Hour*. In the January 9, 1970 issue of *Life*, a two-page full-color ad enticed viewers to watch this "exciting story of youthful adventure . . . from the warmth of your easy chair." Not just the "best adventure show of the season," another promotion exclaimed, this was a genuine opportunity. Because the school "accepts applicants from all over, young viewers" could have more than a vicarious experience; "they can even dream of participating," joining the small cadre of adventurous teens they saw on TV.[2]

That a recently established outdoor training program, based in a remote section of Wyoming, that so far enrolled less than 250 students per summer, could be the focus of such a coordinated nationwide publicity campaign pointed to some major shifts in the camping landscape. This was no loop campground, designed to cultivate democracy. NOLS spoke to different goals and experiences in the outdoors, especially for the younger generation. Petzoldt, born in 1908, seemed an unlikely champion. A lifelong mountaineer who began climbing Grand Teton as a teenager, he was a member of the first American expedition to K2 in 1938 and a trainer for the US Army's 10th Mountain Division during World War II. He alternately ran an outdoor guiding business, an alfalfa farm, a small-town bar, and a used-car dealership before founding NOLS in 1965. His aim was not only to teach young adults technical outdoor skills but also give them opportunities for leadership experience, personal growth, recreational enjoyment, and environmental awareness.[3] NOLS grew slowly in its first few years, but the public attention of 1969–70 paid off. Enrollment for 1970 nearly quadrupled, and by the end of the decade, the organization was enrolling thousands of students at multiple locations, from Alaska to Kenya.

Besides the media blitz, what made American television viewers and young campers ready to embrace the experiences and messages that NOLS offered? Some surely enjoyed the one-hour adventure story—would the kids find their way through the wilderness to safety?—and left it at that. But within the made-for-TV drama, the story resonated with those contemplating a tumultuous world, as that December 1969 issue of *Life* amply demonstrated. The startling eyes of cult leader and mass murderer Charles Manson stared out from the cover. The letters to the editor section was filled with scathing and derisive complaints about youth protestors, drugs, the counterculture, and the women's liberation movement. A two-page spread included dozens of snippets from Americans who had written in to share their wrenching reactions to learning about the My Lai massacre. The very next page brought readers to the story of Petzoldt and the camping expeditions he led. Did they find it a relief amidst the dismaying social problems? Did it suggest a counterweight to the disturbing daily news bulletins about young men in the jungles of Vietnam? Senator McGee believed that NOLS represented a solution for restive youth: it used "the challenges of nature to temper the new generation" and its rebellious tendencies.[4] Petzoldt took a different tack. In "Thirty Days to Survival" and elsewhere, he empathized with the younger generation and their desires to confront rather than dodge the divisive cultural questions of the day.

In the opening moments of "Thirty Days to Survival," the sixty-two-year-old Petzoldt sat on a rocky mountainside, wearing a floppy hat with two yellow flowers stuck in its brim, and spoke of the generational divide. He presented wilderness as a wholesome place for youthful escapades. "They're going to get adventure one way or another whether the old folks like it or not so this is a good way of getting it. Maybe it's even better than LSD, marijuana, hot rods." He cautioned viewers not to write this impulse off as frivolous. "I don't think that the young people are fleeing from anything, boy, I think they're facing reality. I think our generation are the one that fled from things . . . and that's why they don't understand these kids." Petzoldt offered sympathy for young people "suddenly facing all the problems that we've just been sweeping under the rug." Petzoldt rejected the implicit criticism of 1960s youth as trying to escape the responsibilities of work, war, or adulthood. Instead, he reframed their immersion in the wilderness as a "hunger for reality," a disdain for "phony" society where people "talk one thing and do another," a desire for "raw honesty" and a "world with a different set of values."[5]

The style of the film further aligned NOLS with a countercultural ethos. "Thirty Days to Survival" evoked a new genre of cinema verité that employed minimal staging and narration and eschewed slick production values in favor of a "raw footage" feel. It shared this approach with another, more famous documentary produced that summer by the same director, Mike Wadleigh: *Woodstock,* released in theaters in March of 1970.[6] The proximity of the two films was more than chronological. The visual narrative and featured subjects—young men with long hair and beards, young women without makeup, cavorting together in nature—suggested a meaningful connection: three days of peace and music at Woodstock, thirty days of wilderness and self-discovery in the Wind Rivers.

Camping became meaningful in new ways, for a new generation in the 1960s and 1970s, and NOLS was a prototype. Along with belaying ropes and backcountry survival, it taught young people how camping could aid their quest for self-discovery and a generational ethos. Many followed NOLS' courses and ideas into the wilderness and made backpacking a popular pursuit, novel less for its practices than for the emergent identities and values it came to signify. For its acolytes, the backcountry became a newly meaningful part of public nature, beyond the loop campground. If the outdoor world NOLS made was not the campers' republic, it still embodied a social contract where citizens mixed leisure with nature to enact a vision of self and community.

"Call of the Not So Wild"

That children who came of age in the 1960s would come to find liberating and countercultural meanings in camping was not a predictable outcome. Camping in the 1950s was a decidedly mainstream affair. Since the end of World War II it had become a broadly popular choice for the summer family vacation, itself increasingly an expected annual ritual. Families clamored for campsites in the many loop campgrounds in public parks and forest preserves. Touted across the popular press, campgrounds became a prime stage to perform newly idealized family roles and camping a privileged method for producing the coveted sense of "family togetherness."[7] Public agencies had their hands full trying to keep up with the increasing demand. The US Forest Service (USFS), for one, had hosted 1.1 million overnight campers in 1943, when travel was depressed due to the war. By 1950, it was serving 3.9 million campers and ten years later, it struggled to accommodate 10.9 million. As Table 5.1 shows, the National Park Service (NPS) experienced staggering increases as well. Both agencies initiated major infrastructure development plans during the decade—Operation Outdoors (USFS) and Mission 66 (NPS)—which together aimed to increase the number of campsites available nationally, from 41,000 to 125,000. The inadequacy of that goal became clear even before it was realized, and private campground operators began to fill the gap in the early 1960s—such as the Kampgrounds of America (KOA) chain, whose franchised operators could collectively boast more campsites than the NPS by 1970.[8]

Several key factors accounted for the explosive growth of this form of camping. Federal investment in outdoor recreational infrastructure and transportation networks after the war, particularly interstate highways, put campgrounds within easier reach. The success of Emilio Meinecke's formula led many Americans to assume that the government had an obligation to

Table 5.1 National Parks, Monuments, and Recreation Areas Visitor Counts, 1940–1970

Year	Number of Visitors	Growth over previous 10 years	Growth since 1940	US Population	Growth of US Population since 1940	Visitors as % of US pop.
1940	10,830,912	2.0	—	132,164,569	—	8.2%
1950	21,779,905	2.0	2.0	150,697,361	1.1	14.4%
1960	35,539,400	1.6	3.3	179,323,175	1.4	19.8%
1970	66,417,600	1.9	6.1	203,392,031	1.5	32.7%

Source: US Department of the Interior, National Park Service, "Annual Summary Report, 1904—Last Calendar Year," https://irma.nps.gov/STATS/SSRSReports/National%20 Reports/Annual%20Summary%20Report%20(1904%20-%20Last%20Calendar%20Year), (accessed July 15, 2019). Growth numbers appear as a multiple of the previous relevant figure. Year begins October 1 and ends September 30. Figures exclude visitors to National Historic Areas, Memorials, Battlefields, and other site types unlikely to permit regular public camping. The NPS statistics for this era only report total visitation, and do not disaggregate overnight guests, campers, or types of camping. While there were many campers among these visitors, it remains difficult to estimate camping numbers, given the difference in types of parks, lodging options, and uneven campground development. The increase in visitors who camped likely paralleled the rate of increase in visitors overall, but this is conjectural.

provide a low-cost public campsite with modern amenities amidst a peaceful natural setting. A 1961 study concluded that most campers assumed essential amenities would be waiting for them, a "frame of reference" that "presumes the existence of picnic tables, wells, toilets, washrooms and the like."[9] They wrote unceasingly to the Park Service and their Congressional representatives to insist the government make good on these promises. One elementary school teacher from Texas asked her Senator, Lyndon B. Johnson, in 1957 to protect the rights of "us middle-class vacationers," by improving campground conditions, which she found "very primitive for our progressive America." As the thick files of complaint letters suggest, Americans were only raising their expectations of the camping experience.[10]

Keeping costs low for the larger families of the baby boom era remained significant. The oft-touted claim that "a camping vacation costs little more than staying at home, once you've got the camping equipment" may have been an exaggeration, but it was a standard reference in the popular press and had some basis in fact. The National Park Service collected minor entrance fees, but until 1965 charged nothing for campground privileges, even as it continued to upgrade amenities. Yet while camping could be less expensive than some other vacation types, the claim that it was equally available to all Americans, in the same manner, was less obvious. The standard figure cited throughout the era ranged between two and three hundred dollars for a basic complement of gear—not an inconsequential outlay at the time. While the public infrastructure subsidized it, camping was not free. Nor was access universal, as African Americans continued to experience discrimination at public campgrounds.[11]

Another significant factor was the way the campground came to epitomize the era's suburban ideal. In a 1954 magazine article, experienced outdoor adventurer and 10th Mountain Division veteran Hal Burton narrated his embrace of the tamer pleasures of family camping. Burton was sheepish to admit his newfound attraction to car camping, which he had once disdained, but he empathized with his generation in seeking a vacation that was "easy on the pocketbook, soothing to the disposition, and ideal for the family that wants to get away . . . but not too far away."[12] What he had come to appreciate in the campground was the suburban dream come true:

> Happy, flushed youngsters romped among the birches, or splashed on the edge of Moose Brook. Bronzed men, chopping firewood or just relaxing, greeted us with a friendly "Hi" as we walked past their spotlessly tended campsites. Young mothers kept one eye on their tots, and the other on food sizzling over open fireplaces. A sign informed me that firewood was supplied to each tent site, and that there was daily trash collection. It was, all in all, pretty good evidence that camping out . . . wasn't the outdoor version of tenement life I'd gloomily imagined.[13]

Burton's picture of the campground was a rosy one: reliable public utilities and tidy homesteads with hearty children, virile husbands, and happy housewives. This vision seemed to wipe out lingering Depression-era suspicions of camps as refuge for the down and out. In fact, the near disappearance of concerns about tramps or hobos from camping discourse during this affluent era fueled a vision of campgrounds as better at achieving the suburban ideal than suburbia. As the happy campers in Figure 5.1 suggest, the loop campground held out the promise for perfection and satisfaction of postwar social roles in ways that regular work and home life may have fallen short.[14]

The cultural imperative of "family togetherness" thus served as a key stimulus. While family vacations provided general opportunities to practice

FIGURE 5.1 An idyll of family togetherness in the campground. "Camping, Upper Paradise Campground, Mr. Wm. B. Godfrey and family," Sequoia National Park, California, photograph by Harry B. Robinson, 1959, National Park Service, Asset ID: 0294110e-c75d-4022-bed0-bf0a4aa04f68.

togetherness, camping gained acclaim for being uniquely effective at achieving it. Campers echoed these sentiments in their letters to the NPS. One woman from New York applauded the public support of togetherness in 1958. "It is heart-warming to see families camping together . . . from all walks of life. It is a good omen: 'Families which camp together, stay together.'" Whether camping consistently delivered on this promise was less clear, as other letters complained about campers who violated these ideals.[15] In this sense, the campground demonstrated many Americans' commitment to achieving idealized domestic roles and gender dynamics necessary to dominant definitions of family and exposed tensions that underlay the performance of them. Within the domestic paradigms of the Cold War, the social benefits of camping took on heightened levels of importance. Outdoor recreation was understood to promote social stability and family solidarity, bolster the consumer economy, and demonstrate upward mobility—all of which contributed to the moral campaign against communism.[16] Sociological studies tended to reinforce this interpretation: that the white, well-educated, middle-class families who dominated campground populations derived their "major satisfactions"

of camping from the "social system of the camp," the opportunity to perform modern rituals of "companionate marriage and family togetherness."[17]
Recreating an outdoor version of the suburban neighborhood, with loop
upon loop of identically-organized, well-equipped outdoor households,
sustained an image of affluent American leisure for Cold War purposes and
supported the search for the peak togetherness experience.

These factors combined to drive the popularity of camping ever upward
in the 1950s. As the next decade began, many began to wonder whether
increasing crowds were undermining the appeal of the pastime. In July 1961
Time magazine ran a major story on the camping craze, emblazoning the
cover with a double-sized fold-out illustration and a banner that branded
it: "Camping: Call of the Not So Wild."[18] Vividly colored, the cover shown in
Figure 5.2 teems with tents, trailers, cars, hikers, boaters, and wildlife, packed
cheek-by-jowl into every square inch of level ground. Vehicles crammed
with people and gear snake through the panels in bumper-to-bumper lines.
Everywhere people are busy fishing, swimming, reading, taking photographs,
grilling hotdogs, playing ball, blowing up air mattresses, battling a thunder-
storm, ascending switchback trails, fleeing from curious bears. An appealing
and calmer landscape of hills and snow-capped peaks, complete with high-
flying birds, smiling sun and a rainbow, frames the hurly burly below. A closer
look reveals notes of tension. On the crest of a hill, a transmission tower hides
under the letter "M." Two men are engaged in a fistfight while a ranger shakes
a scolding finger. One man spanks his son for sinking the boat, while another
rushes to rescue his daughter on the precipice of a waterfall. Bullies knock a
boy off his canoe. Perhaps most tellingly, on the right a hill frowns in distress
and on the left a grimacing face glares from a storm cloud. Nature, it seems,
does not like being overrun.

The article on the inside, titled "Ah, Wilderness?", took a similarly
conflicted perspective. After directing readers to examine the cover, it began
by quoting Henry David Thoreau's famous passage that starts with "I went
to the woods because I wished to live deliberately" as a laughable mismatch.
Thoreau had been the subject of renewed attention, as the Sierra Club and
other nature organizations put his words in service to a modern push for wilderness preservation. If the reader missed the point, the article suggested that
if Thoreau were to seek out Walden Pond today, he could find it easily by
following the "snort and belch of automobiles" and "the yelps of children,"
the sounds of the "invasion of hundreds of thousands families hungering
for a summertime skirmish with nature." These Americans, it declared, were
"smitten by the call of the not-so-wild"—a not so hidden critique of their

outdoor preferences. The piece aimed to understand "Why this mass move-ment into the world of mosquitoes, snakes and burrs?"[19] But the unstated question it posed was instead this one: Who on earth would want to spend time in the crowded, harried world depicted on the cover?

Upward of 16 million Americans, *Time* predicted, were headed to campgrounds that summer of 1961, "enough to make a forest ranger reach for a cigarette." The federal Outdoor Recreation Resources Review Commission (ORRRC) noted in 1962 that "bumper-to-bumper traffic" and "campground full" signs had become frequent.[20] Debates escalated over the relationship be-tween improving amenities and increasing crowds. Some campers wrote to the NPS to ask for protection from modern intrusions. One woman regis-tered her disappointment in 1961: "Couldn't one little beautiful campground be . . . kept for those of us who still appreciate peace, and quiet, and can still get along quite well without lights and radios?" Others expressed the oppo-site sentiment, requesting long-distance phone service, better roads, precut firewood, and electric light in the restrooms. Almost everyone wanted reli-able hot showers.[21] Occasionally, campers asked for more and less in the same letter, as Frances Archer of New Mexico did in 1966. She expressed "great disappointment" that the NPS would take "the most beautiful section" of Big Bend National Park and "ruin it by building cabins, filling stations and hotels." Rather, she contended, "is it not the main purpose of the National Park System to keep these beautiful sections of our country unspoiled by commercialism?" Yet Archer appended a postscript venting her frustration that the gasoline brand of her choice was not available in the park: "Because I had not a Gulf credit card, I . . . had to cut my park visit short and go outside the park and buy gasoline."[22] Even as campers like Archer recoiled against the ugly sight of filling stations, they relied upon the NPS to provide a host of modern services to facilitate their visits.

Public agencies scrambled to strike the right balance. An NPS adminis-trator laid out the nearly impossible task in 1961: "How to retain the charm, tranquility and beauty of a natural setting in the degree that each indi-vidual would like to see it preserved while permitting each to use the area according to his personal desires."[23] The Mission 66 building program essen-tially doubled down on the Meinecke system to achieve that delicate balance. The NPS Chief of Forestry urged the "continued endorsement of the princi-ples published by Dr. E.P. Meinecke" in order to prevent damage to park re-sources in the rush to increase campground capacity. Yet so far, the one thing the Meinecke formula had produced most spectacularly was more campers.[24] One lamented the feedback loop: "A few 'improvements' are made, then

FIGURE 5.2 Campers throng to the outdoors, hearing the "Call of the Not So Wild." Cover illustration by Boris Artzybasheff, *Time*, July 14, 1961.

people hear that the camp has such amenities. . . . They like the beautiful location but aren't satisfied with the campground. They start 'pressuring' for more
'improvements,' which brings more of the same type of people and the vicious
circle continues."[25]

The *Time* cover satirized the outcome of this process, but the article
hedged. Despite campers' "absurd concessions to civilized living . . . the
great mountains and forests of the U.S. are such indestructible marvels, and
so mysteriously instructive to man's nature, that even the most unabashed
dude and his togetherness-mad neighbor in the sprawl of Tent City return
from a camping trip stronger from their experience." The article contained a
multipage spread of photographs showcasing the rewards of family camping,
picturing tents and trailers amidst beautiful landscapes from the Ozarks to
the Tetons, in Yosemite and Glacier National Parks. Even those who chose
"the new-style, cocktail-slinging mass encampments" might experience a
Thoreauvian "sublime."[26] The article thus concluded by admitting that in offering access to a public nature that fostered American ideals of middle-class
living, even the call of the not so wild had its redeeming qualities.

Despite its happy ending, the *Time* article reflected an undercurrent of doubt. The complaint letters to the NPS also echoed the
uneasiness, encapsulated by economist John Kenneth Galbraith: Was perpetually increasing material progress undercutting social well-being? One of
the most-quoted passages in his bestselling 1958 cultural critique, *The Affluent
Society*, used a family camping vacation as a vehicle to evoke this dilemma:

> The family which takes its mauve and cerise, air-conditioned, power-
> steered and power-braked automobile out for a tour passes through
> cities that are badly paved, made hideous by litter, blighted buildings,
> billboards, and posts for wires. . . . They picnic on exquisitely packaged
> food from a portable icebox by a polluted stream and go on to spend
> the night at a park which is a menace to public health and morals. Just
> before dozing off on an air mattress, beneath a nylon tent, amid the
> stench of decaying refuse, they may reflect vaguely on the curious une-
> venness of their blessings. Is this, indeed, the American genius?[27]

The lingering specter of "camps of crime" and disease combined with new
problems of overcrowding and artificiality to produce an unappealing picture. The ambivalent family vainly in search of nature from their nylon
bunker became, in Galbraith's rendering, a symbol for a self-indulgent and
self-deceptive society.

Among those coming of age in the 1960s, some Americans shared Galbraith's disenchantment and concurred with the critiques the *Time* feature had dramatized. Loop campgrounds, and the domestic aspirations they exemplified, had come to represent aspects of the postwar suburban lifestyle that some found hypocritical and unsustainable. Rather than rejecting the recreational ethos or belief in the power of nature, however, those in the younger generation began to reshape outdoor leisure experiences.[28] By the time NOLS began to hit magazine pages and TV airwaves in the late 1960s, a growing number were primed for its message of self-renewal through a different kind of camping.

"We Hope That They'll Discover Themselves"

The same year that Galbraith published *The Affluent Society*, a very different kind of author voiced similar sentiments. Beat writer Jack Kerouac's semiautobiographical novel *The Dharma Bums* imagined a way out of the "work, produce, consume, work, produce, consume" trap. While ascending a peak in the Sierra Nevada, the characters envision "a great rucksack revolution, thousands or even millions of young Americans wandering around with rucksacks, going up to mountains to pray, making children laugh and old men glad, making young girls happy and old girls happier."[29] This beguiling vision of outdoor travel as respite from modern life was not altogether new. Embedded in a critique of conformity and consumer culture, however, Kerouac summoned a new, generation-specific use of nature to find authenticity and happiness.

Paul Petzoldt seemed to channel Kerouac in the opening minutes of "Thirty Days to Survival." He extolled "the mountains" as a "real" and "complete change" and foresaw young people having transformative outdoor experiences: "Out here I think it's a good opportunity for them to just set and relax and view their whole everything. . . . [W]e hope that they'll discover themselves."[30] These sentiments found a ripe audience in the new generation, as self-discovery and wilderness adventure suggested counterpoints to family camping's suburban togetherness regime. But NOLS did not start with the intention to foster countercultural alternatives. At the outset, it shared much with traditional outdoor practices and approaches. Over time, Petzoldt's program nurtured students' cultural explorations, as new forms and meanings of outdoor recreation emerged.

When NOLS took its first students up into the Wind River Mountains in 1965, it related more to a crowded field of summer camp programs than any incipient rucksack revolution. Since the 1920s, outdoor summer camps had grown in popularity among American parents and their kids. Children went away for weeks at a time to live in cabins, swim in lakes, sing songs, make crafts, and play group games. By the postwar years, as family camping was booming, so too were sleepaway camps. Nearly 5 million kids, or 12 percent of all American children reportedly attended public, private, or religious camps in the summer of 1959 alone. NOLS, Petzoldt insisted, was a demanding course to train a new generation of outdoor leaders, not a traditional sleepaway camp. Still, both fulfilled what *Newsweek* called in 1959 the "desire to expose city-bound children to trees and birds, comradeship and physical well-being, to teach them self-reliance and group cooperation." NOLS thus catered to a specific slice of the summer camp market, particularly older teens who had started to age out of it, and traditional camp leaders shared Petzoldt's concern that "adventure is going out of kids' lives."[31]

Petzoldt's immediate inspiration came from his experience in the Colorado Outward Bound School (COBS), established in Marble, Colorado in 1961. This first US outpost of Outward Bound modeled itself on the British organization begun in 1941 to improve young men's preparation for the armed services. The mission on both sides of the Atlantic was to instill resilience by testing one's physical and emotional limits in outdoor challenges. As *Time* characterized it in 1962, Outward Bound taught "Character, the Hard Way." The daily fare consisted of a "dawn-to-dusk schedule of running, rope climbing, weightlifting, marathon hiking, survival camping, and icy dips in mountain streams. It was a 26-day test of spirit, stamina, and sacrifice," no less than the "moral equivalent of war."[32] Petzoldt signed on as COBS's chief mountaineering advisor in 1963, but became dismayed at the lack of outdoor skills and experience among the enthusiastic instructors. He lobbied to establish an instructor training program to support safe, "healthy, manly, authentic adventure." COBS leadership agreed in principle but rejected his proposal for a satellite school dedicated to instructor training.[33] By then, Petzoldt had developed some reservations about the Outward Bound model itself. If traditional summer camps spent too much time on "fun and games," he believed that COBS overemphasized struggle and treated "the wild outdoors" primarily as an adversary to be conquered. The happy medium, Petzoldt believed, lay in camping, the foundation for outdoor skills and pleasures alike. As he told COBS staff in 1964, "maybe it's more important for the boys to learn . . . how to camp and take care of the forest" than to focus solely on the "physical thing" and confronting "stress/challenge" situations.[34]

Petzoldt decided to build an independent program around camping adventures. In January 1965, he recruited some friends to form a board of directors and incorporated the National Outdoor Leadership School as an independent, nonprofit, educational institution. He began writing dozens of letters a day to high schools and universities and giving slide lectures at elite Eastern prep schools and colleges to recruit students to sign up that summer.[35] In a tape recording of one lecture, he touted the rugged landscape as ripe for adventure and key to the school's appeal: "The classroom is the entire Wind River Mountain Range" where students would learn amidst "beautiful mountains, . . . glacial valleys, . . . and more than a thousand lakes stocked with trout."[36] Before long the 1965 season was fully enrolled.

It was no accident that Petzoldt highlighted the Wyoming backcountry as a unique feature of NOLS. The Wind River Mountains occupy a rugged and remote region of 13,000-foot peaks, glacial lakes and valleys, alpine meadows, and rocky plateaus of granite and limestone. They straddle the Continental Divide and fall within the 2.4-million-acre Shoshone National Forest. Portions also sit within the Wind River Indian Reservation, part of the traditional territory of the Eastern Shoshone, who live there along with relocated Northern Arapaho groups. The political history of the region was complex, as the Wind River Basin also records the presence of and conflict among groups of Crow, Cheyenne, Blackfeet, and Lakota, along with federal treaty negotiations, land cessions and seizures, and law suits. The mountain range anchors the southwestern portion of the Yellowstone ecosystem, with the national park proper on the Northwest side. With the passage of the Wilderness Act in 1964, just a year before NOLS began operations, the Wind Rivers gained protection as one of the first designated areas in the nation's new Wilderness system.[37]

This history made the Wind Rivers a different kind of public nature than the loop campground, though no less so for the remote, seemingly pristine terrain. Cultural investments in ideas and spaces of wilderness fostered new possibilities, and pitfalls. Wilderness areas like the Wind Rivers gained specific protections against most forms of resource extraction and infrastructure development, including roads and campgrounds, and thus became ripe for "backcountry" recreation. The lessons Petzoldt could teach, the experiences campers hoped to have, and the narratives of adventure and survival were possible in the Wind Rivers in a way they weren't in more developed areas. The national attention to these spaces as "wilderness" lent the pursuits of the fledging school a new social significance.[38]

As one hundred students headed toward the small town of Lander, Wyoming and this "new 'college of camping,'" Petzoldt scrambled to get ready for them. He leased a building to serve as headquarters, lured former

COBS staff members, and bought camping equipment from military surplus dealers.[39] He planned the curriculum to include basic skills like orienteering, cooking, fishing, and outfitting, as well as high-altitude breathing techniques and how to wield an axe and butcher game. More thrilling lessons would focus on rock climbing, traversing wild rivers, and navigating glaciers. But, as Petzoldt told a reporter that summer, what they were "really trying to teach" was good judgment, self-awareness, and group cooperation—essential habits of backcountry camping and community building alike.[40] The local press eagerly promoted NOLS, with Lander boosters hoping to raise the area's profile as a tourist gateway. Wire services picked up on the quirky story, which Petzoldt parlayed into wider publicity. He declared success before the summer of 1965 was out, making audacious predictions in the local paper: "We expect to expand the course next year. We'll even have a course for girls."[41] Privately, Petzoldt offered a more sober review of the first season, calling for a series of curricular revisions including "a stronger emphasis" on "practical conservation" as a mechanism for camping skills, individual reflection, and social goals.[42]

As NOLS developed its messages and experience around the social and personal benefits of nature, it created an opening for countercultural interpretations. This convergence was neither a deliberate strategy nor an inevitable outcome. NOLS was, after all, still a program focused on outdoor skills. The backcountry neither harbored innately rebellious tendencies, nor was NOLS populated by self-declared members of countercultural communities. Rather, the School provided a platform where participants used backcountry experiences for personal discovery. Social scientist and public opinion analyst Daniel Yankelovich, among the first to characterize the postwar generation as "baby boomers," set out to understand shifting beliefs and attitudes of college youth in the late 1960s. His research team classified a whole series of countercultural impulses within a broader outlook they labeled "new naturalism." On a basic level, this perspective rendered all things "natural" to be good, and anything synthetic as bad, but it also reflected hopes for a "new world view, a philosophy of nature capable of transforming man's relationship to himself and society." The 1972 report enumerated multiple manifestations, from "living physically close to nature" and prioritizing sensory experience to encouraging self-knowledge and cooperative community.[43] NOLS gave young people a chance to live those values, one month at a time.

The more Petzoldt reached across the generational divide, the more young folks signed up. Where 100 students had enrolled in 1965, the summers of 1966–1968 saw the enrollment climb to an average of 144. In 1969, 231 students, average age nineteen, followed Petzoldt into the Wind Rivers.[44] Given its constituency and the context of the times, it is no surprise that NOLS was entangled with such issues as the Vietnam War, psychedelic drugs, and new social mores.[45] The strongest connections emerged in several components of the new naturalist tendency: validating youth agency and expression, pursuing self-discovery, prioritizing cooperative interdependence above social artifice, and living in close contact with nature.[46]

Petzoldt often empathized with young people's sense of alienation, their distaste for "phoniness," and the frustrations of feeling powerless over their own lives. He told prospective students that NOLS was a place where they would not be "poked in the belly every day by their parents, or by the law, or by their professor telling them what to think and how to think." Instead, he gave the younger generation a vote of confidence: "Kids nowadays are just wonderful. . . . Morally they're so much better than we were. . . . They have more concern for their fellow men; they have more concern for the world and their country. . . . I think they will make the world a helluva lot better place than they found it."[47] Other leaders in organized camping were unconvinced. For them, teenagers who strained against the structure and values of traditional summer camps presented a management problem. As one camp director put it in 1968, "Today's young counselors are different. Many of them come with a strong tendency to use camp for expression of their social convictions and desires for social change. There is a tendency to demonstrate self-determination and the ability to exercise leadership. Attempts are often made to introduce new ways of life." Though one might "try to understand them," camps had to contain these kids and their "new mores" and stave off "hidden or open rebellion."[48] Petzoldt, conversely, embraced these impulses and welcomed youth into NOLS leadership by recruiting new instructors from the ranks of recent graduates. One student promoted to instructor in this era recalled, "It was the best thing in the world for a bunch of young people to have an old man (so he seemed to us) listening to our ideas and letting us do things. . . . We were empowered." Young people had real input in curriculum development and decision-making in the upstart organization and began to shape the NOLS experience in their own image.[49]

Of all the desires embedded in new naturalism, NOLS most strongly dramatized the possibilities of nature as a vehicle for self-discovery. Publicity and teachings were shot through with language about young Americans "finding themselves." Petzoldt tended to embed this in affirmations of the need for adventure, which he saw as a "better way for youth to discover themselves, get confidence, learn what they can do."[50] Students took the idea even farther. More than self-confidence, they made it about finding their whole person, their true and natural self. Part and parcel to this journey were sensory experiences, which took them beyond the constraints of daily life and expectations. "Catching a large trout, glissading down the glaciers, climbing a new peak, expeditioning through spectacular mountains are enjoyments of body and spirit that cannot be translated into words." Such experiences led to "relaxation, recreation, rejuvenation, and self evaluation."[51] Petzoldt was fond of saying that the wilderness was a better target for personal exploration than, say, mind-expanding drugs, and yet they represented two routes to a similar destination: transcendence leading to self-discovery. One student shared the personal insights he gained in the Wind Rivers: one of the "things that I really enjoy up here was hiking, knowing where you are in a map and where you're going because so many people in life they're just running all over like a chicken with his head cut off. They don't really know where they're going and where they're at. . . . Here you learn where your head is."[52]

Self-discovery led not only inside one's own head, but also toward cooperative interdependence. NOLS fostered this move as well, both in concept and practice. Good camping, or "expedition behavior," as Petzoldt preached it, was only possible with solid community relationships, "individual to individual, individual to the group, group to the individual, group to other group." Bad expedition behavior was "a breakdown in human relations caused by selfishness, rationalization, ignorance of personal faults, dodging blame or responsibility." Petzoldt offered the backcountry as a prime spot of public nature to imagine a new social contract, an opportunity to create a better world in microcosm. "This little society we have in the hills has an entirely new system of values."[53] Students took it to heart. As one marveled,

> It's like your whole way of life changes. The values that you use in the city are so different than when you're in the wilderness . . . because what counts is what you're actually doing. . . . It doesn't matter who I voted for or, or the length of my hair or anything. It's just a very real set of values and it gives you a very fine, a very pronounced disgust for, for the other set of values.[54]

NOLS enabled and nurtured visions like this, where wild nature could serve as a meaningful catalyst for personal journeys and cultural change alike.

NOLS also drew from youth activists in challenging social barriers and consumer capitalism. Petzoldt admired the efforts of youth who were "really breaking down the prejudices," and while still largely attracting young white college-going men, he affirmed a belief in diversity in 1968: "We desire students from as many different social, economic and ethnic backgrounds as possible." Partly in order to fill camps in the first summer, Petzoldt came up with a unique scholarship program that served those goals. Anyone who asked for assistance received it and agreed simply to "Pay Back When Able" (PBWA). NOLS continued the open-ended PBWA scholarship in the following years, though by 1969 he worried that it wasn't doing enough to encourage "poor kids and black kids" to sign up.[55] Still, NOLS continued public affirmations of equal access and social justice. Moreover, the PBWA system resonated with countercultural movements like the Diggers and the Yippies who experimented with alternatives to money, consumerism, and capitalism.[56] In a sense, NOLS was operating with a "free store" kind of mentality—giving enrollment away, with the promise to pay back when able, without interest or formal loan terms. The commitment to open access aligned with those who sought to move beyond conventional lines of social authority.

The decision to go coed in 1966 also resonated with challenges to social hierarchies, though it revealed complex cultural tensions. In part as a way to increase enrollment and revenue in the second year, Petzoldt planned a modified course for girls that would parallel, and occasionally merge with, the one for boys.[57] The program started small with eleven young women joining, but by 1971 women comprised one-third of the overall enrollment. Initially women covered fewer miles and carried less weight in their packs, using horses to tote some of the food and equipment. But as films, photographs, and press reports showed, many activities were undertaken together, such as rock climbing and other areas of technical instruction. The end-of-course survival test was optional for women, but when they did join, men and women were fully integrated in the patrols under the same rules. This gradually became the norm.[58]

Despite these moves toward gender parity, a great deal of the publicity surrounding women's participation emphasized the novelty of their appearance in the wilderness and the feminine qualities they brought to it. Writing for the outdoorsmen who read *Field & Stream*, Raye Price pitched her 1968 article about women on NOLS courses as a suburban fantasy: "Imagine your little lady drumming up a supper of fried trout, pilaf, Spring Beauty salad, fresh baked bread, and Apple Betty at 11,000 feet. Not as a hostess in a jet kitchen, mind you, but . . . around your tent in a wilderness imitation of a three-room house, fireplace and all."[59] Remarks about female students' physical appearance reinforced the idea that they retained femininity in the wild. One of the first female instructors, Lee Tapley, noted, "Most persons think

NOLS women students are big, burly P.E. majors. They might be P.E. majors, but the majority are lithe attractive girls who are just as interested in bathing in the icy lakes and tucking wildflowers into their braids as grubbing their way to the top of a pinnacle." In response to a question from the press—"What kind of girl wants to learn about survival in the wilderness?"—Petzoldt put it a little more baldly. "Boy they are attractive! We've had real beauties. Like Nikki Peck, Miss Indiana 1968 (and now Mrs. Joe Nixon)."[60] NOLS leaders regularly hinted at the school's matchmaking roles, perhaps countering fears that female students were lesbians, at the time often lobbed as a pejorative label at feminists and athletic women. Petzoldt defended women's fitness and encouraged their success and female graduates from this era recalled experiences of liberation. Still, gendered tropes about beauty, roles, and heterosexual marriage competed with messages of equality.[61]

By 1969, youth activists hoping for peaceful social and cultural change met with challenges at every turn and more sought a way out of mainstream society by taking refuge in nature. A back-to-the-land movement resurfaced among a new generation. Alongside dreams of self-sufficiency, rural communes envisioned new relationships among people as well as with the land. NOLS was not a commune, but it shared certain outlooks about the benefits of living in close contact with nature. As one frustrated nineteen-year-old woman considering joining a commune wrote, "Right now, I'm trying to keep from being swallowed by a monster—plastic, greedy American society. . . . I need to begin relating to new people who are into taking care of each other and the earth." Many communal experiments proved to be ephemeral, and some failed disastrously, partly due to the lack of experience in rural modes of living or production among young suburbanites, including the letter writer herself, who admitted she knew "nothing about farming." Yet the idea remained an attractive one. Most communes even in their short existence were open to visitors and encouraged nonmembers to come and observe. By some estimates, half a million Americans had done so, and in 1971, some 43 percent of college students reported interest in living off the land for at least a short time.[62]

Abandoning college, career, and urban life for a farm represented a radical choice that only a small minority made. For those who tried to create whole new societies as part of the Open Land movement, particularly in California and the Pacific Northwest, their "outlaw territories" sought to escape the constraints of private property and establish some form of communal guardianship. These efforts often ran afoul of state laws and local codes, resulting in shut downs based on various charges, from health and safety violations, to using tents as "illegal shelters" and operating an organized camp without a permit.[63] For those seeking a more moderate path, NOLS offered back-country camping to connect with people who were "into taking care of each other and the earth" without necessarily questioning private property. In that way, it maintained stronger ties to the recreational ethos and the consumer pursuit of temporary respite than revolutionary approaches. It simultaneously critiqued mainstream culture using sentiments similar to the new back-to-the-landers and reinforced the use of leisure for demonstrating self-reliance.

Why the editors of *Life* decided in 1969 to profile Petzoldt in the magazine and produce a documentary film about NOLS for national distribution remains unclear. The School was certainly riding the crest of a wave of curiosity and Madison Avenue hype about hippies and communes, and a bunch of long-haired kids traipsing about the mountains with an outdoor guru certainly seemed to fit the part.[64] The media organization hired three young filmmakers, Michael Wadleigh (director), Fred Underhill (camera operator), and Charles Grosbeck (sound engineer) to follow a NOLS course that summer. Just twenty-seven, Wadleigh applied his experience as the cinematographer for a handful of independent and experimental films and planned to minimize scripting and prompting. He would capture events as they happened using natural light and sound. Grosbeck recalled, "We didn't affect their experience. We became one of them." Students, most of whom were unaware of the project before arriving, got used to the presence of the cameras, which "were always on. There was never any set up, never any second takes."[65]

The film opened with Petzoldt and his central beliefs about outdoor adventure and admiration for youth but it quickly shifted to the students, as they set up camp, built bonfires, and fished for trout to cook for dinner. It contrasted students' nervous first attempts at cliffside rappels and slow ascents up dramatic snow-covered passes, as the *Life* magazine ad shown in Figure 5.3 featured, with peaceful scenes of hiking in a shaded forest and gathering flowers in a meadow. The physical movements of the students and conversations among them drove the action. The pastiche of experiences portrayed a sense of generational discovery and a feeling of peace and simplicity of nature.[66]

The climax of the film, the survival test, began about forty minutes into the hour. Petzoldt indicated that the goal was to measure "psychological" resilience as much as "raw survival" skills. He admitted, "We know they'll get lost. We know there'll be indecision, argument, and frustration." The question was, how would they respond? Could they find their way out by working together? Zooming in on a coed five-person team led by sixteen-year-old Tom

FIGURE 5.3 Adventures in self-discovery. "The Alcoa Hour: Thirty Days to Survival," *Life*, January 9, 1970, 100–101. Photograph by Martin Epp.

Day, much of the drama revolved around campers' negotiations about what to do with food rations accidentally brought along. The test was supposed to involve living entirely off the land, without back-up meals. Some wanted to burn the unauthorized provisions; others wanted to keep them for emergency purposes. After failing to catch any fish for dinner on the first day, the group embarked on a discussion that resonated with the communal and countercultural ethos. More than the food itself, they wanted to "reach a decision, you know, a *true* decision," as Tom put it.[67] In the end they compromised, allowing a short window for those who wanted to eat, and then burying the remainder.

When the group tumbled down from the hills into the Dry Creek river valley, near Burris, Wyoming, Petzoldt was there to greet them with bear hugs and cups of milk. When the youngest camper pushed to the front, Petzoldt intervened, reminding the thirteen-year-old of the experience he had just survived: "Now you know what civilization is. . . . [T]he only meaning of culture is how much you can control yourself and your own jungle instincts in relation to your fellow men. So why should you grab first? Give it to the girl first."[68] Survival wasn't every man for himself, but rather how to create and preserve a good society. From the protracted negotiations over what to do about the food to Petzoldt's final lesson, the film allowed viewers to witness the re-creation of a new social contract from a state of nature.

Wadleigh and Underhill had barely come out of the Wind Rivers before rushing to the other side of the country to film the Woodstock festival. The director never said that his experience with NOLS influenced *Woodstock*, but the theme of youth "going back to the garden" permeated both films. Wadleigh envisioned the central story of Woodstock as being "like *The Canterbury Tales*, or *Pilgrim's Progress*. It's really a timeless idea where you see kids streaming out of the cities that are so dirty and complex and pollution-ridden and crime-ridden, coming to the countryside. You know, back to the land, back to the garden, to sort of this pristine natural setting that has the lakes and trees and so on, and the innocence of nature."[69] Both films relied on the premise that connecting with nature could be a path out of the troubled world, and that young people were the ones leading the way. In *Woodstock*, like "Thirty Days to Survival," Wadleigh chose to make the kids who made the pilgrimage to be there as much the stars as the musicians. Images of young people, camping and living together outdoors, amidst the beauty of nature, dominated both films, though not all viewers were fans of the hippie style of encampment.[70]

One New York reporter found "Thirty Days to Survival" to be a kind of antidote to the Woodstock scene: "During this time of hippies, junkies and other social dropouts, here was a feature that gave one hope for and renewed one's faith in the youth of this country." And yet college students claimed the show as their own, not a message preached to them from their elders.[71] Whatever viewers took away from these films, Petzoldt was pleased with the exposure "Thirty Days to Survival" netted for NOLS. While he found the film "a little dramatic," he was thrilled with its wide distribution and expected "a considerable increase in inquiries . . . as a result." Rob Hellyer, an instructor featured in "Thirty Days to Survival," remembered that any debate about the accuracy of the film was "quickly drowned out by the sound of the telephone," as viewers clamored to apply.[72] From taking 231 students in 1969, NOLS enrolled 989 in concurrent courses for the 1970 season. Even that did not satisfy demand, and NOLS planned to start winter courses and establish branch outlets, first in New England in 1970, and soon thereafter in Alaska, Baja California, and Tennessee.[73]

Petzoldt's repeated refrains about adventure and self-discovery clearly struck a chord with American youth in 1970. Momentarily isolated from parental and social pressures, students could express new values, try out countercultural identities, and try on new naturalist sensibilities in a land-scape they viewed as untainted and pristine—a wilderness Woodstock in miniature. Tom Day, the group leader from "Thirty Days to Survival," recalled arriving on a PBWA scholarship without much sense that what awaited him would be "a life-changing experience." Petzoldt acknowledged that this was, in many ways, an experience of students' own making. "We don't try to preach. We have nothing to sell. . . . We're not trying to make them establishment or anti-establishment. . . . We do hope that people get a great spiritual feeling and great experience out of the wilderness. They do, but they do it in their own way."[74] In the years that took NOLS from a shoestring start-up to national fame, the younger generation practiced a way of camping attuned to new social outlooks. And for parents who were footing the $450 bill, perhaps there was enough resonance with the ethos of family camping and summer camps that made such expressions seem somehow less threatening than other countercultural choices. Backcountry camping became a kind of rucksack revolution and a popular new segment in outdoor recreation.

"The New Ethic of the Wild Outdoors"

For all the new naturalist sentiments, NOLS had a striking lack of emphasis on conservation and ecology in its early years. Scattered mention of conservation techniques, intended to foster camping enjoyment and preserve wilderness for future recreation, did appear before 1970. Yet "Thirty Days to Survival," its largest publicity vehicle, included no discussion of this issue. Considering that the first Earth Day arrived just three months after the documentary's broadcast, demonstrating rising national concerns about ecology, pollution, and the environment, this seems surprising. Petzoldt had been, as he would claim in 1971, "preaching conservation" for decades, but up to that point ecology had taken a back seat to adventure and self-discovery at NOLS. This changed as a result of the 1970 convergence of the school's surging popularity and the emergence of the environmental movement.[75] The swift growth forced Petzoldt both to look inward, toward the school's own practices, and outward, to relate its teachings to larger ecological dilemmas. Together with students' and instructors' rising interests in ecology, this pushed new understandings of conservation to the forefront of NOLS' mission. Petzoldt aimed to position NOLS as a leader in defining environmental standards for the growing legions of backcountry campers. In the process, outdoor practicalities fused with environmental activism and new visions of the social contract.

That NOLS managed to accommodate nearly one thousand students in 1970 was a logistical feat. In accomplishing it, school leaders began to wrestle with the effects of many more pairs of hiking boots. Petzoldt insisted that NOLS' attention to "clean camping" minimized the group's impact, to the extent that "I have seen a group of four in a camp do more damage conservation-wise in one week than our students do in one year." Whether he could make the same boast with so many more students, was an open question. Many of NOLS' practices remained tied to older traditions of outdoorsmanship. Rifle shooting and dressing game, along with chopping wood and building bonfires, were standard lessons in the late 1960s. Making use of on-site resources was a common assumption of backwoods campers and a central element of the survival test.[76] One student from this era recalled enjoying the chance to carry a .22 caliber rifle, "to slay hundreds of fish and build bonfires," where at the time he would have found "the notion of cruising through the woods and not doing anything, just walking lightly through the woods was weird." Early NOLS courses included more focus on ecology and conservation than students might have remembered, but they did so largely in service to practical skills and personal enjoyment. As Petzoldt told one group of students, "the reason why we're telling you some things about . . . the nature of the country is not that we want to teach you biology or ecology," but rather it is "just another way of learning to enjoy the outdoors."[77]

The growth that came as a result of "Thirty Days to Survival" forced rethinking such practices and the rationale behind them. Following the summer of 1970, NOLS received some local criticism. One woman wrote into the town's newspaper asking, "Why can't they leave our beautiful [landscape] alone?" She objected both to the number and kind of people NOLS brought into the Wind Rivers. "The way some of them was dressed this summer was enough to make you sick." Rumors circulated that fall about NOLS as a hippie bacchanal, laying waste to mountains and morals alike. Others wrote in to defend the School, even as they worried about the increasing impact. One expressed that he was "ashamed" that "the general public is blaming NOLS for their own dirty work" and believed the "unfounded rumors" arose from "prejudice" against the "type of students in your school . . . [the] so-called beatniks." Whether due to environmental or cultural issues, Shoshone and Arapaho communities from the Wind River Indian Reservation also soured on NOLS operations in this era, though evidently continued to grant some permits for programs on their lands. Petzoldt went on a charm offensive in the local papers in hopes of quashing local disgruntlement, though the rift with the Native community lingered for decades.[78]

In response to these external pressures and the challenges of increased enrollment, NOLS redoubled its conservation efforts. Ahead of the 1971 season, Petzoldt admitted that the school's popularity had "exceeded our capacity" and announced an enrollment limit of 900, a 10 percent decrease from the previous year. That spring, the School newsletter, the *Alumnus*, suggested a new emphasis on conservation principles. Teaching "how to live in the wilderness and still leave it in a fit condition for the next person" and training students to "do little or no injury, and leave practically no evidence of their passage" became central.[79] In October, Petzoldt touted, "This summer NOLS made great strides toward working out even better methods of conservation. We now practice methods where we leave no fire scars, no branches broken off trees, no permanent damage of any kind." He further mandated that students, now sporting NOLS badges, remediate any damage they discovered: they "picked up the 'tourist droppings,' cleaned up campsites, and obliterated old fire scars. . . . So instead of harming the beauty (or ecosystem) of the wilderness, we are improving" it.[80] While conservation had long been an element of the curriculum, NOLS had begun to communicate new approaches and commitment to treading lightly on the land, rather than living off it.

This shift became obvious in the changing information NOLS gave prospective students over the course of the early 1970s. Where the 1968 pamphlet held "practical conservation" to be a "second purpose," the 1972 course description elevated it to an "important purpose" though it still followed the standard invocation that "youth demands adventure." The 1973 version led with ecological imperatives: NOLS is "a non-profit organization dedicated to teaching people how to enjoy the natural wilderness without destroying it. Our goal, broadly stated, is to encourage a reverence for our remaining wild areas through training in all aspects of ecology and outdoorsmanship." Lower down was the claim that "a NOLS expedition is an adventure experience."[81] This reversed earlier priorities, yet the combination of ecology and outdoorsmanship suggested that NOLS still had one foot in each of these paradigms. Petzoldt acknowledged that "expansion has forced on us a new concern with conservation" and now hoped NOLS could formulate a "new understanding of what it is to 'go camping.'" By 1974, the School announced plans "to expand and experiment with new and advanced conservation techniques" so that "our wilderness areas" might "stand the test of time."[82]

By the December 1975 issue of the *Alumnus*, NOLS' mission appeared wholly transformed. It incorporated language and concepts almost exclusively from the new, ecological paradigm. Unlike previous covers of the magazine that featured Petzoldt or NOLS students in action—kayaking rapids, digging snowcaves, or performing a rope-traverse—this issue's cover was absent of humans. The subject of the full-page photograph was a stand of trees with a large owl perched on a branch. The inside cover featured an evocative pen-and-ink image of a gnarled, old-growth tree, again unaccompanied by hearty outdoor adventurers. Below the image, a single, centered paragraph issued what looked like a new mission statement: "Conservation practices are the most important part of a NOLS expedition. Our ideas are spreading far and wide, combining with the thinking of others and evolving to fit various environmental requirements. They are not meant to be fixed rules, but tools of consciousness, expressions of our sense of responsibility to our mother earth."[83] The connection to outdoorsmanship was gone, and conservation was presented as the central purpose. "Tools of consciousness" hearkened to the countercultural focus on self-discovery, but here "self" is muted in favor of "responsibility to our mother earth." This shift highlighted the growth of a new ideal of public nature where backcountry recreation forged a new environmental-social consciousness.

NOLS was just one manifestation of this new camping concept, and in the 1970s the popularity of backpacking swelled.[84] The 1962 ORRRC national outdoor recreation survey did not include backpacking among twenty enumerated activities in its initial questionnaire, but by 1982, a similar survey suggested that nine million Americans, as many as twenty percent of all campers, had participated in backpacking in the prior year alone.[85] The tipping point seemed to arrive the early 1970s. The *New York Times* printed a multipage article in 1971 announcing the arrival of "a backpacking boom that has practically revolutionized American outdoor life," estimating, perhaps generously, that as many as 20 million Americans had tried some form of backpacking. The boom touched many public lands, just as family camping had in prior decades. At Shenandoah National Park, for example, backcountry camping climbed from 34,000 in 1967 to 121,000 six years later.[86]

Beyond the numbers, backpacking gained a new set of cultural associations that echoed the trajectory at NOLS. The wave of environmental organizing crested in the early 1970s and spread "new naturalist" outlooks to multiple groups of Americans who sought to connect with nature in a different manner. Whether it arose from interests in wilderness preservation and wildlife protection or movements to control pollution and encourage recycling, new ecological awareness lent backpacking a distinct sensibility. The 1972 Yankelovich study of American youth argued that "among the most potent" of student challenges was the attempt "to stop our frantic rush to bend nature to the human will and instead to restore a vital, more harmonious—and more humble—balance with nature." This involved no less than a complete change in the "conception of man's relationship to a nature, that is no longer seen as infinite, brutish, and something to be mastered with the bulldozer, but as finite, precious, fragile and essentially good." Backpacking and the recreational ethos aligned with this framing. Many now looked to backcountry experience to find harmony more than adventure, or as one scholar termed it, from "*conquering* 'nature' to *communing* with it."[87]

Over the prior decade, sentiment for preservation had been gathering support beyond the younger generation. Legislative breakthroughs like the bipartisan passage of the Wilderness Act in 1964 and the Wild and Scenic Rivers Act in 1968 preserved swaths of land and waterways from most forms of development. Organizations like the Sierra Club gained national prominence as thousands of Americans protested dams, pollution, and other encroachments on wild lands. Well before Earth Day, cultural attitudes toward the outdoors were undergoing something of a metamorphosis. Preservation would continue to be divisive in practice, as competing factions wrestled over the relative costs of protective designations and development in particular places. But the language of the Wilderness Act itself was telling. It committed the nation to preserving spaces explicitly defined "in contrast with those areas where man and his own works dominate the landscape . . . [and] as an area where the earth and its community of life are untrammeled by man, where man himself is a visitor who does not remain." This represented a novel framework for enjoying and advocating for nature.[88]

The Wilderness Act gave a boost to the still niche pursuit of backpacking by constraining development of motorized recreation and permanent infrastructure, including loop campgrounds. The nation's most famous backpacker in the 1960s was Colin Fletcher, who took epic solo treks in the Sierras and the Grand Canyon. Readers followed his adventures and philosophical reveries about backcountry experience in several of his bestselling books, and aspiring backpackers snapped up his how-to guide, *The Complete Walker* (1968). Before 350 pages of practical instructions, the opening chapter asked, "Why walk?" Fletcher's answers praised being "free to go out . . . into the wildest places you dare explore" and emphasized the reward of enlightenment and "release" that came with "sleeping away from officially consecrated campsites." He described this as a process of "re-remember[ing]. . . . By slow degrees, you regain a sense of harmony with everything you move through—rock and soil, plant and tree and cactus, spider and fly and rattlesnake and coyote, drop of rain and racing cloud shadow."[89]

Backpackers—perhaps the one pictured in Figure 5.4—felt the pull of Fletcher's words. The 1971 *New York Times* feature noted that " 'nature,' 'natural,' 'green,' 'clean,' 'silent,' 'simple,' 'unchanging' are words backpackers frequently used when pressed to explain their infatuation with the wilderness." One enthusiast gave his own answer to "Why Walk?": "I go to the wilderness

FIGURE 5.4 A young backpacker contemplates the trail ahead. Captured as part of an effort by the recently created Environmental Protection Agency to "photographically document subjects of environmental concern," backpacking aligned with new ecological mindsets. Photograph by Anne La Bastille, Adirondack Forest Preserve, New York, 1973, for DOCUMERICA, Records of the Environmental Protection Agency, 554570, 412-DA-12118.

to kick the man-world out of me," to find himself as just "a part of the web of life, . . . the wholeness of the universe."[90] NOLS students shared this vocabulary. One student signed up for a 1971 course in hopes of sharing "the beauty of outdoor living" with those who did not treat nature "as a battleground." She was pleased to find that NOLS "was not the usual type of survival school where Man vs. Nature is the usual motto" but instead taught "that man can live with Nature." These images contrasted with the ones emanating from the late phase of the Vietnam War, where the jungle appeared both battleground and enemy, and "survival" was a very different proposition. In the 1972 NOLS film *High on the Wind Rivers*, several students reflected on the feelings of harmony the outdoors could bring under the right conditions. "When you get into an environment such as this it all blends in and there's a oneness about it. Whether it's sitting by a river or climbing a mountain, it's the feeling that you have within you."[91]

If communing with nature pulled many into backpacking, anxiety about overpopulation pushed them out of the city and into the wilderness, seeking relief from the experience of crowds. Concern about population growth, percolating for some decades, spiked in the wake of Stanford biologist Paul Ehrlich's *The Population Bomb* (1968). Talk about population became ubiquitous, shaping discussions at the policy level and in the popular press around a host of social, cultural, and economic issues.[92] It even found its way into the Wilderness Act, which had suggested that preservation of natural spaces could alleviate population pressure. "To assure that an increasing population . . . does not occupy and modify all areas," represented a key reason to set aside for "present and future generations the benefits of an enduring resource of wilderness." This open space might in fact prove crucial for future "survival"—a buzzword permeating much environmental rhetoric—on multiple levels. As a former NOLS instructor turned medical student put it, "good mental and physical health is dependent in large part upon a clean, natural environment," and "outdoor living" offered a "solution" to the problems that came with crowded cities. He quipped: "This communing with nature thing may sound trite, but we may be headed the way of the lemmings!"[93] Backpacking and NOLS sat in the thick of this discourse about the dangers of overpopulation.

Preserving wilderness might not reduce unsustainable population growth rates, but it could address what Ehrlich labeled the "feel" of overpopulation, which drove a good deal of the cultural dialogue around population issues.[94] Outdoor recreation venues like national parks became key areas to measure the impact of this feeling, as these ostensible counterpoints to congested cities instead became poignant examples of the effects of overcrowding. An Interior Department report, titled *The Race for Inner Space*, testified to this as early as 1964. The opening pages juxtaposed cookie cutter suburbs with majestic redwoods, a packed parking lot in the shadow of Yosemite's Half Dome. Set against the fascination with exploring outer space, the imperative to figure out how to share space on "this earth" loomed large. The more people crowded in on each other, the more they needed "close contact with the natural environment" to maintain "emotional balance and spiritual equilibrium." Despite Interior's efforts to provide such opportunities, it bemoaned its own inability to keep pace: "Against the mounting pressures from population, pollution, and the intensifying battle for elbow room . . . our seeming gains fall short even of holding our own." The report feared a time when "even our small scraps of wilderness will have to be rationed . . . [and] the rest of our outdoor experience may have to come from packed amusement parks, shoulder to shoulder beaches, and table-to-table picnic grounds."[95] Or, tent-to-tent loop campgrounds.

When the very spaces that were supposed to provide relief from the stress of overcrowding—parks and campgrounds—were packed to the gills, anxieties escalated. In *Life*'s special issue on outdoor recreation, published in

September of 1971, the whiplash between the joys of being outdoors and the problems of overpopulation was dizzying. Articles and images veered back and forth from extolling sublime nature to descrying "apocalyptic weekend traffic jams" and the inevitable culture clash between "an older generation of mechanized campers and young people trying to re-create Woodstock, complete with drugs, amplified music, and casual nudity." What happened when "more and more of us head into less and less country," only to find places "increasingly similar to what it was we were trying to escape"?[96] A 1973 US Forest Service survey found that among people who had a negative image of camping, 32 percent listed "crowded conditions" as one of the top two problems. The figure was even higher among those who reported having given up camping, temporarily or permanently, suggesting that it was a leading cause driving people away. Even among those who held a positive image of camping, "uncrowded" was seldom mentioned as a favorable characteristic.[97]

Desires for contact with nature and desperation to escape crowds drove interest in backpacking as a temporary respite from the feel of overpopulation. The Wilderness Act had included as one of its rationales the "outstanding opportunities for solitude" found in "primitive and unconfined type[s] of recreation." Colin Fletcher endorsed the sentiment: "By walking out alone into wilderness I can elude the pressures of the pounding modern world, ... in the sanctity of silence and solitude—the solitude seems to be a very important part of it."[98] The 1971 *Life* special issue featured "Six Wild Havens" where one could "go to get away from the people who are getting away from it all." It promised reward for the effort to seek out hidden "pockets of public land" that still felt empty. A 1972 *National Geographic* issue detailing Yellowstone's overcrowding problem included a long feature on a backpacking trip in remote sections of the park. The author noted that his group encountered "few people in the vast area of backcountry," despite the fact that a "motorized cavalcade of humanity" circled just a few miles away. The closing image—a lone backpacker hiking through light snow—beckoned: "Solitude and unspoiled nature can be found even in a park that plays host to two million visitors a year."[99]

Backpacking may have seemed to offer a way out of the crowds, but as more took up the practice, the crowds came with them. Tucked at the end of a 1973 National Geographic ode to *Wilderness U.S.A.* was "A Backpacking Primer" that hinted at this. In contrast to the sublime nature photography of the previous 300 pages, largely devoid of people other than small groups of adventurers playing in unpeopled landscapes, the illustration for the how-to guide, shown in Figure 5.5, was jarring. In a remarkable parallel to the "Call of

FIGURE 5.5 The crowded trail to a hopeful backcountry paradise at the end of the rainbow. Illustration by Dill Cole, in Seymour L. Fishbein, ed., *Wilderness U.S.A.* (Washington, DC: National Geographic Society, 1973), 328.

the Not So Wild" cover of *Time* from 1961, it crammed rows of backpackers, marching in lockstep through a wasteland of stoplights and fire hydrants toward the rainbow's end. Their packs toted unlikely contraptions into the wilderness: toilets and bathtubs, televisions and antennas, bedframes and refrigerators. If the green space and blue skies they hiked toward seemed a welcome respite after the heavy traffic, that all these backpackers could share the space or find solitude there seemed questionable. Given the crush, the author recommended techniques and equipment that would allow the backpacker to "lessen his impact on the wild lands," which was "crucial . . . if wilderness is to survive."[100] The illustrator seemed less sure of the efficacy of this compromise. Was the wilderness at the end of the rainbow paradise, a mirage, or an endangered sanctuary soon to be overrun?

In the spring of 1973, *Backpacker* magazine was born on the horns of this dilemma: how to share the passion for communing with nature without exacerbating the problems that came with so many communers. In his opening "Note from the Publisher," William Kelmsley Jr. admitted that the editorial team had debated the morality of their endeavor: "Since the increased numbers of backpackers are now threatening the backcountry from overuse, how then could we justify publishing a magazine which would probably encourage more backpacking?" Even if wilderness experience might make individuals "more respectful of the environment, . . . the great influx" of backcountry users meant that it was "safer not to encourage more backpacking."[101] The solution Kelmsley presented was awkward at best. They planned to "*limit circulation* as far as possible to those who are already backpacking," enrolling subscribers only through equipment retailers or hiking clubs and keeping issues off the shelves of newsstands or bookstores where they might attract new enthusiasts. Moreover, the magazine would not "*print stories that directly entice newcomers to the backcountry*—no stories telling how to get started, no descriptions of unspoiled paradises (which would immediately be inundated by readers) and no gushy eulogizing of the outdoors." Whether the editors could prevent the magazine from falling into the wrong hands or stop themselves from writing about their favorite places seemed doubtful. The final principle took a different tack. *Backpacker* would zealously "*promote the 'new backcountry ethic'*"—a modern, ecological social contract based on recreational contact with untrammeled wilderness. The opportunity "to encourage a deeper reverence for planet Earth, in whatever way we can" presented the most "compelling reason" for publishing.[102] Perhaps they hoped that more would adopt this perspective by reading the magazine than hitting the crowded trails.

Backpacker readers continued the debate in letters to the editor, with some endorsing the cause and the compromise and others lambasting the probable outcomes: "popularize the mass destruction of our wilderness areas" and "encourage more abuse no matter how good your intentions."[103] NOLS graduates considered similar questions in the pages of the *Alumnus*. H. B. Smith worried about the increasing "conflicts between people" as they competed for access to outdoor space but believed disseminating good conservation practices was the answer. He encouraged fellow graduates to be outdoor leaders and to help federal agencies "develop techniques and guidelines for all kinds of outdoor use." Ken Goddard replied with a more dire assessment: "The rapid growth of population . . . is a threat to us as human beings and as lovers of the wilderness. . . . Even if all visitors to wilderness areas were to practice NOLS practical conservation as they traveled and camped, the wilderness can only hold so many people before it is trampled to death, and many fewer before it ceases to give us pleasure." Without strict limits on visitor numbers, he warned, we "are cutting our own throats by introducing more people to the woods."[104] Limiting access, even as it protected landscapes, served to define backpacking as an exclusive domain, where those who already possessed the appropriate knowledge, mindset, and wherewithal could decide whether to invite new practitioners into their space.

A natural-born publicist, Petzoldt balked at this solution. He believed that reserving wilderness areas was merely "a stop-gap," reducing access "a temporary help." The only "real solution is educating ALL wilderness users in techniques of practical conservation so that they can enjoy an area and leave it in a similar state for others." Petzoldt pushed NOLS to be an incubator for improving practices and its graduates to be frontline educators.[105] In May 1973, the *Alumnus* initiated a continuing education series to keep NOLS graduates "up to date on new techniques" the school was honing. Especially for participants in earlier years, Petzoldt wanted to share newly defined "optimum behavior patterns by which we can take a group through the wilderness with virtually no damage to the environment." The long list of "essential techniques," for example, began with an eight-step protocol for fire use. Unlike the earlier days of roaring bonfires, NOLS now stipulated that fires should be small and built in holes that were refilled. Moreover, fires should not be used "for warming or social purposes," but only for cooking if a portable stove was not available. The new code permitted only the gathering and breaking of downed wood and ended instruction in "axemanship." It then continued to outline new standards for waste disposal, locating campsites, food packaging, soap use, and respect for wild animals.[106] Many items expressed rationales aimed, at least partly, to preserve experience: campers should strive to avoid "visual pollution for others," by wearing "natural colored clothing and equipment . . . to camouflage use." They should be sure to "camp out of sight" and away from meadows and lake shores where tents marred the view of "beauty spots."[107]

Petzoldt shared these recommendations with state agencies and outdoor programs and charged NOLS graduates with "spread[ing] a revolutionary wilderness outlook and camping ethic." Still, he worried. "If the wilderness is to survive the onslaught of use it is going to receive in the coming years, it is absolutely essential that users be taught to follow behavior standards such as those we have developed at NOLS." Petzoldt decided to write a book presenting NOLS' backcountry techniques to a wider audience.[108] Appearing on bookshelves in the spring of 1974, *The Wilderness Handbook* "intended to help all outdoorsmen," from beginners to veterans. The chapters included conceptual explications of survival and expedition behavior along with practical instructions on camping, climbing, and hiking. Throughout, Petzoldt accentuated the importance of minimal-impact techniques and a whole "a new code of outdoor behavior, a new ethics of outdoorsmanship."[109] In essence, the *Handbook* provided a manual for modern ecologically-minded citizens, codifying the details of a social contract grounded in the ideal of backcountry recreation as a new form of public nature. The goal of mixing one's leisure with nature was to produce greater environmental consciousness and a more sustainable future.

A chapter titled "Camping for Conservation" explained that even well-intentioned campers left eyesores and lasting damage: "fire scars along the lake shore, grasses trampled, . . . bits of food from dishwashing, where not only grease and leftovers but soap and detergent pollute pure mountain water. Flies swarm over a deserted garbage dump and piles of human excrement can be found behind bushes and rocks, ready to be washed into lake and streams." Education in proper technique was vital "to protect the environment, an increasingly vital issue which is inseparable from the art of camping."[110] While these minimal-impact techniques were yet "known only to a few," Petzoldt hoped that "if all of us can learn to use the wilderness with so little disturbance," then more rather than less might experience the joys of the backcountry and work to protect it. The *Wilderness Handbook* bore little trace of the overpopulation anxiety that gripped other outdoor leaders. Petzoldt worried more about the many who had not yet learned to experience enjoyment, solitude, and "self-renewal" in the outdoors.[111]

In *The New Wilderness Handbook*, a slightly revised version published a decade later, Petzoldt gathered personal experience, ecological responsibility, and political outlook under the single banner of "The New Ethic of the Wild Outdoors." Looking back over his lifetime, he reflected that "our ways of production, living, and coexisting" had changed dramatically. The effects of this were "very apparent in our usage and concern for the wild outdoors" as well as "revisions of our moral considerations." This entailed a new sense of collective effort, where "no longer can we tolerate the personal jeopardy and damaging environmental consequences of an outdoorsman's selfish practices." The enumerated "Standards for the New Ethic" began with self and community relationships: "Honest Self-Evaluation" and "Honesty to Others." It added benchmarks for "Conservation," "Responsibility," and "Respect" in order to protect the wilderness for the enjoyment of "the peoples of tomorrow."[112] This "New Ethic of the Wild Outdoors" represented the convergence of NOLS' philosophy, new naturalist values, backpackers' debates, and the discourse of popular environmentalism as they had evolved over the previous two decades.

The transformation of NOLS into an organization that viewed its primary mission as one of environmental awareness paralleled larger cultural shifts that had pushed issues of planetary harm and population growth to the forefront. The "minimum impact practices" Petzoldt advocated served equally to enhance personal experience and express one's environmental commitment. This form of camping thus brought political values and outdoor behavior into closer alignment. *Backpacker*'s "new backcountry ethic" offered a similar formula: "simply walking in the backcountry" cultivated "a deep respect for nature" that the editors hoped would translate into greater environmental advocacy.[113] This fusion of practice, politics, and identity made new claims on public nature, shifting the goal from the campers' republic to the ethic of the wild outdoors, from togetherness and democracy to self-discovery and environmental responsibility. What they still shared was the recreational ethos and a social contract based on leisure and consumption, a framework that led to some unintended consequences.

"Equipment That Buyers Can Trust with Their Lives"

In the years following the publication of *The Wilderness Handbook*, Petzoldt aspired to promote this New Ethic on the broadest scales. He focused on two key possibilities: developing a nationwide backcountry certification system and marketing outdoor gear to support minimum-impact practices. Petzoldt came to see that NOLS had limits to its power to disseminate knowledge and increase participation. His efforts to form a national alliance for certification and to develop his gear business would bring Petzoldt into acute tension with the still growing NOLS in the mid-1970s. These attempts highlight how increased desires to practice environmental responsibility went hand in hand with a growing consumer market in outdoor equipment such that clothing and gear could become a sign of one's environmental outlook and identity, invoking public nature far from the wilderness.

The last chapter of *The Wilderness Handbook* laid out Petzoldt's radical plan to ensure that backcountry campers learn and employ ideal methods. In short, he called for an enforcement system, whereby only those who had demonstrated their competence in minimal-impact techniques would be allowed to camp freely. "No one must be allowed in the wild outdoors until he can prove he is ecologically housebroken or at least traveling with a certified leader who will keep his group under control." A national association, financed through user fees, would oversee an education program and a "permit system" with a mandatory "test on general outdoorsmanship. . . . In time, only parties having a licensed leader would be allowed access . . . beyond the roadhead." The book included a sample "Certification Test," which called for both written answers and practical demonstrations. What he was calling for resembled the SCUBA certification system developed over the previous decade and a half, where all users were required to undergo education and training before gaining access to dive on their own. Like the SCUBA system, Petzoldt hoped certification might protect users and environment alike. There was no basis, he argued, to safeguard "freedom for the selfish, ignorant, or incompetent to pillage and destroy. . . . We must restrict some of our own rights" in order to preserve "the delights of recreation in the wild outdoors."[114]

Petzoldt hoped that NOLS could serve as a catalyst for the certification system and began to cultivate a network of public land managers, government officials, professional educators, and wilderness advocacy organizations toward that end. The Summer 1975 issue of the *Alumnus* carried a new title that exemplified this outward-facing approach: *Outdoor Education Bulletin*.[115] The public outreach, however, drew Petzoldt's attention away from internal management and into some conflict with the NOLS Board. Not least among the problems were organization finances, which had been administered in a fairly haphazard way. By 1974, the Internal Revenue Service (IRS) started looking into the books, and the following year, the board removed Petzoldt from his position as director, eventually naming him Senior Advisor and limiting his responsibility to external relations. In December 1975, the magazine, under its original title, reassured its readers that, despite the transition, "NOLS is the same school it has always been."[116]

One of the key issues that raised IRS eyebrows was the relationship between the nonprofit NOLS and Petzoldt's equipment business. Given Petzoldt's insistence on proper outdoor gear and clothing as critical to the success and enjoyment of backcountry travel, the school had always loaned students items they were unlikely to own—sleeping bags and tents as well as wool and waterproof clothing. In the 1960s, he had cobbled together NOLS supplies from a combination of military surplus and cast-off gear, which Thelma Young, an essential early staff member, then customized. By 1969, Petzoldt spun off this in-house department into an independent manufacturing company, first called Outdoor Leadership Supply. The company's mission focused on streamlining the gear supply for NOLS and developed innovative products for a general market with a potential to generate income for the school and its leaders. Based in Lander, the company began to design cutting-edge sleeping bags, parkas, rain gear, tents, and pack systems using synthetic materials, with NOLS students testing prototypes. Catalogs offered the items for sale by mail, and the *Alumnus* notified graduates that they could get Petzoldt-approved gear at a discount. In late 1970 the name changed to Paul Petzoldt Wilderness Equipment (PPWE), in part in an attempt to differentiate it from NOLS, though this failed to resolve the organizational tensions.[117]

The relationship between the school and the equipment company would remain fraught, but in its short life PPWE exemplified the merging of minimum impact camping practices, environmentalist identities, and a modern consumer orientation. Petzoldt argued that new synthetic materials provided improved mechanisms for lessening impact, despite its seeming conflict with ecological principles. A prominent feature on the front-page of the 1975 catalog, titled "About Polyester Fillings," extolled DuPont's insulating materials Dacron 88, Fiberfill II, and Polarguard and PPWE's prototypes using these materials before they were "generally available to other manufacturers." Petzoldt connected his pioneering of synthetics with his vision of NOLS as an incubator of environmentally responsible camping practices.

> We were the first to test and help perfect the synthetic fibers that are safer, more dependable, and more economical. We are proud that our designs and ideas are being copied because it is also our purpose to educate the public and upgrade American outdoorsmanship. We are proud that we were the first work out the way to use the wilderness without harming it, yet with comfort and enjoyment.[118]

New materials and new practices went hand in hand and synthetics became essential to this "new ethic of the wild outdoors." They enabled campers to buffer themselves from the elements and rely less on the land itself to provide warmth, shelter, or fuel. For example, when it came to insulating a sleeping bag from the cold, hard ground, he recommended new forms of "synthetic padding" over the traditional practice of piling up tree boughs. Preserving wild spaces came to require replacing natural and local materials with imported and artificial ones, which embodied a conflicted trade-off: idealizing backcountry experience while obscuring its dependence upon and its environmental costs to urban-industrial-consumer society.[119]

Tying these consumer products to an environmentalist mindset may have seemed like a harder sell, given the countercultural critique of consumerism and the environmental impact of the production of synthetics. To make a case for this form of consumption, PPWE had several models to emulate, including *The Whole Earth Catalog*, an idiosyncratic countercultural publication series first launched in 1968. Provocateur Stewart Brand had modeled *Whole Earth* on the L. L. Bean catalog but hoped that it could become a vehicle for sharing information and creating new communities around a combination of countercultural values, practical technology, and environmental commitments. Without allegiance to any manufacturers, it presented a dizzying array of equipment and book reviews, articles about emerging technologies and traditional techniques for ecological living, photographs, and poetry, which added up to, as one historian put it, "a new alchemy of environmental concern, small-scale technological enthusiasm, design research, alternative lifestyles, and business savvy." The *Catalog's* "Nomadics" section highlighted the new enthusiasm for backpacking and NOLS-style approaches to camping. It included a review of Colin Fletcher's *Complete Walker* and much of its featured equipment was made of new, synthetic products. In the *Whole Earth* sensibility, this represented not an irony but a prime example of "appropriate technology" and the spirit of invention in the service of an optimistic environmental culture.[120]

Yvon Chouinard and Tom Frost's influential 1972 catalog of their innovative climbing gear offered an even tighter fusion of outdoor recreation with environmental mindsets. The two men penned a foreword laying out the philosophy of "clean climbing" that drove their outdoor practices, equipment designs, and business strategies alike. It laid out a by-then familiar dilemma: the growth in popularity of an outdoor pastime, without a parallel rise in sensitivity, created increasing damage to the environment. The "deterioration of the climbing environment . . . is twofold, involving the physical aspect of the mountains and the moral integrity of the climbers." They insisted that the material solutions contained in the pages that followed, offering their products for sale, should be used "in meaningful combination" with this new "ethic." Interspersed with the carabiners and crag hammers was a longer essay detailing the technical aspects of how to "climb clean" and the elevated joys that came with the attempt. Chouinard and Frost, who would go on to found the highly successful company, Patagonia, were leaders among a group of likeminded outdoor entrepreneurs, who were forging a novel green business model from a blend of adventure sports, countercultural consumerism, and environmental advocacy.[121]

Petzoldt, a fellow climber and entrepreneur who advocated for "clean camping," shared much with Chouinard and Frost, and he pitched PPWE in a similar fashion, if to less eventual worldwide success than Patagonia. Both Chouinard and PPWE emulated the visual and rhetorical style of the *Whole Earth Catalog* in the sense of an underground publication that invited readers to join a cutting-edge group of backcountry enthusiasts. A review of the *Chouinard Equipment* catalog described this common approach: "Here's what you need; here's how to use it; don't buy it unless you need it; We've Personally Picked out Everything For You."[122] Addressing the buyer as "Dear Friend," Petzoldt declared PPWE a "small, personalized company" which "resisted the temptation to sell to large corporate complexes." Instead, the company focused on connecting a select group of consumers with a carefully curated set of products, where the consumer transaction furthered a larger educational mission to teach the public ideal outdoor "methods, techniques, philosophy and how to properly select and use equipment." Petzoldt welcomed potential buyers as fellow prototypers by highlighting the "thousands" of NOLS students who field-tested this equipment. He contrasted his crowd-sourced method with outdoor manufacturers that relied only on "a few highly accomplished mountaineers," perhaps hinting at the likes of Chouinard and Frost. The implication was that PPWE was both "passing along the results of this testing" and engaging users as vicarious, or in the case of NOLS graduates, actual, participants in the process. Together these messages imagined that innovative synthetic products in the hands of ordinary folks with the right attitudes could advance outdoor enjoyment and environmental causes.[123]

The visual style of the PPWE catalog reinforced this message. The plain black and white type, line-drawings, and newspaper format, along with listings for gear manufactured by other companies, suggested that it was sharing information as much as advertising its products. The goal, Petzoldt indicated, was "not to make some pretty thing just to sell, but to make equipment that is the best of its kind, equipment that buyers can trust with their lives." On the one hand, Petzoldt meant actual survival—that staying warm and dry wasn't just a matter of comfort but of life and death. On the other hand, trusting one's life to one's gear also underwrote a certain identity: trusting specific products to faithfully represent one's outlook on life. It was both classically consumerist—building lifestyles through consumer choices—and created an opening for an anti-consumption consumer ethic. Buyers understood themselves as purchasing products not because of slick marketing by profit-hungry companies, but for their underlying values.[124]

Another facet of this approach was PPWE's product descriptions, which echoed the "product reviews" featured in *Whole Earth* and *Backpacker*. This common element facilitated conversations about specialized gear that made backpacking an intense consumer experience. *Whole Earth* relied on readers themselves to supply independent and personalized reviews and refused to sell any ad space or listings to the supply companies themselves. *Backpacker* aimed for a similar kind of appeal, though it used its own staff to do product testing and accepted copious advertising from a wide range of outdoor retailers, as well as other travel and lifestyle products. Each issue profiled a different segment of the equipment market—starting with frame backpacks, tents, sleeping bags, and hiking boots—helping buyers determine which brands and models to trust. The language was informal, pulled few punches, and invited both endorsements and challenges from readers (and occasionally companies) which the magazine printed, suggesting an exchange of information.[125]

Underlying the freewheeling prose was an increasingly high-stakes proposition. Finding reliable equipment to trust with your life and to embody a commitment to the "new ethic" could be a daunting process. *Backpacker* promoted its "trail tested evaluations" as a guide to help readers find their way through the dizzying consumer "maze intelligently." It suggested bringing a copy of the magazine "with you into the store, and read each one with the relevant pack right in front of you." While *Backpacker* disavowed allegiance to any particular manufacturer, it declared its loyalty to the consumer experience writ broadly—that knowledgeable consumption was critical to the practice of backpacking and the backpacker identity.[126] While the magazine continued to agonize over the growing numbers of backcountry campers, the constant focus on consumption seemed to suggest that one solution lay in assembling the right combination of products that demonstrated a commitment to environmental awareness.

Just as magazines like *Backpacker* embedded consumer practices in the "new ethic," so did equipment manufacturers incorporate environmental values and minimum impact ideals in their sales pitches. Backpacking equipment and clothing had grown into a $400 million-per-year industry, as *Backpacker* reported in 1974. Large retail and sporting goods chain stores began to carry previously niche equipment; specialty tent and pack manufacturers like Sierra Designs, Kelty, and Jan Sport were being gobbled up by larger conglomerates like General Mills and Johnson Wax. Independent retailers, like REI, founded in 1938 as a co-op by Seattle climbers, grew as well, reporting "sales of $15 million in 1973, a 25% increase over 1972, and double what they were in 1970." Many companies, *Backpacker* noted, were adopting the social values that backpackers had been expressing and taking leading roles "in the environmental movement." Sales catalogs began to emulate the Chouinard model, interleaving conservation-oriented articles with featured products, such as REI's "'Being Kind to the Land,' educating novice campers in the 'new ethic.'"[127] And yet these companies were also procuring materials from corporations like Dow Chemical. The environmental impacts of Fiberfill, Dacron, Gore-Tex, and other sought-after synthetic materials were significant, though not in the backcountry places where recreational campers used them. This allowed both individuals and outdoor retailers to tout an image of environmental consciousness in pristine wilderness spaces, while eliding the impacts those uses generated elsewhere.[128] Whether buyers realized these relationships or followed new practices, purchasing or using products from these companies could signal belonging to the new crowd.

In the late 1970s, a spate of new camping and backpacking guidebooks joined *Backpacker* and Petzoldt's *Wilderness Handbook* in advocating for new environmentally sensitive methods.[129] A good deal of the discussion revolved around the selection and purchase of proper equipment as a necessary step toward environmental stewardship. John Hart, author of the Sierra Club's *Walking Softly* (1977), urged readers to seek out "specialty shops" and mail order catalogs and consult *Backpacker* magazine to help "navigate the equipment labyrinth." This daunting process, he insisted, was crucial to the ultimate goal of lessening the impact of one's "passage on the land," though he noted a keen irony at work: "The stronger our wish to preserve the wild places, the less we can meet them on their own terms, the more sophisticated, civilized, and complex become the gadgets we must bring into them." Despite any misgivings, guidebook authors of this era baked consumption of proper gear into the "new ethic" of environmental protection.[130]

Petzoldt had an easier time attracting buyers of his sleeping bags than advocates to his proposal for a certification system. Still, he was not ready to give up on the idea. He helped to bring university outdoor education programs and public land managers together to form the Wilderness Education Association (WEA) in 1977. An umbrella organization that defined curriculum and standards for certification, the WEA merged the recreational ethos with a public educational project. The organization decided to work through existing higher education programs, targeting students already "majoring in an outdoor-related career . . . people who would be in the field . . . teaching others." Petzoldt's efforts to promote such a national alliance carried him yet farther from NOLS, and after another financial kerfuffle in 1978, he was forced to sever all ties with the school. Instead, he focused on building the WEA and by the end of 1980, he claimed, "several hundred students, teachers and professionals had been certified" and the WEA's program was becoming the national standard.[131]

The WEA persisted, growing to include as many as two dozen organizational members in the United States and abroad, but the certification system fell well short of becoming a prerequisite for backcountry access. For all the anxiety about crowds, backpackers were skeptical. Backpacking, as NOLS and others had popularized it, had represented a way out of standardized campgrounds and mainstream constraints. Establishing common principles for minimum impact was one thing; submitting one's self to standardized testing was something else. While guidebooks insisted on the necessity of low-impact practices, they also suggested that backpackers were likely to find heavy-handed restrictions on their behavior unappealing. Hart noted that too many constraints, even in the name of protecting wild lands, would abrogate "one of the chief pleasures" of the backcountry, namely "independence of the traveler and his freedom from formal rules."[132]

If the certification system gained less traction than Petzoldt hoped, the consumer model attracted legions of campers, backpackers, and environmentalists alike. Hart confessed his "genuine" pleasure in the consumer experience "of dealing with good gear": the allure of "iridescent" colors that lent "a stack of fine equipment that curiously valuable look" and the pursuit of "what truly suits you." Firmly embedded in the recreational ethos, backpackers found consumerism and environmental advocacy more compatible than one might expect, given origins in the 1960s revolt against mainstream culture and the 1970s ecological awakening. As outdoor gear and clothing in particular came to have symbolic as well as practical uses, items could signify one's attachment to wilderness without being used for their original purposes.[133] They became an expression of identity.

Petzoldt pushed against this trend, choosing certification over consumerism. While he still listed PPWE as a supplier for specialized gear in his *New Wilderness Handbook* and insisted on the critical pairing of "skillful camping procedures and use of lightweight, modern equipment," he declined to expand the company. His partner Rob Hellyer noted that PPWE might have capitalized more on the swiftly expanding market, but that neither he nor Petzoldt were interested in trying to compete with national brands or in running a "mail order business from behind a desk" full-time. In the mid-1980s, Petzoldt shut his operation down, amidst a fast growing outdoor industry.[134] While Petzoldt might have agreed with many of his colleagues that being a good camper started with being a good shopper, he didn't want the definition to end there. Into his late eighties, he kept hiking Grand Teton despite suffering from glaucoma, kept writing about the need for outdoor education, and kept giving interviews to anyone who would listen about the wonders of the wilderness. Eventually reconciling with NOLS, the outdoor community widely recognized him as an architect of the modern backcountry ethos. Featured in *Outside Magazine*'s annual "Camping Special" a few years before his death in 1999, Petzoldt was, as one journalist put it, an "icon of the outdoors, the man who's taught more campers to move lightly through the wilderness than anyone else in history."[135]

WHILE PAUL PETZOLDT's dream of a nationwide, enforceable permit system would not materialize, he and NOLS both contributed to formulating the concise list of principles that would become common parlance in the outdoor recreation world: Leave No Trace. NOLS, in partnership with the US Forest Service, National Park Service, and Bureau of Land Management issued a pamphlet in 1987 called *Leave No Trace Land Ethics*. It condensed into a few concise pages many evolving practices and thorny issues backpackers had wrestled with over the previous two decades—the desire for solitude and the troubles that came with increasing crowds, the need to protect fragile lands and the wilderness experience alike. It focused as much on the issue of visual pollution as environmental protection, suggesting a simple rubric: "Practicing a NO-TRACE ethic is very simple if you remember two things: (1) MAKE IT HARD FOR OTHERS TO SEE YOU AND (2) LEAVE NO TRACE OF YOUR VISIT."[136] Momentum for changing outdoor behavior built around this stock phrase. An outdoor recreation summit, convened in 1993 by NOLS and other outdoor nonprofit organizations, federal land management agencies, and, notably, outdoor manufacturers and industry associations, resulted in the formation of an independent entity called Leave No Trace, Inc. (LNTI). A nonprofit corporation, partly funded by contributions from outdoor manufacturers, LNTI shepherded the distillation of six (and later seven) Leave No Trace principles, including: Travel and Camp on Durable Surfaces, Leave What You Find, Be Considerate of Other Visitors. Campers could soon encounter these instructions at multiple points of their outdoor experience: in a wayside sign on a hike, at a summer camp, or sewn into the label of a new backpack or sleeping bag.[137]

That campers came to look for the Leave No Trace logo as a kind of brand suggested the success of the consumer model. LNTI was leveraging the ever-expanding outdoor clothing and equipment industry to make these principles more widely known—even if buyers weren't required to practice them. It also cemented the "new ethic of the wild outdoors" to the practice of consumption. This merger generated tension on several levels. If to "go light" and "leave no trace" entailed consuming products made with synthetic materials in order to reduce impact at the wilderness destination, it often contributed to environmental degradation elsewhere, in their far-flung places of manufacture. While companies like Patagonia began experimenting with using recycled plastics to produce their fleece jackets, in the 1970s and 1980s when these products came on the scene, they were not particularly "eco-friendly" and they continue to have ripple effects, such as shedding microplastics in the wash and into waterways.[138]

Leave No Trace also contributed to what would become a growing social divide in outdoor recreation. The primacy of the consumer driven model of "the new ethic" may indeed have increased access and awareness, but the tone of the marketing, the lingering protective exclusivity of *Backpacker*, and the rising price-points of such gear created a more class-specific appeal. Moreover, the polarization of environmental politics in the later 1970s both tightened the links between Leave No Trace practices, gear manufacturers, and ecological mindsets and epitomized the deepening fissures between outdoor recreationists. That a particular brand could function as shorthand for an environmentalist stance might make it simultaneously more appealing to one crowd and alienating to another.[139]

Wearing a Patagonia Snap-T Synchilla fleece on a trip to the grocery store as a marker of class status and political outlook in 1985 might seem pretty far removed from the rag-tag band of young backpackers in "Thirty Days to Survival," and even from the practice of camping itself. And in many ways it is. Far more people buy and wear these jackets than take them on backcountry expeditions. And yet the generational alchemy that organizations like NOLS fostered, where countercultural mindsets and an ecological ethos imbued a particular form of camping with new meaning, fostered the rise of this connection. Melding personal hopes for self-discovery with environmentalist politics may have increased the audience for minimum-impact practices, but that it did so through the consumer marketplace bequeathed a complex legacy. The history of NOLS and the continuing salience of Leave No Trace, the combination of backcountry recreation with specialized technology made ever more demanding claims on public nature. This new twist on the recreational ethos called for an environmentally-centered social contract that remained dependent upon mixing leisure with nature.

Along with the trade-offs of preserving local places while outsourcing environmental damage, consumption drove ever narrower market niches that mapped onto other social inequalities. Both in terms of consumer gear and the Leave No Trace practices they symbolized, this generational transformation of camping reinforced a divided sense of who belonged in the campground. For some—typically, white, middle-class, educated Americans who espouse a particular kind of environmental politics—the only proper use of the wild outdoors is to Leave No Trace. This framing, however, tends to exclude those looking for more mechanized adventures or traditional outdoor pursuits like hunting and fishing. In researching contemporary cultural divides, economists found that among the top consumer habits predicting an individual held liberal politics was *not* owning fishing equipment. It also fails to encompass Americans with alternate or nonrecreational relationships to nature, as a result of culture or a function of labor.[140] As campers jostled for places in the right back to nature crowd, competing claims on public nature testified to a social contract again in transformation, where both the role of the state and the recreational ethos came upon new challenges.

6

Occupying Public Ground

BY THE TIME South Carolina Congressman Trey Gowdy asked National Park Service Director Jonathan Jarvis to define camping in 2012, the question had been asked and answered many times over. Multiple forms of camping, as claims on public nature, had evolved alongside the social contract across the previous century and a half. Members of the Occupy Wall Street movement camped as part of an explicit challenge to the terms of a social contract that was showing signs of strain. The housing collapse and financial crisis of 2008, and the subsequent recession, undermined both the material and symbolic stability of the American Dream. Precipitated by speculation on an essential premise of the nation—property, homeownership—the economic calamity revealed the shifting foundations of the social contract. While the expectations of citizens and the role of government had been fluctuating since the 1970s, most would have trusted property ownership and home equity as bedrock for individuals and the nation alike.

The Great Recession pulled the rug out from under from millions of Americans. Many began to question the terms of the social contract, as the government looked unable to hold up its end of the bargain and provide citizens with a "secure enjoyment of their properties." If this Lockean formula had survived the transition between the producer-agrarian ideal to the homeowning recreational ethos, from a basis of labor to one of leisure, where would it go from here? The fury of Occupy, and the frustration on the part of many Americans, sprang from this disorienting conundrum.

The Occupy Wall Street movement galvanized public attention in the fall of 2011 by agitating for new visions of the nation in the post–Recession era, even if the details remained murky. In the initial poster campaign that sparked the movement, the central objective remained an open question: "What is our one demand?" Those drawn to participate shared a sense of outrage with economic inequality and alienation from the political process but generated little initial consensus on a list of specific reforms to demand. The form of protest, however, was precise—instructions indicated a date, a place, and a single instruction: "Bring Tent." The tactic took off in ways that surprised both organizers and observers. At the height of its initial wave that fall, Occupy encampments sprouted in hundreds of cities in the United States and beyond, with at least fifty substantial and lasting tent protests in major urban areas from the original location in lower Manhattan to Oakland, California.[1] Initially, the tent might have promised nothing more than basic practical protection from the elements and simple visual testimony to an intent to stay. In the months that followed, however, the tent occupation became a powerful symbol, demonstrating how camping on public nature continued to offer compelling grounds for national debate, if measured only by the hyperbolic reaction it provoked among public officials.

Two major sites in Washington, DC established in October of 2011 testified to the movement's politically supercharged occupation of public nature: one in the concrete Freedom Plaza near the National Mall, the other in McPherson Square, a park a few blocks north of the White House.[2] Both lasted well into the new year, but they were neither the first nor the longest political encampments in the nation's capital to trigger such alarm and debate. In fact, camping had appeared in a surprising number of spaces in Washington, DC, and in federal courtrooms, Oval Office discussions, and front-page news stories in the modern era.

In 1984, Supreme Court Justices had considered the case of a homeless advocacy group planning a DC encampment. Justice Lewis F. Powell wondered why and how to "draw a distinction between sleeping all night and demonstrating all night?" Justice Thurgood Marshall doubted one could draw "a bright line between sleeping and not sleeping."[3] A decade before that, the Supreme Court had weighed in on another camping case begun when the District Court of Washington, DC supported the Government's position barring the Vietnam Veterans Against the War (VVAW) from camping on the National Mall in 1971. As organizer John Kerry tried to explain the encampment as part of a suite of symbolic protest actions against the war, District Court Judge George L. Hart snapped, "What is a simulated campsite? . . . You mean you simulate cooking and you simulate a sump pit? What are you talking about?" A US Park Police officer, contemplating having to arrest veterans who camped in defiance of the government ban, wondered aloud, "What is the definition of camping? You tell me. I don't know."[4]

Three years before the VVAW event, the Southern Christian Leadership Conference held a six-week camp out on the Mall to protest racism and poverty, dubbed Resurrection City. That spring of 1968 President Lyndon Johnson received bags of complaint mail: "How can you permit the 'Poor People's March' to set up camp . . . in the heart of Washington, the capitol of our country"? If an "ordinary family" would be "denied camping rights on these hallowed grounds . . . why is this group given preference?" These demands put pressure on Johnson to decide how to treat the encampment, and Cabinet officials debated how best to handle the situation and minimize the political blowback— something President Herbert Hoover had done decades before, and President Richard Nixon would do a few years later.[5] As Figure 6.1 shows, encampments in the capital, stretching back to the late nineteenth century, made claims on the nation and posed challenging questions. Who can camp? Is camping a right or a privilege? What is the difference

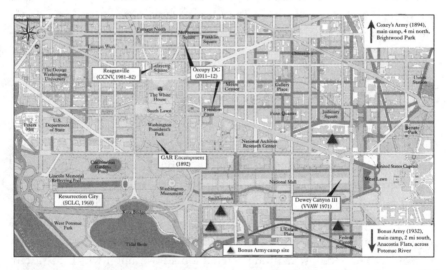

FIGURE 6.1 Capital encampments, 1892–2012. Map by George Chakvetadze compiled from: "The National Encampment: Preparations for the 26th Meeting of the G.A.R.," *National Tribune*, September 15, 1892, 12; Lucy G. Barber, *Marching on Washington: The Forging of an American Political Tradition* (Berkeley: University of California Press, 2002), 31, 91; Gordon K. Mantler, *Power to the Poor: Black-Brown Coalition and the Fight for Economic Justice, 1960–1974* (Chapel Hill: University of North Carolina Press, 2013), 94–97; "Vets Disobey Court Order, Sleep on Mall," *Washington Post*, April 22, 1971, A1; "'Reaganville' Camp Erected to Protest Plight of the Poor," *New York Times*, November 27, 1981, B14; Meredith Somers, "For D.C. Occupy Camps, It's Divided They Stand," *Washington Times*, January 20, 2012, A1.

between sleeping outside and camping? When are they necessities and when are they symbolic acts?

There are no simple answers to these questions. After a century and a half of cultural evolution since the Civil War, camping persists as a multivalent and potent practice. At key moments since the 1960s, protest camping became a highly visible mode of making claims on the nation, sparking political controversy and Constitutional questions, debated by prominent legal minds, elected officials, and ordinary citizens. A careful look at these often intricate deliberations exposes the growing tension between the campers' republic of state-sponsored outdoor leisure and the changing social contract.

Occupy demonstrated the latent potential of camping for making political claims on the nation, at the same time that leisure camping and homeless encampments were surging. Occupiers used camping to petition the state to take action for the public good while also operating within assumptions that camping was quintessentially recreational. The collision of these two frames—one that appeared explicitly political and the other that masqueraded as apolitical—produced the urgency of Gowdy's demand to pinpoint "what camping is and what it is not."[6] The Occupy movement resisted any simple definitions, pushed public nature into the headlines, and demonstrated once again why camping matters.

"Yes We Camp"

In urging protestors to "Bring Tent," the leaders of Occupy Wall Street initially positioned themselves as the inheritors (and hopeful translators) of the energy of 2011's Arab Spring. In the July 2011 public blog post that initiated the call to Occupy Wall Street on September 17, the editors of the Vancouver-based radical magazine *Adbusters* explicitly modeled its strategy on one aspect of the protests in Tahrir Square against President Hosni Mubarak's regime: "incessantly repeating" an uncomplicated demand "in a plurality of voices." For Occupy, camping offered a platform upon which to sustain a similar drumbeat of protest. "If we can hang in there, 20,000 strong, week after week against every police and National Guard that tries to expel us," the editors reasoned, the nation would have to pay attention. The post ended with a call to "screw up our courage [and] pack our tents."[7]

Images of protestors defending their camps against frantic attempts to dislodge them quickly attracted attention despite difficulty identifying the "one demand" among a diverse set of activists. Thus, in the face of public pressure to define what Occupy was all about, the General Assembly, the consensus-oriented representative body for the Wall Street occupation and proxy voice of the national movement, began to veer away from the language of demands. Instead "they opted to make their demand the occupation itself—and the direct democracy taking place there," hoping that the "tent cities and model communities, demonstrations that occupy and transform space" would galvanize broader participation and demands for government action.[8] The tents were having the hoped-for effect. Choosing their ground, and trying to hold it, these protestors unnerved leaders in urban centers and university campuses across the country. Critical or no, people were noticing Occupy.

A poster designed by the staff at *Adbusters* as part of the initial call to action suggests why the tents proved to be a compelling aspect of the protest. An early example of Occupy's visual communication style, the "Yes We Camp" poster shown in Figure 6.2 combined bold graphics, catchy phrases, and glossy satire.[9] Front and center is the cheeky play on the "Yes We Can" message of Barack Obama's 2008 presidential campaign. Recurring on handwritten signs, printed buttons, and graphic memes, the "Yes We Camp" slogan attempted to tap into that political energy while critiquing its naivete. It explicitly linked the tent to electoral politics, projecting an outside-the-booth strategy to achieve change. The tent symbol, however, specifically evoked the standard Park Service icon for "campground." As such, it also conjured the thick history of the national parks and their promise to link recreational camping and citizenship. The logo remains shorthand for the "campers' republic," where the state promotes camping as a social and civic good.

In deploying the campers' republic here, Occupy implicitly relied upon these historical meanings to open a line of argument about access to public nature and national belonging. Set against the columns of the New York Stock Exchange, the tent logo provoked viewers to reimagine Wall Street—a space dedicated to private gain—as they might a national park: as a space regulated for the public good. Zuccotti Park in Lower Manhattan, the first site of occupation, inhabited an increasingly common blend of public and private space. One Occupy commentator described it as privately-owned space that allowed public access in exchange for developers' ability to "build higher than zoning laws permit (colonizing shared sky as well as land)." Use of National Park Service (NPS) iconography worked to take back that "shared" land and sky, bolstering the "decision to take a stand there—in a sliver of 'public' land carved out from rapaciously expanding privatized space."[10] Occupy leaned on well-established NPS visions about the great outdoors and national belonging. And yet Occupiers explicitly disavowed recreational assumptions

FIGURE 6.2 Repurposing the National Park Service campground logo for a new claim on public nature. "YES WE CAMP," *Adbusters*, August 16, 2011.

that came with the symbol, despite the fact that the NPS became one of the few public agencies defending Occupy as a First Amendment action.[11]

As the Grand Army of the Republic (GAR), Coxey's petition in boots, and the Bonus marchers evidenced, the nation's capital has long been a potent place to camp out for a cause. Occupy's commitment to a narrative about its impromptu origins, and the desire to share in contemporary transnational protest energies, tended to obscure these historical relationships. But if Occupiers themselves were reticent to connect the dots, journalists sought out historical parallels for their analyses of Occupy. Most often these stories gravitated toward the Bonus Army, which had camped in Washington in 1932. Dozens of radio, television, and newspaper stories connected Occupy to the Depression-era protest of World War I veterans, to different ends. One radio story speculated on Occupy's long-term prospects for success as compared to the effect the Bonus Army may have had in fostering later support for veterans' benefits, like the G.I. Bill. Other reports paralleled the forceful evictions of the Bonus Army and Occupy camps as a cautionary tale of how heavy hands can come back to haunt those who wield them. Others saw a lesson in the Bonus Army's failure to achieve its immediate goal, arguing that while public sympathy might reject violent suppression, support for a fringe group making a mess of public spaces was likely to wane over time.[12]

What historical lesson the Bonus march might bequeath to Occupy was unclear. Did the tradition of the Bonus Army bolster Occupy's claims? Or was the latter a pale copy of the former? In the context of the emerging campers' republic, Bonus Army marchers emphasized their status as military veterans and thus special citizens, and they worked hard to showcase their commitment to order. But their camp still raised suspicions that it was a hobo jungle that augured social unrest. Whether Americans viewed them as patriots or panhandlers, the protestors did voice a clear-cut, single demand—pay the veterans' Bonus early—but it failed. Occupiers neither claimed to be special citizens (instead characterizing themselves as the 99%) nor articulated a singular demand. The connections lay elsewhere, in the economic issues at the heart of each movement, the call for investment in a public good, and the use of camping as a vehicle for getting political grievances heard, if not remedied.

In his testimony about Occupy in 2012, NPS Director Jonathan Jarvis pointed to two different DC precedents: the Farmers' Vigil, when 6,000 family farmers parked their tractors on the National Mall for seven weeks in the winter of 1979 to call attention to the inequities of US agricultural policy, and Resurrection City, the 1968 encampment of the Poor People's Campaign, which occupied the Mall for six weeks that spring. The agency's "success . . . in managing these demonstrations," Jarvis argued, guided the "reasoned and measured" approaches the agency and the Park Police took to Occupy and other such encamped protests.[13] The Farmer's Vigil alarmed Washington residents at the time, and later served as evidence for Jarvis's defense of the right to protest despite public criticism of the method. Yet for all the colorful press the tractorcade produced, it did not prompt the depth of national questioning around the rights to camp out for a cause as did either Occupy or the other historical case he cited, Resurrection City.[14]

The encampment of the Poor People's Campaign (PPC) became a national lightning rod amidst the troubled times of the late 1960s. More than 2,600 protestors occupied the National Mall for forty-three days in May and June of 1968, living in tent-shaped shelters made of wood frames and plastic sheeting. The multiracial coalition aimed to focus public attention on issues of poverty and generated significant media attention.[15] Resurrection City occasionally appeared in stories about Occupy, though less frequently than the Bonus Army. A *Washington Post* feature from 2011 called the 1968 encampment "The 99 percent, First edition" and suggested that the PPC faced "many of the same criticisms that dog the Occupy Wall Street movement," including both creating a public nuisance and failing to articulate clear demands.[16] A closer look at Resurrection City demonstrates tighter links than Jarvis, Occupy activists, or media commentators realized.

Resurrection City emerged out of a desire to create a different form of protest. In late 1967, Rev. Martin Luther King Jr. announced his "determination to have a 'camp-in,'" where "waves of the nation's poor and disinherited" would travel to the capital "to demand redress of their grievances." He insisted that "this will be no mere one-day march in Washington, but a trek to the nation's capital by suffering and outraged citizens who will go to stay until some definite and positive action is taken." Alluding to the famed 1963 March on Washington as a "mere one-day" event, surprising though it may be, revealed shifting Civil Rights strategies. Specifics remained unclear—maybe protestors would set up tents in strategic locations throughout the city—but King insisted that the movement had to think differently in this "last desperate demand" to use nonviolence to confront "directly and dramatically" the problems of race and poverty amidst the "chaos, hatred, and violence" of the past three summers.[17]

From Washington to Selma, dramatic marches, along with prolonged indoor actions, such as sit-ins, had been provocative and effective in previous years. Now, Southern Christian Leadership Conference (SCLC) organizers considered how a different form of outdoor protest might capture new attention. At one point, one of King's lawyers and close aides, Stanley Levinson, suggested a plan modeled specifically after the Bonus March, which he viewed as "an effective form of political theater." Organizing this event proved to be complex, however, and the PPC floundered for months. In late March, some publicly considered calling it off. King's assassination in April of 1968 lent a new sense of urgency and increased the flow of donations and volunteers to support a sustained occupation. Rather than "a single dramatic event," they aimed to "to act continuously to illustrate the heavy and continual weight of the Poor People's burden."[18]

The campaign had no easy time securing a permit to build housing for two thousand demonstrators. Local and federal officials had opposed the plan, and members of Congress sponsored dozens of bills attempting to prevent it, fearing an outbreak of violence. President Lyndon Johnson was initially averse to the encampment but aides worked to persuade him to appease the PPC with "small victories." The attorney general and the secretary of the interior both advocated granting the permit at least in part by consulting the same history Levinson had. A White House aide circulated excerpts of historian Arthur Schlesinger's 1957 account of the Bonus Army, which was critical of President Hoover's callous disregard and "unforgiving" eviction of the marchers—actions which Schlesinger argued all but secured Hoover's loss in the 1932 election. The Johnson administration vowed to "learn from their mistakes" and granted a thirty-seven-day renewable permit for the PPC to encamp alongside the Reflecting Pool. The site was something of a compromise; the strip of grass was prime symbolic real estate in the "monumental core" of the city, with the high symbolism of the Lincoln Memorial as backdrop, but it was also "isolated a bit," a less-trafficked area of the Mall.[19]

That relative quiet was soon to end, as hundreds began to settle into the plywood and plastic A-frames laid out into neat rows, as shown in Figure 6.3. The SCLC considered repurposing recreational tents, but worried that impoverished participants did not own them. Instead, designers came up with a simple-to-construct base that marchers could build themselves and establish consistency for organizing the "city." Residents modified the structure of their wooden "tents," decorated the interiors and grounds with scrounged materials, and used the sides as message boards. Some residents noted that these spartan structures provided more shelter than their permanent homes. As one woman from Marks, Mississippi put it to the *New York Times*, "I'm living better here than I ever did there." Moreover, she enjoyed getting to take her children to the beach for some outdoor recreation. "We don't have any beaches in Marks, only one swimming pool, and it's for white people only." *Time* magazine described the "unique throbbing" community that emerged as "a revival meeting within a carnival within an army camp."[20]

Environmental and social problems, however, took up a large share of reporting. Construction of basic infrastructure, such as sewer lines, ran behind schedule. Heavy spring rains during the first two weeks of the protest turned the whole area into a sloppy mud pit that roused fears of health problems and critiques of disorder. Reports of petty theft and internal conflicts also drew negative attention. Some understood the irony, as Calvin Trillin pointed out in a *New Yorker* article in mid-June. While campaign leaders tried to explain

FIGURE 6.3 The encamped community at Resurrection City, with the Washington Monument in the background. "Photographic slide of the Poor People's Campaign," photograph by Robert Houston, 1968. Object Number 2015.245.15. Collection of the Smithsonian National Museum of African American History and Culture. © Robert Houston.

that "the poor people in America . . . live in mud all their lives," news stories only focused on how the encampment had made a germ-ridden muddy mess of the Mall. Trillin observed, "The poor in Resurrection City have come to Washington to show that the poor in America are sick, dirty, disorganized, and powerless —and they are criticized daily for being sick, dirty, disorganized and powerless."[21] If the PPC bore some responsibility for failing to anticipate the possibility of bad weather and finding itself without a "contingency plan," journalists tended to overemphasize the shantytown's problems and to downplay the Campaign's successes.[22]

Watching this all play out in televised reports and newspapers, many Americans communicated their reactions in letters and telegrams to President Johnson. Some avowed support for the campaign, urging Johnson to double down on his work to eradicate poverty. As one woman from Maryland wrote, "while it may not be the most pleasant thing in the world to have the Poor People camping by the reflecting pool, it certainly is a worthwhile endeavor on their part." Another from California suggested, "I know you know why they are camping," but likely many "comfortable Americans" did not. "So while it may be slightly embarrassing to have a shantytown in view of our

White House," she hoped it would help "make our nation aware of how the problems of the poor affect all of us."[23]

Recognizing shared fates or endorsing the strategy of encampment, however, was less common than criticism of the protesters and their tactics. One man from Texas complained that "Those gorgeous parks & monuments belong to ALL Americans and our rights and property are being violated a great deal more surely than the 'poor' people who incredibly have the time & money to spend on a summer vacation on public grounds." Another from Illinois lamented "the desecrations" of "hallowed ground in memoriam to great Americans," now "taken over by a hoard of locusts."[24] For these writers, camping did not engender a sense of shared citizenship, but instead pitted Americans against a dehumanized and swarming poor.

The explicit politics of the encampment disturbed many writers, who judged the demonstration against a more pleasant vision of recreational camping. When writers demanded to know why the PPC was "given preference" when "an ordinary family who wished to camp in Washington would not be allowed to camp at any chosen place," the NPS responded by explaining that "demonstrations in the exercise of rights" under the First Amendment, like Resurrection City, had "no bearing on . . . recreation purposes."[25] While this may have satisfied some, others rejected the logic. As the writer from Illinois complained, "to deny the Boy Scouts the same privileges that are accorded the negro people is an insult to the intelligence of the American citizen." Not only did he scoff at the idea that camping could be a legitimate form of protest, but he also implied that such protests denigrated the "wholesome" camping practiced by the Boy Scouts. Moreover, contrasting "negro people" with the Boy Scouts (which officially permitted segregation until 1974) reinforced historical assumptions that African Americans did not belong in the camping landscape. One woman from South Carolina extended this reasoning in her sardonic and derogatory request for information about "our newest Camp Grounds" on the Mall: "Is electricity available at the sites? . . . Do we need reservations? We are coming just for sight seeing, and have no march planned. (Although at the rate things are going, we may march to be treated equal to the negroes.)"[26] This sense that camping should only be practiced without politics suggests how engrained assumptions about recreational camping were by this point.

Resurrection City came to a swift end in the early hours of June 24, 1968. Five days after a march that drew 50,000 in support of the Poor People's Campaign, Washington, DC police provoked a confrontation, fired multiple tear-gas canisters into the camp, and drove out the 500 remaining denizens. Sensationalized fears of crime and Communist infiltration had accelerated in the weeks before this action, though Johnson had hoped to avoid such strong-arm tactics.[27] Suspicion of communism dogged the activists. With many leaders already under active surveillance, rumors circulated among Black leaders and left-leaning activists that the government was planning to round them up and put them in detention camps. The incarceration of Japanese Americans in "relocation camps" during World War II was an ominous example, and at least one letter writer to Johnson suggested that Resurrection City might be repurposed along those lines. This southern California woman proposed, "Why not make the new 'resurrection city' a concentration camp" to quarantine its radicals and Communists who "threaten violence and fire to destroy this country. . . . [Y]ou did that to the japs that hadn't done anything, only lived in this country and raised beautiful gardens & worked hard from daylight till dark—They were not on welfare nor were they criminals."[28] This connection dialed up the intensity of the debate about national belonging and citizenship, as the line between a camp for political expression and a camp to constrain political expression stretched thin.

In a reflection published in *Ebony*, PPC leader Jesse Jackson criticized the press for focusing on "incidentals" like "the record downpour of rain and the resulting mud." While the SCLC returned to more traditional strategies, Jackson insisted that the legacy of Resurrection City was not "a mudhole in Washington, but . . . rather an idea unleashed in history." The 2011 feature in the *Washington Post* that connected Resurrection City to Occupy quoted Jackson's prediction and then observed: "The idea was dormant for a long time, but it seems to have been awakened in Freedom Plaza and McPherson Square. What will come of it this time?"[29] Part of what came of it was a replay of many of the same arguments about the uses of public grounds, cultural divides, and suspicions about explicitly political forms of camping.

Asked to enumerate any times besides Resurrection City and the Farmers' Vigil when the Park Service allowed protest camping, Jarvis could not come up with additional examples, but another witness hinted at one. Law professor Timothy Zick indicated that a 1975 case in the US Court of Appeals for the DC Circuit, *Quaker Action v. Morton,* remained the governing decision around protest camping. While Zick testified that there was "nothing new in the jurisprudence," he believed that Occupy's "use of a public place, in this fashion" was "unprecedented."[30] While this case received no further mention in the hearing, a closer look reveals an overlooked precedent. *Quaker Action v. Morton* is shorthand for the final decision in a series of cases adjudicated over the prior six years, including one regarding an encampment that presaged many of the debates about Occupy. In the spring of 1971, Vietnam Veterans Against the War proposed a six-day event which included a camp-out on the eastern side of the Mall, directly across from the Capitol Building. The NPS sought to bar the encampment, prompting legal proceedings and public debate around the symbolic potential of camping and what the government's responsibility was to support or constrain it.

Launched by a small group of dissenters in 1967, Vietnam Veterans Against the War grew substantially following the invasion of Cambodia and the National Guard shootings at Kent State University in 1970. With perhaps 12,000 members by the spring of 1971, the VVAW hoped to capture national attention with a multiday event at sites around the capital. Like the leaders of the Poor People's Campaign, the VVAW believed that this strategy would be more effective than a one-day march. The group planned to upend any expectations of routine protest with an event dubbed "Dewey Canyon III." Dewey Canyon I and II were code names for US-led secret operations in Laos in 1969 and 1971, actions that the VVAW and veterans themselves had exposed in hopes of increasing the condemnation of the war. Operation Dewey Canyon III, a "limited incursion into the country of Congress," called for an encampment on the National Mall to serve as a base for testifying at hearings, guerilla theater, and other attention-getting actions. A newsletter to VVAW members called for veterans to descend on Washington on April 19, with their "own ponchos, sleeping bags, old uniforms and medals," for peaceful protest actions that would culminate in a mass march on April 24.[31]

Officials in the Nixon administration were wary. The FBI was already keeping a close watch on VVAW activities and the Interior Department had become far more hostile to the encampment idea, and to large protests in general, than it had been in 1968. When the VVAW cited the permit issued to the PPC as a precedent, the move backfired. Another Resurrection City was precisely what federal officials were trying to avoid. Though PPC organizers and participants themselves shouldered most of the public's blame, the event had put the Johnson administration in an unenviable position. Nixon officials, working to shore up support for the war, had no desire to give the VVAW the same kind of platform and denied the permit.[32] In an April 15 letter notifying the group of this decision, Acting Secretary of the Interior Mitchell Melich suggested that allowing Resurrection City had been a mistake, causing "serious damage to park values." The lesson the agency learned was to practice "strict adherence" to camping policies, no matter the VVAW's invocation of the First Amendment, which it regarded as "so insubstantial as to be overridden by the basic . . . responsibility to protect and conserve" the

Mall as a park for "tourists and visitors." Melich did permit the possibility of "simulating a camp in Viet Nam," so long as this did not include tents, fires, or campsite activities.[33] He did not, however, explain how one might simulate camp without such tools.

While pursuing a legal remedy, the VVAW encouraged "veterans and their families to come here despite the government ban and start camping Monday night." They would respect the instruction not to pitch tents or start campfires and instead would "sleep under ponchos or shelter halves and eat food prepared in nearby churches."[34] Shelter halves, which resembled the squares of tarp issued to Union army soldiers in the Civil War, weren't exactly tents, but neither were they not tents. Rather, along with the more Vietnam-specific ponchos, they highlighted a particular, military style of camp shelter. Where the PPC could not assume protestors owned recreational tents, here the VVAW did presume that vets would have access to army surplus, a resource on which previous veterans' encampments, like the Bonus Army and the GAR before it, had relied.

The VVAW request for a stay on the government ban landed in the middle of the *Quaker Action* cases, in the same District Court that heard those disputes over the right to occupy space in the capital. The presiding judge, George L. Hart Jr., later called the *Quaker Action* cases among the most challenging of his career, as they required finding an elusive balance between Constitutional freedoms and public safety.[35] The origin of these cases lay in the complaint of several organizations, headed by the Quaker Action Group, that NPS policies regulating public gatherings in the White House area infringed upon their First Amendment rights. Government lawyers countered with two rationales for restricting protests: one, preserving "park values" and two, protecting the safety of the President, the White House, and the public at large. In *Quaker Action I* (1969) and *Quaker Action II* (1970), the District Court, the Appeals Court, and the Interior Department failed to reach consensus on how to accommodate all of those needs simultaneously. Appeals Judges called twice for a fuller exploration of the issues, rebuked the NPS for failing to produce "a set of coherent park policies" to govern First Amendment events, and implied that the government was not acting in good faith to support free speech and peaceable assembly.[36] Beyond the specific questions they addressed—how many people could gather, for how long, to engage in which kinds of protest—these cases opened a new era of negotiating public nature.

While camping did not come up in these initial cases, the ongoing litigation and efforts by the government to restrict protest created a potent context for adjudicating the VVAW's claim that camping was a form of expressive speech necessary to their petition for redress. The VVAW came before Judge Hart in on April 16, just a few days before the encampment was to begin. The issue hinged on whether the veterans would be allowed to sleep overnight on the Mall; the NPS allowance for the "simulated campsite" was for "daylight hours." Hart tried to narrow the grounds for debate to the act of sleeping. In his mind, this precluded any possibility of First Amendment expression. Hart telegraphed his beliefs, declaring in the early minutes, "We are not talking about freedom of speech now, we are talking about freedom to sleep."[37] Such a representation made the idea seem absurd.

The VVAW called one witness to rebut Hart's assertion: John Kerry, a major architect of Dewey Canyon III. The record does not reflect what Kerry wore to court that day, but he likely appeared in the same Army fatigues that he would wear while presenting riveting testimony the following week at televised Senate hearings about the war. In District Court, Kerry made equally incisive arguments for the broader significance of camping to the Veterans. "We feel the campsite is part of our freedom of speech" because it was "the only way" to truly "tell our story to the people of this country." More than "a march alone" or a "lobby effort alone," the encampment was the glue that held all of the components of the "five-day teach-in" together. It was necessary both because of its symbolic nature in representing the war, and its support role for the demonstration. Kerry explained that neither the veterans, many of whom were disabled and unemployed, nor the VVAW were in a position to pay for hotel rooms. In order to allow "the men who lost their legs and arms" to express themselves at the Capitol, the VVAW needed to house them at a convenient location and in an inexpensive manner.[38]

Kerry also sought to assuage fears that this might become another Resurrection City by emphasizing the brevity of the campout and the skill of the campers. The VVAW requested merely "four nights with men that have been taught how to police their area, how to take care of themselves out doors." While Kerry invoked a sense of common cause with the poor, he also suggested that the Veterans were better prepared than PPC demonstrators, acquainted as they were with spartan bivouacs. One of the VVAW lawyers highlighted the significance of "men who served, who risked their lives ... coming to their government, camping on the grounds here," to make "their presence felt at the seat of Government"—not unlike what World War I veterans had done in the Bonus Army. The idea of veterans as citizens with special standing did not get much credence in Judge Hart's court, but shaped public reaction in the days that followed.[39]

Judge Hart worried more about the slippery slope this argument might generate: "If we permit you to camp out . . . then we must permit all other unemployeds [sic] to camp out . . . and pretty soon nobody can use the Elipse [sic] except unemployed camped out there." He worried that this might require the government to allow camping on federal property to "anybody, any group, any number of people who feels that they want to protest and who can't they say afford to pay their sleeping places." If one camp-out was granted, what was the basis for denying another?[40] To forestall this possibility, Hart pushed back on the idea that camping, or crucially, the physical act of sleeping, could communicate protest. "I don't really see that it's necessary for your protest at all. . . . We are not talking about a demonstration. We are talking about sleeping-in." Hart simply could not see how camping activities could "express a single idea, not even one." Kerry tried to concede that narrow point to win the larger argument. "We are not even trying to say sleeping itself is a First Amendment freedom. What we are saying is that this event, as it is construed in its entirety, is a First Amendment freedom, and if part of that entails sleeping, then so be it."[41]

The attorneys for the VVAW tried a different tactic. Why did the NPS allow noisier "all-night activities on the Mall," such as music and speeches, but ban "quiet activities, people lying down?" Judge Hart's answer was telling: "Well, the sleeping has the connotation of taking over the place." And in that, Hart implied that sleeping outdoors could express an idea. "The parks are for all the people. . . . [Y]ou can't just simply take over the park for your own purpose and deprive the other people of a right to use them." By the end of the hearing, Hart appeared even more strongly opposed to the VVAW's argument than at the beginning and he upheld the camping ban.[42] But his judgment echoed the thorny questions Resurrection City had raised. Who was taking over from whom here exactly? If protestors aren't the people, then who were they?

The VVAW raced to appeal the decision, issued at 3:20 pm on Friday. With the imminent arrival of the veterans in the capital, Dewey Canyon organizers decided to go forward as planned. As the *Washington Post* quoted John Kerry, "You can't tell veterans who have been fighting an illegal war that they cannot sleep illegally."[43] Back in court on Monday, the VVAW presented the Appeals Judges with the absurdity that the government had allowed the veterans to "demonstrate through the night and sleep through the day" but "forbidden sleeping at night." Their motion emphasized that the campground should not be "viewed in isolation" but as crucial to their "continued presence before the Congress of the United States—a bearing of witness to the . . . idea that the war in Vietnam must end." This time the argument worked, and the

Court of Appeals agreed that this represented a "legal symbolic encampment" and in line with such varied actions in the past as Boy Scout Jamborees and Resurrection City. It was a short-lived victory for the Veterans. The government immediately applied to the Supreme Court to reinstate the District Court's decision, and on Tuesday April 20, Chief Justice Warren Burger agreed, issuing a summary order upholding the ban, without recording an opinion.[44]

That evening the veterans were in a quandary. They were already encamped on the east end of the mall, just opposite the Capitol steps, and had just begun their slate of actions when the order came down to cease their "camping activities" by the next night, Wednesday, April 21. The *Washington Post*, which ran front-page stories on the court proceedings, reported that the Veterans were "defiant" and most had decided that they were "not moving, no matter what." Others worried that a clash with police might damage the positive image they had so far built—marching with Gold Star mothers, lobbying Congress, acting out mock search and destroy missions. Well into the evening, the veterans debated the issue. Eventually, they voted 480 to 400 to stay, defy the Supreme Court's order, and await reaction.[45]

Press treatment of the VVAW encampment, unlike Resurrection City, remained largely positive, even after the Supreme Court declared it illegal. National television news programs featured it each night, highlighting the campsite, the courtroom drama, and moving excerpts of veterans' testimony. Coverage tended to characterize veterans as upright citizens and loyal soldiers and the camp as peaceful and orderly. While the camp had "a scruffy look," one *Washington Post* article maintained, "it is fairly well policed so far." Reporter Carl Bernstein noted that despite the prevalence of "unmilitary length" hair, the encampment resembled a "basic training company." Other articles noted the visits by Congressional representatives including Senators Ted Kennedy (D-MA) and Phillip Hart (D-MI), accompanied by his wife. Hart commented, "We let the Boy Scouts use this park. We let the poverty people use this park and it's ridiculous not to let the veterans use it." Nixon studiously ignored the encampment but was dismayed at the positive press it received, fearing it accelerated a decline in both support for the war and his approval ratings.[46]

Though Nixon had summoned additional security forces to the capital and possessed the go-ahead to deploy them, neither he nor law enforcement were eager to take that step. As Figure 6.4 shows, the veterans were still encamped on the morning of April 22. The *Post* noted that "police looked on and appeared to ignore the 'camping' aspects of the scene," and were reluctant

FIGURE 6.4 Veterans begin to emerge from their tents, sleeping bags, and blankets at the VVAW encampment, the morning after US Park Police declined to enforce the Supreme Court order. Photograph by Brig Cabe, April 22, 1971. Reprinted with permission of the DC Public Library, Star Collection. © Washington Post.

to make any arrests. One officer realized the bad optics such arrests might create: "We are not going in there at 1 in the morning and pick up some wounded veteran and throw him into the street. . . . We don't treat people like this." Though the Police had taken similar such actions against denizens of Resurrection City, the presence of wounded veterans changed the calculation. It was not unlikely that some of those officers were veterans themselves, whether or not they sympathized with the VVAW. Or, perhaps what gave pause was the bad press the NPS had drawn the day before for preventing veterans and Gold Star Mothers from entering Arlington National Cemetery to lay wreaths at soldiers' graves. The US Park Police, moreover, struggled to define camping when confronted with the scene. The *Post* reported a telling comment from Captain Archie Finagin of the Park Police, himself a World War II Navy veteran: "about 3 a.m.," as "Finagin looked across the sleeping-bag-paved Mall," a reporter asked him "why, since the veterans were camping in defiance of a court order, arrests weren't being made." Finagin replied, " 'What's the definition of camping? You tell me. I don't know.' "[47]

The next day, Nixon and his aides furiously debated options while the veterans staged a memorable protest at the Supreme Court, planned well before Justice Burger's ruling. One woman arrested at the protest noted the irony: "All we want the Chief Justice to do is rule on the constitutionality of the war, and all he's done this week is tell us we can't sleep on the Mall." Perhaps with the recurrent example of Hoover's blunder in evicting veterans on his mind, Nixon reversed course.[48] The government went back to District Court to ask that the original restraining order be dissolved. This proved to be embarrassing. Judge Hart complied but chastised the administration for failing to enforce a court order and for contradicting itself by then issuing a permit for a larger and even "more militant" group of antiwar protestors—the People's Coalition for Peace and Justice—to camp for two weeks in West Potomac Park. In the aftermath, the Justice Department conceded that it "made an error in judgment" but pleaded that it had no way of knowing that the protest would be a peaceful action by "bonafide ex-GI's," rather than "radical street people, sympathizers, and other hangers on." As the *Post* reported, the "government's initial overreaction and subsequent total backdown" earned it a justified "tongue-lashing" from Judge Hart and quite possibly reduced its leverage in trying to constrain the People's Coalition.[49]

The government's retreat on this point contributed to the general view of the success of the VVAW encampment, which led into continuing antiwar protests that May. The court fight over camping had indeed heightened attention to the action as a whole. The *Post* suggested that what had begun as "a small, unconventional prelude to another springtime surge of antiwar protest" had become a "major event," symbolized most memorably by the VVAW's "encampment on the Mall, an outpouring of public emotion and the federal government's unsteady reaction to an unfamiliar army." It even suggested that this action had revived the efficacy of mass demonstrations altogether, served to "widen public sentiment against the war," and stepped up the pressure for US withdrawal from Vietnam.[50] While political expression through camping worked in this instance, the different outcome from Resurrection City suggested that veterans—even dissenting ones—possessed a special claim on the nation. It was veterans in the GAR, after all, that had arguably established the tradition of the encampment as political lobbying technique, memorably at the 1892 National Encampment, just a few blocks west on the Mall, between the White House and the Washington Monument.

By the time the *Quaker Action IV* decision came down in 1975, the Appeals Court could look back on the history of how the NPS had handled recent protests. In this final opinion, the Court expressed dismay at "a recurring Park Service theme that the use of parks for demonstrations is 'not an appropriate use of Federally-owned park lands.'" How would such activity not be "part of the 'basic mission' of the Park Service" or demonstrators somehow not be "'bona fide' visitors"? Instead, it asserted that "the use of parks for public assembly and airing of opinions is historic and one of its cardinal values. Public assembly for First Amendment purposes is as surely a 'park use' as any tourist or recreational activity." It balked at a policy that treated expressive conduct "on a lesser footing" than commemorative events or recreational activities. The case concluded with instructions to the government to accommodate longer and larger protests and again charged the Park Service with developing a coherent policy based on a "thorough and reflective consideration of park values, including First Amendment rights."[51] The case, however, exposed rather than resolved the tension between political and recreational claims at the heart of shifting understandings of the social contract, where rights as consumer citizens and rights to Constitutional freedoms increasingly came into conflict.

By insisting that the NPS include protest as a core "park value," alongside tourism and recreation, the *Quaker Action* cases bequeathed a lasting principle that found its way into the Occupy hearing three decades later. The "reasoned and measured" approach that Jarvis touted had resulted from legal pressure. Even as the Park Service was prodded to expand its notion of "park values," the *Quaker Action* cases failed to dislodge the centrality of mainstream recreational, family, and Boy Scout style camping. The agency embodied the way recreation had become a democratic right and protest encampments appeared an exception to the norm. Despite the success of Dewey Canyon III, in the ensuing years, camping out for a cause only grew more at odds with the beliefs that camping was fundamentally about personal recreation, not political expression. By the time of the Occupy hearing, the converse also had a powerful hold; baseline political rights were best exercised through recreation and freedom to consume rather than free speech.

"The Tent City Is Not Merely a Symbol"

Legal and public advocates for Resurrection City and Dewey Canyon III defended their encampments as First Amendment activities by arguing that they were primarily symbolic and only secondarily about logistical needs. Though the courts had not clearly established symbolic camping as a right, the Park Service learned to accommodate some level of protest encampments on the basis of symbolism. Occupy tried a different argument. Once again in DC District Court, a suit initiated on behalf of the McPherson Square occupiers in December of 2011, argued that the functional practices of camping could also embody protest. Where John Kerry had argued vehemently that the VVAW camp was crucial to the symbolism of the protest and not merely sleeping, Occupy DC's complaint in *Henke v. Department of the Interior* took the reverse angle: "The tent city is not merely a symbol" but rather, the physical act of "sleeping overnight" enacted the central "message of taking back the city to create a more just, economically egalitarian society."[52] In some ways this ratcheted up the symbolism, further pushing the idea that sleeping itself could be expressive speech, a claim Judge Hart and others had rejected on its face.

With the claim that the camp was "not merely a symbol," however, Occupy added a new wrinkle to this debate. In a handout distributed to Occupiers at McPherson Square in October, the NPS quoted its current definition of camping, as "the use of park land for living accommodation purposes such as sleeping activities, or making preparations to sleep . . . or storing personal belongings, or making any fire, or using any tents or shelter . . . for sleeping." Regulations defined symbolic camping (which could be allowed) in opposition to this more functional version (expressly prohibited outside of designated campgrounds). Despite its resistance to symbolic encampments like Dewey Canyon III, the NPS had in fact long promoted its spaces in symbolic terms: outdoor pleasure grounds for rituals of citizenship. If, as the *Henke* complaint contended, the functional acts of camping could also be symbolic, then how might the NPS draw any meaningful distinction?[53] This was, in some ways, Hart's slippery slope—where did physical or economic need end, and symbolic protest against the social conditions that produced those needs begin?

Occupy intertwined functional and political camping in a performance of social precarity. Labeling the tent city a "permanent occupation," as the *Henke* complaint did, hid the inevitable in plain sight. Tents were inherently mobile structures, and these too would eventually be folded up and moved elsewhere. In fact, by the first weeks of 2012, everywhere but the District of Columbia, it seemed, Occupy encampments were being evicted, often forcibly. These tents, as representations of impermanence and transience, thus broadcast another key piece of Occupy's message about the increasing instability or precarity of life in a context of "extreme economic inequality" that was "harming people and destroying communities." In the visual resemblance of "living in public space" and in the eviction experience, the tents of Occupy thus evoked the escalating twin crises of housing and homelessness.[54]

At times Occupy groups were careful to differentiate their camping from that of individuals experiencing homelessness. At other times, Occupy messages explicitly cited the homeless crisis as evidence of the social damage wealth inequality and government neglect could inflict. In some camps Occupiers shared food, tents, blankets, and medical care with unsheltered folks. Yet the relationship between Occupy campers, many of whom had jobs or school to go to during the day and homes to return to if evicted, and those who had none of those things could be tense. Protestors occasionally blamed homeless people for freeloading, causing problems and bad press. In some cities, longer term homeless residents expressed resentment that Occupy monopolized their usual camping areas and received laxer enforcement of trespass and anti-camping laws.[55] In the Congressional hearing on McPherson Square, one representative asked NPS Director Jarvis, "how do you distinguish between D.C. Occupy protesters and homeless people who might find their way into McPherson Square?" Jarvis skirted that question but registered his concern that "some homeless people have moved in to join the occupiers and have taken advantage of the situation there."[56] Again, the quandary arose: how to differentiate and why to prioritize symbolic over functional camping?

This uneasy overlap had happened before, as far back as Coxey's Army in 1894. A few journalists explored its historical parallel with Occupy, noting that each addressed a similar set of economic complaints at a time of financial crisis and proposed greater government responsibility. One commentator praised leader Jacob Coxey for his long-term influence, despite the short-term failure, as his seemingly radical plans for public investment would later gain acceptance as a federal responsibility. The implication was that "Occupy Wall Street should be so lucky" as to be a harbinger of future reforms. A closer kinship might be found in the way Coxey's Army had been derided as a "motley aggregation of homeless wanderers."[57] Many cities approached Occupy as they did homeless encampments, though with greater urgency. The legal structures designed to control how people experiencing homelessness used public outdoor space served as a primary rubric for managing Occupy. If these camping protests made their complaints more visible in the public eye, they also exposed the depth of national fears of the seemingly rootless poor, those that could not maintain stable connections to property or leisure. That was as much the legacy of Coxey's Army as was the fact that its proposal for federal jobs and infrastructure programs would eventually become standard expectations.

A little noticed but consequential forerunner of the Occupy encampments was "Reaganville," a Washington protest meant to call attention to the problems of homelessness in 1981 and 1982.[58] The Community for Creative

Non-Violence (CCNV), a peace and social justice organization with Christian roots, sponsored the action. Leader Mitch Snyder devised a plan to heighten awareness of the growing homeless crisis in the first year of Ronald Reagan's presidency. After serving its annual free Thanksgiving dinner in Lafayette Park, one block north of the White House, CCNV put up a dozen tents along with a sign that read: "Welcome to Reaganville—Reaganomics at Work—Population Growing Daily." CCNV hoped to "dramatize the plight of thousands of homeless people who scavenge for food and sleep wherever they can outdoors, atop sidewalk heating grates, in parks or entrances to buildings." They planned to continue the occupation through the winter of 1981–82 to "make increasingly obvious the devastation wreaked by the Reagan Administration's drastic cutback in social spending."[59]

The day after Thanksgiving was a slow news day, and multiple newspapers ran a feature on the quirky incident, highlighting the juxtaposition of the tents, the poor, and a "soup line," with the stately White House, trimmed out for a day of feasting, in the background. The story might have died there, had the US Park Police not gone in the next morning to arrest six demonstrators who had slept overnight. Though charged with "camping . . . and demonstrating without a permit on national park property," CCNV quickly negotiated with the NPS and obtained a seven-day renewable permit that allowed "nine 'symbolic' tents" but remained surprisingly silent on the issue of sleeping. The CCNV provided functional shelter for people who had none while simultaneously expressing a political grievance. For participants experiencing homelessness, use of the tents as living accommodations and as symbolic protest could not easily be separated. These ambiguities touched off another round of legal wrangling over the definition of camping, including a 1984 Supreme Court decision that held as precedent through the Occupy protests.[60]

Reaganville highlighted both the continuity of camping in negotiations over the social contract and brought new issues to the table. It explicitly referenced Depression-era Hoovervilles, the last time mass homelessness was in full public view. Yet the early 1980s marked the onset of what has been labeled the "new homelessness," and a renewal of fears of transience not seen since the 1930s. Functional outdoor transience had receded so noticeably from the postwar landscape that researchers predicted that it was likely to disappear entirely and it largely ceased provoking cultural alarm. Federal investment in the war effort and the postwar emphasis on housing contributed to a sharply declining population of transients. Research showing that transients were most likely to be older, unmarried men added to the assumption that homelessness would, literally, die out. Moreover, as transients tended to find housing in urban "skid row" districts rather than resort to outdoor living strategies their relationship to camping diminished. Recreational camping articles from the 1950s and 1960s markedly lacked the warnings of previous decades to avoid tramp-like appearances or worries about camping trailers encouraging rootlessness. The reduced numbers and visibility made it seem like those difficult earlier problems had been—or were soon to be—definitively solved.[61]

The 1980s reversed those rosy predictions. Downturns and transformations in the economy, declines in funding for public housing and other social programs, the closing of state psychiatric hospitals, all of which accelerated during Reagan's first term, contributed to a spike in the homeless population and a renewed cultural visibility.[62] Unlike the rump of skid row transients from the earlier era, the "new homeless" both included different populations (typically younger and more nonwhite people, including women and children as well as those addicted to drugs or mentally ill) and they tended to be entirely unhoused, sleeping outdoors in public spaces. New terminology accompanied the shift. Those who had once been called vagrants, tramps, hobos, or transients, became "the homeless" or sometimes "street people." Whether observers of this resurgent phenomenon rendered unsheltered people as a human tragedy to be met with compassion or a social nuisance to be scorned, they shared a belief that people should not be sleeping outside— unless as a form of recreation and with a waiting roof at home. Much homeless advocacy focused upon expanding shelters and bringing outdoor lodgers inside.[63] Simultaneously, urban redevelopers worked to make outdoor public spaces less hospitable for sleeping.[64] These increasingly restrictive urban rules about space, together with the way camping had become synonymous with outdoor recreation during a period of low transience, marginalized functional outdoor sleeping in new ways.

Set against this context, the efforts of CCNV to hold onto its encampment demonstrated how people experiencing homelessness attempted to reassert a place for themselves in the city. Whether there were simply not enough spaces for indoor shelter or whether individuals were loath to exchange personal autonomy for a bed in rigid and alienating facilities, even a precarious outdoor camp made a claim to public belonging and could sometimes be the best among bad options. That homeless people could act rationally did not substantiate what President Reagan would later declare, that "the people who are sleeping on the grates . . . are homeless, you might say, by choice."[65] The new label of "homeless" itself contained an incipient critique of those who either willfully, tragically, or through lack of perseverance failed to participate in a social contract based on home-based property and leisure. As Figure 6.5 suggests, Reaganville became a platform for unsheltered people to affirm their desires for civic voice while at the same time testifying to their loss of social and economic power. One resident noted, "Being at Reaganville is how I can write a letter to my Congressman."[66] The CCNV's efforts to hold onto a portion of public nature challenged assumptions that favored the citizens for whom parks served as place of leisure over those who used them on a basis of need.

In early December, Reaganville was in limbo. The permit that the NPS issued to the CCNV allowed "symbolic tents" but prohibited camping activities. The District Court of DC again served as a forum to sort this out. The Judge heard testimony from several Reaganville campers and even undertook a nighttime inspection of Washington streets to observe their plight first-hand. Later that month the court ruled in favor of the CCNV and the government appealed. The Appeals Court came back to the consequential but still unresolved issue: whether "regulations prohibiting camping" inherently banned associated "sleeping activities." It ruled in CCNV's favor as well, maintaining that where individuals were clearly engaged in a First Amendment activity, NPS "regulations plainly allow" participants "to sleep in the tents as an intrinsic part of their protest against governmental policies which they allege

FIGURE 6.5 The Reaganville encampment claimed the public nature in Lafayette Park for people experiencing homelessness as both a mechanism to assert civic voice and a place to sleep. Photograph by Scott Stewart, October 12, 1984. AP Photo/Scott Stewart.

contribute to their lack of shelter." The decision indicated that "in this case sleeping itself may express the message that these persons are homeless and so have nowhere else to go." The judges on the appeals panel chose to recognize the unique convergence of functional with symbolic in this case.[67]

Appeals Judge George MacKinnon, who was not on the three-member panel that made the ruling, dissented with his colleagues. Though his request for a rehearing was rejected, MacKinnon's brief reanimated the slippery slope argument. Pointing to the CCNV's stated goal to extend its permit all the way through March 1982, MacKinnon feared that this ruling "opens the door for virtually any group of demonstrators . . . to convert national monuments, symbols and grounds into sites for sleeping accommodations of indefinite duration." MacKinnon also signaled that this decision sat at odds with the Supreme Court's 1971 order in the first VVAW case, as well as overlooked its own decision in a second VVAW case in 1974, one on which he had ruled.[68] In this second case, the Appeals Court upheld the NPS's prohibition of sleeping as part of a VVAW demonstration on the Mall, calling the "unfettered exercise" of protest camping "not crucial to the survival of democracy."[69] MacKinnon cited this 1974 ruling as establishing that "sleeping can never be a form of expressive speech." But the Appellate decision on CCNV instead cited a 1976 precedent which held that under some cases sleeping could be "sufficiently expressive" as to qualify for First Amendment protection. The latter case, *United States v. Abney*, was idiosyncratic in its focus on the sleeping of an individual protestor maintaining a constant vigil, rather than an organized group encampment. Though cited here, *Abney* figured less prominently in most camping-related cases that followed.[70] MacKinnon bypassed *Abney* and emphasized VVAW in order to establish a simple logic proposition: if "sleeping in a tent is 'camping,'" and camping was prohibited, then sleeping is prohibited.[71] For the moment, MacKinnon's was the minority voice.

The government complied with the appellate decision, allowing the CCNV to remain encamped for the full four months. As Reaganville closed up on the first day of spring, 1982, CCNV reported that up to two dozen "homeless people had slept in the tents each night since late January." Based on this success CCNV planned to hold an expanded demonstration along the same lines during the winter of 1982–83, with twenty tents in Lafayette Park and forty additional tents on the Mall. The NPS granted a permit for "Reaganville II" that was identical to the one the year before in all but one respect: it explicitly prohibited sleep.[72] The CCNV went back to District Court, using the argument that had worked before: sleeping was central to demonstrating the plight of homeless people who had no place to sleep.

What the CCNV did not count on was that between the close of Reaganville I and the plan for Reaganville II, the NPS changed the wording of its policy. The new language prohibited camping "when it reasonably appears . . . that the participants . . . are in fact using the area as a living accommodation regardless of the intent . . . or the nature of any" associated activities. The District Court ruled in favor of the NPS this time, affirming the constitutionality of the new regulations separating the content of a protest from camping activities. As the US Attorney who argued the case told the press: CCNV had a permit to engage in a wide range of protest activities and "the only thing denied was camping. . . . The poor could bring their cots to show their plight but could not sleep on them." The CCNV protested the absurdity of that position: "We can put up tents, put up cots with blankets, lie down and close our eyes but we can't go to sleep."[73] The hairsplitting rules that separated sleeping from camping seemed especially unreasonable when applied to people for whom these symbolic tents were the only shelter they had.

The Appeals Court reversed this ruling to allow sleeping, but beyond that provided little guidance on the matter. The full panel of eleven judges produced six separate opinions on the way to a narrow decision in favor of the CCNV. Even some of those joining the majority only partially concurred or included a caveat. The lead opinion registered a thin consensus that, in this particular case, the "NPS failed to establish" what government interests would be served by preventing sleeping when it had already permitted the encampment.[74] Yet the multiple dissenting and concurring opinions offered by appellate judges suggested that this case provided inadequate precedent for resolving future dilemmas. Judge Antonin Scalia argued that the Constitution protected only "spoken and written thought," while Judge Ruth Bader Ginsburg countered that the majority opinion did not go far enough in endorsing symbolic speech. In her own call to the NPS to develop more "sensible, coherent, and sensitive" regulations, she suggested they take into account the full "mixture of motives" rather than try to enforce a blanket no-camping rule. While prior decisions had indicated that a total ban on camping outside of designated campgrounds could be constitutional if enforced with complete obliviousness to content, Ginsberg found both this draconian approach to be overly "arbitrary," with a "less-than-fully baked flavor." While Scalia's argument might appear "tight, tidy analysis," she continued, it was "not a rational rule of order to forbid sleeping while permitting tenting, lying down and maintaining a twenty-four hour presence." The majority opinion concluded by expressing "doubt that this will be the last occasion that the court" would have to attempt this "difficult reconciliation"—and it was cor-rect.[75] The case had a ticket to the Supreme Court.

In oral arguments on March 21, 1984, CCNV's lawyer Burt Neuborne, National Legal Director of the American Civil Liberties Union, maintained that the government should be able to discern intent, whether the genuine motives of "homeless men," who had few outlets to express "what it means to be without shelter," or folks with "some sham reason" to camp.[76] The government's lawyer, Solicitor General Paul M. Bator pushed for a clear dis-tinction around practice, between sleeping and a twenty-four-hour vigil. At one point, Justice Thurgood Marshall chided him, "How do you tell when somebody's sleeping and when they're not sleeping? I know people that sleep with their eyes open." While a low chuckle spread across the court-room, Justice William Brennan tried to clarify the seemingly absurd terms of the CCNV permit: "So you can enter a tent and lie down and lie there all night . . . as long as you don't sleep?" Bator confirmed that yes, that was the case. To defend this "very important line," he echoed Judge Hart's rea-soning that camping had the connotation of "taking over the place." Sleeping supported "continuous and intense . . . occupation" that interfered with other park uses.[77]

Wrangling over these fine distinctions pointed to larger issues at stake. Essentially the justices' consideration hinged on two questions: whether the government could prohibit camping as part of a First Amendment demon-stration and whether sleeping, as a defining characteristic of camping, could be expressive speech. In a 7–2 decision, the Court ruled in favor of the gov-ernment on the first question and sidestepped the second. In reversing the Appellate decision, *Clark v. CCNV* held that even if sleeping might consti-tute expressive conduct with some measure of First Amendment protection, the government could still restrict or ban it altogether. So long as protestors had access to alternate outlets to communicate political messages, then the government's interest in protecting the parks outweighed the right of citizens to sleep or camp. Moreover, the decision indicated that the Park Service had the authority and responsibility for "maintaining the parks in the heart of the Capital" in a particular form: "an attractive and intact condition, readily available to the millions of people who wish to see and enjoy them."[78] Here, the decision reinforced the recreational ethos over both functional and po-litical camping. Yet the oral arguments, along with a testy concurrence by Chief Justice Burger and a powerful dissent by Justice Marshall, suggested that this instance of camping raised significant underlying issues. Who were the parks for? Whose uses of outdoor space, whose claims on public nature should prevail? Which forms of citizenship should take precedence: leisure and consumption, or speech and assembly?

Assuming for the sake of argument that overnight sleeping could be expressive conduct, without taking a position on whether it was, allowed the Court to sidestep consideration of the nature of the protest itself and established a cleaner basis for the government prerogative to restrict. Camping now fell within a range of First Amendment activities that could be restricted in time, manner, or place so long as some expressive activities were allowed. This relieved the justices of having to determine those fine shades of meaning that separated camping, sleeping, and sleepless twenty-four-hour vigils. In essence, the decision endorsed a content-neutral standard. As one legal scholar put it, "The Court adopted an all-or-nothing approach: either everybody could camp, or nobody could." It ruled that the NPS should not be in the business of distinguishing between more or less compelling cases for encamped protests.[79] This satisfied Chief Justice Burger, who had ruled against the VVAW encampment back in 1971, and now judged sleeping as without meaning, "irrelevant," and plainly "not speech." In decoupling camping from the content of protest, it also offered a compromise for those, like Justice Stevens, who had worried in oral arguments whether banning encampments would have prevented the "veterans march of many years ago or Resurrection City or some massive demonstration in the city of Washington for a very, very important cause." The decision indicated that large demonstrations could continue, simply without the overnight camping aspect.[80]

Justice Marshall did not find this a reasonable solution. His dissent faulted the Court for avoiding a more serious examination of the relationship between the medium (camping) and the message (homelessness). Rather, he countered, "The proper starting point for analysis of this case is a recognition that . . . sleeping in a highly public place, outside . . . for the purpose of protesting homelessness—is symbolic speech protected by the First Amendment." Marshall called sleeping "the central fact of homelessness" and forcefully reminded his colleagues of the importance of context:

It is true that we all go to sleep as part of our daily regimen, and that, for the most part, sleep represents a physical necessity, and not a vehicle for expression. But these characteristics need not prevent an activity that is normally devoid of expressive purpose from being used as a novel mode of communication. Sitting or standing in a library is a commonplace activity . . . not conduct that an observer would normally construe as expressive conduct. However, for Negroes to stand or sit in a "whites only" library in Louisiana in 1965 was powerfully expressive; in that particular context, those acts became "monuments of protest" against segregation.[81]

If the simple act of sitting could become a widely recognized symbolic act in defiance of segregation, why could sleeping not also become a monument of protest against homelessness?

Not only did the symbolic aspects of this protest emerge directly from the lived facts of their existence, but Marshall also suggested that homeless people had limited capacity to broadcast political messages through mainstream channels. Content-neutrality, far from ensuring equal access, placed further constraints. "A content-neutral regulation that restricts an inexpensive mode of communication will fall most heavily upon relatively poor speakers and the points of view that such speakers typically espouse." Encampment, as far back as Coxey's Army, had been a consistent strategy for those with lesser means to get their point across, to render invisible issues and marginalized people visible on the public landscape. Marshall further cautioned the Court not to treat the homeless demonstrators as "supplicants seeking to wheedle an undeserved favor from the Government. They are citizens raising issues of profound public importance."[82]

Underlying these debates about medium and message were bedrock beliefs about who were the rightful park users and which uses of public nature were primary. Justice White's majority opinion began by citing the 1916 Organic Act, which "admonished" the NPS with its dual mission: "to conserve the scenery" and "provide for the enjoyment" of it. He then gave a rundown of the history of the Mall and Lafayette Park, focusing entirely on their role in the city's planning, where Lafayette was conceived as a "Garden park" with "formal landscaping." The opinion highlighted these parks' popularity with visitors, but their history as spaces for protest appeared only as a brief aside. Marshall's dissent noted this omission: "Missing from the majority's description is any inkling that Lafayette Park and the Mall have served as the sites for some of the most rousing political demonstrations in the Nation's history."[83] That the majority downplayed this to emphasize visitors' enjoyment of scenery was telling.

The highest use of the parks, in this decision, was as a space of leisure. Justice Burger doubted any rationale for activities that might hinder the "hundreds of thousands of tourists who . . . want to take pictures, walk around the flowers." Justice Rehnquist ventured that maybe the government should just ban all demonstrations in Lafayette Park because they prevented visitors from enjoying the space. "They like to see the park just as kind of like a green pleasant place. They don't like the hassle of demonstrations." He was doubtful that the government had constitutional obligations to respect such protests: "I don't think that's necessarily true when the Government's dealing with its own property." Neuborne found this an alarming, "extraordinary statement. The parks are the property of the people," not the government.[84]

In his concurring opinion, Burger weighed in on this debate, suggesting that the people best asserted claims to that "property" through the recreational ethos, rather than political expression. Not only did he find Reaganville an "absolutely absurd" and "wholly frivolous" effort that "trivializes the First Amendment," but he also believed that such protests detracted from "the purposes for which [the Park] was created. Lafayette Park and others like it are for all the people, and their rights are not to be trespassed even by those who have some 'statement' to make. Tents, fires, and sleepers, real or feigned, interfere with the rights of others to use our parks." White's majority opinion imagined protestors not as citizens raising significant issues, but as negligent campers, a group "readily understood" by national park visitors who have "observed the unfortunate consequences of the activities of those who refuse to confine their camping to designated areas."[85] The frame of reference in each of these opinions is revealing. The analogy repeated the notion that the primary and proper function of public nature should be as a space for recreation. Homeless folks and people with "statements" to make appeared as trespassers on the green and pleasant places of the nation.

CCNV lost its case but its hearing in the highest court punctuated the reemergence of outdoor transience in the 1980s. As Neuborne had reminded, the case was not about "whether or not homeless people will sleep in the parks." The decision would not change the fact that they would "be in Lafayette Park, they'll be on the Mall, they'll be in the parks of virtually every city in the nation. The truth is we are prepared to tolerate their presence sleeping in the parks."[86] The question was whether the nation was prepared to see them as citizens making political claims on the public, rather than intruders on a seemingly nonpolitical public lawn. Reaganville challenged the universality of the recreational ethos and called into question the social contract on which it was based.

Following *Clark v. CCNV*, restricting camping became key to municipal legal responses to homeless populations. Municipalities enacted urban camping bans in the ensuing decades, laws that tended to define camping as sleeping "with a shelter" on public or private property in order to "conduct activities of daily living, such as eating or sleeping." Daytime napping and picnicking were usually exempt, but shelter could mean anything from a conventional tent to a makeshift lean-to, or even "any cover or protection from the elements other than clothing." Under this definition, sleeping bags could be considered shelter. Given that the courts prevented municipalities from banning all sleeping in public, camping as shelter or living accommodations became a mechanism to control the functional use of outdoor urban space.[87] While municipal anti-camping ordinances usually identified shelter as the key difference between lawful sleeping outside and unlawful camping, in the case of encamped protests, the act of sleeping rendered a tent occupation unlawful.

These legal developments marked nonrecreational camping as deviant. Recreational camping, whether of the loop campground or backcountry adventure variety, had become the assumed norm between the 1940s and 1960s, an interlude marked by the relative absence of mass outdoor transience or encamped protests. As functional camping reappeared in dramatic ways in the early 1980s, it garnered growing suspicion. The logic that the *CCNV* decision laid out built on the campers' republic and expanded its reach into political life, supporting a belief that the best manifestation of democracy is access to leisure, recreation, consumption, and personal fulfillment, not the "hassle" of political debate and First Amendment expression.

The tent cities that swelled following the onset of the Great Recession in 2008 intensified this divide even as they echoed the collision of symbolic expression and lived experience. Made homeless by foreclosure, unemployment, or loss of retirement savings, some deliberately sought out spaces of urban nature to pitch their tents and ride out their own economic storm. Many of the foreclosed and unemployed, in fact, relied upon an array of camping equipment—lanterns, coolers, tents, trailers—perhaps originally purchased for leisure purposes. While camping elsewhere received positive press as a frugal option for family vacations in tough times, recession encampments became symbols of both nature and economy gone awry. Sympathetic observers, profit-minded developers, and conservationists alike worried about tent cities as distressing "third worlds" in America, ruining outdoor spaces and symbolizing the public tragedy of the times.[88]

Occupy emerged while the nation was still in the throes of the Great Recession, in part to argue for a recovery that might assuage rather than exacerbate the inequality of wealth. Though the movement did not always make common cause with homeless advocates, its practices drew attention to the economic issues and social disinvestments driving increases in homelessness. Occupiers also revealed how public camping was subject to surveillance.

The police forces of cities from Providence, Rhode Island, to Sacramento, California, employed thermal imaging to ascertain whether protesters were, in fact, sleeping in their tents at night and thus violating the prohibition on sleeping during a twenty-four-hour vigil. Homeless people, on the other hand, could be cited not for sleeping, but for using shelter. Whichever side of these laws one might run afoul of, the infrared night-vision turned nonrecreational campers into suspicious targets. The tactics suggested a fear of the semiprivate space tents created in a public place. What were people doing in there? The material consequences of the reaction to Occupy encampments, however, fell more heavily on unsheltered people than on protestors. Many cities responded to Occupations by tightening regulations or enacting new emergency bans on "urban camping" or closing off public space to any nighttime presence. From one angle, Occupy provided municipalities an expedient catalyst for further restricting functional campers. For example, in 2019 voters in Denver reaffirmed the City's camping ban—first enacted in response to Occupy—not due to renewed protest, but to the alarming increase in homeless populations and encampments as a result of sharply rising costs of housing.[89]

Unlike unsheltered people or CCNV's homeless protestors, Occupiers were better equipped to work in the realm of the purely symbolic. The tent could become a symbol for making camp not just upon a physical space but as an idea, and a way of being seen. As Figure 6.6 shows, a protestor from Occupy Denver demonstrated how the tent provided a unique vehicle for broadcasting political messages about corporations, money, and politics. Occupiers often used their tents for such purposes, but this tent was more mobile than most and mischievously subverted the whole point of a tent itself—to provide shelter. Why in this instance use a tent at all? A sign might have been a more practical choice for publicizing the message. University of California, Berkeley students took this tactic further. Instructed to strike their camp, Occupiers instead affixed helium balloons and floated several empty tents above their space, hanging improbably a dozen feet in midair.[90] These performative uses of tents functioned as uncanny, eye-catching symbols of the impulse to occupy.

The argument Occupy DC made in *Henke*, however, was that the tents were not merely symbolic. The "24-hour-a-day physical occupation" enacted the movement's myriad goals of creating a "more just and egalitarian society," ending "corporations' permanent occupation of the government," and "taking back the City of Washington." The language of "occupation" was precise, as the complaint studiously avoided any reference to sleeping, camping, or the First Amendment. Instead of an encampment, what was happening at

FIGURE 6.6 An Occupy protestor sports a tent as a symbolic bid for visibility. "Occupy Denver introduces protest tent," Not My Tribe blog, October 19, 2011. Photograph by Eric Verlo.

McPherson Square and other sites were "symbolic, round-the-clock, peaceful protests, or 'occupations.'" In that, Occupiers (or their lawyers) were clearly aware of the precedent and the letter of NPS regulations. The language on the handout the NPS had circulated in McPherson Square in October, reminding Occupiers of the prohibition on camping, remained identical to the regulations developed between the two Reaganville demonstrations, which the Supreme Court upheld. Occupy DC thus eschewed "any reliance on the First Amendment," a move the District Court Judge called a "a wise concession because *Clark* [*v. CCNV*] indeed forecloses a First Amendment argument." Instead, the *Henke* complaint made Fourth and Fifth Amendment claims, that "tents are protected from seizure and destruction." The strategy failed, as the judge did not find enough evidence to support those claims either.[91]

Curiously, the District Court's decision detailed how the judge mediated several related disputes in early January 2012 and secured a promise from the NPS to provide twenty-four hours' notice if it decided to evict Occupiers from McPherson Square. On January 27, three days after the Congressional hearing, the NPS issued a "Camping Enforcement Notice," indicating that the

US Park Police would begin to arrest Occupiers still encamped in McPherson Square on January 30, providing close to seventy-two hours' notice. What had changed was not the regulations but the position of the NPS. Resisting earlier tendencies, it held out as long as possible from enforcing its anti-camping regulations, tried to grapple with the complex fusion of medium and message, and defended its reasoning to a largely hostile Congressional committee. The "reasoned and measured" approach that Jarvis articulated may have emerged from an era when the courts compelled the NPS to consider and reconsider its regulations, but in approaching Occupy the agency chose not to take the most restrictive path the *Clark* decision invited.[92]

"Using a Tent ≠ Camping"

At the Congressional hearing that prompted the NPS to start shutting down Occupy DC, Trey Gowdy, who chaired it, and California representative Darrell Issa, chair of the subcommittee that sponsored it, aimed to get to the bottom of what they saw as a clear conflict. How could the government reconcile the official NPS ban on camping with obvious evidence "that sleeping, cooking and camping are taking place." They wanted to know who was responsible for wasting "thousands of dollars in taxpayer money" by allowing this situation to continue.[93] NPS Director Jarvis, and those more sympathetic with Occupy's efforts, tried to separate the movement from common assumptions about camping, instead emphasizing links with the long history of protest in the city. Issa, Gowdy, and those less supportive of Occupy, continued to see the action through the lens of recreational camping, if a baffling never-seen-before perversion of it.

Jarvis walked representatives through guidelines, carefully constructed through decades of experience and court instructions, that governed "public assembly and political demonstration." The NPS took Occupiers at their word, that they were "maintaining a site of protest," and thus according to the guidelines, they were engaged in "round-the-clock demonstration vigils" and "expressive activities" protected by the First Amendment. As such, barring an emergency or imminent threat to public health or safety, Jarvis believed that the Occupy "demonstrators in McPherson Square and elsewhere" were "allowed to continue their vigil." Moreover, he stressed that the McPherson Occupiers were not technically required to obtain a permit, because their protest involved less than 500 people (a threshold set by the final *Quaker Action* case). At its height, the Occupy encampment at McPherson Square held about 350 participants.[94]

As to whether those participants were camping, Jarvis believed that tents were "permissible" so long as they acted to advance a "symbolic message or to meet logistical needs." If some individuals were using these tents primarily for "living accommodation" purposes, and thus in violation of the camping prohibition, Jarvis explained that this did not invalidate the entire group's action. He defended the NPS strategy to educate and gradually bring protestors into compliance with the regulations through cooperation rather than resorting to arrests or other heavy-handed tactics. So far, Jarvis noted, this approach avoided the volatile confrontations seen in cities like New York and Oakland and allowed the Park Police to make progress in gaining compliance.[95]

That a vigil might employ tents for symbolic and logistical means, but somehow not signify camping, drew skepticism. Issa and Gowdy had opened the proceedings with doubt that there could be a "difference between camping and a 24-hour vigil, especially when that 24-hour vigil lasts several months." Like Judge Hart, Chief Justice Burger, and others, they reverted to a simpler, I-know-it-when-I-see-it definition of camping. Together the two Congressmen drove the questioning of Jarvis and other witnesses from a standpoint of recreational camping as a governing framework and balked at the idea that there could be any other legitimate uses of tents. Issa derived his definition from personal experience. He knew what camping was supposed to look like because, he stated, "I'm an avid camper, both RV and tent over the years, and a very old Boy Scout."[96] The RV and Boy Scout camp invoked a quite different historical reference than did Jarvis's links to late-1960s protestors and recalled precisely the kinds of cultural rifts that had animated those earlier moments.

Gowdy dismissed the "measured and reasoned approach" of the NPS and demanded a clear-cut answer. Calling himself an "old country prosecutor," he told Jarvis, "I need a definition of camping. Because I need to go back to South Carolina and tell everyone who wants to spend the summer in one of our parks what camping is and what it is not." Jarvis reluctantly offered up sleep as the key factor. In a vigil, protestors remain awake to distribute information, whereas camping is "defined as sleeping or preparing to sleep at the site." Even if, Jarvis admitted, there was some sleeping going on at McPherson, the vigil remained the primary purpose of the encampment and the sleeping a secondary concern. For Gowdy, as for others before, the introduction of sleeping into a First Amendment discussion introduced a new level of befuddlement. If the "linchpin of the definition of camping" is sleeping, was there a difference between "First Amendment sleeping versus recreational sleeping"? Jarvis, in a rare display of frustration, shook his head and replied, "I don't really understand that question."[97] It is difficult not to empathize with Jarvis.

On its face, without the longer history of debate on this question by major legal figures in the nation's history, the question sounds ridiculous. Though Jarvis was not deeply versed in this history, he continued to present the NPS approach: once an action was identified as a demonstration with expressive content, then any camping or sleeping was viewed in light of that primary character, not in abstract.

For Gowdy, this raised the specter of the slippery slope. If the NPS allowed Occupy to continue its encampment, without permit or penalties, how would it prevent other people from setting up camp anywhere in the United States as long as "they say they're in protest of something"? It rankled Gowdy that protest was the key criteria, and that if anyone should be allowed to use the space it should be those who camped for recreational reasons. From his standpoint, it looked like protest campers had an unfair privilege over recreational campers, who should have a higher claim on what it meant to camp and on the use of public nature. Issa concurred, lamenting that innocent tourists could not "pitch a tent in McPherson Square if they're camping for fun" while those "camping in protest of fun" had free rein.[98] Along with minimizing Occupy's grievances, this reasoning reinforced the recreational ethos as the preferred expression of citizenship.

One of the key factors underlying this dispute was whether one perceived inhabiting public outdoor space as a right or a privilege. This too had evolved historically. The state had not always exerted authority to dictate where individuals could and could not camp. From the informal practices of the nineteenth century to the early days of automobile camping, travelers largely assumed the right to camp where they pleased. The regulations that accompanied the development of the loop campground in the 1930s put the government in the position of both sponsoring and limiting recreational camping. The campers' republic depended upon this formula, as camping increasingly became an activity performed on public ground with permission of some public agency (or, as in homeless camping, in violation of those rules). This was the default from which Gowdy and Issa operated, though without understanding it as a product of history. For them, it was an axiomatic definition: sleeping outside was a privilege fundamentally regulated by the state. Campers could not assume any tacit permission or right.

Issa proffered an example. Park rangers routinely "check to see if somebody is allowed to be a camper" and, if finding them in violation or outside of "lawfully designated areas," then "they're ushered out . . . if necessary at gunpoint." Jarvis quickly countered these assumptions, asserting citizens' right to be (if not necessarily to camp) in national parks, most of which were

open twenty-four hours a day, 365 days a year. This recalled the scrap between Justice Rehnquist, who saw the Parks as the government's "own property," and CCNV's startled lawyer, who reminded him that the parks were
"the property of the people." In Issa's logic, demonstrators had no right to
camp and instead should "come with candles and stand" and then "get hotel
rooms." He questioned why Occupy refused to conform to these standard
protest expectations, exemplified at a recent anti-abortion rally: "They
came, they protested, they left."[99] Issa wanted to impose a standard of appropriate political action and use of public space where citizens' expression
was controlled by their ability to pay for hotel rooms or by a Park Ranger's
firearm. This was one of the hazards of content-neutral standards Justice
Marshall had warned about; it constrained those with fewer means to get
their views across in more conventional ways. Eleanor Holmes Norton, the
nonvoting Congressional Delegate for the District of Columbia, echoed this
sentiment in refuting Issa. Arguing that protest tactics should not be held
to a format preferred by those in power, she compared Occupy to 1960s-era
protests like Resurrection City and sit-ins, which "nobody much wanted"
then either.[100] Issa's proffered formula—they came, they stood with candles,
they left—posited a circumscribed vision of citizen participation, precisely
what Occupy sought to resist.

At least part of the issue revolved around the location of the protest,
shown in Figure 6.7. McPherson Square, more so than the National Mall
or Freedom Plaza, the swath of concrete where the other Occupy group
was encamped, seemed a space for local, outdoor leisure rather than politics. The Park Service had recently completed a $400,000 rehabilitation
of the pocket park with refurbished benches, repaired drinking fountains,
fresh paint, new fences, and significantly, an acre of grass sod. The new lawn
quickly began to show wear and tear, as Occupiers expanded their footprint to up to three-quarters of the square. One woman who lived near
McPherson Square wrote to the NPS to complain about the damage to her
neighborhood park: "Now the ducks are gone, the squirrels are gone and my
park bench no longer available thanks to Occupy DC. The grass is ruined,
the trash is horrendous and the rat population has at least tripled." While
both Occupy sites contained a similar collection of individual tents, outdoor kitchens, overnight campers, and, presumably, rats, only McPherson
drew such ire.[101]

What McPherson Square had was greenery—trees, flowers, and grass. The
fact that Occupiers were ruining a lawn—a key symbol of suburban recreational
space—made it all the more problematic. Occupiers did attempt to minimize

FIGURE 6.7 Occupy DC's encampment at McPherson Square, growing toward its height of approximately 350 residents, with the lawn showing early signs of deterioration. McPherson Square, Washington, DC, October 25, 2011. Photograph by Karen Bleier via Getty Images.

their impact, rotating tent placements in an effort to preserve the turf because, as one resident suggested, "This is our home too." Issa rejected the claim of shared ownership, declaring instead that the protestors were "basically using somebody else's asset, the American people's asset" without obeying "regulations set about for all citizens." Here Issa not only prioritized economic costs over public voice, but also defined the Occupiers not as part of the "American people" who jointly owned the Square but as squatters on someone else's property, misappropriating a recreational asset.[102] The occupation of public nature sat at the heart of what Occupy's struggle was all about, as it pushed back on the idea that well-behaved recreation was the preferred exercise of citizenship.

Occupy continued to disavow any connection to the recreational assumptions that their tents implied. McPherson Square protestors taped signs to their tents that announced, in large block letters printed over a background of the Bill of Rights, "WE ARE NOT CAMPING. We are assembling peaceably to petition the Government for a redress of grievances." Red pen circled the First Amendment, and insisted, "THIS IS OUR PERMIT."[103] Though the First Amendment had not protected protest camping in court, the appeal had cultural resonance and supported the explicitly nonrecreational definition.

However strongly Occupy renounced recreational camping, it also depended on the tradition of making claims on public nature. The declaration in Figure 6.8, that "Using a Tent ≠ Camping," sought to amplify Occupiers' claim to seriousness by using common images of camping as a foil. And yet the tent appeared at the intersection of a Venn diagram that held on the one side recreational icons for swimming, hiking, canoeing, and picnicking, and on the other a pencil, a poster, a fist, and a megaphone. This image attempted to separate camping from "petitioning government for redress of grievances"

FIGURE 6.8 A public nature Venn diagram that relied upon standard NPS icons even as it tried to reject the recreational. Occupy* Posters, November 1, 2011. Image by Stephen Ewen, stephen.ewen@gmail.com.

but simultaneously managed to link the two activities.[104] The tent inhabited one circle with all the associated background of the other. Moreover, as in the "Yes We Camp" poster, this continued to use iconography echoing standard NPS signage. The figure holding the sign does not appear fundamentally different than the hiking figures. The tent did not resemble the high-tech dome-style versions most common to Occupy encampments but the archetypal pup tent. The movement's graphics generally featured more traditional canvas-and-frame tents over contemporary models. These choices suggested that Occupy implicitly relied upon the vision of the campers' republic, whose recreational practices it claimed to repudiate.

In a sense, Occupy iterated on Emilio's Meinecke's social design: an organized form of camping that served as a lasting model of democratic community that transformed space and argued for a new social contract. It also resonated with the countercultural version that fostered personal discovery and political identities. Occupy's messages and images often invoked a "back to nature" theme. Whether emphasizing their organic communal kitchens, what one reporter termed its "borrowed-cup-of-sugar community," or the way these model communities were possible because they were outside of the normal constraints of modern society, Occupy employed a version of "new naturalism" alongside its politics—and recombined them in compelling ways.[105] Moreover, Occupy's claim of "model communities" echoed the social contracts National Outdoor Leadership School participants had to work out to survive an expedition. They too expressed preferences for consensus and direct democracy and emphasized getting away from the deceit and artifice of mainstream society and enacting a better world in microcosm. While they denied recreation, they sought a kind of "occupiers' republic."

Occupy's use of public space for these ends captivated architectural critics, who admired the improvisational and "vibrant urbanism" that Occupiers achieved where planners usually failed. Such observations linked Occupy to, as one observer of McPherson Square labeled it, "DIY urbanism," a movement that sought "to engage ordinary people in a hands-on approach to shaping and claiming public space." A piece in the Style section of the *Washington Post* about five weeks after the encampment had begun showcased Occupy as a living example of how "people, working through consensus, can solve basic problems such as how to regulate public space, security and infrastructure." The architecture critic of the *Los Angeles Times* declared that "2011 turned out to be the Year of the Tent. . . . Whatever your feelings about their political merits, the Occupy gatherings clearly represented a new chapter in the long history of the relationship between protest and civic life—and urban design."

They spoke to our "notions of civic space," weaving critique of inequality and models of democracy into the spontaneous design of the camps. Moreover, they might serve as a reminder of the illusion of permanence. In light of the "apocalyptic qualities" of recent natural disasters in California, he concluded, "maybe you could argue that we are all just camping here in any case."[106]

Envisioning encampments as hopeful novel settlements amidst a tightly regulated urban landscape, where protestors invented their model communities through the occupation of space, played into Occupy's arguments of resisting the status quo and establishing a permanent beach-head. Yet this framing tends to obscure another set of historical meanings of occupations. Tents have not always been a mechanism for resistance by the less powerful. They can and have served to displace others, and not just tourists. They have been tools of state occupation, used to colonize rather than to protest. In the nineteenth century, for example, both the US Army and American settlers pursued conquest in part by first making camp on Native lands. They too understood themselves as creating model communities, establishing a new civilization in wilderness. The claim of "we are all just camping here" elides this legacy. Some groups have insisted on rights to permanence for themselves over others, often by force. On what layers of displacement did Occupy rely?

The message of the eye-catching "Take Back Wall Street" poster shown in Figure 6.9 suggests this complexity. It referenced the European takeover of Indigenous land as a prior—and harmful—form of occupation. Wall Street's origins lie in the wall erected by Dutch settlers in the 1640s. Built by both white colonists and enslaved Africans, the wall's purpose was to establish the northern boundary of the New Amsterdam colony in opposition to Indigenous people inhabiting the rest of the island as well as for protection from incursions by English colonists. The wall grew to a twelve-foot-high fortification of substantial strength before colonists took it down in 1699 to allow urban expansion. The new residents kept the name Wall Street, preserving its legacy of European occupation and locus for commercial trade.[107] In this sense, the poster suggested the possibility of reversing a bad occupation with a good one, liberating Native Manhattan simultaneously from seventeenth-century colonizers and twenty-first-century financiers.

The poster was a clever twist on the Occupy meme, bringing the colonial conquest into the present. Yet the quaintly-styled font and tinted historic photograph of an early twentieth-century Lenape woman in traditional dress shaped the message as a remnant from the past. The woman appeared less as a person with a modern claim to make than as historic guilty conscience, the ghost of occupy past. Instead of using Occupy to bolster Native land

FIGURE 6.9 Occupy, seventeenth-century style, suggests the legacy of displacement. The photograph is cropped from an original taken of Jennie Bobb (Lenape) and her daughter around 1915 (Negative 56928, National Anthropological Archives, Smithsonian Institution). "Take Back Wall Street," from the *Social Design Notes* blog, October 7, 2011. Image by John Emerson.

claims, the "Take Back Wall Street" poster used an image of an Iindigenous woman to strengthen the claims of Occupy. A solidarity of the 99% made a powerful claim, but in part by occluding the specific anti-colonial politics of Native people, who comprised almost precisely 1% of the US population in the 2010 census. In an "Open Letter to the Occupy Wall Street Activists," JohnPaul Montano (Anishinabe) pointed out how the framing of the 99%

served to exclude Indigenous people, rendering them more as mascots than participants. Different messages were possible, from Toronto artist's Ryan Hayes's call to "(Un)Occupy Canada: Respect Indigenous Sovereignty" to the art and activist collective, DignidadRebelde's reminder that "Oakland is Occupied Ohlone Land—Decolonize the 99%." Indigenous sovereignty and decolonization offered alternative way to conceptualize the movement. Acknowledging both the history and the contemporary claims of Native people invited both Occupy participants and critics to rethink the strategy of "occupation" itself.[108] The legacy of appropriation in "Take Back Wall Street"—vanished Indian as metaphor for the subjugation of non-Indian people—heightened the visibility of Occupy at the expense of Native political claims. Whose ground did Occupy occupy?

By the time Trey Gowdy gaveled open the Congressional hearing in late January 2012, McPherson Square and Freedom Plaza were among the last major Occupy encampments standing. Most others had been shut down weeks, if not months, before. The original camp in Zuccotti Park in Manhattan, along with Philadelphia, Oakland, and Los Angeles, were all gone by November; Boston, Richmond, and Denver followed in December, and Baltimore, one of the larger holdouts, by mid-January. A handful of smaller camps in cities like Houston, Miami, and Charlotte were still hanging on in late January, but Occupy DC essentially became the nucleus for the national movement. Plans for an "Occupy Congress" based around the two camps drew an influx of protestors to Washington from cities whose encampments had shut down. Knowing it was among the last remaining encampment contributed to Occupy DC's staunch vow to hold onto McPherson Square, despite the increasing pressure from Congress and the city. Occupiers knew that the reason they had outlasted the camps in other cities was because of the NPS's commitment to protecting demonstrations in the capital. As one demonstrator told a reporter in January, "The No. 1 reason why we're still here? We're in D.C."[109] It continued to push the Park Service to uphold that principle.

The NPS began to buckle to the pressure following the Congressional hearing and announced it would enforce the camping prohibition at both sites on January 31. Many Occupiers complied peacefully, closing the kitchen, packing their personal belongings, and emptying their tents—some of which were left unoccupied "as symbols rather than living spaces." The Park Police was initially pleased that they were making progress with "voluntary compliance." But the denouement dragged out and the NPS conduced a pre-dawn raid on February 5, which included eleven arrests and some violent confrontations. Even after that it continued to monitor McPherson Square, as a few Occupiers persisted in sleeping on-site, evading the letter of the regulations by, ironically, moving their tents to the sidewalks for overnight sleeping and moving them back into the park during the day. By June, they were just using the park for general assembly meetings, which dwindled over time as organizers found that "without the park as a hub, communication" became "more difficult." Restoration of the lawn and flower beds proceeded throughout that spring. The work was estimated to cost on the order of $7,000, far less than the alarmist figures Issa had cited. Occupiers were glad to see the new landscaping, through their offer to help with the planting was rebuffed and the protective fencing frustrated their attempts to hold gatherings.[110]

What Occupy had to confront was how to sustain the movement without the encampments. Many called for Occupy to "move out of their tents and start engaging the political process in a more significant way," say by running for office. If that might support specific causes, was it still Occupy? One man who joined the McPherson Square encampment from Minnesota wrestled with this question. "Occupy is supposed to mean occupy. You know, like [the United States] has occupied other countries." He told a reporter about a rumor that a Virginia man was inviting protesters "to occupy his land," but remarked, "that's not really the point." As the reporter interpreted it, "Occupying a yard that you have been invited to stay in isn't really occupying. It's just being a houseguest. And occupying a park that you're no longer sleeping in . . . is that occupying? Or is that just standing around with a protest sign?" This dilemma called attention to the way the strategy of "occupation" represented a potent, complex use of public nature that needed actual ground on which to enact the protest. Reporters observed the scene as Occupiers packed up "the bedrolls and blankets and crusty Nalgene bottles, the comfy camp accoutrements that have, over the course of four months, turned McPherson Square into a radical protest experiment, communal living cooperative and REI advertisement."[111] To mount its challenge, Occupy involved all three elements of camping— political, functional, and recreational—in a unique combination.

Although active camping and consistent media coverage linked to Occupy largely disappeared as the decade wore on, the memory of the movement and the mobilization of the tent as political logo has left significant cultural traces. Perhaps it influenced protests that emerged later in the decade, from the protectors fighting the Dakota Pipeline in 2016 to Black Lives Matter encampments in 2020. Highlighting the 1%–99% divide brought the issue of wealth inequality to the forefront in a way that reframed discourse on inequality for years afterward. In its attempt to use occupations to represent "the enormity of the problem" and to model an impossible reimagining of society, it spoke to the core of the nation's social contract through claims on public nature, even if the platform ultimately proved unstable.[112]

RESURRECTION CITY, Dewey Canyon III, Reaganville, and Occupy DC. Poverty, war, homelessness, inequality. Different issues, driven by different coalitions of American activists. All pursued a similar form of encamped protests in the nation's capital to draw greater attention to their cause. And they all ran up against public criticism, even outright alarm, often from government agencies. Each time these groups set up camp, the National Park Service struggled to adapt. Initially, the NPS was inclined to forbid camping in the National Mall and other green spaces in the Memorial core, but the courts pushed the agency to explain precisely why it needed to do so. Once it settled on a stable method—a seemingly "content-neutral" ban on camping for "living accommodations"—the courts backed off. But by the time it had come around to trying to prohibit camping while also supporting Occupy, the NPS found itself back in a muddle. While the NPS sustained and shielded Occupy DC encampments far longer than most municipalities, in the end it could not defend its nuanced approach to the satisfaction of those who desperately wanted a bright line between camping and not-camping.

Much of the fear of protest encampments, and their uncomfortable melding with functional or recreational camping, came from the oft-cited slippery slope. Judge Hart had not even been the first to raise it. He implicitly relied on Justice Hugo Black's dissent to the same 1966 Supreme Court decision cited by Justice Marshall in *Clark v. CCNV*, which ruled that sit-ins protesting segregation deserved First Amendment protection. Justice Black railed against this decision, which he deemed as requiring public officials "to stand helplessly by while protesting groups advocating one cause or another . . . take over." In this case it was desegregating libraries, but in the future, "other groups will assert the right to do so" in other public spaces for less appealing causes, paralyzing the state's ability to maintain those spaces for their original purposes. How would the government be able to enforce the difference between legitimate and sham causes? None of the encamped protests that followed bore out such fears. Yet Trey Gowdy reawakened them in his closing remarks at the McPherson Square hearing. If there was no singular definition of camping that could be applied in all spaces to all groups, he warned, "the fabric of this republic is going to unravel."[113] The idea that a handful of protest campers could cause the nation to unravel suggested that camping continued to be a potent mode for political expression.

Ironically, these protest campers were in fact trying to tug on a few threads and start to unravel some aspects of how the republic operated—how it marginalized poor, nonwhite, and unsheltered people, how it maintained foreign wars and domestic inequalities. That these groups fell short did not take away from the continued evolution of encamped protests in meaningful public spaces. An Occupy advocate, reflecting on the legal history, concluded that if the movement had "any chance of success, [it] must engage in the expressive activity for which it was named. . . . [I]t must continue to occupy space." The battles Occupy waged to hold onto its encampments bequeathed to future movements the recognition that "the occupation of physical space is important and resonant" not only for "those who remain day after day and night after night, but the full participation of the rest of us." The sustained encampments "reinvigorated the meaning of the public forum and civic participation."[114]

Occupy evoked a sense of civic belonging and public responsibility that the campers' republic had embodied, calling for the government to renew its commitment to the public good but questioning the recreational ethos as the standard for citizenship. The movement contested an ascendant neo-liberalism that was championing not just recreation and consumption, but individual responsibility as the prime source of public good. Gowdy and Issa's apparently nostalgic vision of camping typified this new twist that took a thin view of the government role in supporting public nature as a civic resource for the nation. Instead many came to see the outdoors as a kind of marketplace for Americans in search of recreation for personal benefit. While Occupy in some ways used the outdoors to summon a sense of connection that such neo-liberal formulas were severing, responses to it underscored how public nature increasingly operated more as a commodifiable asset than as common ground.

Epilogue

"WE MUST CAMP"

OUTDOOR RETAILER REI titled one of its 2017 marketing campaigns with the inviting suggestion "Let's Camp," but many individual advertisements took a more adamant tone. One insisted, "We MUST camp," and proceeded to lay out the reasons: "We need dirt. And air that smells like air. We need to gather wood and our favorite people, to stuff our faces with marshmallows and bodies into sleeping bags. We need to ponder a pinecone—or nothing at all. Now more than ever, we must camp." This appeal echoes some of the attractions that recreational camping acquired over a century or more. The outdoors promised the chance to escape from everyday stressors and commune with nature. It also beckoned as a place for social connection and sensory experience. Missing from the scene, however, is much trace of the campers' republic and its physical or philosophical infrastructure. As Figure E.1 shows, two young campers appear snug in their puffy sleeping bags as they gaze out at a pristine mountain valley. No driveway, picnic table, or fire ring. No sense of how they and their hip camping gear arrived at that panoramic perch. A different ad in this series framed the scene this way: "Camping is an instinct. It's an outside homesickness constantly trying to get our attention. With summertime here, we must tune in to it. We must camp."[1] Here camping entails hardly any choice at all, much less infrastructure. People camp to satisfy innate urges or universal bodily needs. The imperative tense, the ALL-CAPS command, demands following our instincts and heading straight into the wilds—with a quick stop at REI, of course.

The idea that camping, or other leisure time spent in nature, can fulfill human biological needs is not limited to REI marketing strategies. Outdoor

We need dirt. And air that smells like air. We need to gather wood and our favorite people, to stuff our faces with marshmallows and bodies into sleeping bags. We need to ponder a pinecone—or nothing at all. Now, more than ever, we must camp.

FIGURE E.1 Camping as a human biological need, where sleeping bags and marshmallows are key ingredients in a new "nature cure." REI Co-op, "Let's Camp," email to subscribers, May 31, 2017.

recreation promoters and environmental advocates alike have increasingly adopted this reasoning. Perhaps an innate, physiological, or even genetic drive for nature proposes a novel, present-day answer to the question of why camping matters. The biological case for outdoor recreation, however, does not account for history and culture. Nor does it consider the variable social and political contexts for sleeping outside, which remain as critical as in earlier eras. This book began by tracking the emergence of camping as a meaningful way to claim public nature as the old agrarian social contract faded in the late nineteenth century. It ends by reflecting on the legacies of the recreational ethos that rose to dominance by the mid-twentieth century and the changing terms of that social contract. Does this new formulation and camping as ful-filling a biological need suggest an incipient transition toward a new social contract? Or is the role of public nature, and the idea of a social contract itself eroding? The contemporary landscape for recreational, functional, and polit-ical camping provides some clues.

IRONIC OR NO, the onset of the COVID-19 pandemic in 2020 revealed intriguing dimensions of the camping landscape and highlighted Americans' desires to get outdoors. In many communities, outdoor recreation was declared an essential activity for mental and physical health, one of the few permitted reasons to leave the house under stay-at-home orders.[2] As many campgrounds remained closed, however, REI shared "CFH (camp from home) tips" for transforming a living room or a deck into a "full blown campsite." The store's Instagram followers posted their attempts at "indoor camping," from lounging in a cozy tent to "streaming a campfire, a starry sky, or forest sounds" from myriad devices.[3] As the weather warmed, the idea of backyard camping, as a whimsical and nostalgic quarantine activity, began to circulate. While backyard campers might miss "the piney cathedral of the woods," outdoor fun, complete with s'mores, could still be had. The absence of the usual hassles—packing up the car, fusty public bathrooms, or "the thick, slow and steady traffic to your campsite"—might even amplify the charm.[4] As soon as public campgrounds started to open up in early summer, however, Americans scrambled to reserve sites. Reduced capacity, combined with a sense that camping represented a safe travel choice, meant that campgrounds filled quickly. Campers turned to "dispersed camping" beyond regulated campgrounds, travel by camper vans or RVs, and sought out "glamping" resorts. Any of these choices might support what *Outside* magazine called "the ultimate socially-distanced weekend" in "the fresh air, the trees, the sense of escape, and the quality time by the campfire."[5]

The pandemic-driven enthusiasm for camping rested on a decade of surging interest and promotional efforts following a brief period of rel-ative decline in campers at the turn of the twenty-first century. The Great Recession that began in 2009 served as one catalyst, as the affordability of camping increased its appeal in comparison to other vacation types.[6] The tem-porary closing of the national parks during a federal government shutdown in the Fall of 2013 provided another. While the shutdown affected myriad critical government functions, closed signs barring entrance to the parks gave

Americans particular offense. They underscored how much people had come to view recreational access to public nature as a right.[7] A new generation discovered a love for camping through novel options like the plush amenities of glamping, the convenience of online reservation systems, and the connectedness of on-site wi-fi and cell phones.[8]

The National Park Service (NPS) and other public agencies had also embarked on projects to expand access to outdoor recreation, especially to historically marginalized groups. As the nation continued to diversify demographically, campers and visitors to the national parks remained whiter and older than the general population, as did its employees. Attracting Americans from all segments of the population became a goal for many outdoor organizations. In collaboration with corporate sponsors, including REI, Subaru, Humana, and Disney, the NPS launched a new multimedia marketing campaign, "Find Your Park/Encuentra Tu Parque," in 2016. The intention was twofold: to celebrate the agency's centennial and to attract younger and more diverse visitors. "Find Your Park" featured a multiethnic cast of spokespeople promising a renewed vision of the national parks, both leaning on historical sentiments and rebranding the venerable agency for a new generation.[9]

NPS Director Jonathan Jarvis reflected on the motivations behind "Find Your Park" in 2018. They included both "a parochial interest in building constituency" and a broader desire to remove any "sense of barrier to participation in the outdoors from all Americans." While Jarvis remained unsure whether the NPS had created this barrier or exactly "how to fix" it, he affirmed his belief that no "demographic or segment of our society" should miss out on the "inherent human benefits" of the outdoor experience that should be "common to all people. I mean you can take pretty much anybody to the South Rim of the Grand Canyon and they'll be in awe, right? It doesn't matter what their socioeconomic or ethnic background is."[10] Jarvis assumed that the barrier was getting people to the outdoors, presuming that the experiences they would have when they arrived would be universal. Class or racial barriers appear here as surface effects of a deeper human experience, rather than part and parcel of the development of the national parks or outdoor recreation practices. The rationale of "inherent human benefits" took a page from the new biological need paradigm which did not account for the social history that often made public nature a policed and unequal space. It also embodied the tightening connections between forms of camping and individual identity or lifestyle. Telling personal stories has been a key ingredient in the development of recreational camping, from the Shaybacks' temporary home to the backpackers seeking self-discovery. Today's search for

Instagram-worthy outdoor adventures further elevates camping as a vehicle for self-expression. You are how you camp. Find *Your* Park.

Matching, and perhaps surpassing, the uptick in recreational camping has been a rise in the number of Americans engaged in some form of functional camping or transience. Pinpointing how many Americans are homeless and regularly unsheltered, or houseless and essentially nomadic is difficult. Still, most evidence suggests that both groups are growing. Reporter Jessica Bruder has written revealingly of the resurgence of itinerant work, particularly for those at or near retirement age whose nest eggs were wiped out by the Great Recession. Taking to the roads in used RVs, older model vans, and camping trailers, they have swelled the stream of "workampers" who chase seasonal jobs across the nation, for modest wages and a free or low-cost campsite. They work concessions at amusement parks and sporting events, they run fireworks stands, pumpkin patches, and Christmas tree lots, they guard oil fields and state hunter check stations, they process the sugar beet harvest, and increasingly they handle the seasonal rush at Amazon's "Fulfillment Centers." Branded as CamperForce, Amazon targets recruitment among this nomadic population, promoting its demanding physical work of picking, packing, stowing, and receiving as "Your next RV adventure."[11]

The irony of recruiting temporary labor as if advertising a vacation is only heightened in the common workamping job of "campground host." Drawn by the promise of earning money while living for free in the great outdoors, the thousands who take these minimum-wage positions labor under often difficult conditions, managing unruly campers, cleaning latrines, and dealing with late-night emergencies. Despite this, recruiters who used to have to beg for applicants now routinely turn them away by the tens of thousands. This new "shadow economy," like the older one at the turn of the last century that employed bindlestiffs, the Reeves family, and others, depends on the willingness of workers to do without a permanent address. It is especially poignant that many of these workers service the outdoor recreation economy and extractive industries alike, and that they work largely for private concessionaires contracted to manage public lands.[12] Not only does it testify to the complex relationships between functional and recreational camping but it also points to shifts in the social contract. Arriving at an ostensibly public campground, managed by private companies and staffed by workampers, are campers still guests of the nation, or citizens of Aramark?

Getting a sense of how many Americans live without even such mobile dwellings is also tricky. The Department of Housing and Urban Development enumerates people experiencing homelessness, but cautions that its numbers represent only rough approximations. In 2018, it estimated that 554,000 people were homeless on any given night, with close to 35 percent of them classified as "unsheltered"—living outdoors without benefit of shelters or transitional housing. These numbers have ticked steadily upward in recent decades. New York City, for example, averaged about 22,000 people experiencing homelessness each night in the 1980s and 1990s, and 34,000 in the early 2000s, but the expansion since then has been dramatic. The Great Recession years (2009–2015) pushed nightly counts to 49,000, and since 2016 they have averaged over 63,000.[13] As in earlier waves, multiple factors have contributed to this sharp rise, including lack of treatment for mental illness and drug addiction, now especially opioids. Steep costs of housing in prosperous areas and disinvestment in affordable housing programs, however, have played increasingly significant roles. Advocates trying to address these problems report frustration with a persistent "myth that people experiencing homelessness decline help or prefer to live outdoors." As with earlier waves of tramps and transients, such beliefs say less about the preferences of people without housing than the fears observers hold for society. Sleeping outside persists as a rational means of last resort in cities with skyrocketing costs of living and dwindling will to build affordable alternatives.[14]

For people without permanent shelter, however, opportunities to camp lawfully can be hard to come by. Though most public campgrounds operate without regard to an individual's housing status, they have not proved a reliable option. Not only can these be far away from urban support systems, but some recreational campers have also voiced fears about functional campers infiltrating the great outdoors. Sporadic proposals to use organized campground facilities for homeless campers have met with strident resistance.[15] Meanwhile, recreational forms of urban camping have flourished in recent years, despite the tightened urban camping bans instituted in the wake of the Occupy movement. City law enforcement has largely tolerated modern traditions of camping out on sidewalks for Black Friday doorbuster sales or the debut of new Apple products. Urban Parks and Recreation departments have also begun to develop programs to encourage families to camp in local parks. New York City's agency holds a lottery for coveted spots in its popular summer series of campouts in Central Park and other city greenspaces. To get a spot, a city resident must register online and provide a permanent address.[16] Whether any of the more than 63,000 New Yorkers without housing might qualify is unclear.

In late 2019, the Supreme Court chose to leave intact a lower court's ruling that people experiencing homelessness "cannot be punished for sleeping outside on public property in the absence of adequate alternatives." Cities were scrambling to evaluate the constitutionality of their camping bans in the wake of this ruling when the COVID-19 pandemic arrived to shuffle the dynamic.[17] Suddenly, states and municipalities were renting out hotel rooms to house the unsheltered in fear of the virus spreading rampantly in crowded shelters and tent cities. As Figure E.2 shows, cities like San Francisco concurrently moved to support outdoor encampments, opening "safe sleeping villages" that provided occupants with social distancing as well as meals, restrooms, running water, and trash service. Both efforts—free individual housing and authorized encampments—marked major reversals in municipal approaches to functional campers. Whether this new willingness to try such strategies lasts, especially in the face of a likely wave of people losing their homes due to pandemic-induced economic fallout of unemployment, eviction, and foreclosure, remains to be seen.[18] These debates will continue to play out in a context of retreat from the goals of President Franklin Roosevelt's Second Bill of Rights and the Federal Housing Act of 1949 which committed the nation to "a decent home and a suitable living condition for every American family."[19] The vast infrastructure that supported the camper's republic depended upon parallel investments in housing. That both functional

FIGURE E.2 Socially-distanced, municipally-supported homeless encampment in San Francisco's Civic Center. "Rectangles designed to help prevent the spread of the coronavirus by encouraging social distancing," photograph by Noah Berger, May 21, 2020, AP Photo/Noah Berger.

outdoor transience and mass outdoor recreation continue to rise suggests increasingly fraught future contests over public nature.

The realm of political camping exemplified this complexity. Four years after the Occupy camps closed down, a new encampment galvanized public attention. Thousands of people from across the country, including members of more than one hundred different Native groups, along with environmental activists, camped out in 2016 in an attempt to halt the Dakota Access Pipeline. Designed to move oil from North Dakota's Bakken fields to an Illinois riverport, the pipeline's route crossed ancestral lands of the Standing Rock Sioux, desecrating sacred sites and threatening the water supply. The effort to halt the completion of this project centered on two encampments: Sacred Stone and Oceti Sakowin. They both sat on the edge of the Standing Rock Sioux Reservation, about an hour south of Bismarck, North Dakota, and in the direct path of the pipeline already under construction.[20] While the camps echoed earlier encamped protests from Coxey's Army and the Bonus marchers to Resurrection City and Occupy, activists adopted a stance as "protectors" rather than protestors, as Figure E.3 highlights. This choice distinguished their encampment in key ways. LaDonna Bravebull Allard, one of the initiators of the Sacred Stone camp on her family's land, and a Tribal

FIGURE E.3 The protectors at Sacred Stone camp block the Dakota Access Pipeline and provide a new vision of public nature. Photograph by Joe Brusky, September 2, 2016, Joe Brusky / Overpass Light Brigade.

Historic Preservation coordinator who investigated local impacts under the Environmental Protection Act, explained the stance: to keep the pipeline from "wiping out our most important cultural and spiritual areas" and thus erasing "our footprint from the world . . . [and] us as a people."[21] The action and the language of protection linked the camps to a continuous line of resistance to colonization, abrogation of treaty agreements, and forcible occupation of their lands. The protectors weren't occupying unpeopled space to create a new model community; they were protecting an enduring community of people with historical presence on the land against those who sought to occupy it.

Withstanding multiple attempts to dislodge the camp, the protectors gained global media attention and a brief victory. But by February 2017, the new presidential administration issued directives to resume pipeline construction and to shut down the camps. The legal battles continued as the oil began to flow, though the persistence of the protectors resulted in a July 2020 ruling that ordered at least a temporary shutdown pending further environmental review.[22] While the ultimate fate of the pipeline remains in the courts, the language of protection bequeathed a new framing for political encampments that deepened the emphasis on shared stakes in the land and ongoing relationships to nature. Sacred Stone Village, a Native community organization that emerged out of the Standing Rock protests, envisioned convening a kind of "permanent village that can teach by example how to live and thrive in an ecologically and spiritually sustainable community." In addition to calling for a seasonal "return to camp life along the Cannonball River," the organization hopes to prototype new bases for establishing community on the land: "sharing traditional indigenous lifestyles and wisdom" and practicing "food sovereignty, technological self-reliance through 'green' energy, and sustainable architecture" at this "precarious time when all life is threatened by climate change."[23]

Multiple groups have adopted the language of protection, the strategy of encampment, or both, in recent years. Indigenous protectors in Hawai'i employed similar tactics in the latest rounds of their resistance to the building of the Thirty Meter Telescope on the sacred mountain of Mauna Kea. In 2019, more than 2,000 people starting camping on the access road to the summit for five months. While protectors agreed in December to move their camp off the road itself to allow access, they continued to forestall the onset of construction.[24] In Harlan County, Kentucky, laid-off coal miners camped out for several months that same summer to pressure their former employer which had filed for bankruptcy and left the workers with weeks of unpaid wages.

As the company tried to sell its already-mined coal to pay creditors, a few miners blockaded the railroad tracks to prevent the trains from delivering their payloads. The encampment grew, garnering national attention, and perhaps played a role in the preliminary bankruptcy settlement that awarded the workers an unusually large share of the initial payout.[25]

Given this renewed attention to political encampments, perhaps it was not surprising that the extraordinary 2020 Black Lives Matter protests resulted in at least one revival of Occupy. In early June, Americans mounted mass protests following a recent spate of police killings of Black people, particularly those of George Floyd and Breonna Taylor, along with so many others in previous months and years. The movement evolved into an international uprising against police violence and entrenched racism. By the end of the month, protestors in New York City seeking to pressure municipal authorities to reduce the city's $6 billion annual police budget started to bring tents and camp out. They dubbed it "Occupy City Hall," and tried to replicate some of the organizational strategies of the earlier movement, if complicated by the ongoing pandemic. While the City Council agreed to some of the demands, Occupiers vowed to continue the encampment to sustain attention to a broad swath of related issues. Maintaining this space quickly proved to be difficult. Occupiers encountered challenges in attempting to include unsheltered folks "who were drawn to the compound for its free food, open-air camping and communal sensibility." After several confrontations, concerned New Yorkers, even those who voiced support for the goals of Black Lives Matter, worried that it "has turned into a disorderly shantytown where violence has occurred."[26] The confluence of political and functional camping contained echoes that hearkened back to Reaganville and Resurrection City. These contemporary encampments built on multiple models for claiming public nature in order to foster collective efforts to revive and revise the social contract.

THE CONTEMPORARY CAMPING landscape, with its dizzying array of possibilities, exhibits novel patterns, historical echoes, and perplexing contradictions. Together, they suggest that Americans are immersed in yet another transition. Is the social contract changing or is it disappearing? What role will public nature play? How do rising beliefs about the biological need for outdoor recreation figure into these developments? Unpacking this new imperative, interrogating the notion that "We MUST Camp," provides additional insight.

The 2005 publication, *Last Child in the Woods*, diagnosed the nation as suffering from a new social ailment, "nature-deficit disorder," sparking popular interest and dismay. Author Richard Louv listed the "human costs of alienation from nature, among them: diminished use of the senses, attention difficulties, and higher rates of physical and emotional illness," as well as "high crime rates, depression, and other urban maladies." These symptoms resulted from too much technology and too little opportunity to explore the outdoors, especially among children.[27] The cure for this syndrome has emerged as the "nature fix": a few days communing with the outdoors, hiking a tree-lined trail, sleeping on the ground, and sitting around a campfire to restore well-being and improve health. A growing crop of social and medical studies have suggested that even small amounts of time spent "outdoors" in "nature" can improve cognitive processing and academic performance, reduce stress and anxiety, ward off childhood obesity, mitigate behavioral and mood disorders, and increase individual productivity and environmental commitments.[28]

Just go outside. Could it really be that simple? This elegant answer to a complex set of worrisome social problems holds a compelling appeal. Public lands agencies, along with environmental advocacy groups, youth organizations, and outdoor recreation industries, have all begun to speak the language of biological need. This framing offers updated rationales for preserving outdoor spaces and increasing access and participation. The Wilderness Society, for one, pivoted toward this framing in 2013. A series of infographics detailed the costs of nature-deficit disorder and proclaimed the "good news—the cure is free and available to all," with camping listed among the "top five" low-cost options.[29] *Outside* magazine made the case on the cover of its May 2019 issue: "The Nature Cure—Science's Newest Miracle Drug is Free." One in a recurring series, this feature explained how physicians were issuing "nature prescriptions" through a ParkRx app, counted nearly 500 "published studies linking time in nature to better health," labeled the NPS "the country's most important health care provider," and applauded Humana Insurance for rewarding subscribers for visiting local parks. "The Camping Cure" offered a particularly potent remedy, as a "weeklong camping excursion can reset your biological clock" and alleviate the negative effects of stress.[30] During the quarantines of 2020, urban parents especially lamented the reduced availability of this remedy and correlated children's behavioral problems with "a lack of access to outdoor space." This led the *New York Times* to suggest that the pandemic effectively proved that "'Nature Deficit Disorder' is Really a Thing"—a realization that Louv hoped would add a "sense of urgency to the movement to connect children, families and communities to nature."[31]

The history narrated in this book complicates this formula. Arguments for the restorative benefits of connecting with nature have long been part of rationales for recreational camping and before that, for back-to-the-land movements. A discourse of biological need and medical cure, however, has gained new emphasis. While tantalizing, the claim of universal genetics displaces the significant cultural history of outdoor recreation. This vantage point presents recreational camping as a neutral norm: just nature, no politics. Moreover, these narratives of a biological need for nature elevate camping as one of several privileged outdoor activities, but does not ask "What is camping?"—or "What is nature?" Or, whether either of those are really "free."[32] The standard-issue trio of picnic table, parking spot, and fire ring by this point may seem natural, but it is neither free nor the product of biology.

Nor are the purported benefits of the nature cure equally available. One can imagine those for whom walking in nature or camping out may trigger feelings of anxiety rather than assuage them, including those with experiences of being surveilled or memories of feeling unwelcome in such spaces. W. E. B. Du Bois remarked as far back as 1920 on the peculiar equation of "whiteness" with "ownership of the earth," suggesting how feeling entitled to a sense of ownership has not been equally available. Contemporary reports continue to suggest that assumptions about who belongs in nature can have a starkly differential effect on Americans' ability to participate in outdoor recreation.[33] Those for whom camping is a functional rather than recreational endeavor are also left out. If the nature cure were truly universal, then why are those without homes, who camp as a regular mode of living, not the healthiest among us? *Outside* affirmed in 2020 that outdoor sleeping is "more restorative than sleeping indoors. It's science." Whether the science bears out for the unsheltered remained unaddressed. One study defined the "ideal amount of time to spend outside," as 120 minutes per week and indiated that the "benefits of being outdoors . . . appeared to max out" somewhere between 200 and 300 minutes per week, rewarding those who choose to engage with nature for recreation and excluding those who have little choice but to be outdoors for longer stretches. Whether people experiencing homelessness are or are not in need of a nature cure, or if the cure is only a function of leisure, rather than necessity or labor, is a question that largely goes unasked.[34]

Complicating the nature cure need not undermine its positive outcomes. Indeed, some forms of outdoor recreation have shown promise for helping such intractable afflictions as Post-Traumatic Stress Disorder (PTSD), which might alone suggest the merits of the movement.[35] Moreover, those working to address nature-deficit disorder have become more attentive to the fact that there might be diverse paths to connecting with nature. There has been a push for greater inclusivity and for thinking in terms of "equity and capacity" rather than presumed universal or optimal experiences. Many outdoor organizations have made concerted efforts to diversify participation in terms of race, ethnicity, and disability, from NOLS' "Leaders of Color" program to targeted groups established by people of color themselves.[36]

For all the good it might generate, the speedy embrace of the nature cure across multiple outdoor constituencies gives some reason for caution. On the one hand, the focus on the biological need to camp leaves little room for the historical role of public nature as a forum for negotiating the terms of the social contract. On the other, where the biological need argument does reference larger social issues, it tends to echo neoliberal principles, promoting individual investments rather than public goods.

What does the nature cure—and camping—look like in neoliberal terms, where market rationalities have come to inform nearly "all institutions and social actions?" Earlier social contracts had been partially rooted in classical liberalism, where governments sought to maximize free trade and competition in the economic realm and maintain protections for individual freedoms and formal equality in the political sphere, all while keeping a critical distance between economy and politics. Neoliberal frameworks, arguably ascendant since the 1970s, parrot some of the language of liberalism but collapse the space between economy and politics. Instead of a social contract, individuals acting within the market become "the organizing . . . principle" for society, as government backs away from its role as "provider of public welfare." One result of this, political theorist Wendy Brown suggests, is that one's "moral autonomy is measured by their capacity for 'self-care'—the ability to provide for their own needs and service their own ambitions" and where inability to do so leads to "a 'mismanaged life.'" The "model neo-liberal citizen" makes strategic individual choices from existing "social, political, and economic options," rather than contesting the arrangement of their life options.[37]

The language of biological need tends to treat "the outdoors" as a value proposition and the nature cure as an option for self-care. The Outdoor Industry Association (OIA)—a trade group representing some 1,200 manufacturers, suppliers, and retailers of gear and services—offers a case in point. In addition to arguing for the significance of public lands, its 2017 annual report touted the power of the outdoor recreation market, which generated a total of $887 billion in economic activity that year. Camping accounted for $167 billion in spending, $23.5 billion in federal, state, and local taxes, and 1.4 million jobs.[38] The report deployed these numbers as a demonstration of how "outdoor recreation makes America stronger," even beyond the dollar figures.

The OIA deftly braided older understandings of public nature with a neoliberal framing.

> America's outdoor recreation assets are its citizens' common trust. Our public lands and waterways belong to every American, and they are the backbone of our outdoor recreation economy. They hold the promise of prosperity and well-being. It is as much our responsibility to invest in them as it is our right to enjoy them. . . . Investments in outdoor recreation on public lands and waters earn compounding returns in the form of healthier communities, healthier economies and healthier people. . . . Likewise, it is an underappreciated and underfunded weapon against crime, poor academic performance and rising health care costs.[39]

While it echoes the campers' republic in its sense of shared ownership and "common trust," the defense of public lands now comes by way of market rationality, measured in terms of assets and return on investment. Moreover, it shifts responsibility onto individual decisions to invest in personal well-being by enjoying nature in order to address social issues such as crime, education, and health care.

While market metaphors have become "common sense" assumptions, neoliberalism has not gone uncontested, including in the camping landscape. Employing such arguments does not alone mean wholesale capture by this neoliberal calculus.[40] The NPS and other organizations have maintained commitments to protecting public lands against market rationalizations. Major outdoor retailers such as Patagonia and REI, which operate as a Benefit Corporation and a Co-op, respectively, eschew the typical corporate model, and aim to make decisions with both environmental concerns and social justice ideals in mind, despite also relying on synthetic consumer products and fossil-fuel driven outdoor experiences.[41] New political encampments, from New York and Kentucky to North Dakota and Hawaii keep pushing to expand the ground for political claims, perhaps as the seeds of a new social contract built around the concept of protection. They are reminders of the broader concept of public nature, beyond a space for personal enjoyment. If, as some have suggested, neoliberalism may be waning as a viable economic theory, its cultural effects continue to resonate in this struggle over how deep market sensibilities run and where they should end.[42]

Employing neoliberal language to combat such neoliberal moves as divesting from public lands may signal a particular contemporary predicament, but it is also counterproductive. The OIA report remains optimistic about the power of public nature: "By enjoying these places, we invest in our own well-being and affirm our shared history. In challenging times, when disagreements appear sharper and differences seem harder to bridge, it is the outdoors that reconnects us."[43] It is such an appealing vision amidst difficult days. In a moment of climate crisis, political polarization, and global pandemic, it suggests that enjoyable respites in the great outdoors can keep our problems and our disagreements at bay. Yet the mechanism for healing these divisions themselves arrives not through collective action but through individual efforts to "invest in our own well-being." It makes nature more of a private asset, even when the government seeks to preserve spaces or promote access. Moreover, even as this framing elevates the investment of one's leisure time in the outdoors, it obscures the concomitant marginalization of camps made under duress or by force. If participating in recreational camping still demonstrates one's belonging to the nation, camps of necessity or penalty render their occupants "stateless" in a way, with constrained access to individual rights and community.[44]

Ultimately, reliance on neoliberal and biological arguments risks an impoverished sense of public nature, where the outdoors is simply a place in which we spend time as individuals instead of the basis for how we work out relationships to each other, to the nation, and to the places we inhabit. Moreover, if the nature cure movement has become more attentive to those who have been left out of recreational access, the biological need argument still offers little basis for understanding functional needs or political claims. This runs counter to the more holistic approaches our contemporary challenges, not least the climate crisis, demand.

Camping, recreational or otherwise, is neither the problem nor the cure. Instead, a careful look at its history suggests that it serves as a bellwether for changes in the social contract and how we envision the role of public nature. Insofar as it exhibits neoliberal tendencies, camping suggests that the idea of a social contract, and public nature as a space to enact it, is eroding. Attending to the entwined history of recreational, functional, and political camping, however, demonstrates how public nature has operated, and might persist, as a forum in which we wrestle toward some new social contract. Without nostalgia for the campers' republic, a vision that embedded social divisions even as it fostered connections to the outdoors and a sense of national belonging,

how might we use public nature to remind us of the public good, and re-
vise it for a new era? Our survival at a time of global environmental perils
will come not by individual pursuit of leisure in the outdoors, or even in the
preservation of wild lands for that purpose. Instead we might seek grounds
for working toward a social contract that recognizes recreational, functional,
and political acts and upholds our collective stakes in protecting nature and
ourselves.

Notes

INTRODUCTION

1. U.S. Congress, House Subcommittee on Health Care, District of Columbia, Census and the National Archives, *Hearing on McPherson Square: Who Made the Decision to Allow Indefinite Camping in the Park, Focusing on the Impact of the Ongoing "Occupy" Encampment on Public Health and Public Safety Inside and Outside the Park,* 112th Cong. (January 24, 2012), (testimony and statement of Jonathan Jarvis, Director, National Park Service, and questions by Trey Gowdy, R-SC). A video recording of the full hearing is available at https://www.c-span.org/video/?303866-1/occupy-washington-dc-mcpherson-square-permit-decision.

2. U.S. Congress, *Hearing on McPherson Square* (testimony of Jarvis); "Camping," National Capital Region, Special Regulations, Areas of the National Park System, Code of Federal Regulations (36 CFR § 7.96(i)(l)), quoted in National Park Service, "Help Us Preserve McPherson Square," McPherson Use Handout, October 26, 2011, National Park Service Documents on Occupy Movement, https://archive.org/details/NPS-Occupy-FOIA.

3. Monica Hesse and Paul Farhi, "A Protest That's Not in the Bag," *Washington Post*, January 31, 2012, C1–2.

4. See, for example, Cindy S. Aron, *Working at Play: A History of Vacations in the United States* (New York: Oxford University Press, 2001); Warren James Belasco, *Americans on the Road: From Auto-camp to Motel, 1910–1945* (Baltimore: Johns Hopkins University Press, 1979); Matthew De Abitua, *The Art of Camping: The History and Practice of Sleeping Under the Stars* (New York: Penguin, 2011); Rachel Gross, "From Buckskin to Gore-Tex: Consumption as a Path to Mastery in Twentieth-Century American Wilderness Recreation" (PhD diss., University of Wisconsin-Madison, 2017); Roderick Frazier Nash, *Wilderness and the American Mind*, 5th ed. (New Haven, CT: Yale University Press, 2014); William Philpott, *Vacationland: Tourism and Environment in the Colorado High Country* (Seattle: University of Washington

Press, 2013); Susan Sessions Rugh, *Are We There Yet? The Golden Age of American Family Vacations* (Lawrence: University Press of Kansas, 2008); Susan Snyder, *Past Tents: The Way We Camped* (Berkeley, CA: Heyday Books, 2006); Paul S. Sutter, *Driven Wild: How the Fight Against Automobiles Launched the Modern Wilderness Movement* (Seattle: University of Washington Press, 2005); David Wescott, *Camping in the Old Style* (Salt Lake City: Gibbs Smith, 2000); James Morton Turner, "From Woodcraft to 'Leave No Trace': Wilderness, Consumerism, and Environmentalism in Twentieth-Century America," *Environmental History* 7, no. 3 (July 2002): 462–84; Dan White, *Under the Stars: How America Fell in Love with Camping* (New York: Henry Holt, 2016); and Terence Young, *Heading Out: American Camping since 1869* (Ithaca, NY: Cornell University Press, 2017).

5. Karl Jacoby, *Crimes Against Nature: Squatters, Poachers, Thieves, and the Hidden History of American Conservation* (Berkeley: University of California Press, 2001); Jonathan Peter Spiro, *Defending the Master Race: Conservation, Eugenics, and The Legacy of Madison Grant* (Lebanon, NH: University of Vermont Press, 2009).

6. Charlie Hailey, "More Notes on Camp: A Formulary for a New (Camping) Urbanism," *Thresholds* 33 (Summer 2008): 28. Felicity Scott seeks to examine such "outlaw areas" as the "Woodstockholm" encampment at the United Nations Conference on the Human Environment in 1972, and Palestinian refugee camps, among other sites. Charlie Hailey places Guantanamo Bay, Burning Man and many others, in provocative and uncomfortable juxtapositions across what he calls the "unsettling range of camp's historical functions." He both proposes a taxonomy of camps according to three categories—camps of autonomy, of control, and of necessity—and a typology of various stages of camp: siting, clearing, making, and breaking camp. But he also explicitly imagines his books as manuals, guides, or scrapbooks that eschew historical or narrative resolution. Felicity D. Scott, *Outlaw Territories: Environments of Insecurity/Architectures of Counterinsurgency* (New York: Zone Books, 2016); Charlie Hailey, *Camps: A Guide to 21st Century Space* (Cambridge, MA: The MIT Press, 2009), 13–17; Charlie Hailey, *Campsite: Architectures of Duration and Place* (Baton Rouge: Louisiana State University Press, 2008), 1–2, 9–10; William Mangold, Review of *Camps: A Guide to 21st-Century Space* by Charlie Hailey; *Campsite: Architectures of Duration and Place* by Charlie Hailey; and *A Manufactured Wilderness: Summer Camps and the Shaping of American Youth, 1890–1960* by Abigail A. Van Slyck, *Journal of Architectural Education* 64, no. 2 (March 2011): 176–78.

7. Marguerite S. Shaffer and Phoebe S. K. Young, "The Nature-Culture Paradox," in *Rendering Nature: Animals, Bodies, Places, Politics*, ed. Marguerite S. Shaffer and Phoebe S. K. Young (Philadelphia: University of Pennsylvania Press, 2015), 1–17; William Cronon, "The Trouble with Wilderness: Or, Getting Back to the Wrong Nature," *Environmental History* 1, no. 1 (January 1996): 7–28.

8. Mark Hulliung, *The Social Contract in America: From the Revolution to the Present Age* (Lawrence: University Press of Kansas, 2007), 2–42. Hulliung suggests that

the revolutionary generation, Patriots and Loyalists alike, hotly debated and incorporated pieces not only of Locke's framing but also those from several of his predecessors. Locke's version, however, became dominant in such seminal documents as Thomas Paine's *Common Sense* and Thomas Jefferson's Declaration of Independence. Hulliung, *Social Contract*, 2.

9. John Locke, *The Second Treatise on Civil Government* (Buffalo: Prometheus Books, 1986 [1690]), 49–50, 54, 69–72, 77; Hulliung, *Social Contract*, 2, 18. Scholarly inquiries into the concept of property are voluminous and longstanding. For a glimpse of this larger discussion, see, for example, Jill Frank, *A Democracy of Distinction: Aristotle and the World of Politics* (Chicago: University of Chicago Press, 2005), 54–80; Samuel A. Butler, "Arendt and Aristotle on Equality, Leisure, and Solidarity," *Journal of Social Philosophy* 41, no. 4 (Winter 2010): 470–90.

10. Locke, *Second Treatise*, 20–22, 26, 30; Hulliung, *Social Contract*, 76–77; Lisi Krall, *Proving Up: Domesticating Land in U.S. History* (Albany: SUNY Press, 2010), 11–12.

11. Thomas Jefferson, *Notes on the State of Virginia* (1787), Query XIX, hypertext edition, http://xroads.virginia.edu/~hyper/jefferson/ch19.html.

12. Hulliung, *Social Contract*, 76–107; Steven Stoll, "Farm Against Forest," in *American Wilderness: A New History*, ed. Michael Lewis (New York: Oxford University Press, 2007), 58–59; David Danbom, "Romantic Agrarianism in Twentieth-Century America," *Agricultural History* 65, no. 4 (1991): 2; Leo Marx, *The Machine in the Garden: Technology and the Pastoral Ideal in America* (New York: Oxford University Press, 2000 [1964]), 73–144; Krall, *Proving Up*, 4–5, 9–30; Elijah Gaddis, "Locating the Agrarian Imaginary in Tillery, North Carolina" (MA thesis, University of North Carolina–Chapel Hill, 2013), 6.

13. Madison, quoted in Hulliung, *Social Contract*, 77; Hulliung, *Social Contract*, 76–77, 88–89; Krall, *Proving Up*, 24–29.

14. Steven Stoll, *Larding the Lean Earth: Soil and Society in Nineteenth-Century America* (New York: Hill and Wang, 2002), 13–68; Hulliung, *Social Contract*, 85–107; Krall, *Proving Up*, 5; Richard White, *Railroaded: The Transcontinentals and the Making of Modern America* (New York: Norton, 2012).

15. Donald Grant Mitchell, *My Farm of Edgewood: A Country Book* (New York: C. Scribner, 1863), 285; Dona Brown, *Back to the Land: The Enduring Dream of Self-Sufficiency in Modern America* (Madison: University of Wisconsin Press, 2011), 3–15; Lawrence Buell, *The Environmental Imagination: Thoreau, Nature Writing, and the Formation of American Culture* (Cambridge, MA: Belknap Press of Harvard University Press, 1995).

16. *Fourteenth Census of the United States Taken in the Year 1920: Population 1920*, Vol. I: *Number and Distribution of Inhabitants* (Washington, DC: Government Printing Office, 1921), 43. In 1920, 51.4% of inhabitants were classified as living in urban areas, and 48.6% in rural areas. In 1910, 45.8% had been urban, and 54.2% rural, continuing a trend the Census Bureau noted as "manifested conspicuously

in the United States ever since 1820." It was clearly accelerating, however, as even as late as 1880, 71.4% of the population still lived in rural areas.

17. *Fourteenth Census of the United States Taken in the Year 1920: Population 1920*, Vol. IV: *Occupations* (Washington, DC: Government Printing Office, 1923), 34. In 1920, 26.3% of the people were employed in "agriculture, forestry, and animal husbandry," and 30.8% in "manufacturing and mechanical industries." In 1910, those numbers had been 33.2% for agriculture, and 27.8% for manufacturing.

18. Krall, *Proving Up*, 2–3; Mark Spence, *Dispossessing the Wilderness: Indian Removal and the Making of the National Parks* (New York: Oxford University Press, 1999); Jacoby, *Crimes Against Nature*.

19. Brown, *Back to the Land*, 24–30, 51. David Danbom notes the particularly male character of "romantic agrarianism," as men experienced the apparent loss of "independence" more keenly than women, many of whom found modern urban life to be relatively more liberating. Elijah Gaddis and Kimberly Smith suggest the ways the "agrarian imaginary" has also privileged whiteness, both subjugating African Americans and providing a potential route to undermining that subjugation. Danbom, "Romantic Agrarianism," 5; Gaddis, "Agrarian Imaginary," 7–9; Kimberly Smith, "Black Agrarianism and the Foundations of Black Environmental Thought," *Environmental Ethics* 26, no.3 (2004): 273.

20. Brown, *Back to the Land*, 30–34; Danbom, "Romantic Agrarianism," 2, 11–12; David Shi, *The Simple Life: Plain Living and High Thinking in American Culture* (New York: Oxford University Press, 1983); T. J. Jackson Lears, *No Place of Grace: Antimodernism and the Transformation of American Culture, 1880–1920* (New York: Pantheon Books, 1981).

21. Truman A. DeWeese, *The Bend in the Road, and How a Man of the City Found It* (New York: Harper and Brothers, 1913), ix, 2–3, 10–11; Brown, *Back to the Land*, 54; "Country Lure: *The Bend in the Road* by Truman A. DeWeese," *New York Times*, July 13, 1913, Review 398.

22. Thorstein Veblen, *The Theory of the Leisure Class* (New York: Macmillan, 1899).

23. Historians of consumer culture have yet to fully contend with the role of nature in this context. For scholars that have examined this connection, see Aron, *Working at Play;* Catherine Gudis, *Buyways: Billboards, Automobiles, and the American Cultural Landscape* (New York: Routledge, 2004); Jennifer Price, *Flight Maps: Adventures with Nature in Modern America* (New York: Basic Books, 1999); Sarah Schrank, *Free and Natural: Nudity and the American Cult of the Body* (Philadelphia: University of Pennsylvania Press, 2019); Marguerite S. Shaffer, *See America First: Tourism and National Identity, 1880–1940* (Washington, DC: Smithsonian Institution Press, 2001); Sutter, *Driven Wild*.

24. While cultural anxieties about modernity played a role in the rise of outdoor recreation, the prevailing tendency among scholars to see them as the central root of such apparently anti-modern activities like camping has obscured more complex relationships to modern systems. For a close look at camping as a form of

modernity, see Phoebe S. Kropp [Young], "Wilderness Wives and Dishwashing Husbands: Comfort and the Domestic Arts of Camping Out, 1880–1910," *Journal of Social History* 43, no. 1 (Fall 2009): 5–29.

25. Louis S. Warren, *The Hunter's Game: Poachers and Conservationists in Twentieth-Century America* (New Haven, CT: Yale University Press, 1997), 10–13.

26. Theodore Roosevelt, *The Strenuous Life: Essays and Addresses* (New York: Charles Scribner's Sons, 1903), 3–4, 9, 150. Roosevelt also used his promotion of the strenuous life to celebrate the conquest of Native people and to justify imperial ambitions.

27. Emphasis added, National Park Service Organic Act (16 U.S.C. sec. 1), August 25, 1916 (39 Stat. 535); Marguerite S. Shaffer, "Performing Bears and Packaged Wilderness: Reframing the History of National Parks," in *Cities and Nature in the American West*, ed. Char Miller (Reno: University of Nevada Press, 2010), 137–53.

28. E. P. Meinecke, et. al, "Recreation reports," misc. typescript notes, 1938, Box 19, Folder 6; E.P. Meinecke, "Human Aspects of Conservation," TS, paper read at meeting of the discussion group on philosophy of conservation at the University of California (Berkeley), Department of Geography, [ca. 1935], Box 2, Emilio Pepe Michael Meinecke Collection, California Academy of Sciences Archives, San Francisco, California.

29. Throughout this book, and especially in chapter 2, I have endeavored to employ terminology that is both respectful and historically appropriate. I have been guided by the work of several scholars, including Ryan Hall, Rosalyn R. LaPier, Coll Thrush, and Louis Warren, in making the following choices: "Indigenous" generally indicates people living on or lifeways associated with original lands, "Native" or "Native American" refers to a broader population, and "Indian" appears only when part of an official title or serves to highlight white constructions of Native identity operant at the time. Ryan Hall, *Beneath the Backbone of the World: Blackfoot People and the North American Borderlands, 1720–1877* (Chapel Hill: University of North Carolina Press, 2020), 10; Roslyn R. LaPier, *Invisible Reality: Storytellers, Storytakers, and the Supernatural World of the Blackfeet* (Lincoln: University of Nebraska Press, 2017), xi; Coll Thrush, *Native Seattle: Histories from the Crossing-Over Place* (Seattle: University of Washington Press, 2007), xv–xvi, 98–101; Louis Warren, *God's Red Son: The Ghost Dance Religion and the Making of Modern America* (New York: Basic Books, 2017), xiii.

CHAPTER I

1. William T. Sherman, "Camp-Fires of the G.A.R. [Grand Army of the Republic]," *North American Review* (November 1, 1888): 497–98, 502. Sherman's *Memoirs* sold by the tens of thousands and he avidly sought out the opportunity to lecture at soldiers' reunions, in part to foreclose Southerners' attempts to reinterpret the war.

David Blight, *Race and Reunion: The Civil War in American Memory* (Cambridge, MA: Harvard University Press, 2001), 161–62.

2. Sherman, "Camp-Fires," 502.

3. John Mack Faragher, *Women and Men on the Overland Trail* (New Haven, CT: Yale University Press, 1979); Susan Johnson, *Roaring Camp: The Social World of the California Gold Rush* (New York: Norton, 2000); Paul K. Conkin, *Cane Ridge: America's Pentecost* (Madison: University of Wisconsin Press, 1990).

4. Sherman, "Camp-Fires," 497; Stuart McConnell, *Glorious Contentment: The Grand Army of the Republic, 1865–1900* (Chapel Hill: University of North Carolina Press, 1992), 15, 24, 36–37; James Marten, *Sing Not War: The Lives of Union & Confederate Veterans in Gilded Age America* (Chapel Hill: University of North Carolina Press, 2011), 246. Enrolling just 27,000 members in 1875 (merely 2% of eligible veterans), the GAR rose to its apex in 1890 at 400,000 (roughly 39% of surviving Union veterans, enumerated at 1,034,073 in the 1890 census) and then went into gradual decline as members aged and died. David Blight, *Race and Reunion*, 157; Department of the Interior, *Report on the Population of the United States at the Eleventh Census: 1890* (Washington, DC: Government Printing Office, 1895), 803; John A. Casey Jr., *New Men: Reconstructing the Image of the Veteran in Late-Nineteenth-Century American Literature and Culture* (New York: Fordham University Press, 2015), 110.

5. There is a vast library attending to the history of the creation of the lost cause mythology, the role of the United Confederate Veterans and associated organizations, and the reconciliation between the regions. See, for example, Blight, *Race and Reunion*; Gaines M. Foster, *Ghosts of the Confederacy: Defeat, the Lost Cause, and the Emergence of the New South* (New York: Oxford University Press, 1987); Nina Silber, *The Romance of Reunion: Northerners and the South, 1865–1900* (Chapel Hill: University of North Carolina Press, 1997); Caroline E. Janney, *Remembering the Civil War: Reunion and the Limits of Reconciliation* (Chapel Hill: University of North Carolina Press, 2013).

6. William David Barry, "No Detail Escaped Gould's Diaries," *Portland (ME) Press Herald*, March 1, 1998, 6E; William B. Jordan, "Preface" to John Mead Gould, *The Civil War Journals of John Mead Gould, 1861–1866,* ed. William B. Jordan, (Baltimore: Butternut and Blue, 1997), i–iii; Richard A. Sauers, "Introduction" to Gould, *Civil War Journals*, iv–v. Where most diaries cut off abruptly with the cessation of conflict, Gould narrated the messy mop-up phase of the war, the occupation of the South (in which he remained a soldier in Georgia and South Carolina until March of 1866), his experience as a carpet-bagger trying to establish a lumber business, and the readjustment to civilian life back home—all of which are rare subjects in the bulk of diaries. Unlike many soldiers who kept a diary (or sent letters) only during the war, Gould's war diaries are merely five volumes out of a seventy-five-year set. Gould's war experiences appear as part of a recorded continuum; the war was a defining experience of his life and he continued to wrestle with the meaning

of the war long after its conclusion. His diaries, before, during and after the war, are unusually expressive, recording not just daily events, but the evolution of his inner emotional life, his reaction to political events, the books he read, the places he visited, the nature around him, social behaviors, personal relationships, and moral commitments. Marten, *Sing Not War*, 8, 10.

7. Some aspects of Gould's outlook and background (i.e., his teetotaling and religiosity, as well as his work as a banker) and his military experience (i.e., promotion to the rank of major and five years' service without sustaining major injuries) gave his observations a particular cast. However, extensive reading in other published and digitized manuscript Union soldiers' diaries and letters suggests a strong similarity with many of the themes about camp life emphasized here: dealing with the elements, social relationships, and the comforts and precarity of camp. Including material from the extensive set of Union Army soldiers' writings on the subject for the purposes of comparison with Gould was unfeasible in the scope of this chapter. Some helpful guides to Civil War soldiers' diaries and letters include: Library of Congress, *Civil War Diaries and Personal Narratives: A Selected Bibliography of Books in the General Collections of the Library of Congress* (Washington, DC: Library of Congress, 1998); *The American Civil War: Letters and Diaries* (Alexandria, VA: Alexander Street Press, 2020), https://alexanderstreet.com/products/american-civil-war-letters-and-diaries; Steven E. Woodworth, ed., *The American Civil War: A Handbook of Literature and Research* (Westport, CT: Greenwood Press, 1996); Alan Nevins, James I. Robertson Jr., and Bell I. Wiley, eds., *Civil War Books: A Critical Bibliography*, 2 vols. (Baton Rouge: Louisiana State University Press, 1967–1969); C. E. Dornbusch, comp., *Regimental Publications and Personal Narratives of the Civil War: A Checklist*, 2 vols. (New York: New York Public Library, 1961–1972).

8. Joseph W. A. Whitethorne "Blueprint for Nineteenth-Century Camps: A Castramentation, 1778–1865," in *Huts and History: The Historical Archaeology of Military Encampment During the American Civil War*, ed. David G. Orr, Matthew B. Reeves, and David R. Geier (Gainesville: University of Florida Press, 2006), 30; Orr, Reeves, and Geier, "Introduction" to *Huts and History*, 11; James I. Robertson Jr., *Soldiers Blue and Gray* (Columbia: University of South Carolina Press, 1988), 43. In 1862, General Daniel Butterfield wrote an expanded manual that recommended the most beneficial practices for health, comfort, and safety, adding tips to help soldiers to keep the elements at bay. The US Sanitary Commission also inspected hundreds of camps and made recommendations to preserve health. Daniel Butterfield, *Camp and Outpost Duty for Infantry* (New York: Harper and Brothers, 1863); Julia Lorrilard Butterfield, ed., *A Biographical Memorial of General Daniel Butterfield, Including Many Addresses and Military Writings* (New York: Grafton Press 1904), 119–21; *The Sanitary Commission of the United States Army* (New York: U.S. Sanitary Commission, 1864); Charles J. Stillé, *History of the United States Sanitary Commission* (Philadelphia: J. B. Lippincott & Co., 1866).

9. Gould, *Civil War Journals*, 2. Among Gould's initial preparation was to work out a plan to transmit his diary, which he largely stuck to for the duration. He would write up his entries and send them in installments first to his father to share with local family and friends, who would then send them all on to his dearest friend, Edward Sylvester Morse, for safekeeping until after the war. Morse and Gould had met as teens and would remain close friends throughout their entire lives, though Morse avoided serving in the army and instead studied under Louis Agassiz at Harvard, later becoming renowned in the fields of natural history, ethnography and art history. Gould, *Civil War Journals*, 4–5, 6n15; Scott M. Martin, "Maine's Remarkable Edward Sylvester Morse: Quintessential Naturalist," *Maine Naturalist* 3, no. 2 (1995): 81–102.

10. "Counsel to Volunteers," *Boston Daily Journal*, April 23, 1861, 2; Gould, *Civil War Journals*, 7; John M. Gould to Edward S. Morse, April 25, 1861, box 5, folder 6, Edward Sylvester Morse (1838–1925) Papers, E 2, Phillips Library, Peabody Essex Museum, through Adam Mathew Digital, *Meiji Japan: The Edward Sylvester Morse Collection from the Phillips Library at the Peabody Essex Museum* (2008–2011), http://www.aap.amdigital.co.uk (hereafter Morse Collection).

11. C. L. R., "The Practical Wants of the Army," *New York Times*, May 7, 1861, 5; "Health of the Army—The Sanitary Commission," *New York Times*, June 25, 1861, 4. Many articles in this "advice to soldiers" genre made the rounds in Boston and New York papers that spring, though they often communicated conflicting recommendations.

12. Gould, *Civil War Journals*, 5, 7, 11.

13. Gould, *Civil War Journals*, 11–14.

14. Gould, *Civil War Journals*, 36.

15. Gould, *Civil War Journals*, 37–42.

16. Gould, *Civil War Journals*, 145; Robertson, *Soldiers Blue and Gray*, 43–46; James S. Hutchins, "An 1860 Pamphlet on the Sibley Tent," *Military Collector & Historian* 57 (Summer 2005): 70–79; Mark R. Wilson, "The Extensive Side of Nineteenth-Century Military Economy: The Tent Industry in the Northern United States during the Civil War," *Enterprise & Society* 2, no. 2 (June 2001): 297–337. Union troops in the Civil War lodged more frequently in tents than armies of earlier wars, which quartered in houses or buildings when they could, and in the field relied more on makeshift structures like huts or lean-tos made of boughs and other gathered materials.

17. Gould, *Civil War Journals*, 83. Gould became Regimental Sergeant Major, the senior enlisted soldier of the 10th Maine, on October 1, 1861. On April 7, 1862, he became the Second Lieutenant of Company E and Regimental Adjutant, responsible for keeping personnel and other records for the regiment, later rising to First Lieutenant of his company. On December 20, 1864, he was elected Major of the 29th Maine, third in command of the regiment. Gould, *Civil War Journals*, 65, 114, 439.

18. Gould, *Civil War Journals*, 211.

19. Gould, *Civil War Journals*, 445; Roberston, *Soldiers Blue and Gray*, 43–46; John U. Rees, "'Soldiers are Ingenious Animals': American Civil War Campaign Shelters," *Military Collector & Historian* 56 (Winter 2004): 248–66. For discussion of the wide-ranging effects of the war on the landscape, see Megan Kate Nelson, *Ruin Nation: Destruction and the American Civil War* (Athens: University of Georgia Press, 2012).

20. Gould, *Civil War Journals*, 26–28, 37, 40.

21. Gould, *Civil War Journals*, 151, 244.

22. Gould, *Civil War Journals*, 165.

23. Gould, *Civil War Journals*, 137.

24. Gould, *Civil War Journals*, 138, 141–43.

25. Gould, *Civil War Journals*, 154, 159.

26. Gould, *Civil War Journals*, 220, 327.

27. Gould, *Civil War Journals*, 377.

28. Gould, *Civil War Journals*, 241–43, 249.

29. Gould, *Civil War Journals*, 332.

30. Gould, *Civil War Journals*, passim; James M. McPherson, *For Cause and Comrades: Why Men Fought in the Civil War* (New York: Oxford University Press, 1997), 85–90; McConnell, *Glorious Contentment*.

31. See, for example, Gould, *Civil War Journals*, 44, 263.

32. Gould, *Civil War Journals*, 232, 253. Gould's frustration with the lack of religion in the army grew significantly after his born-again experience while home on hiatus in the summer of 1863. The 10th Maine had disbanded in May and while in Portland, serving as a recruiter for a new regiment, the 29th Maine, Gould became infatuated with a young woman who had herself recently adopted a fervent Christianity and helped him become "'born again' . . . in the new religion." Gould wasn't the only one in or out of the Union army hoping to foster religious commitments. The US Christian Commission distributed bibles to the troops by the tens of thousands as well as other supplies and comforts in the name of recalling men to their faith. Gould, *Civil War Journals*, 286; David A. Raney, "In the Lord's Army: The United States Christian Commission, Soldiers, and the Union War Effort," in *Union Soldiers and the Northern Home Front: Wartime Experiences, Postwar Adjustments*, ed. Paul A. Cimbala and Randall M. Miller (New York: Fordham University Press, 2002), 263–92.

33. Gould, *Civil War Journals*, 232, 373.

34. Keith P. Wilson, *Campfires of Freedom: The Camp Life of Black Soldiers During the Civil War* (Kent, OH: Kent State University Press, 2002), 6–7; David A. Cecere, "Carrying the Home Front to War: Soldiers, Race and New England Culture during the Civil War," in Cimbala and Miller, *Union Soldiers*, 300.

35. Gould, *Civil War Journals*, 38, 184, 347.

36. Gould, *Civil War Journals*, 208, 224–26.

37. Gould, *Civil War Journals*, 465, 472.

38. Gould, *Civil War Journals*, 484. For data and experiences at Florence Stockade, see "'Comfortable Camps?' Archeology of the Confederate Guard Camp at the Florence Stockade," National Park Service, March 27, 2020, https://www.nps.gov/articles/-comfortable-camps-archeology-of-the-confederate-guard-camp-at-the-florence-stockade-teaching-with-historic-places.htm; John Harrold, *Libby, Andersonville, Florence: The Capture, Imprisonment, Escape and Rescue of John Harrold. A Union Soldier in the War of the Rebellion* (Philadelphia: W. B. Selheimer, 1870). For experiences in Civil War prison camps in general see, Evan A. Kutzler, *Living by Inches: The Smells, Sounds, Tastes, and Feeling of Captivity in Civil War Prisons* (Chapel Hill: University of North Carolina Press, 2019).

39. Walter Kittredge, *Tenting on the Old Camp-ground*, song sheet (New York: H. De Marsan, 1863); "Tenting Tonight: Civil War Song Endures 150 Years Later," New England Historical Society (2014), http://www.newenglandhistoricalsociety.com; Christian McWhirter, *Battle Hymns: The Power and Popularity of Music in the Civil War* (Chapel Hill: University of North Carolina Press, 2012).

40. Walt Whitman, "Camps of Green," *Drum-Taps* (New York: n.p., 1865), 57–58; Charles M. Oliver, *Critical Companion to Walt Whitman: A Literary Reference to His Life and Work* (New York: Facts on File, 2006), 55–56. "Camps of Green" later appeared in the *Leaves of Grass* editions of 1871 and 1881.

41. John Mead Gould, *History of the First-Tenth-Twenty-Ninth Maine Regiment* (Portland, ME: Stephen Berry, 1871), 471.

42. Marten, *Sing Not War*, 4, 18, 29, 245.

43. Marten, *Sing Not War*, 7, 54; Casey, *New Men*, 48–73.

44. Marten, *Sing Not War*, 6, 18–19; Casey, *New Men*, 17–47.

45. Robert B. Beath, *History of the Grand Army of the Republic* (New York: Bryan, Taylor & Co., 1889), 30–31. Beath, from Philadelphia, was commander of the first GAR post established in Pennsylvania and became the 12th Commander in Chief of the National Encampment in 1883.

46. See, for example, Walt Whitman, "The Veteran's Vision," *Drum-Taps*, 55–56; Oliver, *Critical Companion*, 34–35; Betsy Erkkila, *Whitman the Political Poet* (New York: Oxford University Press, 1989), 215–20; Blight, *Race and Reunion*, 184.

47. George S. Merrill, "The Grand Army of the Republic in Massachusetts," *New England Magazine* 4 (1886): 118. Merrill, from Massachusetts, served as the 10th Commander in Chief for the GAR in 1881–82.

48. In the 1860s and early 1870s, the GAR was one of several veterans' organizations working openly with the Republican Party fighting for the cause of Radical Reconstruction. Zachery A. Fry, "'Let Us Everywhere Charge the Enemy Home': Army of the Potomac Veterans and Public Partisanship, 1864–1880," in *The War Went On: Reconsidering the Lives of Civil War Veterans*, ed. Brian Matthew Jordan and Evan C. Rothera (Baton Rouge: Louisiana State University Press, 2020), 15–36; Scott Ainsworth, "Electoral Strength and the Emergence of Group

Influence in the Late 1800s: The Grand Army of the Republic," *American Politics Quarterly* 23, no. 3 (July 1995): 323; McConnell, *Glorious Contentment*, 24–27; Oliver M. Wilson, *The Grand Army of the Republic under Its First Constitution and Ritual* (Kansas City, MO: Franklin Hudson Publishing Co., 1905), 195.

49. McConnell, *Glorious Contentment*, 31–33; Cecilia O'Leary, *To Die For: The Paradox of American Patriotism* (Princeton, NJ: Princeton University Press, 2000), 37. O'Leary suggests that a "persistence of localism" also served as a brake on the organization's growth in the 1860s, along with tough economic times and the collapse of Reconstruction in the 1870s.

50. Wilson, *Grand Army of the Republic* 195; Merrill, "The Grand Army," 118; O'Leary, *To Die For,* 37. Wilson, who was from Indiana, was among the eight founding members of the GAR in 1866 and served as the Department commander for Indiana in 1869.

51. Marten, *Sing Not War*, 252–55; Earl J. Hess, *The Union Soldier in Battle: Enduring the Ordeal of Combat* (Lawrence: University Press of Kansas, 1997), 165, 181–85, and ch. 9 generally; Alice Fahs, *The Imagined Civil War: Popular Literature of the North and South, 1861–1865* (Chapel Hill: University of North Carolina Press, 2001), 255, 311–14; Blight, *Race and Reunion*, 142–44; McConnell, *Glorious Contentment*, 169–74; Mitchell, *Civil War Soldiers*, 24, 28, 76–77; Gerald F. Linderman, *Embattled Courage: The Experience of Combat in the American Civil War* (New York: Free Press, 1987). Hess categorizes veterans' memoirs in four types: those that recalled their faith in the cause; rejected the cause and patriotism as hollow goals; reoriented their faith from cause to comrade or personal development; and avoided the dark side of war experiences to focus on "amusing Camp stories, the excitement of living out doors, the comradeship of good friends, and the novelty of military life." Hess, *The Union Soldier*, 164.

52. Gould, *Civil War Journals*, 36, 44, 63.

53. Gould, *History of the First-Tenth-Twenty-Ninth*. In 1866, Gould married a local woman, Amelia Jenkins Twitchell, who taught freedpeople in Beaufort, South Carolina, in 1864–65. They then returned to South Carolina where Gould tried to start a lumber mill, a venture that soon failed. Their first child was born shortly after they returned to Portland later in 1867. Gould gained mention in the veterans' newspaper, *The National Tribune* at least seventeen times between September 19, 1889, and September 3, 1908. "John Mead Gould Papers, 1841–44," Collection Guide, Archives and Manuscripts, Duke University Libraries, https://archives.lib. duek.edu/catalog/gouldjohn/ (accessed July 26, 2019).

54. Blight, *Race and Reunion*, 149–50, 172–98; Hess, *The Union Soldier*, 158–90; Casey, *New Men*, 74–103; Andre Fleche, "'Shoulder to Shoulder as Comrades Tried': Black and White Union Veterans and Civil War Memory," *Civil War History* 51, no. 2 (June 2005): 181.

55. Founded by Union veteran and leading pension attorney, George E. Lemon, the *Tribune* began publication as a monthly paper out of Washington, DC, but soon

became a weekly affiliated with the GAR, though it remained independent and reported on veterans' issues beyond the GAR. Circulation rose from less than 10,000 in 1882 to 100,000 in 1887 and maintained 300,000 throughout the 1890s. The Library of Congress has digitized the entire run of the *National Tribune.* "About the *National Tribune* (Washington, DC) 1877–1917," *Chronicling America,* The Library of Congress, http://chroniclingamerica.loc.gov/lccn/sn82016187/ (accessed June 15, 2013); Steven E. Sodergren, "'Exposing False History': The Voice of the Union Veteran in the Pages of the *National Tribune,*" in Jordan and Rothera, *The War Went On,* 137–39; Richard A. Sauers, *"To Care for Him Who Has Borne the Battle": Research Guide to Civil War Material in the National Tribune* (Jackson, KY: History Shop, 1995); O'Leary, *To Die For,* 48–54.

56. "Our Paper," *National Tribune,* January 1, 1879, 4; Sodergren, "Exposing False History," 137–56.

57. John Goodmiller, "To the Editor: He Wants More Fun and Less Gore," *National Tribune,* August 5, 1886, 3, 6.

58. For examples of these stories, see among others, "At Fredricksburg," *National Tribune,* October 8, 1881, 3; Dr. C. C. Bombaugh, "Ourselves," *The National Tribune,* April 22, 1882, 6; Anon., "Echoes from the Old Campground," *National Tribune,* May 13, 1882, 3; Harvey Reid, "A Post Camp-Fire," *National Tribune,* October 18, 1883, 6; John McElroy, "Camp-Fires of Old, As Recalled After Twenty Years of Peace," *National Tribune,* December 20, 1883, 7.

59. "The Grand Army of the Republic and Kindred Societies," *The Library of Congress,* September 13, 2011, https://www.loc.gov/rr/main/gar/garintro.html.

60. Theodore O'Hara, "Bivouac of the Dead," c1847; Susan Bullitt Dixon, "Theodore O'Hara; His 'Bivouac of the Dead'—The Correct Version and the Incorrect Ones," *New York Times,* August 11, 1900, BR5; *Journal of the Nineteenth Annual Session of the Department of Indiana Grand Army of the Republic, held at Columbus, May 18 and 19, 1898,* Vol. XV (Indianapolis: Sentinel Printing Co., 1898), 235; *Journal of the Twentieth Annual Session of the Department of Indiana Grand Army of the Republic, held at Terre Haute, May 24 and 25, 1899,* Vol. XVI (Indianapolis: Sentinel Printing Co., 1899), 192.

61. Terence Young, *Heading Out: A History of American Camping* (Ithaca, NY: Cornell University Press, 2017), 21–48.

62. John Mead Gould, April 1875: Review, Diary of John Mead Gould, Collection 1033, Collections of the Maine Historical Society (hereafter cited as Gould, MHS Diary). Thanks to Jamie Kingman-Rice and Jo Harmon for research assistance with this diary.

63. Gould to Morse, November 6, 1875; Gould to Morse, March 13, 1876, box 5, folder 6, Morse Collection. After Appleton's and Leypold & Holt declined to publish the book, Gould negotiated with Armstrong and agreed to forego royalties on the first 1000 copies sold, with a 10% rate on copies after that. This was evidently on

the low side of normal for what Scribner's was offering authors at the time. Gould believed this was "favorable" for him but fretted that "it is a mighty bad year for such a book to come out." Scribner's sold the book for $1.00, fairly standard for a lower priced book on Scribner's lists. Legal Records, Book Agreements with Authors: 1866–1906, Box 858, Folder 1, 1866–1894: *Series 14: Legal Records, 1846–1982; Scribner, Armstrong & Co.'s List of New Books* (New York: Scribner, Armstrong & Co., April 1877), Series 5: Book Catalogs and Lists, 1855–1996, box 672, folder 16, 1877, Archives of Charles Scribner's Sons, C0101, Princeton University Library, Department of Rare Books and Special Collections, Manuscripts Division (hereafter Scribner's Archives); Gould to Morse, March 13, 1876, box 5, folder 6, Morse Collection.

64. John Mead Gould, *How to Camp Out: Hints for Camping and Walking* (New York: Scribner, Armstrong & Co., 1877), 6; *Scribner . . . List of New Books* (April 1877), Scribner's Archives; *Publishers' Weekly*, March 31, 1877, 371; *Publishers' Weekly*, March 3, 1877, 237; *Scribner, Armstrong & Co.'s List of New Books* (New York: Scribner, Armstrong & Co., June 1877), *Scribner, Armstrong & Co.'s List of New Books* (New York: Scribner, Armstrong & Co., July 1877).

65. Review of *How to Camp Out, Daily Evening Bulletin* (San Francisco), May 19, 1877, 1.

66. Review of *How to Camp Out, The Nation*, April 19, 1877, 240. Scribner's quoted *The Nation's* review in its July 1877 book list. *Scribner . . . List of New Books* (July 1877).

67. Gould, *How to Camp Out*, 5.

68. Following conflict between Indigenous peoples and English settlers, Cape Elizabeth was a site for commercial harvesting of natural resources—fish, forest, and furs. By the mid-nineteenth century, it had become more of a recreational "resort for fishermen," though relatively undeveloped in terms of tourist amenities. In 1870, it held a permanent population of about 5,000 and by the late 1880s would be served by suburban railways. A. J. Coolidge and J. B. Mansfield, *A History and Description of New England, General and Local*, Vol. I (Boston: Austin J. Coolidge, 1859), 85–86; George J. Carney, "History of Cape Elizabeth, Maine," *A gazetteer of the state of Maine* (Boston: B. B. Russell, 1886); John F. Bauman, *Gateway to Vacationland: The Making of Portland, Maine* (Amherst: University of Massachusetts Press, 2012), 7, 79.

69. Gould, MHS Diary, November 9, 1871–December 31, 1877; Bauman, *Gateway to Vacationland*, 109.

70. Gould, MHS Diary, May 26–27 and June 29, 1875.

71. Gould to Morse, July 23, 1877, box 5, folder 6, Morse Collection.

72. Gould MHS Diary, August 5, 1876.

73. Gould, *How to Camp Out*, 12, 24.

74. Gould, *How to Camp Out*, 50, 52, 53, 55.

75. Gould, *How to Camp Out*, 26–29.

76. Gould MHS Diary, June 8, 1875, June 5–6, 1877. Major Joseph Prentice Sanger was a career officer in the US Army who taught Military Science and Tactics at Bowdoin College in the 1870s—which is presumably where Gould met him. Jeremiah E. Goulka, *The Grand Old Man of Maine: Selected Letters of Joshua Lawrence Chamberlain* (Chapel Hill: University of North Carolina Press, 2004), 44–45.

77. Randall H. Bennett, *The White Mountains, Alps of New England* (Charleston, SC: Arcadia, 2003); Candace Kanes, "Hiking, Art & Science: Portland's White Mountain Club," *Maine History Online,* Maine Historical Society, https://www.mainememory.net/sitebuilder/site/1414/page/2078/display (accessed September 10, 2016). For more on the formation of the White Mountain Club, the Appalachian Mountain Club, and other hiking organizations during this era, see Silas Chamberlin, *On the Trail: A History of American Hiking* (New Haven, CT: Yale University Press, 2016), 30–65.

78. Gould to Morse, May 23, 1878, box 5, folder 6, Morse Collection.

79. Gould, *How to Camp Out,* 9.

80. Gould, MHS Diary, July 8, 1872. See also entries for August 6, 1874 and May 31, 1875.

81. Gould to Morse, April 7, 1879; Gould to Morse, April 22, 1879, box 6, folder 8, Morse Collection.

82. Gould, *How to Camp Out,* 107–12.

83. Emphasis from the original, Gould, *How to Camp Out,* 14.

84. Gould, *How to Camp Out,* 15–16.

85. Gould, *How to Camp Out,* 33.

86. Gould, *How to Camp Out,* 55–57, 97–98.

87. Gould, *How to Camp Out,* 105, 129.

88. Gould, *How to Camp Out,* 97.

89. Gould to Morse, July 23, 1877, box 5, folder 6, Morse Collection.

90. Scribner, Armstrong & Co., to John M. Gould, April 21, 1877; Scribner, Armstrong & Co., to John M. Gould, May 17, 1877; Scribner, Armstrong & Co., to John M. Gould, September 22, 1877, Series 15: Letterbooks, Subseries 15E: J.B. Scribner, Box 933, Vol. 5 (Oct. 1876–Sept. 1877), Scribner's Archive; Gould MHS Diary, March 16, 1876, January 1877 review, July 1877 review. Scribner's records did not include sales figures or estimates for the book. In September 1877, Scribner's apologized that the first royalty check was "not for a larger amount"—though that Gould was receiving anything suggests that the book had sold more than 1000 copies. Gould mentioned in an April 25, 1878 letter to Morse that "some hundreds of my 'How to Camp' were sold at a great 'trade sale,'" but by the end of the year he reported great disappointment. Gould to Morse, April 25, 1878, Gould to Morse, July 19, 1878, Gould to Morse, December 5, 1878, box 5, folder 6, Morse Collection.

91. Scribner's book and price lists are contained in Series 5: Book Catalogs and Lists, 1855–1996, Box 672, Folder 17 (1878); Box 673, Folders 1–12 (1879–1890), Scribner's Archive.

92. The GAR played a key role in electoral politics. President Grover Cleveland failed in his reelection bid in 1888 in part due to his prior veto of a Dependent Pension Bill that the GAR had favored, whereas his victorious opponent, Benjamin Harrison gained support with veterans in part because of his firm support of pension legislation. McConnell concluded that "especially in the ultrapatriotic context of the 1890s, it had real political consequences. By tying the preservation of the Union to the preservation of the antebellum Northern social order, the GAR put forth a strong proposition about American nationalism, a proposition to which future versions of the 'nation' would feel obligated to respond." McConnell, *Glorious Contentment*, 220–22; "The Grand Army of the Republic and Kindred Societies."

93. Emphasis from the original, John A. Logan, quoted in Beath, *History of the Grand Army*, 109–10.

94. O'Leary, *To Die For*, 48, 54.

95. John Ireland [speech], *Journal of the Thirty-First National Encampment 1897* (Lincoln, NE: State Journal Company, 1897), 228; O'Leary, *To Die For*, 48–49.

96. As an example of the operation of a typical GAR post, the manuscript records of the General Lander Post of the GAR from Lynn, Massachusetts are available online. The meeting minutes usually included reports of illness and death of members or other area veterans, elected officers, plans to decorate graves and donations for indigent veterans as well as widows and orphans. The post built a banquet room in the basement where they typically held campfires, inviting members of other posts as well as students of local high schools to come and witness the "reminiscences by comrades." Records of the General Lander Post 5 of the GAR, Lynn MA, 1897–98; January 7, 1897, March 10, 1898, Boston Public Library, https://archive.org/details/recordsofgeneral1897gran.

97. [Robert B. Beath], "The Grand Army. Opening of the Eighteenth Annual Encampment. Gen. Beath's Address," *National Tribune*, July 24, 1884, 1.

98. *Journal of the Twenty-Third Annual Session of the National Encampment, Grand Army of the Republic, Milwaukee, Wis., August 28th, 29th and 30th, 1889* (St. Louis, MO: A. Whipple, 1889): 198–99.

99. "Robert Chivas Post Camp," *Milwaukee Daily Journal*, September 18, 1885, 1.

100. George Morgan, "Bronze Button Heroes: A Study of the G.A.R.," *Lippincott's Monthly Magazine* 64, no. 381 (September 1899): 439.

101. "The Encampment: Preparations for 22d National Encampment," *National Tribune*, August 30, 1888, 6; "The G.A.R. Encampment," *New York Tribune*, September 4, 1899, 2.

102. "Reunited Veterans-Annual Encampment of the Illinois Department of the Grand Army of the Republic," *The Daily Inter Ocean* (Chicago), January 29, 1880, 3. For example, the New York plan for state encampments of 1884 and 1885 published negotiated rates for various hotels for events to be held in Buffalo and Utica, but nothing in regard to tents or camping except for the Grand Camp-Fire planned to be held at the Music Hall in Buffalo. *Proceedings of the Semi-Annual*

and *Annual Encampments of the Department of New York, Grand Army of the Republic, Convened at Buffalo, N.Y. July 3 and 4, 1884 and Utica, N.Y., Feb 4 and 5, 1885 and General Orders and Circulars* (New York: Willis McDonald & Co., 1884).

103. Hess, *The Union Soldier*, 168; McConnell, *Glorious Contentment*, 255; Blight, *Race and Reunion*, 189; Larry M. Logue, *To Appomattox and Beyond: The Civil War Soldier in War and Peace* (Chicago: Ivan R. Dee, 1996), 39, 167, 113.

104. Emphasis from the original, Palmer quoted in "The National Encampment, The Address of the Commander-in-Chief at Washington," *National Tribune*, September 22, 1892, 1.

105. Palmer quoted in "National Encampment."

106. Joseph Lovering quoted in Beath, *History of the Grand Army*, 223–24.

107. Miles O'Reilly [Charles Graham Halpine], "The Canteen" (c. 1866), quoted in Warner, [speech], "The Grand Army," *National Tribune*, April 25, 1889, 8.

108. McConnell, *Glorious Contentment*, 104.

109. Fleche, "'Shoulder to Shoulder,'" 176; Blight, *Race and Reunion*, 193–96; Donald R. Shaffer, *After the Glory: The Struggles of Black Civil War Veterans* (Lawrence: University Press of Kansas, 2004), 143–68; George Washington Williams, *A History of the Negro Troops in the War of the Rebellion, 1861–1865* (New York: Harper & Bros, 1888), 213.

110. Beath's history records multiple statements in defense of race-blind membership, in support of Black veterans' needs, and in praise of their contributions and heroism. Membership statistics were not recorded by race, though some posts sometimes carried the designation "colored." Beath, *History of the Grand Army*, 110–13, 488, 539. Nothing referencing race appeared in the *Rules and Regulations for the Government of the Grand Army of the Republic* (Philadelphia: Grand Army of the Republic, 1887).

111. Williams, *History of Negro Troops*, x; Blight, *Race and Reunion*, 193–96.

112. "The Encampment: Preparations for 22d National Encampment," *National Tribune*, August 9, 1888, 6; "The National Encampment: Preparations for the 26th Meeting of the G.A.R.," *National Tribune*, September 15, 1892, 12. For examples of notices for and participation of Black posts, see "The Colored Troops," *National Tribune*, August 11, 1887, 1; "The Encampment," *National Tribune*, August, 21, 1890, 1; Joseph T. Wilson, *The Black Phalanx; A History of the Negro Soldiers of the United States in the Wars of 1775–1812, 1861–'65* (Hartford, CT: American Publishing Co, 1890), 11; Fleche, "'Shoulder to Shoulder,'" 182–84.

113. Fleche's studies showed that the vast majority of GAR members, both rank and file and national leadership, sided with Black veterans. Fleche, "'Shoulder to Shoulder,'" 196.

114. James Sexton, quoted in *Journal of the Thirty-Second National Encampment of the Grand Army of the Republic, Cincinnati, Ohio, September 8th and 9th, 1898*

(Philadelphia: Town Printing, Co, 1898), 52; J.F. Lovering, quoted in Beath, *History of the Grand Army,* 223.

115. Blight cites paeans to the Soldier's Faith (as articulated by Oliver Wendell Holmes) and the sentimentalist view of campfire camaraderie as contributing to the racist reconciliationist view that allowed northerners to back away from their commitments to Black freedom and to animate a sense of Americanism based on shared whiteness (even with former rebels). McConnell views the GAR's de facto segregation as fundamentally undermining its commitment to a more racially in-clusive view. Fleche challenges this suggesting that the GAR's focus on veterans as a unified group in general and defense of Black veterans in particular was one of the few bulwarks against a full-throttled segregationist vision. Blight, *Race and Reunion,* 96; McConnell, *Glorious Contentment,* 213-18; Fleche, "'Shoulder to Shoulder,'" 176–82, 184. See also, Shaffer, *After the Glory,* 143–68.

116. Hess, *The Union Soldier,* 167–68; Charles Robinson, "My Experiences in the Civil War," *Michigan History Magazine* 24 (Winter 1940): 50; O'Leary, *To Die For,* 37.

117. "A few of our enterprising and energetic citizens are taking steps to secure for St. Louis the Selection," *St. Louis (MO) Globe-Democrat,* June 21, 1886, 4; "Official Programme For the Encampment of the Grand Army of the Republic in St. Louis Next Month," *The Galveston (TX) Daily News,* August 29, 1887, 2.

118. "Grand Army Reunion," *San Francisco Examiner,* February 4, 1886, 5; Marguerite S. Shaffer, *See America First: Tourism and National Identity 1880–1940* (Washington, DC: Smithsonian Institution Press. 2001), 7, 11.

119. "Camp Agnus," *National Tribune,* June 24, 1882, 4.

120. Gould, MHS Diary, June 21–24, 1885. For reports of debates over and consump-tion of alcohol at the 1885 National Encampment, see, for example, "The Grand Army in Maine," *Los Angeles Daily Times,* June 23, 1885, 1.

121. Emphasis from the original, Gould, MHS Diary, June 22–23, 1885.

122. Gould, MHS Diary, June 21–23, 1885. Gould served as the Association's secretary and historian for more than three decades. When the Association presented him in 1896 with two easy-chairs, a revolving bookcase and an onyx clock in thanks for his years of service, Gould replied that this work had been "the greatest pleasure of his life." *National Tribune,* August 27, 1896, 6; John Mead Gould, *Directory of the First—Tenth—Twenty-ninth Maine Regiment Association, Compiled for the Use of the Association* (Portland, ME: Stephen Berry, 1889); John Mead Gould, *Additions and Corrections to the 1-10-29 Maine Regiment. Correcting all errors that have been noticed up to February, 1893* (n.p., 1893); Committees from the Maine Regiments, *The Maine Bugle,* Campaign IV, Call IV, October 1897, 334; Crompton B. Burton, "'The Dear Old Regiment': Maine's Regimental Associations and the Memory of the American Civil War," *The New England Quarterly* LXXXIV, no. 1 (March 2011): 110–11; "Reunion of the 1-10-29th Me.," *National Tribune,* October 30, 1902, 6.

123. Emphasis from the original, Gould, MHS Diary, April 5–10, and August 18–21, 1884.
124. Sherman, "Camp-Fires," 499–500.

CHAPTER 2

1. John Muir, *Our National Parks* (Boston: Houghton, Mifflin and Co., 1901), 1; Donald Worster, *A Passion for Nature: The Life of John Muir* (New York: Oxford University Press, 2008), 487n9.
2. John Muir, "The Forests of the Yosemite Park," *Atlantic Monthly* 85, no. 510 (April 1900): 493. *Our National Parks* was largely compiled from a series of *Atlantic* essays, published in the preceding years. A revised version of "The Forests of the Yosemite Park" appeared as chapter 4 of *Our National Parks*. Worster, *Passion for Nature*, 372–77.
3. Susan Schulten, *Mapping the Nation: History and Cartography in Nineteenth-Century America* (Chicago: University of Chicago Press, 2012), 86; Conevery Bolton Valencius, *Health of the Country: How American Settlers Understood Themselves and Their Land* (New York: Basic Books, 2002), 2–7, 86–92. In the years after the Civil War, epidemic diseases of malaria, yellow fever, cholera and later smallpox, which had earlier come under a modicum of control in the North, ran rampant in the Southern lowlands.
4. Michael Willrich, *Pox: An American History* (New York: Penguin Books, 2012), 14–20.
5. Worster, *Passion for Nature*, 9.
6. Laura Dassow Walls, *Henry David Thoreau: A Life* (Chicago: University of Chicago Press, 2017); Thomas Andrews, "Beasts of the Southern Wild: Slaveholders, Slaves, and Other Animals in Charles Ball's *Slavery in the United States*," in *Rendering Nature: Animals, Bodies, Places, Politics*, ed. Marguerite S. Shaffer and Phoebe S. K. Young (Philadelphia: University of Pennsylvania Press, 2015), 21–47.
7. The graveyard then known as "Old Bonaventure" had been a family cemetery attached to a plantation established in the eighteenth century by the loyalist John Mulryne. Seized during the American Revolution and later purchased by Josiah Tattnall, the Bonaventure plantation continued to use the burial ground until Tattnall's son sold the property in 1846. At the time of Muir's visit, it was owned by the Wiltberger family, who began to operate it as a commercial enterprise catering to prominent white Georgia families. In 1907 the city of Savannah purchased and expanded it. Featured in John Berendt's popular murder mystery novel, *Midnight in the Garden of Good and Evil* (1994), Bonaventure gained literary fame and became a popular tourist attraction. "History," *Bonaventure Historical Society* (2017), https://www.bonaventurehistorical.org/history-bonaventure-cemetery/. For discussion of pastoral cemeteries as public park space, see Jeffrey

Smith, *The Rural Cemetery Movement: Places of Paradox in Nineteenth-Century America* (Lanham, MD: Lexington Books, 2017); and, James R. Cochran and Erica Danylchak, *Grave Landscapes: The Nineteenth-Century Rural Cemetery Movement* (Columbia: University of South Carolina Press, 2018).

8. John Muir, *A Thousand-mile Walk to the Gulf* (Dunwoody, GA: N. S. Berg, 1969, c. 1916), 73–76. Muir's posthumously published book largely reproduced his original manuscript journal verbatim, with several important exceptions, which will be noted. To aid reference, I cite the published version unless it diverges significantly from the original text.

9. Aaron Sachs, *The Humboldt Current: Nineteenth-Century Exploration and the Roots of American Environmentalism* (New York: Viking, 2006), 4, 27–29.

10. Wilbur R. Jacobs, "Francis Parkman: Naturalist-Environmental Savant," *Pacific Historical Review* 61, no. 3 (May 1992): 347. Muir did meet Parkman many years later, on a trip to Boston in 1893 and later acquired Parkman's twelve-volume *Works* (1902) for his personal library, but there's no evidence that Parkman influenced Muir's earlier travels or thinking. For his part, Parkman made no mention of Muir in his papers or correspondence. Worster, *Passion for Nature*, 334–35; Richard F. Fleck, *Henry Thoreau and John Muir Among the Native Americans* (Portland, OR: WestWinds Press, 2015), 114n2; Jacobs, "Francis Parkman," 344.

11. Francis Parkman, *The Journals of Francis Parkman*, ed. Mason Wade (New York: Harper Brothers, 1947), 1:3.

12. Emphasis from the original, Parkman, quoted in *American Habitat: A Historical Perspective*, ed. William A. Koelsch and Barbara Gutmann Rosenkrantz (New York: Free Press, 1973), 325–26; Francis Parkman, "Exploring the Magalloway," *Harper's New Monthly Magazine* 29, no. 174 (November 1864): 735–41.

13. Jacobs, "Francis Parkman," 352; Howard Doughty, *Francis Parkman* (New York: Macmillan, 1962), 114, 203–204, 222, 358, 385, 411.

14. Charles P. Horton, "A Vacation Ramble," *Harvard Magazine* 3, no. 1 (January 1857): 18; William Koeslch, "Antebellum Harvard Students and the Recreational Exploration of the New England Landscape," *Journal of Historical Geography* 8, no. 4 (1982): 365–67.

15. "In the Woods," *Harvard Magazine* 5, nos. 6, 7 (July and September 1859): 246–53; Henry George Spaulding, "Among the Mountains," *Harvard Magazine* 4, no. 8 (October 1858): 338; Koelsch, "Antebellum Harvard," 366.

16. Horton, "A Vacation Ramble," 18; Koelsch, "Antebellum Harvard," 366; "In the Woods," 246–53; Spaulding, "Among the Mountains," 338; Christopher Sellers, "Thoreau's Body: Towards an Embodied Environmental History," *Environmental History* 4, no. 4 (October 1997): 486–92; Dona Brown, *Inventing New England: Regional Tourism in the Nineteenth Century* (Washington, DC: Smithsonian Institution Press, 1995), 46–52, 72; Roderick Nash, *Wilderness and the American Mind*, 5th ed. (New Haven, CT: Yale University Press, 2014), 44–66.

17. *Report of the Class of 1857 in Harvard College, Prepared for the Twenty-fifth Anniversary of its Graduation* (Cambridge, MA: John Wilson and Son, 1882), 77–78.

18. Worster, *Passion for Nature,* 89.

19. Worster, *Passion for Nature,* 74–91. With his brother, Muir joined perhaps as many as 15,000 draft evaders in British North America. Technically, since his name was never called, Muir was a draft avoider rather than an illegal draft evader, the label for those who failed to report for examination were called. A full 20%, or about 160,000 of all those ordered to report decided to evade illegally, rather than try to raise the $300 commutation fee or find a substitute—legal ways to avoid being drafted. One of the areas with the highest rates of draft evasion was in Milwaukee, Wisconsin, partly due to physical proximity to the Canadian border. Muir was thus hardly alone in his decision to strike out for Canada in fear of the draft. Peter Levine, "Draft Evasion in the North in the Civil War, 1863–1865," *Journal of American History* 67, no. 4 (March 1981): 816–34; Robin W. Winks, *The Civil War Years: Canada and the United States,* 4th ed. (Montreal: McGill-Queen's University Press, 1998), 202–205.

20. Worster, *Passion for Nature,* 92–95. President Lincoln had announced amnesty for draft evaders in March 1865, so Muir had little to worry about in returning.

21. Worster, *Passion for Nature,* 102–14.

22. Muir, *Thousand-mile Walk,* 2.

23. John Muir, Journal, July 1867—February 1868 [Journal 01]: The "thousand mile walk" from Kentucky to Florida and Cuba (hereafter cited as Journal, "thousand mile walk"), Muir Papers, MSS 048, Holt-Atherton Special Collections, University of the Pacific Library, (hereafter cited as Muir Papers). Muir did not record the particulars of his sleeping arrangements on six occasions.

24. Maxwell Whiteman, "Notions, Dry Goods, and Clothing: An Introduction to the Study of the Cincinnati Peddler," *Jewish Quarterly Review* 53, no. 4 (April 1963): 312; David Jaffee, "Peddlers of Progress and the Transformation of the Rural North, 1760–1860," *Journal of American History* 78, no. 2 (September 1991): 511–24; Susan Strasser, *Waste and Want: A Social History of Trash* (New York: Henry Holt, 1999), 77; Seymour Dunbar, *A History of Travel in America* (New York: Tudor Publishing Company, 1937), 329–31.

25. Muir, *Thousand-mile Walk,* 60, 64.

26. Muir, *Thousand-mile Walk,* 12, 15–16.

27. A. K. Sandoval-Strausz, "Travelers, Strangers, and Jim Crow: Law, Public Accommodations, and Civil Rights in America," *Law and History Review* 23, no. 1 (Spring 2005): 53–94; A. K. Sandoval-Strausz, *Hotel: An American History* (New Haven, CT: Yale University Press, 2007).

28. Steven J. Holmes, *The Young John Muir: An Environmental Biography* (Madison: University of Wisconsin Press, 1999), 99; Jonathan Ned Katz, *Love Stories: Sex Between Men before Homosexuality* (Chicago: University of Chicago

Press, 2001), 34. Katz indicates that taverns were typical places in the mid-nineteenth century for men to meet other men in search of physical companionship or sex. Thanks to Kevin Leonard for the suggestion to interrogate the phrase "uncordial kindness."

29. Muir, *Thousand-mile Walk*, 93–95, 110; Holmes, *Young John Muir*, 130–32, 164; John P. Herron, *Science and the Social Good* (New York: Oxford University Press, 2010), 60–64.

30. Kathryn E. Holland Braund and Charlotte M. Porter, eds., *Fields of Vision: Essays on the Travels of William Bartram* (Tuscaloosa: University of Alabama Press, 2010); "Inquiries: John Muir and William Bartram," *John Muir Newsletter* 2, no. 2 (Spring 1992), reprinted at https://vault.sierraclub.org/john_muir_exhibit/john_muir_newsletter/william_bartram_and_john_muir.aspx.

31. William Bartram, *Travels Through North & South Carolina, Georgia, East & West Florida, the Cherokee Country, the Extensive Territories of the Muscogulges, or Creek Confederacy, and the Country of the Chactaws* (Philadelphia: James & Johnson, 1791), 11, 107–108, 111, 124, 138–39, 426, electronic edition, *Documenting the American South*, University of North Carolina at Chapel Hill, 2001, http://docsouth.unc.edu/nc/bartram/bartram.html; Robert Sayre, "William Bartram and Environmentalism," *American Studies* 54, no. 1 (2015): 67–87.

32. Muir, *Thousand-mile Walk*, 65–67, 72.

33. Muir, *Thousand-mile Walk*, 71. Muir was quite enamored of the live oaks at Bonaventure and elsewhere, including several images and descriptions of them in the diary. Whether Muir was aware of the strong symbolic association his contemporary Walt Whitman drew between the "live oak" and male genitalia in several editions of *Leaves of Grass* in the decade before one can only guess. Katz, *Love Stories*, 103, 118.

34. Muir, *Thousand-mile Walk*, 84. For environmental devastation in the South wrought by the war, see Megan Kate Nelson, *Ruin Nation: Destruction and the American Civil War* (Athens: University of Georgia Press, 2012), 61–102.

35. Reiko Hillyer, *Designing Dixie: Tourism, Memory, and Urban Space in the New South* (Charlottesville: University of Virginia Press, 2014), 30; C. Vann Woodward, "Whitelaw Reid: Radical Pro Tem: Introduction to the Torchbook Edition," in Whitelaw Reid, *After the War: A Tour of the Southern States*, ed. C. Vann Woodward (New York: Harper & Row, 1965; c. 1866).

36. Reid, *After the War*, 1, 10, 138, 339, 403, 419, 441.

37. Reid, *After the War*, 139–41; Lori Robison, "Writing Reconstruction: Race and 'Visualist Ideology,' in Whitelaw Reid's *After the War*," *Journal of Narrative Theory* 29, no. 1 (Winter 1999): 85–109.

38. Muir, *Thousand-mile Walk*, 66, 72–73.

39. Throughout the war, division commanders reacted differently to the presence of contraband refugees, employing policies that spanned a spectrum from allowing Southern masters into camps to search for fugitives to enticing slaves to leave their

plantations and enter the protection of the army camp. See Benjamin Quarles, *The Negro in the Civil War* (New York: DaCapo Press, 1989; c. 1953), 58–92; James Oakes, *Freedom National: The Destruction of Slavery in the United States, 1861–1865* (New York: Norton, 2014), 105, 196, 242, 370–97, 416–17; Leon F. Litwack, *Been in the Storm So Long: The Aftermath of Slavery* (New York: Vintage Books, 1980), 52–59, 64–103; Steven Hahn, *A Nation Under Our Feet: Black Political Struggles in the Rural South from Slavery to the Great Migration* (Cambridge, MA: Harvard University Press, 2005), 71–72; Chandra Manning, "Working for Citizenship in Civil War Contraband Camps," *Journal of the Civil War Era* 4, no. 2 (June 2014): 172–204.

40. Sherman, quoted in Oakes, *Freedom National,* 417; Cam Walker, "Corinth: The Story of a Contraband Camp," *Civil War History* XX (March 1974): 8. For the numerical estimate of self-emancipated slaves that ran through the military and federal system before April 1865, see Gregory P. Downs, *After Appomattox: Military Occupation and the Ends of War* (Cambridge, MA: Harvard University Press, 2015), 41–42; Hahn, *Nation Under Our Feet,* 82–83.

41. Walker, "Corinth," 6–8, 19–20; Manning, "Working for Citizenship," 181–90; Quarles, *Negro in the Civil War,* 175, 282; Chaplain John Eaton Jr., General Superintendent of Contrabands, Department of the Tennessee, "Interrogatories," March, 1863, in *Free at Last: A Documentary History of Slavery, Freedom and the Civil War,* ed. Ira Berlin, Barbara J. Fields, Steven F. Miller, Joseph P. Reidy, and Leslie S. Rowland (New York: The New Press, 1992), 187.

42. Aid worker quoted in Manning, "Working for Citizenship," 190–92. For an example of military leaders' efforts, see *Private and Official Correspondence of Gen. Benjamin F. Butler,* Vol. 2 (Norwood, MA: Plimpton Press, 1917), 244–45. On disease in contraband camps, see Berlin, et. al., *Free at Last,* 186; Walker, "Corinth," 7; Oakes, *Freedom National,* 419.

43. Eaton, Interrogatories, 190–92; Oakes, *Freedom National,* 418–20. This risk fell particularly harshly on women, who suffered sexual abuse at the hands of soldiers. Jacqueline Jones, *Labor of Love, Labor of Sorrow: Black Women, Work, and the Family from Slavery to the Present* (New York: Basic Books, 1985), 49.

44. Oakes, *Freedom National,* 419; Jones, *Labor of Love,* 49; Keith P. Wilson, *Campfires of Freedom: The Camp Life of Black Soldiers during the Civil War* (Kent, OH: Kent State University Press, 2002), 203–205. The Camp Nelson incident, where families of Black soldiers encamped near their regiment in Kentucky were expelled during a particularly cold November, resulting in more than a few deaths of women, children, and elderly relatives, became a national scandal. Berlin, et. al., *Free at Last,* 393–97, 493–95; Oakes, *Freedom National,* 418; Wilson, *Campfires of Freedom,* 186–88.

45. Hahn, *Nation Under Our Feet,* 84; Oakes, *Freedom National,* 414.

46. Boston Blackwell, *Born in Slavery: Slave Narratives from the Federal Writers' Project, 1936–1938, Arkansas Narratives,* 2:173–74, https://www.loc.gov/resource/mesn.021/?sp=173; Manning, "Working for Citizenship," 192.

47. General Benjamin F. Butler to President Abraham Lincoln, November 28, 1862 in Butler, *Private and Official Correspondence,* 447–50; Joseph P. Reidy, "Coming from the Shadow of the Past: The Transition from Slavery to Freedom at Freedmen's Village, 1863–1900," *Virginia Magazine of History and Biography* 95, no. 4 (October 1987): 406; Hahn, *Nation Under Our Feet,* 82; Oakes, *Freedom National,* 419–20. In many cases, freedpeople did not leave the camps to return to labor on plantations voluntarily but were coerced by the army. William Cohen, *At Freedom's Edge: Black Mobility and the Southern White Quest for Racial Control, 1861–1915* (Baton Rouge: Louisiana State University Press, 1991), 10–11.

48. Hahn, *Nation Under Our Feet,* 73. See also, Quarles, *Negro in the Civil War,* 77 and Manning, "Working for Citizenship," 173, 182.

49. Booker T. Washington, *Up from Slavery: An Autobiography* (Garden City, NY: Doubleday, 1901), 19–23; Hahn, *Nation Under Our Feet,* 116–17; Litwack, *Been in the Storm,* 296–300; Lee W. Formwalt, "Moving in 'That Strange Land of Shadows': African-American Mobility and Persistence in Post-Civil War Southwest Georgia," *Georgia Historical Quarterly* 82, no. 3 (Fall 1998): 510.

50. Reid, *After the War,* 389.

51. Jacqueline Jones, *The Dispossessed: America's Underclasses from the Civil War to the Present* (New York: Basic Books, 1992), 22; Hahn, *Nation Under Our Feet,* 119; Litwack, *Been in the Storm,* 305–16.

52. Jones, *Dispossessed,* 22; Reid, *After the War,* 325–26; Downs, *After Appomattox,* 79.

53. Formwalt, "Moving," 507–32; Willrich, *Pox* 42; Jones, *Dispossessed,* 24–25; Litwack, *Been in the Storm,* 319. See Cohen, *At Freedom's Edge,* 32–35 on vagrancy laws. Nine states adopted vagrancy laws in 1865–1866 (Alabama, Florida, Georgia, Louisiana, Mississippi, North Carolina, South Carolina, Texas, and Virginia); all but North Carolina provided for the hiring out of convicted vagrants, and most vagrancy laws remained in place in some form after the initial Black Codes were struck down.

54. Cohen, *At Freedom's Edge,* 3–4, 27; Oakes, *Freedom National,* 490; Downs, *After Appomattox,* 48–49; Jones, *Dispossessed,* 26. Staying in one place did not necessarily provide a safe haven. "Night riders," gangs of armed white men, descended upon Black families in their homes at night, holding them captive, subjecting them to physical and sexual abuse, and destroying their property. Kidada E. Williams "The Wounds that Cried Out: Reckoning with African Americans' Testimonies of Trauma and Suffering from Night Riding," *The World the Civil War Made,* ed. Gregory P. Downs and Kate Masur (Chapel Hill: University of North Carolina Press, 2015), 162–64.

55. Jones, *Dispossessed,* 24; Reid, *After the War,* 456; Oakes, *Freedom National,* 489; Downs, *After Appomattox,* 110; Hahn, *Nation Under Our Feet,* 153.

56. Note that Muir's route did not venture into areas where slave populations were concentrated most densely (at least as recorded in 1860). National Park Service, "Contraband Locations (1863–65) compared to slave population density (1860),"

https://www.nps.gov/hdp/exhibits/african/images/ContrabandData_110128.jpg (accessed August 1, 2019).

57. Muir, *Thousand-mile Walk*, 6–7, 51–53, 29–30; Muir, Journal, "thousand mile walk," 55; Worster, *Passion for Nature*, 121, 128. Worster notes a key change in Muir's wording on this point. In the original journal, Muir writes that "The negroes are very lazy and merry," while in the published version the word "lazy" is changed to "easy-going."

58. Muir, *Thousand-mile Walk*, 93, 110.

59. Muir, *Thousand-mile Walk*, 27–28, 31, 61.

60. Muir, *Thousand-mile Walk*, 106–107.

61. As Holmes noted about the drawing of the Black family, "Muir's experiences and responses were leading him not to a straightforward value dichotomy between wilderness and civilization but rather to a complex array of emotionally charged associations and images, with natural and human elements in complex juxtaposition, held together by a personal psychological logic." I see the connection as much social and political as "personal psychological." Holmes, *Young John Muir*, 180.

62. Muir, *Thousand-mile Walk*, 109–10, 135–36.

63. Valencius, *Health of the Country*, 88–89.

64. Reid, *After the War*, 326, 456.

65. Litwack, *Been in the Storm*, 319–20.

66. Willrich, *Pox*, 14, 18–20, 41; Schulten, *Mapping the Nation*, 90, 107.

67. Worster, *Passion for Nature*, 140–47.

68. Muir, Journal, "thousand mile walk," 18b; Muir, *Thousand-mile Walk*, 186, 188, 188n1 (inserted by editor, Fredrick William Badé), xxv; John Muir, Journal, March 1868 [Journal 02], Crossing the Panama Isthmus, Muir Papers; Worster, *Passion for Nature*, 462.

69. In 1867, Muir's friend Jeanne Carr recommended he get someone to read him descriptions of the Valley while his eyes recovered. Once able to see, he became enthralled by images in an illustrated Yosemite brochure, which perhaps included lithographs and stereographs circulating since the 1850s or reprints of Carleton Watkins's mammoth plate photographs first exhibited in New York in 1862, or Albert Bierstadt's painting *Looking Down the Yosemite Valley* which toured the Midwest in 1866. John Muir to Jeanne Carr, April 6, 1867; Jeanne Carr to John Muir, April 15, 1867; John Muir to Jeanne Carr, May 2, 1867, John Muir Correspondence, Muir Papers (hereafter cited as Muir Correspondence); Rebecca Solnit, *Savage Dreams: A Journey into the Hidden Wars of the American* West (Berkeley: University of California Press, 2014), 236–45.

70. John Muir to Merrills and Moores, January 6, 1868; John Muir to David Gilrye Muir, March 3, 1868, Muir Correspondence.

71. John Muir to David Muir, July 14, 1868; John Muir to Jeanne C. Carr, July 26, 1868, Muir Correspondence. Muir did experience a relapse of malarial fever on the trip up to Yosemite, but it proved mild and brief.

72. Charles Nordhoff, *California: For Health, Pleasure and Residence* (New York: Harper & Brothers, 1872), 109. See also John E. Baur, *The Health Seekers of Southern California* (Berkeley: University of California Press, 2010; c. 1959).

73. John Muir, Journal, January—May 1869 [Journal 03], "Twenty Hill Hollow," January 1, 1869, Muir Papers; Robert Bauer, "Shepherd of the Plains: John Muir at Twenty Hill Hollow" (MA thesis, California State University, Stanislaus, 2001).

74. Muir, journal "Twenty Hill Hollow," February 13, 1869; [John Muir] to John and [Margaret Muir Reid], January 13, 1869, Muir Correspondence.

75. John Muir, "Twenty Hill Hollow," *Overland Monthly* 9, no. 1 (July 1872): 80.

76. Muir, "Twenty Hill Hollow," 80; Muir, *Thousand-mile Walk,* 210–12.

77. [John Muir] to Dan[iel H. Muir], April 17, 1869; [John Muir] to Mary [Muir], May 2, 1869; [John Muir] to [Jeanne C. Carr], May 16, 1869, Muir Correspondence.

78. John Muir to [Jeanne C.] Carr, July 11, [1869], Muir Correspondence.

79. John Muir, *My First Summer in the Sierra* (Minneola, NY: Dover Publications, 2004, c. 1911). Muir initially reworked the journal in 1887 and threw the original away, so his raw impressions are lost. The few letters that remain, including a couple where he copied journal entries, suggest that Muir made extensive alterations to the original, and continued to modify it up through its 1911 publication. The discarded journal continued the story after the "Twenty Hill Hollow" journal, which chronicled the first five months of 1869 and survives. Worster, *Passion for Nature,* 160, 474n13.

80. Muir, *My First Summer,* 67; John Muir to Sarah [Muir Galloway], August 1, 1869, Muir Correspondence.

81. Muir, *My First Summer,* 102–103.

82. Muir, *My First Summer,* 17, 59.

83. Muir, *My First Summer,* 48, 52, 58.

84. Muir, *My First Summer,* 12–13, 44; Kevin DeLuca and Anne Demo, "Imagining Nature and Erasing Class and Race: Carleton Watkins, John Muir and the Construction of Wilderness," *Environmental History* 6, no. 4 (October 2001): 552–53.

85. Muir, *My First Summer,* 1, 81; Worster, *Passion for Nature,* 159–62; DeLuca and Demo, "Imagining Nature," 553.

86. Muir, quoted in Worster, *Passion for Nature,* 160, 165; Muir, "Twenty-Hill Hollow," 80, 86; David Hickman, "John Muir's Orchard Home," *Pacific Historical Review* 82, no. 3 (August 2013): 335–61.

87. Muir, *My First Summer,* 17, 35; Muir, journal, "Twenty Hill Hollow," 71.

88. Jen A. Huntley, *The Making of Yosemite: James Mason Hutchings and the Origin of America's Most Popular Park* (Lawrence: University Press of Kansas, 2014), 55–57, 126–29.

89. Muir, quoted in Richard F. Fleck, "John Muir's Evolving Attitudes toward Native American Cultures," *American Indian Quarterly* 4, no. 1 (February 1978): 20; John

Muir, *The Yosemite* (San Francisco: Sierra Club Books, 1988, c. 1914), 168–74; Huntley, *Making of Yosemite,* 77–79.

90. Solnit, *Savage Dreams,* 268–70; Albert Hurtado, *Indian Survival on the California Frontier* (New Haven, CT: Yale University Press, 1988), 1; Huntley, *Making of Yosemite,* 77; M. Kat Anderson and Michael J. Moratto, "Native American Land-Use Practices and Ecological Impacts," in *Sierra Nevada Ecosystem Project: Final Report to Congress* (Davis: University of California, Centers for Water and Wildland Resources, 1996), 2:191.

91. Emphasis from the original, "Address of the Indian Agents," *Daily Alta California* (San Francisco), January 14, 1851, 2; Huntley, *Making of Yosemite,* 55–56; Solnit, *Savage Dreams,* 272; Brendan C. Lindsay, *Murder State: California's Native American Genocide* (Lincoln: University of Nebraska Press, 2015), 240–43.

92. Solnit, *Savage Dreams,* 219, 273–74; Huntley, *Making of Yosemite,* 56; Hurtado, *Indian Survival,* 135–36; Benjamin Madley, *An American Genocide: The United States and the California Indian Catastrophe, 1846–1873* (New Haven, CT: Yale University Press, 2016), 188–94.

93. "Address of the Indian Agents"; Huntley, *Making of Yosemite,* 56–59; Solnit, *Savage Dreams,* 272–73; Hurtado, *Indian Survival,* 136–49.

94. Hurtado, *Indian Survival,* 162; Huntley, *Making of Yosemite,* 56–57; Solnit, *Savage Dreams,* 280–84; Craig D. Bates and Martha J. Lee, *Tradition and Innovation: A Basket History of the Yosemite-Mono Lake Area* (Yosemite National Park, CA: Yosemite Association, 1990), 31; Albert D. Richardson, *Beyond the Mississippi: From the Great River to the Great Ocean* (Hartford, CT: American Publishing Co., 1867), 428.

95. J. Neely Johnson, US Indian Commissioner, "Speech to the Mariposa Battalion," quoted in Huntley, *Making of Yosemite,* 27; Yosemite Indians, *Petition to the Senators and Representatives of the Congress of the United States in Behalf of the Remnants of the Former Tribes of the Yosemite Indians,* [ca. 1891], 7, http://www.yosemite.ca.us/library/yosemite_indian_petition_to_the_us.html (accessed March 1, 2017).

96. Solnit, *Savage Dreams,* 236–37; Huntley, *Making of Yosemite,* 57–58; DeLuca and Demo, "Imagining Nature," 554.

97. Muir, *My First Summer,* 30; Solnit, *Savage Dreams,* 224–30; Rebecca Solnit, *River of Shadows: Eadweard Muybridge and the Technological Wild West* (New York: Penguin Books, 2003), 92; DeLuca and Demo, "Imagining Nature," 546–48.

98. Michael Redmon, "Who Was Davy Brown?" *Santa Barbara (CA) Independent,* September 26, 2011, http://www.independent.com/news/2011/sep/26/who-was-davy-brown/; Shirley Contreras, "Early Settler Davy Brown Remembered as Area's Most Colorful and Adventurous," *Santa Maria (CA) Times,* February 5, 2012, http://santamariatimes.com/lifestyles/columnist/shirley_contreras/early-settler-davy-brown-remembered-as-area-s-most-colorful/article_f5897412-4fb8-11e1-b7c8-0019bb2963f4.html.

99. Emphasis added, Muir, *My First Summer*, 17.

100. "Digger" was a catch-all term with which white Californians had been reducing the state's diverse Indigenous groups for decades. It connoted contempt for them as extremely primitive; white Californians frequently judged them the most primitive among all Native North American cultures because of the subsistence practices of gathering roots and grubs—the origin of the "digger" term which most whites equated with rudimentary intelligence and lack of civilization. Solnit, *Savage Dreams*, 270–71; J. J. Rawls, *Indians of California: The Changing Image* (Norman: University of Oklahoma Press, 1984), 48–49.

101. Muir, *My First Summer*, 30; DeLuca and Demo, "Imagining Nature," 553–54; Solnit, *River of Shadows*, 92.

102. Eadweard Muybridge, *The Indians of California* (series) ([San Francisco]: Bradley & Rulofson, 1872), *Lone Mountain College Collection of Stereographs by Eadweard Muybridge*, BANC PIC 1971.055, The Bancroft Library, University of California, Berkeley; Solnit, *River of Shadows*, 90–94.

103. [John Muir] to John and [Margaret Muir Reid], January 13, 1869, Muir Correspondence; Solnit, *Savage Dreams*, 260–61; Huntley, *Making of Yosemite*, 171.

104. John Muir to Dan[iel Muir Jr.], September 24 [1869] Muir Correspondence; Muir, *My First Summer*, 41–46. In the letter, Muir indicated that he copied entries "direct from my diary" from July 2–5. In the published version of *My First Summer*, Muir talks about how the Eskimo "gets a living far north of the wheat line, from oily seals and whales. Meat, berries, bitter weeds, and blubber, or only the last, for months at a time; and yet these people all around the frozen shores of our continent are said to be hearty, jolly, stout, and brave." This addition probably came from his experience traveling among the Inuit in 1879 (and again in Alaska in 1880, and 1890) and developing a greater appreciation for Indigenous lifeways than he had the decade before. Muir, *My First Summer*, 43; Fleck, "John Muir's Evolving Attitudes," 19–31; John Muir, *Travels in Alaska* (Boston: Houghton Mifflin Company, 1915).

105. Muir, *My First Summer*, 41–42; Solnit, *Savage Dreams*, 266.

106. Muir, *My First Summer*, 124–25.

107. Muir, *My First Summer*, 114, 124–25.

108. Muir, *My First Summer*, 32–33; M. Kat Anderson, *Tending the Wild: Native American Knowledge and the Management of California's Natural Resources* (Berkeley: University of California Press, 2005), 108–11.

109. Muir, *My First Summer*, 121.

110. Gaylen D. Lee, *Walking Where We Lived: Memories of a Mono Indian Family* (Norman: University of Oklahoma Press, 1998), 139. More specifically, Lee identified himself as Cha:tiniu Nim (Nim being the Monos' word for themselves) who lived in the Sierra Nevada near the San Joaquin River for generations. Cha:tiniu is the name for a large meadow about 45 miles from the village of North

Fork in Madera County, CA. The Grandpa to whom Lee refers was commonly known as Charlie "Hotshot" Moore. Lee, *Walking Where*, 1.

111. Muir, *My First Summer*, 32–33; Anderson and Moratto, "Native American Land-Use Practices," 187–200; Solnit, *Savage Dreams*, 224–30, 304–307. For more on Indigenous cultivation practices in California, see also Anderson, *Tending the Wild*; Bates and Lee, *Tradition and Innovation*; T. C. Blackburn and M. Kat Anderson, eds., *Before the Wilderness: Native Californians as Environmental Managers* (Menlo Park, CA: Ballena Press, 1993).

112. [John Muir] to [Jeanne C. Carr], May 16, 1869, Muir Correspondence; Worster, *Passion for Nature*, 181.

113. Muir, *My First Summer*, 33; John Muir to Jeanne Carr, October 7, 1874, Muir Correspondence.

114. Muir, "Twenty Hill Hollow," 80.

115. John Muir to R[alph] W[aldo] Emerson, [May 8], 1871, Muir Correspondence; Worster, *Passion for Nature*, 164, 209.

116. Muir, *Our National Parks*, 131–36.

117. Muir, *Our National Parks*, 134–35.

CHAPTER 3

1. S[amuel] J. Barrows, "The Shaybacks in Camp—Part I," *Outing* 4, no. 5 (August 1884): 361; Samuel J. Barrows and Isabel C. Barrows, *The Shaybacks in Camp: Ten Summers Under Canvas* (Boston: Houghton, Mifflin, and Co., 1887), 67 .

2. Barrows and Barrows, *Shaybacks in Camp*, v, xxx. Samuel June Barrows (1845–1909) rose from a poor family to attend Harvard Divinity School. He served as a correspondent for the *New York Tribune*, assigned to accompany Col. David S. Stanley's Yellowstone Expedition (1873) and Lt. Col. George Armstrong Custer's Black Hills Expedition (1874), as the editor of the *Christian Register* (1880–1896), and as a one-term Representative to the U.S. Congress (1897–1899). He advocated for women's suffrage and education, African American rights, and prison reform, among other issues. Isabel Chapin Barrows (1845–1913) worked as a stenographer for the US State Department and the US Congress. She was among the first women to study ophthalmology at the University of Vienna and practiced in the Washington, DC Freedmen's Hospital, although she could not sustain a private practice. She later coedited the *Christian Register* with her husband and shared interest in the same causes. Leslie H. Fishel, "Barrows, Samuel June," *American National Biography Online* (February 2000); "Mrs. Isabel C. Barrows [obituary]," *New York Times*, October 26, 1913, 15; Thaddeus Russell, "Isabel Barrows," *American National Biography* (Oxford: Oxford University Press, 1999), 2:246.

3. Barrows, "Shaybacks in Camp—Part I," 362.

4. John McCook, "Tramps," *Charities Review* 3, no. 2 (December 1893): 39. Usage in outdoor recreation publications echoed this linguistic transition. While in the 1880s "tramp" indicated a hike as often as a transient, by 1900 "tramp" nearly always meant a wandering homeless person.

5. Todd DePastino, *Citizen Hobo: How a Century of Homelessness Shaped America* (Chicago: University of Chicago Press, 2002), 68–71, 138.

6. Michael Willrich, *Pox: An American History* (New York: Penguin, 2011), 20, 41; Eric H. Monkkonen, *Walking to Work: Tramps in America, 1790–1935* (Lincoln: University of Nebraska Press, 1984), 207; Carlos Schwantes, *The Pacific Northwest: An Interpretive History* (Lincoln: University of Nebraska Press, 1989), 250–65; Paul Groth, *Living Downtown: The History of Residential Hotels in the United States* (Berkeley: University of California Press, 1994), 131–67.

7. See Tara Kathleen Kelly, *The Hunter Elite: Manly Sport, Hunting Narratives, and American Conservation, 1880–1925* (Lawrence: University Press of Kansas, 2018) for discussion of *Outing*'s editors and history. At its height, an issue of *Outing* cost twenty-five cents, ran upward of 100 pages, included many illustrations and few advertisements. The most prominent editors were Poultney Bigelow, Caspar Whitney, and Albert Britt. Simply titled *Outing* for most of its run, it was also briefly titled *Outing and the Wheelman*, between January 1884 and March 1885 and then later went by *The Outing Magazine*, between April 1905 and April 1913, at which point it reverted to *Outing* until its last issue in April 1923. For clarity, it will be referenced here as *Outing* for all periods. *Field and Stream, Outdoor Life*, and *Sports Afield* all began publication in the 1880s and 1890s and featured many of the same themes and writers. Frank Luther Mott, *A History of American Magazines, 1741–1930* (Cambridge, MA: Belknap Press of Harvard University Press, c. 1958–1968), 4 (*1885–1905*): 633–38.

8. *Outing* also featured extensive coverage of amateur athletics and frequent discussion of lawn sports, such as croquet or golf, unrelated to camping.

9. Cindy S. Aron, *Working at Play: A History of Vacations in the United States* (New York: Oxford University Press, 1999); Marguerite S. Shaffer, *See America First: Tourism and National Identity 1880–1940* (Washington, DC: Smithsonian Institution Press, 2001).

10. Aron, *Working at Play*, 15–100.

11. "Camping Out," *Scribner's Monthly* 10, no. 2 (June 1875): 245–46. For similar arguments, see also "Tenting," *Outing* 8, no. 6 (September 1886): 678; "Pleasure Travel and Resorts: Cutler," *Outing* 10, no. 3 (June 1887): 286.

12. Barrows, "Shaybacks in Camp—Part I," 362; Barrows and Barrows, *Shaybacks in Camp*, 20–21, 107–109, 260. For more about the Barrows family and this region, see, J. I. Little, "Life without Conventionality: American Social Reformers as Summer Campers on Lake Memphremagog, Quebec, 1878–1905," *Journal of the Gilded Age and Progressive Era* 9, no. 3 (July 2010): 281–311.

13. G. O. Shields, *Camping and Camp Outfits: A Manual of Instruction for Young and Old Sportsmen* (Chicago: Rand, McNally & Co., 1890), 9–10. Shields published *Recreation* and *Shields* magazines, wrote hunting and fishing guides, books about Native people and the American West, and at least one dime novel. Kelly, *Hunter Elite*, 78–79, 111–12, 250–52; James A. Tober, *Who Owns the Wildlife? The Political Economy of Conservation in Nineteenth-Century America* (Westport, CT: Westport Press, 1981), 235n40.

14. Aron, *Working at Play,* 160–61. For more on H.H. Murray, see Terence Young, *Heading Out: A History of American Camping* (Ithaca, NY: Cornell University Press, 2017), 21–48; and David Strauss, "Toward a Consumer Culture: 'Adirondack Murray' and the Wilderness Vacation," *American Quarterly* 39, no. 2 (Summer 1987): 270–86.

15. Ripley Hitchcock, "Trout Fishing in Maine," *Outing* 8, no. 3 (June 1886): 349; Lillian H. Shuey, "The Starry Chamber," *Outing* 10, no. 6 (September 1887): 576–77. Shuey suggested that the benefits of outdoor sleeping could also be had by sleeping on a balcony or porch. Sleeping porches became a popular fad, especially in temperate climates like California. See for example, Elizabeth Farwell and Lucia Thompson, "Open-Air Sleeping," *Sunset* 23, no. 2 (August 1909): 200–204.

16. Aron, *Working at Play*, 30–32. For more on the history of camp meetings, see Kenneth O. Brown, *Holy Ground: A Study of the American Camp Meeting* (New York: Garland Publishing, Inc., 1992); Paul K. Conkin, *Cane Ridge: America's Pentecost* (Madison: University of Wisconsin Press, 1990); and Charles A. Johnson, *The Frontier Camp Meeting: Religion's Harvest Time* (Dallas: Southern Methodist University Press, 1955). Camp meetings were also related to the Chautauqua movement, founded in 1874 as an institution to train Sunday School teachers and which became rustic resorts for adult education and culture. Hundreds of thousands of Americans participated in Chautauquas each year during this era. See Aron, *Working at Play*, 111–26; Theodore Morrison, *Chautauqua: A Center for Education, Religion, and the Arts in America* (Chicago: University of Chicago Press, 1974); Andrew C. Rieser, *The Chautauqua Moment: Protestants, Progressives, and the Culture of Modern Liberalism* (New York: Columbia University Press, 2003).

17. Barrows and Barrows, *Shaybacks in Camp*, 4, 18, 21.

18. Barrows and Barrows, *Shaybacks in Camp*, 102–103, 208, 217–18.

19. "Editor's Open Window," *Outing* 5, no. 1 (October 1884): 62–63.

20. Barrows, "Shaybacks in Camp—Part I," 365.

21. Emphasis from the original, F.G., "The Miseries of Camping Out," *Lippincott's Magazine* 26 (September 1880): 387–88. See also Sadie S., [pseud.], "A Calamitous Camping Out," *Overland Monthly* 16, no. 96 (December 1890): 596–607; A Camper, [pseud.], "Camping and Its Drawbacks," letter to the editor, *New York Times*, May 17, 1900, 23.

22. Warwick S. Carpenter, "In the Heart of the Tall Timber," *Country Life in America* 12, no. 3 (May 1907): 71. Aron argues that a major factor in the rise of camping

was that it suggested a "working vacation" rather than indolent leisure. See Aron, *Working at Play,* 156–80.

23. [Clipping], *Boston Journal,* July 1, 1887, in Isabel Chapin Barrows, "Diary, 1887–1912," Folder 1, Barrows Family Papers, MS Am 1807–1807.5, Houghton Library, Harvard University (hereafter Barrows Family Papers).

24. Charles S. Greene, "Camping in Mendocino," *Overland Monthly* 22, no. 130 (October 1893): 338, 347–48; The Outing Club, *Outing* 7, no. 1 (October 1885): 86.

25. Barrows, "The Shaybacks in Camp—Part I," 361–62. For Barrows' writings and experiences on the Yellowstone Expedition, see M. John Lubetkin, ed., *Custer and the 1873 Yellowstone Survey: A Documentary History* (Norman: The Arthur H. Clark Company, an imprint of the University of Oklahoma Press, 2013).

26. John E. Crowley, *The Invention of Comfort: Sensibilities and Design in Early Modern Britain and Early America* (Baltimore: Johns Hopkins University Press, 2001); Katherine C. Grier, *Culture and Comfort: Parlor Making and Middle-Class Identity, 1850–1930* (Amherst: University of Massachusetts Press, 1988), viii–ix; Daniel Horowitz, "Frugality or Comfort: Middle-Class Styles of Life in the Early Twentieth Century," *American Quarterly* 37, no. 2 (Summer 1985): 239–59; Phoebe S. Kropp [Young], "Wilderness Wives and Dishwashing Husbands: Comfort and the Domestic Arts of Camping Out, 1880–1910," *Journal of Social History* 43, no. 1 (Fall 2009): 6–8.

27. Frank R. Stockton, "Camping-Out at Rudder Grange," *Scribner's Monthly* 16, no. 1 (May 1878): 104, 113, 115.

28. T J Jackson Lears, *No Place of Grace: Antimodernism and the Transformation of American Culture, 1880–1920* (Chicago: University of Chicago Press, 1994), 91–94.

29. DePastino, *Citizen Hobo,* 3–39; Tim Cresswell, *The Tramp in America* (London: Reaktion Books, 2011), 11–12, 48; Paul T. Ringenbach, *Tramps and Reformers, 1873–1916: The Discovery of Unemployment in New York* (Westport, CT: Greenwood Press, 1973). For a prehistory of tramps, particularly in early modern Europe, see Cresswell, *Tramp in America,* 17–19; Mark Wyman, *Hoboes: Bindlestiffs, Fruit Tramps, and the Harvesting of the West* (New York: Hill & Wang, 2010), 30–38.

30. Allan Pinkerton, *Strikers, Communists, Tramps, and Detectives* (New York: G. W. Dillingham Co., 1878), 47; DePastino, *Citizen Hobo,* 17–18; Brian Jordan, *Marching Home: Union Veterans and Their Unending Civil War* (New York: Liveright, 2016), 58–59, 172–76.

31. Pinkerton, *Strikers,* 51, 66; Wyman, *Hoboes,* 38; DePastino, *Citizen Hobo,* 19; Cresswell, *Tramp in America,* 23.

32. Wyman, *Hoboes,* 39; DePastino, *Citizen Hobo,* 20–22. Vagrancy laws continued to serve as a mechanism to control African Americans, and when fused with fears about tramps, escalated white racism. Charles Crowe, "Racial Violence and Social Reform—Origins of the Atlanta Riot of 1906," *Journal of Negro History* 53, no. 3 (July 1968): 246–47.

33. Cresswell, *Tramp in America*, 9–10, 19–21; John Allen, *Homelessness in American Literature: Romanticism, Realism, and Testimony* (New York: Routledge, 2004), 55–58.

34. Henry George, *Social Problems* (1883), quoted in DePastino, *Citizen Hobo*, 41; Kenneth C. Wenzer, ed., *Henry George: Collected Journalistic Writings*, Vol. I (Armonk, NY: M. E. Sharpe, 2003), xxiv–xxvi; Cresswell, *Tramp in America*, 14–16.

35. For discussion of tramps and the crisis of free labor ideals see DePastino, *Citizen Hobo*, 3–58.

36. Monkkonen, *Walking to Work*, 6–9; Frank Higbie, *Indispensable Outcasts: Hobo Workers and Community in the American Midwest, 1880–1930* (Champaign: University of Illinois Press, 2004), 4.

37. Wyman, *Hoboes*, 7, 102.

38. Pinkerton, *Strikers*, 38, 58–66.

39. "Tramps," *Unitarian Review* 8 (October 1877): 439, quoted in DePastino, *Citizen Hobo*, 25; DePastino, *Citizen Hobo*, 68–71, 138; Monkkonen, *Walking to Work*, 207; Schwantes, *Pacific Northwest*, 250–65; Groth, *Living Downtown*, 131–67; David T. Courtwright, *Violent Land: Single Men and Social Disorder from the Frontier to the Inner City* (Cambridge, MA: Harvard University Press, 1996), 170–97.

40. McCook compiled Aspinwall's letters and interviews with other tramps into a serialized investigation published as "Leaves from the Diary of a Tramp." For more on Aspinwall and McCook, see DePastino, *Citizen Hobo*, 47–58. For the phenomenon of middle-class social investigators see Higbie, *Indispensible Outcasts*, 98–133 and Mark Pittenger, *Class Unknown: Undercover Investigations of American Work and Poverty from the Progressive Era to the Present* (New York: NYU Press, 2012).

41. Aspinwall, quoted in John J. McCook, "Leaves from the Diary of a Tramp, V," *The Independent*, January 16, 1902, 159–60; Joanna Dyl, "Transience, Labor, and Nature: Itinerant Workers in the American West," *International Labor and Working-Class History* 85 (Spring 2014): 97–117. Aspinwall served in the 47th Indiana Volunteer Infantry from 1861 to 1865 and was wounded at the battle of Champion Hill in Mississippi in 1863. David Williamson, *The 47th Indiana Volunteer Infantry: A Civil War History* (Jefferson, NC: McFarland & Co., 2012), 142–43.

42. McCook, "Diary of a Tramp, V," 158; John J. McCook, "Leaves from the Diary of a Tramp, IV," *The Independent*, January 2, 1902, 27.

43. Jack London, *The Road* (1907), ed. Todd DePastino (New Brunswick, NJ: Rutgers University Press, 2006); Dyl, "Transience, Labor and Nature," 102–106, 111; Kenneth L. Kusmer, *Down & Out and On the Road: The Homeless in American History* (New York: Oxford University Press, 2002), 137; John Lennon, *Boxcar Politics: The Hobo in U.S. Culture and Literature, 1869–1956* (Amherst, MA: University of Massachusetts Press, 2014); Alan Trachtenberg, *The Incorporation of America: Culture and Society in the Gilded Age* (New York: Hill and Wang, 2007), ix–xxi, 38–69.

44. Pinkerton, *Strikers*, 26.

45. Emphasis from the original, Lee Meriwether, "Preface to 4th edition," *A Tramp Trip or Europe on Fifty Cents a Day* (New York: Harper & Brothers, 1886), 7. Meriwether traveled Europe in 1885–86 after dropping out of college and was subsequently hired by the US Department of Labor to study labor conditions. *A Tramp Trip* served as his report on Europe, replete with observations about working classes and conditions. He was then assigned to research and report on similar subjects in the United States. The resulting book, *The Tramp at Home,* offered less encouragement to travel in tramp style for pleasure, and belonged more to the genre of social investigations of tramps and the working class, although he expressed relative sympathy with their plight and lamented the growing divergence in wealth. Meriwether, *The Tramp at Home* (New York: Harper & Brothers, 1889); James B. Lloyd, ed., *Lives of Mississippi Authors, 1817–1967* (Jackson: University Press of Mississippi, 2009), 332.

46. William John Warburton, "By Canoe from Lake George to the Atlantic," *Outing* 22, no. 6 (September 1893): 464.

47. Higbie, *Indispensible Outcasts*, 75–77; Pittenger, *Class Unknown, 9–41;* Daniel E. Bender, *American Abyss: Savagery and Civilization in the Age of Industry* (Ithaca, NY: Cornell University Press 2009), 154–55, 217–19.

48. Dan O'Hara, "Camp Cooks," *Outing* 6, no. 2 (May 1885): 207.

49. Mrs. Larz Anderson, "Camping for Women," *Country Life in America* (June 1910): 176; John F. Kasson, *Rudeness and Civility: Manners in Nineteenth Century Urban America* (New York: Farrar, Straus and Giroux, 1990), 205–14. For more discussion of the issue of appetites, food, and eating in camp, see Kropp [Young], "Wilderness Wives," 21–23.

50. Pinkerton, *Strikers*, 51. For more on the demographic composition of tramps, who were largely white, native-born (although with some European immigrants), city-dwellers, see Kusmer, *Down & Out*, 137; Higbie, *Indispensable Outcasts*, 98–133.

51. Aspinwall, quoted in James McCook, "Leaves from the Diary of a Tramp, VI," *Independent*, February 6, 1902, 337. Aspinwall here echoed the language of so-called Fresh Air reformers. See Barry Muchnick, "Nature's Republic: Fresh Air Reform and the Moral Ecology of Citizenship in Turn of the Century America" (PhD diss., Yale University, 2010).

52. Barrows, "Shaybacks in Camp—Part I," 361–62; "Tenting," 678.

53. John Mead Gould, *How to Camp Out: Hints for Camping and Walking* (New York: Scribner, Armstrong & Co., 1877), 35.

54. Ralph K. Wing, "Canoeing on the Genessee," *Outing* 3, no. 3 (December 1885): 309–10.

55. Ed. W. Sandys, "Rod and Gun," *Outing* 20, no. 5 (August 1892): 102.

56. Walter Laidlaw, "A Camping Tour to Yosemite," *Outlook*, June 5, 1897, 321. See also Ernest Ingersoll, "Practical Camping," *Outlook*, June 5, 1897, 324. For public "campgrounds" in this era, see John H. Barber, "Camping in a Government Forest

Reservation," *Overland Monthly* 33, no. 197 (May 1899): 449–55; Walter A. Dyer, "Camping in the Adirondacks," *Country Life in America* 8, no. 3 (July 1905): 344.

57. McCook, "Diary of a Tramp, IV," 24. Tramps, too, made efforts to showcase their honorable (if not recreational) status through appearance and behavior. DePastino, *Citizen Hobo*, 39.

58. Carlos Schwantes, *Coxey's Army: An American Odyssey* (Lincoln: University of Nebraska Press, 1985), 13–14. See Lucy G. Barber, *Marching on Washington: The Forging of an American Political Tradition* (Berkeley: University of California Press, 2004), 44–74, for discussion of the origins of the movement and for the use of the label "Army."

59. *Commercial Gazette* (Pittsburgh) quoted in Barber, *Marching on Washington*, 22; DePastino, *Citizen Hobo*, 59–66; Barber, *Marching on Washington*, 11–12, 21–43. Labeling working class radicals as tramps was a common tactic employers used to undercut their legitimacy.

60. Ella W. Ricker "Only an Accident," *Outing* 10, no. 6 (September 1887): 541.

61. H. A. Hill, "Camping in Comfort," *Outing* 32, no. 5 (August 1898): 505.

62. Edward W. Sandys, "Camps and Camping," *Outing* 30, no. 4 (July 1897): 377.

63. Barrows and Barrows, *Shaybacks in Camp*, 41–45.

64. Emphasis from the original, Charlotte Reeve Conover, "A Family Camp in the Rockies, Part 1," *Outing* 22, no. 5 (August 1893): 360. Conover was a mother of eight and a prominent member of Dayton, Ohio society, where she wrote books and articles on local history. "Charlotte Reeve Conover, Dayton Historian, Dead," *Dayton (OH) Herald*, September 23, 1940, 1, 4.

65. Conover, "Family Camp, Part 1," 360–62. For similar negotiations, see Mrs. Jacob Barzilla Rideout, *Camping Out in California* (San Francisco: R. R. Patterson, ca. 1889), 9; Lenore M. Lybrand, "The Island of Delight," *Outing* 36, no. 5 (August 1900): 501–507; Katherine A. Chandler, "Housekeeping in the Summer Camp," *Sunset* 9, no. 1 (May 1902): 24.

66. Charlotte Reeve Conover, "A Family Camp in the Rockies, Part 2," *Outing* 22, no. 6 (September 1893): 421; Barrows and Barrows, *Shaybacks in Camp*, 77; Mary A. Barr, "Camping for Women," *Outing* 6, no 2 (May 1885): 234.

67. Kelly, *Hunter Elite*, passim; Dyer, "Camping in the Adirondacks," 344. Camping in this era has often appeared synonymous with the manly version of roughing it. Historian Roderick Nash typified this overemphasis by characterizing late-nineteenth-century camping as "masochistic—in that it provided a chance to play the savage, accept punishment, struggle, and, hopefully triumph over the forces of raw nature." Roderick Nash, *Wilderness and the American Mind*, 5th ed. (New Haven, CT: Yale University Press, 2014, c. 1967), 154.

68. Emily Palmer, "Family Camping," *Outing* 26, no. 6 (September 1895): 479; "Contents of Volume XXVI: April to September 1895," *Outing* 26 (April to September, 1895), n.p.

69. Barrows, "Shaybacks in Camp—Part I," 361.

70. Isabel C. Barrows, "Summer Camping in the Woodland: Holiday Life for Boys and Girls," *New England Magazine* 24, no. 6 (August 1898): 732, 734–36. See Little, "Life without Conventionality," 294–96 for more on issues of gender equality in the Shaybacks' camp.

71. Barrows and Barrows, *Shaybacks in Camp*, 105–106, 110. The Barrows family did have at least one regular maid working in their household. Barrows, [Diary], April 7, 1897, Folder 7, Barrows Family Papers.

72. Ruth Schwartz Cowan, *More Work for Mother: The Ironies of Household Technologies from the Open Hearth to the Microwave* (New York: Basic Books, 1983), 42, 121–22; Steven Mintz and Susan Kellogg, *Domestic Revolutions: A Social History of American Family Life* (New York: The Free Press, 1989), 123–25. For the social history of domestic servants and servant-related discourse see also Faye E. Dudden, *Serving Women: Household Service in Nineteenth-Century America* (Middletown, CT: Wesleyan University Press, 1983); David M. Katzman, *Seven Days a Week: Women and Domestic Service in Industrializing America* (New York: Oxford University Press, 1978); Daniel E. Sutherland, *Americans and their Servants: Domestic Service in the United States from 1800 to 1920* (Baton Rouge: Louisiana State University Press, 1981).

73. Martha Haskell Clark, "Co-Operative Gipsying," *Country Life in America* 18, no. 1 (May 1910): 59; Martha Coman, "The Art of Camping. A Woman's View," *Outlook*, June 7, 1902, 373.

74. Charles Ledyard Norton, "How to Camp Out," *Sunday Inter Ocean* (Chicago), July 15, 1888, 19; Barr, "Camping for Women," 234; Warren J. Belasco, *Americans on the Road: From Autocamp to Motel, 1910–1945* (Baltimore: Johns Hopkins University Press, 1979), 52; Cowan, *More Work for Mother*, 4–8, 175–78.

75. Anderson, "Camping for Women," 177, 180; Bergthara [pseud.], "A Woman's Outing on the Nepigon," *Outing* 30, no. 6 (September 1897): 483. See also John R. G. Hassard, "Camping Out in California," *Century Magazine* 33, no. 5 (March 1887): 736–50.

76. Caroline Mae Turner, Journal of a Camping Trip, with Mr. & Mrs. C.R. Van Hise, in Ontario, Canada, 1908, MS, Frederick Jackson Turner Collection, TU Vol. XI, Henry E. Huntington Library. Caroline was the wife of historian Frederick Jackson Turner, the "Fred" referred to in the quotations from the journal.

77. Herbert L. Jillson, "The Maine Guide and the Maine Camp," *Outing* 38, no. 6 (September 1901): 651–52. Jillson, originally of Worcester, Mass., held various positions on the executive board of the Pinehurst Country Club in North Carolina. "Country Club Officers," *Pinehurst Outlook*, April 23, 1910, 14. For more on the complicated sportsman-guide relationship, see Kelly, *Hunter Elite*, 2-12, 187-220, and Annie Gilbert Coleman, "Rise of the House of Leisure: Outdoor Guides, Practical Knowledge, and Industrialization," *Western Historical Quarterly* 42, no. 4 (Winter 2011): 437-57.

78. Robert Dunn, "The Fallacies of 'Roughing It,'" *Outing* 46, no. 6 (September 1905): 645; Biographical Note, "Finding Aid: The Papers of Robert (Steed) Dunn, MSS-42, Dartmouth College Library, https://ead.dartmouth.edu/html/stem42.html (accessed April 10, 2017).

79. Karl Jacoby, *Crimes Against Nature: Squatters, Poachers, Thieves, and the Hidden History of American Conservation* (Berkeley: University of California Press, 2001); Louis S. Warren, *The Hunter's Game: Poachers and Conservationists in Twentieth Century America* (New Haven, CT: Yale University Press, 1997).

80. Dunn, "Fallacies of 'Roughing It,'" 645–46.

81. Dunn, "Fallacies of 'Roughing It,'" 646.

82. Mrs. Alphonso Reeves, Diary of family's travels in South Dakota, Wyoming and Montana, 1900–1906, HM 53214, Henry E. Huntington Library (hereafter Reeves Diary), n.p.

83. Reeves Diary, November 28, 1901; October 8, 1900; April 24, 1901; April 29, 1901; May 6, 1901; July 5, 1901.

84. Reeves Diary, September 11, 1900; May 24, 1901; September 27, 1901; July 16, 1901.

85. Reeves Diary, September 16, 1900; May 26, 1901; June 1, 1902; June 7, 1902; December 11, 1900; October 26, 1902; August 11, 1903; September 3, 1903; 1904–1906, passim. For the soldiers in Yellowstone, see Jacoby, *Crimes Against Nature*, 99–120.

86. Monkkonen, *Walking to Work*, 3–6; Andrew Lyndon Knighton, *Idle Threats: Men and the Limits of Productivity in Nineteenth-Century America* (New York: NYU Press, 2012), 117–19; Dyl, "Transience, Labor, and Nature," 106–10. That mobile Western workers like the Reeveses were difficult to capture in census data or occupational categories was not uncommon. The family largely seemed to elude the census, with research made especially difficult given that Mrs. Reeves' first name remains unknown. An Alphonso Reeves appeared in the 1910 census, born in Iowa (which Mrs. Reeves noted was her family home), approximately the right age, then divorced and living as a tenant-farmer in Nebraska, one of the places the family had earlier tried to homestead. It's not verifiable that this is the Phonso from the diary, but if so, it suggests the continuing fluctuation of family fortunes, outcomes, and travels. "Alphonso Reeves, Milan, Sheridan, Nebraska," United States Census, enumeration district 209, sheet 2A, family 23, NARA microfilm publication T624 (Washington, DC: National Archives and Records Administration, 1982), roll 855, accessed through FamilySearch, "United States Census, 1910," database, https://familysearch.org/ark:/61903/1:1:LHQ-C7D (accessed April 22, 2017).

87. Carlos A. Schwantes, "The Concept of the Wageworkers' Frontier: A Framework for Future Research," *Western Historical Quarterly* 18, no. 1 (Winter 1987): 41, 46–47, 51–52.

88. Schwantes, "Wageworkers' Frontier," 44–46; Wyman, *Hoboes*, 5, 106, 228.

89. T. J. Morgan, "A Plea for the Papoose: An Address at Albany, NY, February 1892," *Baptist Home Mission Monthly* 18, no 2. (December 1896): 404; Margaret D. Jacobs, *White Mother to a Dark Race: Settler Colonialism, Maternalism, and the*

Removal of Indigenous Children in the American West and Australia, 1880–1940 (Lincoln: University of Nebraska Press, 2011), 42–43.

90. United States, Office of Indian Affairs, *Annual Report of the Commissioner of Indian Affairs, for the Year 1885* (Washington, DC: Government Printing Office, [1885]), CXII, http://digital.library.wisc.edu/1711.dl/History.AnnRep85 (accessed April 12, 2017); Catherine Cahill, *Federal Fathers and Mothers: A Social History of the United States Indian Service, 1869–1933* (Chapel Hill: University of North Carolina Press, 2011), 5–6, 54.

91. Rebecca S. Wingo, "Dr. Ferdinand Shoemaker's Traveling Photographs from the Crow Reservation, 1910–1918," *Montana: The Magazine of Western History* (Winter 2016): 26, 30–32.

92. Wingo, "Dr. Ferdinand Shoemaker's," 31, 33; Jacobs, *White Mother,* 44; Knighton, *Idle Threats,* 92; Cahill, *Federal Fathers,* 190–93, 226.

93. Louis S. Warren, "Wage Work in the Sacred Circle: The Ghost Dance as Modern Religion," *Western Historical Quarterly* 46, no. 2 (Summer 2015): 149–56; Brian C. Hosmer, *American Indians in the Marketplace: Persistence and Innovation* (Lawrence: University Press of Kansas, 1999).

94. Farwell and Thomson, "Open-Air Sleeping," 200; Wingo, "Dr. Ferdinand Shoemaker's," 31; Howard Henderson, *Practical Hints on Camping* (Chicago: Jansen, McClurg & Co., 1882), 27; Muchnick, "Nature's Republic," 275–80.

95. Ralph K. Wing, "Paddle, Camp, and Baby," *Outing* 34, no. 6 (September 1899): 615. For "playing Indian" in multiple aspects of American culture, see Philip J. Deloria, *Playing Indian* (New Haven, CT: Yale University Press, 1999). For the shift from negative to positive associations of "skin-darkening" among whites, see Catherine Cocks, *Tropical Whites: The Rise of the Tourist South in the Americas* (Philadelphia: University of Pennsylvania Press, 2013).

96. James Weir Jr., M.D., "A Little Excursion into Savagery," *Outing* 26, no. 4 (July 1895): 305.

97. Horace Kephart, *Camping and Woodcraft: A Handbook for Vacation Campers and for Travelers in the Wilderness* (Knoxville: University of Tennessee Press, 1988, c. 1906), 1: 17–21. For more on Kephart and his influence, see Jim Casada, "Introduction," to *Camping and Woodcraft*, 1: vii–xxxiii; Young, *Heading Out*, 16–19, 59–78.

98. Kephart, *Camping and Woodcraft*, I: 6–7; Katharina Vester, *A Taste of Power: Food and American Identities* (Berkeley: University of California Press, 2015), 73–85.

99. Shields, *Camping and Camp Outfits*, 9. "Woodcraft," learning to use the wilderness for survival, aligned with the "do-it-yourself" fad among elite Americans who feared losing touch with the "artisan" spirit and knowledge amidst an era of intense modernization and technological change. Lears, *No Place of Grace,* 59–95; James Morton Turner, "From Woodcraft to 'Leave No Trace': Wilderness, Consumerism, and Environmentalism in Twentieth-Century America," *Environmental History* 7, no. 3 (July 2002): 462–82.

100. Horace Kephart, *Camping and Woodcraft: A Handbook for Vacation Campers and for Travelers in the Wilderness*, rev. ed. (New York: Macmillan, 1919, c. 1916–17), 1:21.

101. Norton, "How to Camp Out," 19; Dunn, "Fallacies of 'Roughing It,' " 64; Hill "Camping in Comfort," 505. For the perennial novelty of "women in camp" and further discussion of gender issues, see Kropp [Young], "Wilderness Wives," 5–30.

102. T. C. Yard, "Practical Camping-Out Near Home," *Outing* 34, no.3 (June 1899): 270; Andrea Smalley, "'Our Lady Sportsmen': Gender, Class, and Conservation in Sport Hunting Magazines, 1873—1920," *Journal of the Gilded Age and Progressive Era* 4, no. 4 (October 2005): 355–80.

103. Katherine L. Storm, "Two Girls and a Bulldog Camp Out," *Ladies' Home Journal* 22, no. 8 (July 1905): 15. Storm was a Clinical Instructor in Medicine and Surgery at the Woman's Medical College of Pennsylvania and a Surgical Clinician at the Woman's Hospital of Philadelphia. *The Woman's Medical College of Pennsylvania, North College Avenue and Twenty-First Street, Philadelphia. 53d Annual Announcement, Session of 1902–1903* (Philadelphia: n.p, ca. 1902), 6, 34.

104. Grace Gallatin Seton-Thompson, *A Woman Tenderfoot* (New York: Doubleday, Page and Co., 1900), 15, 361; Tiffany Johnstone, "Grace Gallatin Seton-Thompson: Frontier Adventure Literature and the Dawn of Suffrage," *Women Suffrage and Beyond* (January 29, 2013), https://womensuffrage.org/?p=21040; Kelly, *Hunter Elite*, 200. Well-known outdoor author Ernest Thompson Seton was born with the name Ernest Thompson, but as a young man added the name "Seton" to advertise a presumed connection to a prominent English family. At the time he married Grace Gallatin, he was going as Ernest Seton-Thompson, which is the name she then took. However, five years later he legally changed his name to Ernest Thompson Seton, which is the name he is primarily known by, although his wife, whom he later divorced, partly over objection to her suffrage activities, retained the original order. This has led to some confusion. "Seton, Ernest Thompson (1860–1946)," *Encyclopedia of World Biography* (Detroit: Gale, 1998), *Gale Academic OneFile*, https://www.gale.com/c/academic-onefile.

105. Barrows and Barrows, *Shaybacks in Camp*, 105–106, 110; [newspaper clipping], *Boston Journal*, Barrows Family Papers. See Little, "Life without Conventionality," 292–94 for more on Isabel's professional life and the camp routines.

106. A. S. B. [Alice Stone Blackwell], "Women in Camp," *The Woman's Journal* (Boston, MA) 21, no. 28 (July 12, 1890): 1; A. S. B. [Alice Stone Blackwell], "Camp Jottings," *The Woman's Journal* (Boston, MA) 26, no. 36 (September 7, 1895): 1. Lucy E. Anthony, Susan B. Anthony's niece was also a camp regular. Barrows herself made a similar argument, advocating for women to run children's camps. Barrows, "Summer Camping," 737.

107. Margaret Bisland, "Women and Their Guns," *Outing* 15, no. 3 (December 1889): 227; Shields, *Camping and Camp Outfits*, 24; Sara Stokes Baxter, "A Woman's Camping Outfit," *Outing* 54, no. 6 (March 1910): 634, 637. For the

history of corsets, see Valerie Steele, *The Corset: A Cultural History* (New Haven, CT: Yale University Press, 2001); Jennifer Hargreaves, *Sporting Females: Critical Issues in the History and Sociology of Women's Sports* (London: Routledge, 1994).

108. Emily A. Thackvay, "Camps and Tramps for Women," *Outing* 14, no. 5 (August 1889): 335–36; Barr, "Camping for Women," 233; Seton-Thompson, *Woman Tenderfoot*, 19, 22, 29.

109. Zephine Humphrey, "Five Women on the Trail, Parts 1–2," *Outing* 54, no. 2 (May 1909): 197–98; Zephine Humphrey, "Five Women on the Trail, Parts 7–9," *Outing* 54, no. 6 (September 1909): 66. See Seton-Thompson, *Woman Tenderfoot*, 22–29 for descriptions and a rough pattern of the astride riding skirt. Zephine Humphrey (1874–1959) was born in Philadelphia, graduated from Smith College in 1896, and upon her marriage moved to Dorset, Vermont, where she became a noted writer of essays, fiction, travel, and regional history. "Biography," Collection Summary, The Zephine Humphrey Papers, Special Collections, University of Vermont Library, http://cdi.uvm.edu/findingaids/collection/humphrey.ead.xml (accessed April 21, 2017).

110. Kephart, *Camping and Woodcraft*, 1:163; Emerson Hough, *Out of Doors* (New York: D. Appleton, 1915), 116. For similar sentiments, see Alfred Balch, "Camp Lore, With Notes on Outfit and Equipment," *Outing* 14, no. 5 (August 1889): 372; Sandys, "Camps and Camping," 376.

111. Seton, *Woman Tenderfoot*, 30.

112. Rena A. Phillips, "A Woman on the Trail," *Outing* 44, no. 5 (August 1904): 585.

113. Phillips, "Woman on the Trail," 585–89.

114. Bisland, "Women and their Guns," 226–27. As Virginia Scharff has suggested "We understand movement—in the grossest sense, as the desire and capacity to get the body from one place to the next with one end in mind—in fundamentally gendered terms." Scharff, *Twenty Thousand Roads: Women, Movement, and the West* (Berkeley: University of California Press, 2003), 3.

115. Seton, *A Woman Tenderfoot*, 21–22, 357–361.

116. Aron, *Working at Play*, 166. For similar questions around gender, femininity, and camping, see discussions of the earlier nonrecreational overland trail experiences. John M. Faragher, *Women and Men on the Overland Trail* (New Haven, CT: Yale University Press, 1979); Julie Roy Jeffrey, *Frontier Women: The Trans-Mississippi West, 1840–1880* (New York: Hill & Wang, 1979); Lillian Schlissel, *Women's Diaries of the Westward Journey* (New York: Schocken Books, 1982).

117. Rena A. Phillips, "The Woman in the Woods," *Outing* 46, no. 4 (July 1905): 475–76.

118. Companionate marriage also reaffirmed monogamy, heterosexuality, and expectations that brides and grooms would find their partners within the same race, ethnicity, and religion. See Stephanie Coontz, *Marriage, a History: From Obedience to Intimacy; or, How Love Conquered Marriage* (New York: Penguin Books, 2005); Nancy Cott, *Public Vows: A History of Marriage and the Nation*

(Cambridge, MA: Harvard University Press, 2000); Rebecca L. Davis, "'Not Marriage at All, but Simple Harlotry': The Companionate Marriage Controversy," *Journal of American History* 94, no. 4 (March 2008): 1137–163; Elaine May, *Great Expectations; Marriage and Divorce in Post-Victorian America* (Chicago: University of Chicago Press, 1980) 137–55; Christina Simmons, *Making Marriage Modern: Women's Sexuality from the Progressive Era to WWII* (New York: Oxford University Press, 2011), 58–137.

119. Seton-Thompson, *Woman Tenderfoot*, 15–17. For the camping honeymoon, see, for example, Iva Cooley Colliver, "Yosemite Honeymoon, 1915" *Pacific Historian* 15, no. 2 (1971): 75–82; and Vivian Gurney, "An Auto-Burro Honeymoon," *Sunset* 43, no. 3 (July 1919): 40–42, 66–67.

120. Phillips, "Woman on the Trail," 589.

121. Charles S. Greene, "Camping for Two," *Sunset* 15, no. 4 (August 1905): 357.

122. Barrows, "Shaybacks in Camp—Part 1," 365.

123. Hough, *Out of Doors*, 109–10, 112–24.

124. Shields, *Camping and Camp Outfits*, 10–11; Hough, *Out of Doors*, 3.

125. Samuel J. Barrows, "The Beacon Street Tramp," typescript, 3–4, Barrows Family Papers.

126. Barrows, "Beacon Street Tramp," 68–79, 97–98, Barrows Family Papers. "Pokie" was a camp nickname for "Pocahontas."

127. Barrows, "Beacon Street Tramp," 9, 12, 21–22, 32–33; *The Beacon Street Tramp,* program, Barrows Family Papers. The play was staged in 1894 as a benefit for the Massachusetts Prison Association.

CHAPTER 4

1. W. W. Wagener, Carl Hartley, and J. S. Boyce, "Obituary: Emilio Pepe Michael Meinecke, 1869-1957," *Phytopathology* 47, no. 11 (November 1957): 633–34. Meinecke was born in Alameda, California to German parents who settled in San Francisco as early as 1850. After earning his PhD in Botany at Heidelberg, he worked in Germany and Argentina, before returning to California in 1909.

2. E. P. Meinecke, "Human Aspects of Conservation," paper read at meeting of the discussion group on philosophy of conservation at the University of California (Berkeley) Department of Geography, [ca. 1935], TS, box 2, Emilio Pepe Michael Meinecke Collection, California Academy of Sciences Archives, San Francisco (hereafter Meinecke Collection).

3. Lizabeth Cohen, *A Consumer's Republic: The Politics of Mass Consumption in Postwar America* (New York: Vintage Books, 2004).

4. Paul Sutter, *Driven Wild: How the Fight Against Automobiles Launched the Modern Wilderness Movement* (Seattle: University of Washington Press, 2002), 19–30; Warren Belasco, *Americans on the Road: From Autocamp to Motel, 1910-1945* (Cambridge, MA: MIT Press, 1979), 73–74. For highway expansion, see

Owen D. Gutfreund, *Twentieth-Century Sprawl: Highways and the Reshaping of the American Landscape* (New York: Oxford University Press, 2004); I. B. Holley Jr., *The Highway Revolution, 1895-1925: How the United States Got out of the Mud* (Durham, NC: Carolina Academic Press, 2008).

5. Hrolf Wisby, "Camping Out With an Automobile," *Outing* 45, no. 6 (March 1905): 739, 745; Belasco, *Americans on the Road,* 33–35.

6. George W. Sutton Jr., "Are You a Motor Gypsy?" *Vanity Fair* 18, no. 4 (June 1922): 79, 90; Belasco, *Americans on the Road,* 92–99.

7. D. L. Lane, "Camping de Luxe," *Sunset* 57, no. 1 (July 1926): 10–11; William R. Mulvane, "Tenting on the New Camp Ground," *Sunset* 55, no. 1 (July 1925): 13, 58.

8. L. W. Peck, "Practical Hints for the Motor Camper," *Sunset* 36, no. 6 (June 1916): 74, 76, 80; Peter J. Schwab, "Camping is an Art!" *Sunset* 58, no. 5 (May 1927): 20–21; F. E. Brimmer, *Motor Campcraft* (New York: MacMillan, 1923), 15.

9. "Dealers; Advertising Cut Service," Coleman Camp Stoves—Quick-Lite Lanterns (Wichita, KS: Coleman Lamp Co., 1926): 12, box 3, folder 1, Coleman Company Collection, RH MS 837, Kenneth Spencer Research Library, University of Kansas; Schwab, "Camping is an Art," 21; Sheldon Coleman and Lawrence M. Jones, *The Coleman Story: The Ability to Cope with Change* (New York: The Newcomen Society in North America, 1976); Kathleen Franz, *Tinkering: Consumers Reinvent the Early Automobile* (Philadelphia: University of Pennsylvania Press, 2005), 28–32. The "Quick Lite Lantern" got a boost from sales to the US Army during World War I.

10. Emphasis from the original, Frank E. Brimmer, *Coleman Motor Campers Manual* (Wichita, KS: The Coleman Lamp Co., 1926), 13, 19.

11. Mary L. Seelhorst, "Ninety Years of *Popular Mechanics,*" in *Possible Dreams: Enthusiasm for Technology in America*, ed. John L. Wright, (Dearborn, MI: Henry Ford Museum & Greenfield Village, 1992); Frank Luther Mott, *A History of American Magazines, 1741-1930* (Cambridge, MA: Belknap Press of Harvard University Press, c. 1958–1968), 4 (*1885-1905*): 320. For the relationship of tinkering, *Popular Mechanics,* and auto-camping, see Sutter, *Driven Wild,* 33–34 and Franz, *Tinkering,* 43–73.

12. See for example, "Motorists' Kitchen Chest Convertible into Tables," *Popular Mechanics* 26, no. 1 (July 1916): 108; "Berths Add to the Comfort of Automobile Touring," *Popular Mechanics* 37, no. 1 (January 1922): 75; "Auto Seat with Folding Back Converts Car into Bed," *Popular Mechanics* 44, no. 2 (August 1925): 274; "Tourists' Stove Heated by Exhaust Gas," *Popular Mechanics* 53, no. 5 (May 1930): 857.

13. "Auto Trailer for Tourists Makes Camping Easy," *Popular Mechanics* 38, no. 5 (November 1922): 714; "Elaborate House on Wheels for Country Tours," *Popular Mechanics* 37, no. 1 (January 1922): 160.

14. Belasco, *Americans on the Road,* 100–102; Franz, *Tinkering,* 30–41; Sutter, *Driven Wild,* 33–35.

15. "Municipal Camp Grounds," *Los Angeles Times,* June 6, 1920, VI:6; "To View Site of Auto Camp," *Los Angeles Times,* February 22, 1922, III:1; Denver Tourist Bureau, "Motoring and Camping in the Colorado Rockies," ca. 1923, Clipping File: Camping—Colorado, Western History and Genealogy Department, Denver Public Library. Auto-camps also spawned new configurations of casual roadside lodging, such as cabin courts and motels, all of which added to travelers' options rather than eclipsing camping. See Sutter, *Driven Wild,* 37–42 and Belasco, *Americans on the Road,* 41–104.

16. W. I. Hutchinson, "A Dollar-a-Day Vacation," *Sunset* 59, no. 1 (July 1927): 36; Mulvane, "Tenting on the New," 12; Allison Edwards, "Camping in Comfort," *Sunset* 55, no. 1 (July 1925): 39; Schwab "Camping is an Art," 82; Sutter, *Driven Wild,* 106–29.

17. Sutter, *Driven Wild,* 30–42, 106–29.

18. Marguerite Shaffer, "Performing Bears and Packaged Wilderness: Reframing the History of the National Parks," in *Cities and Nature in the American West,* ed. Char Miller (Reno: University of Nevada Press, 2010), 140–42; Sutter, *Driven Wild,* 103–25; Marguerite Shaffer, *See America First: Tourism and National Identity, 1880-1940* (Washington, DC: Smithsonian Institution Press, 2001); Alfred Runte, *National Parks: The American Experience* (Lincoln: University of Nebraska Press, 1979).

19. Franklin K. Lane, Secretary of the Interior to Stephen T. Mather, Director, May 13, 1918, General Records, Central Classified Files, 1907-49, box 82, file 201–15: Admin./Policy, National Park Service Records, RG 79, (hereafter NPS Records), National Archives and Records Administration, College Park, MD (hereafter NARA II); Richard Sellars, *Preserving Nature in the National Parks: A History* (New Haven, CT: Yale University Press, 1997), 28.

20. Stephen Mather, US Congress, House Committee on Appropriations, *Interior Department Appropriation Bill, 1928, Hearing,* 69th Congress, 2d Session, 1926, 833; Barry Mackintosh, *Visitor Fees in the National Park System: A Legislative and Administrative History* (Washington, DC: Department of the Interior, 1983), at 1b, https://www.nps.gov/parkhistory/online_books/mackintosh3/fees1b.htm; Ethan Carr, *Wilderness by Design: Landscape Architecture and the National Park Service* (Lincoln: University of Nebraska Press, 1999), 133; Sutter, *Driven Wild,* 106–10.

21. "National Park Service Organic Act," 16 U.S.C. § 1 (1916); Craig E. Colten and Lary M. Dilsaver, "The Devil in the Cathedral: Sewage and Garbage in Yosemite National Park," in Miller, *Cities and Nature,* 154–70; US Department of the Interior, National Park Service, "Pubic Use of the National Parks; A Statistical Report, 1904-1940," (1963), Table III, https://irma.nps.gov/Stats/Reports/National; Sutter, *Driven Wild,* 107.

22. Emilio P. Meinecke, *A Report on the Effect of Excessive Tourist Travel on the California Redwood Parks,* State of California, Department of Natural Resources, Division of Parks (Sacramento: State Printing Office, 1928), 1.

23. Emilio P. Meinecke, "Memorandum on the Effects of Tourist Traffic on Plant Life, particularly Big Trees, Sequoia National Park, California," unpublished report in Sequoia-Kings Canyon Archives (May 1926), cited in Lary M. Dilsaver and William C. Tweed, *Challenge of the Big Trees of Sequoia and Kings Canyon National Parks: A Resource History* (Three Rivers, CA: Sequoia Natural History Association, 1990) 144–45; Meinecke, *A Report on the Effect of Excessive Tourist Travel*, 7–9; E. P. Meinecke, "Tree Diseases and Mechanical Damage to Forests," unpublished report for the National Park Service, February 18, 1928, 3, box 7, Meinecke Collection. See also, Linda McClelland, *Presenting Nature: The Historic Landscape Design of the National Park Service, 1916-1942* (Washington, DC: National Park Service, 1993); Dilsaver and Tweed, *Challenge of the Big Trees,* 140–45.

24. Meinecke, "Tree Diseases," 12.

25. Dilsaver and Tweed, *Challenge of the Big Trees,* 144–52, 242; McClelland, *Presenting Nature*, 161–66; Hal K. Rothman, "'A Regular Ding-Dong Fight': Agency Culture and Evolution in the NPS-USFS Dispute, 1916-1937," *Western Historical Quarterly* 20, no. 2 (May 1989): 141–53.

26. Arthur Carhart, "Municipal Playgrounds in the Forests," *Municipal Facts Monthly* 2, no. 7 (July 1919): 7, 14; Sutter, *Driven Wild*, 39, 63–64; Tom Wolf, *Arthur Carhart: Wilderness Prophet* (Boulder: University Press of Colorado, 2008), 54–55, 87–91; Donald N. Baldwin, *Quiet Revolution: Grass Roots of Today's Wilderness Preservation Movement* (Boulder, CO: Pruett Publishing Co., 1972), 5, 11–12, 17–19, 25, 58–59, 69, 77; Arthur Carhart, "Recreation in the Forests," *American Forestry* 26, no. 317 (May 1920): 268, 271; A. H. Carhart, "Denver's Greatest Manufacturing Plant," *Municipal Facts Monthly* 4, nos. 9–10 (September–October 1921): 3–7.

27. Arthur H. Carhart, "Recreation in Forestry," *Journal of Forestry* 21, no. 1 (January 1923): 11–12, 13–14; Arthur Carhart, "Auto Camp Conveniences," *American Forestry* 26, no. 321 (September 1920): 557; Sutter, *Driven Wild*, 66–67; Baldwin, *Quiet Revolution*, 115–18.

28. Meinecke, "Tree Diseases," 3; Meinecke, *Report on the Effect*, 12–14, 18–19.

29. Meinecke, "Tree Diseases," 3; Meinecke, *Report on the Effect*, 12–14, 18–19.

30. E.P. Meinecke, "The Trailer Menace," TS, April 1, 1935, box 11, Meinecke Collection. The extent of Meinecke's participation in the Wilderness Society remained unclear from his papers. His supervisor requested he join partly to serve as a moderating force, protecting forests from "abuses" by "special interests" while also dissuading members "from going too wild in their wildernesses." He resigned in 1940, and later rejoined at the request of leader Robert Sterling Yard. E.I. Kotok, Director, California Forest and Range Experiment Station, USFS, to Meinecke, August 7, 1936; Robert Sterling Yard to Meinecke, June 26, 1940, box 11, Meinecke Collection. See Sutter, *Driven Wild,* for the role of the Wilderness Society in resisting the development of mass public and automobile access to the outdoors.

31. Dilsaver and Tweed, *Challenge of the Big Trees,* 148–52.

32. E. P. Meinecke, *A Camp Ground Policy* (Ogden, UT: US Forest Service, 1932), 1–2, 4–5, 7.

33. Meinecke, *Camp Ground Policy*, 1, 7, 15–16.

34. Meinecke, *Camp Ground Policy*, 1, 7–12, 15–16. This was in part the logic for prohibiting campground fees, a congressional mandate regularly debated but not repealed until 1965. If it cost money to stay in a designated camp but free outside of it, campers would be tempted to head off into the woods to evade the fee and then cause damage. Mackintosh, *Visitor Fees*, at 1d, https://www.nps.gov/parkhistory/online_books/mackintosh3/fees1d.htm.

35. Meinecke, *Camp Ground Policy,* 11–12.

36. Meinecke, *Camp Ground Policy,* 11–12.

37. Meinecke, *Camp Ground Policy*, 9–11; E. P. Meinecke, *Camp Planning and Camp Reconstruction* (California Region: US Forest Service, 1934), 11.

38. Meinecke, *Camp Planning*, 15–16.

39. Meinecke, *Camp Ground Policy*, 11–12.

40. Meinecke, *Camp Planning*, 3–5, 17.

41. Meinecke, *Camp Planning*, 9, 15, 20; Meinecke, *Camp Ground Policy*, 12.

42. Meinecke, *Camp Planning*, 4.

43. Meinecke, "Human Aspects," 7, 11–14; Meinecke, *Camp Planning*, 20.

44. E.P. Leavitt, Superintendent, Hawaii National Park to A.E. Demaray, Acting Director, NPS, July 16, 1932; Memo for all Superintendents, June 14, 1932 from A.E. Demaray, Acting Director, NPS; Horace M. Albright, Director, NPS, to Meinecke, October 12, 1932; Guy D. Edwards, Acting Superintendent, Yellowstone National Park, to Meinecke, November 14, 1932; Meinecke to Albright, November 1, 1932; Demaray to Haven Metcalf, Principal Pathologist, Bureau of Plant Industry, May 18, 1932; Central Classified Files 1907-49, Administration, Policies, box 82, file 201–15: Admin./Policy, NPS Records, NARA II.

45. Demaray to F.D. Richey, Chief, Bureau of Plant Industry, USFS, December 31, 1934, Branch of Forestry, Correspondence & Subject Files, 1928-59, box 58, file 883–10: Campground Protection, NPS Records, NARA II.

46. Demaray, Memorandum for Field Officers, May 14, 1935; J.B Coffman, Chief Forester, NPS to W.G. Carnes, Chief, Western Division, Branch of Plans and Design, NPS, March 26, 1936, Branch of Forestry, Correspondence & Subject Files, 1928-59, box 58, file 883–10: Campground Protection, NPS Records, NARA II; Carr, *Wilderness by Design*, 281; McClelland, *Presenting Nature*, 161–66.

47. Demaray to M.H. Tillotson, Superintendent, Grand Canyon National Park, May 12, 1937; Paul R. Franke, Acting Superintendent, Mesa Verde National Park, to Demeray, May 20, 1937; Thomas Allen Jr., Superintendent, Rocky Mountain National Park, to Demeray, May 25, 1937, Central Classified Fields, 1933-49, box 164, file 0-204-20: Part One—Parks General Inspections and Investigations: Meinecke, NPS Records, NARA II.

48. Meinecke to Lawrence F. Cook, Assistant Chief Forester, NPS, October 10, 1934, Branch of Forestry, Correspondence & Subject Files, 1928-59, box 58, file 883–10: Campground Protection, NPS Records, NARA II.

49. Meinecke to Cook, October 10, 1934; Meinecke to Arno B. Cammerer, Director, NPS, September 24, 1937; Cammerer to Meinecke, November 24, 1937, General Records, Central Classified Fields, 1933-49, box 164, file 0-204-20: Part One, Parks General Inspections and Investigations: Meinecke, NPS Records, NARA II.

50. E.P. Meinecke "Recreation reports," misc. typescript notes, 1938, box 19, folder 6, Meinecke Collection. See also E. P. Meinecke, "Recreation Planning: A Discussion," *Journal of Forestry* 35, no. 12 (December 1937): 1120–28.

51. Meinecke, et. al, "Recreation reports."

52. John A. Jakle and Keith A. Sculle, *America's Main Street Hotels: Transiency and Community in the Early Auto Age* (Knoxville: University of Tennessee Press, 2009), 153.

53. Charles Lubcke, "A Sunset Family Visits the Grand Canyon," *Sunset* 66, no. 1 (January 1931): 19.

54. F. E. Brimmer, quoted in Norman Hayner, "The Auto Camp as a New Type of Hotel," *Sociology and Social Research* 15, no. 3 (March - April 1931): 369.

55. Nels Anderson, *Men on the Move* (Chicago: University of Chicago Press, 1940), 66.

56. Todd DePastino, *Citizen Hobo: How a Century of Homelessness Shaped America* (Chicago: University of Chicago Press, 2002), 17.

57. DePastino, *Citizen Hobo,* 202–205; "Jobless Women in Parks," *New York Times,* September 20, 1931, N2; Lisa Goff, *Shantytown, USA: Forgotten Landscapes of the Working Poor* (Cambridge, MA: Harvard University Press, 2016), 219–49, esp. 225–34; Joan M. Crouse, *The Homeless Transient in the Great Depression: New York State, 1929-41* (Albany: SUNY Press, 1986), 100–101.

58. DePastino, *Citizen Hobo,* 195–200; Lucy G. Barber, *Marching on Washington: The Forging of an American Political Tradition* (Berkeley: University of California Press, 2002), 76 78.

59. Anderson, *Men on the Move,* 54.

60. Gladwin Bland, quoted in DePastino, *Citizen Hobo,* 197; Smedley Butler, quoted in Hans Schmidt, *Maverick Marine: General Smedley Butler and the Contradictions of American Military History* (Lexington: University Press of Kentucky, 1987), 218; DePastino, *Citizen Hobo,* 197–98; Barber, *Marching on Washington,* 82–87.

61. "Hoover Orders Eviction," *New York Times,* July 29, 1932, 1; Barber, *Marching On Washington,* 89–104; "Bonus Hikers Begin Lobbying in House," *New York Times,* June 1, 1932, 7; "Congress Provides Bonus Exodus Fare," *New York Times,* July 8, 1932, 2.

62. Barber, *Marching On Washington,* 89–107. When veterans arrived in Washington again in May of 1933, Roosevelt also rebuffed their pleas for

immediate payment of the bonus but did arrange for several thousand men to reside at an army post in Virginia, with tents, food, and supplies provided courtesy of the government.

63. "Transients Park Camp Scheme Hit," *Los Angeles Times*, December 27, 1933, A1; "City Transient Camps Urged," *Los Angeles Times*, January 21, 1932, A3; "Federal Work Camps to Open," *Los Angeles Times*, December 22, 1933, A1; DePastino, *Citizen Hobo*, 207–209, 232–33; Goff, *Shantytown*, 228, 232–33; Crouse, *Homeless Transient*, 169. Such assessments were based as much on anecdote and cultural belief as on data or social research, as administrators failed to consult detailed federally commissioned studies of transients. See Goff, *Shantytown*, 228; Crouse, *Homeless Transient*, 216.

64. Goff, *Shantytown*, 222; Anderson, *Men on the Move*, 66; Paul Groth, *Living Downtown: The History of Residential Hotels in the United States* (Berkeley: University of California Press, 1999), 131–67.

65. John Steinbeck, *The Grapes of Wrath* (New York: Penguin Classics, 2006; c. 1939), 119.

66. Steinbeck, *Grapes of Wrath*, 134–36, 193, 197.

67. Carleton Beals, "Migs: America's Shantytowns on Wheels," *Forum and Century* 99, no. 1 (January 1938): 11.

68. Steinbeck, *Grapes of Wrath*, 193–94, 196.

69. United States, Department of Commerce, Bureau of the Census, *Census of Business: 1935—Tourist Camps* (May 1937). Figures were collected in 1936 and reported 7,814 tourist camps without filling stations, 2,034 with filling stations, and 1,409 filling stations with some "tourist camp facilities." The latter number was not disaggregated by state, and so the percentage in the Dust Bowl and migrant route states was calculated from the first two categories alone and assumes that the geographical distribution is roughly similar. Dust Bowl and migrant route states include Arizona, Arkansas, California, Colorado, Kansas, Missouri, Nevada, New Mexico, Oklahoma, Texas, and Utah. The total for these 11 states was 4,417 out of 9,848 for a percentage of 44.85%. None of the reports gave a breakdown by type of accommodation offered—cabin, campsite, or a combination. It defined a "tourist camp" as "engaged primarily in furnishing temporary lodging accommodations to tourists in cabins . . . or in furnishing camping space and other camping facilities to tourists for a fee." It did not include private homes renting rooms, municipal camps, or vacation resort "cottage colonies."

70. Steinbeck, *Grapes of Wrath*, 174–75.

71. Steinbeck, *Grapes of Wrath*, 186.

72. Beals, "Migs," 15.

73. Steinbeck, *Grapes of Wrath*, 92, 235, 241–42.

74. DePastino, *Citizen Hobo*, 214–15; Molly Godfrey, "They Ain't Human: John Steinbeck, Proletarian Fiction, and the Racial Politics of 'The People,'" *Modern Fiction Studies* 59, no. 1 (Spring 2013): 107–34.

75. Frances Perkins, quoted in Anderson, *Men on the Move*, 100; Beals, "Migs," 10–11; Crouse, *Homeless Transient*, 75, 97–98.

76. Steinbeck, *Grapes of Wrath*, 254, 271, 296; Charles Wollenberg, Introduction to *Harvest Gypsies: On the Road to the Grapes of Wrath*, by John Steinbeck (Berkeley, CA: Heyday Books, 1988), 5–6, 26–29.

77. United States, *Report of the Administrator of the Farm Security Agency, 1938* (Washington, DC: Farm Security Agency, 1938), 22; Bernard Sternsher, *Rexford Tugwell and the New Deal* (New Brunswick, NJ: Rutgers University Press, 1964).

78. United States, *Report of the Administrator of the Farm Security Agency, 1939* (Washington, DC: Farm Security Agency, 1939), 19–20.

79. *Report of the Administrator of the Farm Security Agency, 1940* (Washington, DC: Farm Security Agency, 1940), 15–17. Camps were built in Arizona, California, Florida, Idaho, Oregon, Texas, and Washington.

80. DePastino, *Citizen Hobo*, 208; camp manager quoted in DePastino, *Citizen Hobo*, 209; Hopkins quoted in Crouse, *The Homeless Transient*, 194–95.

81. John Lennon, *Boxcar Politics: The Hobo in U.S. Culture and Literature, 1869-1956* (Amherst: University of Massachusetts Press, 2014), 107; DePastino, *Citizen Hobo*, 165.

82. Much historical scholarship has focused on Lange and "Migrant Mother." See, for example, James C. Curtis, "Dorothea Lange, Migrant Mother, and the Culture of the Great Depression," *Winterthur Portfolio* 21, no. 1 (April 1986): 1–20; Linda Gordon, *Dorothea Lange: A Life Beyond Limits* (New York: W.W. Norton, 2010), esp. 235–44. I owe some of my interpretation of "Migrant Mother" to conversations with Fraser Cocks at the University of California, San Diego.

83. Leta Foster Ide, "Camping with a Fresh Little Heir," *Sunset* 72, no. 5 (May 1934): 24.

84. L. H. Robbins, "America Hobnobs at the Tourist Camp," *New York Times*, August 12, 1934, M9; John A. Jakle, *The Motel in American Culture* (Baltimore: Johns Hopkins University Press, 2002), 33–34; Belasco, *Americans on the Road*, 125.

85. Maylen Newby Pierce, "Everglades Camping Memories," *Historical Association of South Florida Update* 13, no. 4 (November 1986): 7.

86. F. W. Leuning, *Motor Camping* (Milwaukee: Milwaukee Journal Tour Club, 1926), 1; Doris Hudson Moss, "Ye Who Enter Here Leave All Boiled Shirts Behind," *Sunset* 73, no. 1 (July 1934): 9.

87. "'Collapsible' Idea Rules Camp Items: Ingenious Gadgets for Outdoors Designed to Conserve Space in Autos and Tents," *New York Times*, February 21, 1937, 69; "Secret of Camping Comfort is in the Equipment You Select," *Popular Mechanics* 61, no. 5 (May 1934): 694–95.

88. A. Ruhland, "At Home on the Road in a Trailer," *Popular Mechanics* 57, no. 3 (March 1932): 497; Beals, "Migs," 11; Goff, *Shantytown*, 234.

89. "200,000 Trailers," *Fortune* (March 1937): 105–107, 200, 214, 220–22; "Hitting the Trail, 1935 Style," *Popular Mechanics* 64, no. 1 (July 1935): 40–42; H. W. Magee, "Hitch Your Wagon to a Car," *Popular Mechanics* 66, no. 6 (December 1936): n.p.

90. "Big Gain Reported by Resort Hotels," *New York Times,* November 14, 1935, 19; Jakle and Sculle, *America's Main Street,* 153; Jakle, *The Motel,* 33.

91. [James Agee], "The Great American Roadside," *Fortune* 10, no. 3 (September 1934): 53–56; Norman Hayner "Auto Camps in the Evergreen Playground," *Social Forces* 9, no. 2 (December 1930): 256–66.

92. J. Edgar Hoover with Courtney Ryley Cooper, "Camps of Crime," *American Magazine* 129, no. 2 (February 1940): 14–15, 130–32; "1935 Census of Business." See also, Hayner, "Auto Camps," 265–66; Hayner, "Auto Camp as a New Type," 370; Eleanor N. Knowles "Road Shelters Now Inns," *New York Times*, June 16, 1935, xx15.

93. "200,000 Trailers," 107, 111, 229.

94. Meinecke, "Recreation reports," box 19, folder 6, Meinecke Collection.

95. Louis Warren, personal communication to author, December 27, 2019. Thanks to Louis for sharing this story from his own family history and granting me permission to include it here.

96. National Park Service, "Rules and Regulations," *Federal Register* 2, no. 82 (April 29, 1937): 893–95; Jackson F. Price, Chief Counsel, NPS, to Assistant Director Hillory Tolson, October 10, 1951; Cook, to Tolson, November 3, 1950; *National Forest Service Manual,* Volume 1, Page GA-A3, amended September 1950, Branch of Forestry, Correspondence & Subj. Files, 1928-59, box 58, file 883–10: Campground Protection, NPS Records, NARA II; "Public Campsites in the Forest Preserves," RDA Program Files 1934-47, box 6, file 208: General Rules and Regulations, NPS Records, NARA II.

97. Emilio Meinecke, "The Need for Non-Urban Outdoor Recreation and the Types of Recreation Involved," TS, 5, box 19, folder 8, Meinecke Collection.

98. Meinecke, "Trailer Menace."

99. Meinecke, "The Need for Non-Urban," 7, 38; Sutter, *Driven Wild,* 38–39.

100. Sellars, *Preserving Nature;* Sutter, *Driven Wild,* 49–50; Harlan D. Unrau and G. Frank Willis, *Administrative History: Expansion of the National Park Service in the 1930s,* (Denver: National Park Service, 1983), at 3a, https://www.nps. gov/parkhistory/online_books/unrau-williss/adhi3.htm; Neil Maher, *Nature's New Deal: The Civilian Conservation Corps and the Roots of the American Environmental Movement* (New York: Oxford University Press, 2009), 15, 67–73, 117, 154, 161–64, 215–19, 252n2.

101. Maher, *Nature's New Deal,* 67–73, 84, 92–109, 116, 154, 163–64, 252n2, 254n19; Bryant Simon, "'New Men in Body and Soul': The Civilian Conservation Corps and the Transformation of Male Bodies and the Body Politic," in *Seeing Nature Through Gender,* ed. Virginia J. Scharff (Lawrence: University Press of Kansas, 2003), 80–102.

102. Herbert Evison to Newton B. Drury, Director, NPS, February 11, 1942, Recreational Demonstration Area Program Files 1934-47, box 2, file 120: General Legislation, NPS Records, NARA II.

103. Cammerer to Washington and All Field Offices, September 18, 1939, Memoranda Sent to Field Officers, 1936-42, NPS Records, NARA II; Phoebe Cutler, *The Public Landscape of the New Deal* (New Haven, CT: Yale University Press, 1985), 65. The plan called for RDAs to become State Parks, which most eventually did.

104. J.S. Lasill, Director, The Land Program, FERA, [Recreational Demonstration Areas], December 1, 1934; "History of Recreational Demonstration Projects and Development of Policies," n.d., 7; "[RDA] Policy" (n.d.), 1, Recreational Demonstration Area Program Files 1934-47, box 2, file 1: General History, NPS Records, NARA II; Cutler, *Public Landscape*, 5, 70.

105. Mattias C. Huppuch "An Innovation in Recreational Development" [n.d.]; "For the Guidance of Project Directors in the Selection and Development of Recreational Areas from Sub-marginal Land"; Lasill, [Recreational Demonstration Areas]; [RDA] Policy (n.d.) 2, Recreational Demonstration Area Program Files 1934-47, box 2, file 1: General History, NPS Records, NARA II; Cutler, *Public Landscape*, 8–11, 23, 65, 70–71.

106. "Annual Report of the Director of the National Park Service," 1937, in *Annual Report of the Secretary of the Interior, 1937*, 38–39; Lasill, [Recreational Demonstration Areas]; Cutler, *Public Landscape*, 19; Unrau and Williss, *Administrative History*, at 4i, https://www.nps.gov/parkhistory/online_books/unrau-williss/adhi4i.htm.

107. "History of Recreational Demonstration Projects," 4; "For the Guidance of Project Directors"; Cutler, *Public Landscape*, 64–66, 75–76. The CCC provided much of the labor for RDA construction.

108. Susan Schrepfer, *The Fight to Save the Redwoods: A History of Environmental Reform, 1917-1978* (Madison: University of Wisconsin Press, 1983), 52–78.

109. Henry M. Busch, "Camping," in *Encyclopaedia of the Social Sciences*, ed. Edwin R. A. Seligman and Alvin Johnson (New York: Macmillan, 1937), 3:168–70.

110. Department of the Interior, National Park Service, *An Invitation to New Play Areas*, [Spring 1938]: 4, 12–13, National Park Service, History eLibrary, http://npshistory.com/brochures/year-1930; Charles E. Hendry to Julian H. Salomon, Field Coordinator, NPS, March 2, 1937, RDA Program Files, 1934-47, box 14, file 501: General/Publicity, 1937-43; Unrau and Williss, *Administrative History*, at 4i, https://www.nps.gov/parkhistory/online_books/unrau-williss/adhi4i.htm. RDAs also included group camping facilities available for youth, municipal, industrial, church, and other social groups to lease.

111. F.A. Silcox, Chief, US Forest Service, "Planning the National Forests for Greater Recreational Uses," October 1, 1935, Records Concerning the Recreation Area Study/Competitive Recreation Development, 1935-40, box 1, NPS Records, NARA II; Sutter, *Driven Wild*, 221–24, 230.

112. G.A. Moskey, Assistant Director, NPS, to Ben Thompson, April 30, 1938; Fred T. Johnston, Acting Assistant Director, NPS, to Moskey, May 2, 1938, Records Concerning the Recreation Area Study concerning Competitive Recreation

Development, 1935-40, box 1, NPS Records, NARA II; Sidney S. Kennedy, "Report: Recreational Developments in Adirondack and Catskill Forest Preserves," October 17, 1935; Norman Newton, District Inspector to Belvin Borgeson, Regional Officer Region Two NPS, October 16, 1935; "Special Report to Conrad L. Wirth, Assistant Director, State Park Division," Records Concerning the Recreation Area Study/Records Concerning Competitive Recreation Development, 1935-40, box 2, NPS Records, NARA II.

113. Leonora Philbrook, "Camping in the Sierra National Forest," *Sunset* 72, no. 2 (February 1934): 22.

114. Barbara W. Gardener, Simi, California, to National Park Directors, May 22, 1957; Mrs. Francis Latzke, Los Angeles, California to Conrad L. Wirth, May 22, 1957; Price, Assistant Director, NPS, to Gardener, May 29, 1957; Price to Latzke, June 4, 1957, Branch of Forestry, Correspondence & Subj. Files, 1928-59, box 58, file 883–10: Campground Protection, NPS Records, NARA II.

115. J. R. Eakin and T. Arnold Hill quoted in Terence Young, "'A Contradiction in Democratic Government': W. J. Trent, Jr., and the Struggle to Desegregate National Park Campgrounds," *Environmental History* 14, no. 4 (October 2009): 657–59, 677n23; J. W. Holland, *Black Recreation: A Historical Perspective* (Chicago: Burnham, Inc., 2002), 133–39.

116. A. Wilberforce Williams, "Dr. A. Wilberforce Williams Talks on Preventative Measures" *Chicago Defender*, July 25, 1914, 8; "Is Part of Human Nature," *Chicago Defender*, September 26, 1914, 7.

117. "Society," *Chicago Defender,* May 15, 1920, 10; "Off On Motor Tour," *Chicago Defender*, August 11, 1923, 10; C. Elliott Freeman Jr., "Around the Hub: Boston News," *Chicago Defender*, September 25, 1926, A7; Young, "A Contradiction," 654–55; Gretchen Sorin, *Driving While Black: African American Travel and the Road to Civil Rights* (New York: Liveright Publishing Co., 2020), 80; Colin Fisher, "African Americans, Outdoor Recreation, and the 1919 Chicago Race Riot," in *"To Love the Wind and the Rain": African Americans and Environmental History,* ed. Dianne D. Glave and Mark Stoll, (Pittsburgh: University of Pittsburgh Press, 2006), 70–74; Mark S. Foster, "In the Face of 'Jim Crow': Prosperous Blacks and Vacations, Travel and Outdoor Leisure, 1890-1945," *Journal of Negro History* 84, no. 2 (Spring 1999): 140–41.

118. Ruby E. Stutts-Lyells, "Mississippi's Women Dedicate New Center," *Chicago Defender*, November 27, 1937, 17.

119. "Tough on Acts," *Chicago Defender*, October 25, 1924, 7; George Schuyler, "Keeping the Negro in his Place," *American Mercury* 17, no. 68 (August 1929): 469–76; Foster, "In the Face of 'Jim Crow,'" 140–41; Holland, *Black Recreation*, 157–61.

120. Alfred E. Smith, "Through the Windshield," *Opportunity* 11, no. 5 (May 1933): 142–44; Sorin, *Driving While Black*, 36–39, 80, 291n7. Smith was a long-time advocate for civil rights and worked for the Works Progress Administration

and other New Deal agencies, as well as serving on Roosevelt's Federal Council on Negro American Affairs.

121. Sorin, *Driving While Black,* 178–90; Cotton Seiler, *Republic of Drivers: A Cultural History of Automobility in America* (Chicago: University of Chicago Press, 2008), 106–28; "The Green Book," New York Library Digital Collections, https://digitalcollections.nypl.org/collections/the-green-book#/?tab=about (accessed July 10, 2017); Susan Sessions Rugh, *Are We There Yet?: The Golden Age of American Family Vacations* (Lawrence: University Press of Kansas, 2008); Candacy Taylor, *Overground Railroad: The Green Book and the Roots of Black Travel in America* (New York: Abrams Press, 2020), 26–79. Sorin suggests that the Green Book simultaneously promoted Black freedom and demonstrated "moderate behavior" without overt challenges to segregation. Sorin, *Driving While Black,* 188.

122. *The Negro Motorist Green Book* (New York: Victor G. Green, Co., 1937), Schomburg Center for Research in Black Culture, Jean Blackwell Hutson Research and Reference Division, New York Public Library (hereafter cited as Schomburg Center).

123. See annual editions of *The Negro Motorist Green Book* (New York: Victor G. Green, Co., 1938–1967), 9, Schomburg Center; Taylor, *Overground Railroad,* 218–19.

124. "Accommodations for Colored People," Entry 6, General, Minutes, Sixth National Parks Conference, 1922, quoted in Shaffer, *See America First,* 125–26.

125. Meinecke, "Recreation reports"; Fisher, "African Americans, Outdoor Recreation," 68–69. For connections between the early twentieth century eugenics movement and conservation, see Gerald Allen, "'Culling the Herd': Eugenics and the Conservation Movement in the United States, 1900–1940," *Journal of the History of Biology* 46, no. 1 (Spring 2013): 31–72; Schrepfer, *Fight to Save,* 38–51.

126. Young, "A Contradiction," 658–59.

127. United States, *General Information Regarding Great Smoky Mountains National Park* (Washington, DC: Department of the Interior, 1933): 8, 15; Maher, *Nature's New Deal,* 74, 138–48; Unrau and Williss, *Administrative History,* at 4a, https://www.nps.gov/parkhistory/online_books/unrau-williss/adhi4.htm.

128. Maher, *Nature's New Deal,* 106–10; Edgar G. Brown, *The CCC and Colored Youth* (Washington, DC: Government Printing Office, 1941), 1–2; John Salmond, "The CCC and the Negro," *Journal of American History* 52, no. 1 (June 1965): 75–88; Owen Cole, *The African-American Experience in the Civilian Conservation Corps* (Tallahassee: University Press of Florida, 1999).

129. W. J. Trent Jr. to E. K. Burlew, May 19, 1942, in Lary M. Dilsaver, *America's National Park System: The Critical Documents,* 2nd ed. (Lanham, MD: Rowan & Littlefield, 2016), 145–46; Young, "A Contradiction," 655; Maher, *Nature's New Deal,* 14, 74, 138.

130. Demaray to L. E. Wilson, September 18, 1936; Walter White to Harold Ickes, January 21, 1937, quoted in Young, "A Contradiction"; William O'Brien, "The Strange Career of a Florida State Park: Uncovering a Jim Crow Past," *Historical Geography* 35 (2007): 160–84.

131. Walter Magnes Teller to Drury, October 4, 1940, Wilson to Ickes, September 10, 1936, and Charles S. Johnson to Cammerer, April 23, 1937, quoted in Young, "A Contradiction," 657–59.

132. W. J. Trent Jr., to Ickes, January 3, 1939, quoted in Young, "A Contradiction," 658–65. See Young, "A Contradiction," 651–82 and Terence Young, *Heading Out: A History of American Camping* (Ithaca, NY: Cornell University Press, 2017), 173–207, for more on segregation in this era at the NPS and Trent's role in pressing for the change in policy.

133. "Congress Wins Fight; Cracks Jim-Crow Rule," *Chicago Defender,* April 6, 1940, 4; Drury, "Parks and Redwoods," 469–71; Dilsaver, ed. *America's National,* 143–48.

134. Newton B. Drury, Memorandum for the Regional Director, NPS Region One, June 15, 1942, in *America's National,* 148; Trent Jr., to Burlew, in *America's National,* 145–46; Young, "A Contradiction," 667–72.

135. Nina S. Roberts and Donald A. Rodriguez, "Use of Multiple Methods: An Examination of Constraints Effecting Ethnic Minority Visitors Use of National Parks and Management Implications," *Ethnic Studies Review* 31, no. 2 (Winter 2008): 49–50, 57–59; Carolyn Finney, *Black Faces, White Spaces: Reimagining the Relationship of African Americans and the Great Outdoors* (Chapel Hill: University of North Carolina Press, 2014), 55–60.

136. Drury, "Parks and Redwoods," 2:469–70.

137. Thos. A Vint, Chief Landscape Architect, National Park Service, Memorandum for the Regional Director, Region 4, December 27, 1944, box 6, Meinecke Collection.

138. Franklin D. Roosevelt, "Fireside Chat 28: On the State of the Union," January 11, 1944, Presidential Speeches, Miller Center, University of Virginia, https://millercenter.org/the-presidency/presidential-speeches/january-11-1944-fireside-chat-28-state-union; Marc A. Weiss, *The Rise of the Community Builders: The American Real Estate Industry and Urban Land Planning* (New York: Columbia University Press, 1987), 141–58; Richard Rothstein, *The Color of Law: A Forgotten History of How Our Government Segregated America* (New York: Liveright, 2017), 63–67.

139. United States, Department of the Interior, National Park Service, *A Park and Recreational Land Plan for the United States* (Washington, DC: Government Printing Office, 1941), in Dilsaver, *America's National,* 131–34; Roosevelt, "Fireside Chat 28."

140. W. E. B. Du Bois, *Darkwater: Voices From Within the Veil* (New York: Harcourt, Brace and Howe, 1920), 4, 225–30; Anthony William Wood, "The Erosion of the Racial Frontier: Settler Colonialism and the History of Black Montana, 1880-1930" (MA thesis, Montana State University, Bozeman, 2018), 109–11.

141. Rothstein, *The Color of Law*; George Lipsitz, *The Possessive Investment in Whiteness* (Philadelphia: Temple University Press, 1998), 1–23.

CHAPTER 5

1. "TV and Radio Program Guide: Tuesday's TV Highlights," *The Toledo (OH) Blade*, January 20, 1970, 41; "TV Listings," *Waukesha (WI) Daily Freeman*, January 20, 1970, 8. The reference to Petzoldt's appearance on *The David Frost Show* found at http://www.tv.com/shows/the-david-frost-show/january-14-1970-1127447/ (accessed March 25, 2018).

2. Jane Howard, "Last Mountain Man? Not if He Can Help It," *Life* 67, no. 25 (December 19, 1969): 48–56; Sen. Gale W. McGee (R-WY), "Paul Petzoldt, Mountain Man," *Congressional Record* (16 Dec. 1969): 39285–86; "TV and Radio Program Guide." For the January 9 ad in *Life*, see Figure 5.3.

3. For an institutional history of NOLS from the perspective of the organization, see Kate Dernocoeur, *A Worthy Expedition: The History of NOLS* (Guilford, CT: FalconGuides, 2017). For a general biography of Paul Petzoldt, see Raye C. Ringholz, *On Belay!: The Life of Legendary Mountaineer, Paul Petzoldt* (Seattle: The Mountaineers, 1997).

4. McGee, "Paul Petzoldt," 39285; *Life*, December 19, 1969, cover, 19, 46–47.

5. Petzoldt, in *The Alcoa Hour*, episode one, "Thirty Days to Survival," directed by Mike Wadleigh (New York: Time/Life Films, 1970), aired on January 20, 1970 on the Hughes Television Network; Petzoldt, quoted in Howard, "Last Mountain Man," 53.

6. "TV and Radio Program Guide"; *Woodstock: Three Days of Peace and Music*, directed by Mike Wadleigh (New York: Wadleigh-Maurice, 1970, distributed by Warner Bros.); Dave Saunders, *Direct Cinema: Observational Documentary and the Politics of the Sixties* (London: Wallflower Press 2007), 99–125. Cinema verité, or direct cinema, was associated with younger, independent filmmakers, and with protest movements. This was a new genre for the "nature film," and differed significantly from the earlier styles of *Disney's True Life Adventures* or *Mutual of Omaha's Wild Kingdom*—two popular nature documentary TV series that had preceded it. Gregg Mitman, *Reel Nature: America's Romance with Wildlife on Film* (Seattle: University of Washington Press, 2009).

7. Susan Sessions Rugh, *Are We There Yet? The Golden Age of American Family Vacations* (Lawrence: University Press of Kansas, 2008); Peter Boag, "Outward Bound: Family, Gender, Environmentalism, and the Postwar Camping Craze, 1945–1970," *Idaho Yesterdays* 50, no. 1 (Spring 2009): 5.

8. Ethan Carr, *Mission 66: Modernism and the National Park Dilemma* (Amherst: University of Massachusetts Press, 2007); Paul Hirt, *Conspiracy of Optimism:*

Management of the National Forests since World War Two (Lincoln: University of Nebraska Press, 1996).

9. Gordon L. Bultena and Marvin J. Tavis, "Changing Wilderness Images and Forestry Policy," *Journal of Forestry* 59, no. 3 (March 1961): 167–71.

10. Mrs. J. F. Veit, Corpus Christi, TX to Senator Lyndon Johnson, July 28, 1957, box 24, file A3615, ROMO Numerical Subject Files 97–437, Records of the National Park Service, RG 79, (hereafter NPS Records), National Archives and Records Administration, Denver Regional Office (hereafter NARA Denver). Similar complaints abound in NPS records, found in regional NARA repositories as well as those at National Archives and Records Administration, College Park, Maryland (hereafter NARA II).

11. "Camping," *Motorland* (July–August 1960): 9; Boag, "Outward Bound," 6–7; Rugh, *Are We There Yet?* 121, 147–52; Barry Mackintosh, *Visitor Fees in the National Park System: A Legislative and Administrative History* (Washington, DC: History Division, National Park Service, Department of the Interior, 1983), at 2, https://www.nps.gov/parkhistory/online_books/mackintosh3/fees2.htm.

12. Hal Burton, "Pitch a Tent for Family Fun," *American Magazine* 158, no. 1 (July 1954): 32. Burton was an expert in skiing and climbing who collaborated in the development of Whiteface Mountain Ski Resort in the late 1930s, before becoming an officer in the 10th Mountain Division; afterward he worked as a freelance reporter writing on the outdoors, skiing, and suburban development for popular periodicals. James A. Goodwin, "Harold B. Burton, 1908-1992: In Memoriam," *American Alpine Journal* 35, no. 67 (1993): 333; Pete Nelson, "Lost Brook Dispatches: Hal Burton's Peak," *Adirondack Almanack* (September 8, 2012): n.p., https://www.adirondackalmanack.com/2012/09/lost-brook-dispatches-hal-burtons-peak.html.

13. Burton, "Pitch a Tent," 32–34. A plethora of similar articles in the popular press appeared throughout the 1950s and early 1960s, many of which shared similar features and emphases. Burton's stands in for the highly repetitive and copious stream of family camping features, of which this list is only a brief sample: Edwin L. Brock, "The Whole Family Can Go Camping," *Recreation* 44, no. 2 (May 1950): 86; John Perry, "Weekend Camping," *Harper's Magazine* 203, no. 1214 (July 1951): 41–47; Jan Weyl, "How Young America Lives," *Ladies' Home Journal* 71, no. 7 (July 1954): 91–94, 119–20; Robert C. Orr, "Pack up the Kids and Go Camping," *Parents' Magazine & Family Home Guide* 31, no. 7 (July 1956): 88; Jeanne Olsen, "We're a Week-end Camping Family," *Parents' Magazine & Family Home Guide* 32, no. 8 (August 1957): 64; Joseph N. Bell, "Four Weeks of Camping on a Family Budget," *Popular Mechanics* 107, no. 5 (May 1958): 97–103; "Family Camping, "*American Home* 44, no. 5 (May 1961): 8; "Car Camping Vacation for Your Family," *Field & Stream* 66, no. 10 (February 1962): 38; Bill Conaway, "Big-family Camping," *Field & Stream* 67, no. 11 (March 1963): 48; Robert Charles, "Let's Take a Family Camping Vacation!" *Parents' Magazine & Better Homemaking* 40, no. 4 (April 1965): 110.

14. Boag, "Outward Bound," 7–9. For more on transience during this era, see chapter 6 and Peter H. Rossi, "The Old Homeless and the New Homeless in Historical Perspective," *American Psychologist* 45, no. 8 (August 1990): 954–56; Todd DePastino, *Citizen Hobo: How a Century of Homelessness Shaped America* (Chicago and London: University of Chicago Press, 2003), 220–35; Ronald Tobey, Charles Wetherell, and Jay Brigham, "Moving Out and Settling In: Residential Mobility, Home Owning, and the Public Enframing of Citizenship, 1921-1950," *American Historical Review* 95, no. 5 (December 1990): 1395–422.

15. Doris E. Wood, White Plains, NY, to Secretary of the Interior, September 24, 1958, box 1, file A3615, Glacier National Park Mixed Subject Files 97–436, NPS Records, NARA Denver; Rugh, *Are We There Yet?* 5, 12, 120–21; Boag, "Outward Bound," 9–10. For letters complaining of trouble in paradise, see Mr & Mrs J. V. Colyar, Wenatchie, WA, to Department of the Interior, August 30, 1961; Virginia B. Strong, Kirkland, WA to Harthon L. Bill, Superintendent, Glacier National Park, July 23, 1963; John L. Ergle to Superintendent, Glacier National Park, August 21, 1962, box 1, file A3615, Glacier National Park Mixed Subject Files 97–436, NPS Records, NARA Denver.

16. Erica A. Morin, "'No Vacation for Mother': Traditional Gender Roles in Outdoor Travel Literature, 1940-1965," *Women's Studies* 41, no. 4 (June 2012): 436–56; Rugh, *Are We There Yet?* 121; Annie Gilbert Coleman, *Ski Style: Sport and Culture in the Rockies* (Lawrence: University Press of Kansas, 2004), 125. For more on the connection of outdoor recreation and the Cold War, see Susan A. Schrepfer, *Nature's Altars: Mountains, Gender, and American Environmentalism* (Lawrence: University Press of Kansas, 2005), 182–93.

17. K. Peter Etzkorn. "Leisure and Camping: The Social Meaning of a Form of Public Recreation," *Sociology and Social Science Research* 49, no. 1 (October 1964): 77–79, 83. Citing sociologists became a common feature in popular articles about camping. Scholars had begun in the late 1950s to study both motivation for camping and specific practices, an inquiry that helped to spawn a new subfield, later dubbed Environmental Sociology. William R. Burch Jr., "The Play World of Camping: Research Into the Social Meaning of Outdoor Recreation," *American Journal of Sociology* 70, no. 5 (March 1965): 607–608; William R. Catton Jr. and John C. Hendee, "Wilderness Users. . . What Do They Think?" *American Forests* 74, no. 9 (September 1968): 31; Gordon Bultena and Lowell Klessig, "Satisfaction in Camping: A Conceptualization and Guide to Social Research," *Journal of Leisure Research* 1, no. 4 (Autumn 1969): 348; Patrick C. West and L. C. Merriam Jr., "Outdoor Recreation and Family Cohesiveness: A Research Approach," *Journal of Leisure Research* 2, no. 4 (Fall 1970): 251–59; William R. Freudenburg and Robert Gramling, "The Emergence of Environmental Sociology: Contributions of Riley E. Dunlap and William R. Catton, Jr.," *Sociological Inquiry* 59, no. 4 (October 1989): 439–52.

18. Boris Artzybasheff, "Camping: Call of the Not-So-Wild," illustration, *Time*, July 14, 1961, cover. For background on the illustrator, see Domenic J. Iacono, "1998 Hall of Fame Inductee: Boris Artzybasheff (1899–1965)," *Society of Illustrators: The*

Museum of Illustration, https://www.societyillustrators.org/boris-artzybasheff (accessed on May 16, 2018).

19. "Ah, Wilderness?" *Time,* July 14, 1961, 46. For example, David Brower and the Sierra Club featured the Thoreau quotation, "In wildness is the preservation of the world," on one of its popular coffee-table books in the early 1960s, and invoked him regularly to support modern wilderness preservation. Lawrence Buell, *The Environmental Imagination: Thoreau, Nature Writing, and the Formation of American Culture* (Cambridge, MA: Harvard University Press, 1995), 339–69; Finis Dunaway *Natural Visions: The Power of Images in American Environmental Reform* (Chicago: University of Chicago Press, 2005), 117–30.

20. "Ah Wilderness?" 46; Outdoor Recreation Resources Review Commission (hereafter ORRRC), *National Recreation Survey* (Washington, DC: Government Printing Office, 1962), 86.

21. Mrs. H. Horseman, Moose Jaw, Sask. Canada to Superintendent Glacier National Park, September 20, 1961, box 1, file A3615, Glacier National Park Mixed Subject Files 97–436, NPS Records, NARA Denver. For complaint letters detailing these issues, see for example, box 24, file A3415, ROMO General Correspondence 97–437, NPS Records, NARA Denver; and box 1, file A3615, Glacier National Park Mixed Subject Files 97–436, NPS Records, NARA Denver.

22. Emphasis from the original, Frances Archer, Santa Fe, NM, to Secretary of the Interior Stewart Udall, April 15, 1966, box 7, file A361b, Southwest Regional Office General Correspondence, Files, 1965-67, 93–002, NPS Records, NARA Denver.

23. N. T. Scoyen, Acting Director, NPS, to Senator Mike Mansfield, August 29, 1961, box 1, file A3615, Glacier National Park, Mixed Subject Files 97–436, NPS Records, NARA Denver. Public officials also relied on sociological studies, such as this one commissioned by the USFS: William R. Burch and Wiley D. Wenger Jr., *The Social Characteristics of Participants in Three Styles of Family Camping* (Portland, OR: Pacific Northwest Forest and Range Experiment Station, Forest Service, U.S. Department of Agriculture, 1967).

24. L. F. Cook, Chief of Forestry and Wildlife, to Mr. Davis, Memo Re: National Park Service Camping Policy, April 14, 1959, box 58, file 883–10: Campground Protection, Branch of Forestry, Correspondence & Subject Files, 1928–59, NPS Records, NARA II. Cook mentioned Meinecke's *A Campground Policy* (1932) and *Camp Planning and Camp Reconstruction* (1934) as official NPS policy as referenced in the Administrative Manual. In the late 1960s the NPS was still reprinting Meinecke's pamphlets and crediting him as the "originator" of the modern campground. Newton Bishop Drury, "Parks and Redwoods, 1919-1971, An Interview Conducted by Amelia Roberts Fry and Susan Schrepfer," Bancroft Library, University of California, Berkeley, Regional Oral History Office, c. 1972, 2: 453.

25. Mrs. Irving Boettger, East Helena, MT, to Senator Mike Mansfield, August 15, 1964, box 1, file A3615, Glacier National Park, Mixed Subject Files 97–436, NPS Records, NARA Denver.

26. "Ah, Wilderness?" 47–50, 51, 53. Sales of camping trailers and RVs boomed during this era and widened a perceived cultural divide between tent and trailer campers. See Terence Young, *Heading Out: A History of American Camping* (Ithaca, NY: Cornell University Press, 2017), 208–43.

27. John Kenneth Galbraith, *The Affluent Society* (Boston: Houghton Mifflin Co., 1998, c. 1958,), xi–xii, 187–88; Adam Rome, "'Give Earth a Chance': The Environmental Movement and the Sixties," *Journal of American History* 90, no. 2 (September 2003): 529.

28. Rugh, *Are We There Yet?* 177–79; Rome, "Give Earth a Chance," 541–42; Christopher C. Sellers, *Crabgrass Crucible: Suburban Nature and the Rise of Environmentalism in Twentieth-Century America* (Chapel Hill: University of North Carolina Press, 2012), 277–78.

29. Jack Kerouac, *The Dharma Bums* (New York: Penguin Books, 1976, c. 1958), 97–98; Rome, "Give Earth a Chance," 543; DePastino, *Citizen Hobo*, 239–40.

30. Petzoldt, in "Thirty Days to Survival."

31. Gerald J. Barry, "The Summer Camp Frenzy. . . How It's Growing More So and More Profitable," *Newsweek*, 54, July 13, 1959): 70–72; Leslie Paris, *Children's Nature: The Rise of the American Summer Camp* (New York: NYU Press, 2008), 271, 356; Abigail A. Van Slyck, *A Manufactured Wilderness: Summer Camps and the Shaping of American Youth, 1890-1960* (Minneapolis: University of Minnesota Press, 2006).

32. "Character, the Hard Way," *Time*, August 3, 1962, 38.

33. Paul Petzoldt to Joshua Miner, founder, COBS, February 27, 1964; Joseph Nold, Director, COBS, to Miner, September 26, 1963; Miner to Nold, September 29, 1963; Nold to Miner, December 9, 1963; Miner to Nold, December 13, 1963; Nold to Miner, December 27, 1963; Nold to Miner, March 4, 1964, Outward Bound records, Leadville, CO (hereafter Outward Bound records); Joshua L. Miner and Joe Boldt, *Outward Bound USA: Crew Not Passengers* (Seattle: The Mountaineers Books, 2002), 76–89, 105–13; Dernocoeur, *Worthy Expedition*, 15–24; Delmar Bachert, "The NOLS Experience: Experiential Education in the Wilderness" (EdD Diss, North Carolina State University, 1987), 20–23.

34. Petzoldt, quoted in Howard, "Last Mountain Man," 55; Petzoldt, interview with Delmar Bachert, 1982, quoted in Bachert, "The NOLS Experience," 28; Petzoldt, tape recording directed to COBS staff, 1964, quoted in Bachert, "The NOLS Experience," 24; Paul Petzoldt, tape recording, letter dictated to Raye Price, 1965, quoted in Bachert, "The NOLS Experience," 32–33.

35. Petzoldt to Miner, January 19, 1965, Outward Bound records; Dernocoeur, *Worthy Expedition*, 25–27; Bachert, "The NOLS Experience," 42–43.

36. Petzoldt, tape recording prepared for NOLS slide show, 1965, quoted in Bachert, "The NOLS Experience," 41–42.

37. The Wind River Range now falls within the Bridger Wilderness (1964) and Fitzpatrick Wilderness (1976) areas in the Shoshone National Forest. US

Forest Service, "Welcome to the Shoshone National Forest," https://www. fs.usda.gov/main/shoshone/home (accessed August 6, 2019); James Morton Turner, *The Promise of Wilderness: American Environmental Politics since 1964* (Seattle: University of Washington Press, 2012), 50; Mark Harvey, *Wilderness Forever: Howard Zahnhiser and the Path to the Wilderness Act* (Seattle: University of Washington Press, 2007), 281n33. For the Indigenous history of and US dispossession of Native claims in the Yellowstone region, see Peter Nabokov and Lawrence L. Loendorf, *Restoring a Presence: American Indians in Yellowstone National Park* (Norman: University of Oklahoma Press, 2004); Loretta Fowler, *Arapaho Politics, 1851-1978* (Lincoln: University of Nebraska Press, 1982).

38. Among those who critiqued the Wilderness Act for its definitions of nature was none other than Arthur Carhart, who had become a well-known authority in outdoor recreation planning. Arthur Carhart, *Planning for America's Wildlands* (Harrisburg, PA: Telegraph, 1961); Andrew G. Kirk, *Counterculture Green: The Whole Earth Catalog and American Environmentalism* (Lawrence: University Press of Kansas, 2007), 198, 261n61. See also, for broader debates about defining wilderness, William Cronon, "The Trouble with Wilderness; or, Getting Back to the Wrong Nature," in *Uncommon Ground: Toward Reinventing Nature*, ed. William Cronon (New York: Norton, 1995), 69–90.

39. "Marion Youth, 19, to Attend Camping School," *Cedar Rapids (IA) Gazette*, May 19, 1965, 8C; Petzoldt to Miner, March 10, 1965, Outward Bound records; Dernocoeur, *Worthy Expedition*, 27–34.

40. "Outdoor Leadership School Formed Here," *Wyoming State Journal* (Lander), March 23, 1965, n.p.; "London Times Has Article on Petzoldt School," *Wyoming State Journal* (Lander), August 5, 1965, n.p., Newspaper Clipping Scrapbook, National Outdoor Leadership School Records, National Outdoor Leadership School Headquarters, Lander, WY (hereafter NOLS records); Howard, "Last Mountain Man," 53; Raye Price, "Outdoor Finishing School," *Field & Stream* 72, no. 11 (March 1968): 128.

41. "26 Youths Isolated for 25 Days in Mountains," *Wyoming State Journal* (Lander), August 5, 1965, n.p.; "Icy Plunge Begins Day for Outdoor Leadership School," *Casper (WY) Morning Star*, June 15, 1965, n.p.; Jack Langan, "Outdoors School to Open in Lander this Summer," *Riverton (WY) Ranger*, [1965], n.p.; Addison Bragg, "Adventure—Part of Growing Up," *Billings (MT) Gazette*, January 29, 1967, n.p., Newspaper Clipping Scrapbook, NOLS Records.

42. Paul Petzoldt, "NOLS Review and Report to the Board of Trustees," 1965, 5, quoted in Bachert, "The NOLS Experience," 64; Maurice E. Horn Jr., "Lessons in Adventure," *Parks & Recreation* 1, no. 9 (September 1966): 704–705.

43. Daniel Yankelovich, "The New Naturalism," in Daniel Yankelovich, Inc., *The Changing Values on Campus: Political and Personal Attitudes of Today's College Students* (New York: Washington Square Press, Pocket Books, 1972), 167–71; Robert D. McFadden, "Daniel Yankelovich, Who Mastered Public Opinion

Research, is Dead at 92," *New York Times,* September 23, 2017, D8; Rome, "Give Earth a Chance," 549.

44. Bachert, "The NOLS Experience," 78; Tom Cockerill and Bernard Kelly, "Outdoor Geewhizery," *Denver Post,* May 23, 1971, Newspaper Clipping Scrapbook, NOLS Records. Bachert calculated a total of 431 students enrolled between 1966 and 1968. The age average appeared in the 1971 *Denver Post* piece and earlier years likely represented a similar range .

45. For example, at least one NOLS student was later drafted and killed in Vietnam, while Petzoldt reportedly helped to keep several conscientious objectors employed in NOLS operations and returned draft notices as undeliverable if the student was on course. "Jabberwock," *Alumnus* 1, no. 1 (February 1971): 7, NOLS Records; Charles D. Clack to Petzoldt, October 27, 1970, "Letters to the Editor," *Alumnus* 1, no. 2 (May 1971): 2, NOLS Records; Dernocoeur, *Worthy Expedition,* 71, 91, 143, 330–31; Julie Hwang, "The Pyle Family: Three Generations of NOLS," *Leader* 21, no. 3 (Summer 2005), http://www.nols.edu/alumni/leader/05summer/pyle_family.shtml; Mark Owen, "The Way It Was . . . Wind River Wilderness 8/4/71," *Leader* 20, no. 2 (Spring 2004), http://www.nols.edu/alumni/leader/04spring/thewayitwas.shtml.

46. Yankelovich, "New Naturalism," 169–71; Mark H. Lytle, *America's Uncivil Wars: The Sixties Era from Elvis to the Fall of Richard Nixon* (New York: Oxford Univeristy Press, 2005), 198.

47. Petzoldt, in NOLS, "Paul Petzoldt's films of NOLS in the 1960s" https://www.youtube.com/watch?v=lou5Y8OQBMQ (accessed May 17, 2018); Petzoldt, quoted in "Wilderness Is Their Schoolmaster," *Milwaukee Journal,* May 30, 1971, Newspaper Clipping Scrapbook, NOLS Records; Petzoldt, quoted in Phil White, "Paul Petzoldt— A Man to Match the Mountains," *Branding Iron* 76, no. 18 (February 14, 1969): 8–9.

48. Anne Fried, "Today's Counselors are *Different*," *Camping* 41, no. 2 (February 1968): 8–9.

49. Skip Shoutis, quoted in Dernocouer, *Worthy Expedition,* 48; Dernocouer, *Worthy Expedition,* 60, 68–69; Bachert, "The NOLS Experience," 50.

50. White, "Paul Petzoldt."

51. *High on the Wind Rivers,* directed by Richard Catron and Edward Summer (Brior Cliff, NY: Benchmark Films, 1973); "National Outdoor Leadership School, Wilderness Expedition Course," TS, November 1, 1968, NOLS Records. NOLS Records indicate that *High on the Wind Rivers* was shot either during the summer of 1970 or 1972, and was distributed internally through the NOLS promotional network, not screened on national television as was "Thirty Days to Survival."

52. NOLS student, in *High on the Wind Rivers.* For discussion of the relationship between psychedelic drugs and "new naturalism," see Rome, "Give Earth a Chance," 543; Robert Fletcher, *Romancing the Wild: Cultural Dimensions of Ecotourism* (Durham, NC: Duke University Press, 2014), 80–81, 127; Mark Liechty, *Far Out: Countercultural Seekers and the Tourist Encounter in Nepal* (Chicago: The University of Chicago Press, 2017), 165–68; Sara Porterfield, "The Paradox of

Place: Finding the Colorado River at Home and Abroad" (PhD diss., University of Colorado Boulder, 2018), 230–31.

53. Paul Petzoldt, *The Wilderness Handbook* (New York: Norton, 1974), 130; Paul Petzoldt, "National Outdoor Leadership School, General Information," TS [1968], NOLS Records; Rome, "Give Earth a Chance," 542–43.

54. NOLS student, in *High on the Wind Rivers*.

55. Petzoldt, "National Outdoor Leadership School, General Information"; "After 1st Course, Petzoldt Sure His New School is Needed," *Wyoming State Journal* (Lander), July 13, 1965, n.p., Newspaper Clipping Scrapbook, NOLS Records; Petzoldt, quoted in Howard, "Last Mountain Man," 55–56; Dernocoeur, *Worthy Expedition*, 35.

56. David Swanston, "The Diggers' Mystique: A Hippie Way of Giving," *San Francisco Chronicle*, January 23, 1967, 6; Lytle, *America's Uncivil Wars*, 212–14.

57. The origin story of the decision to take NOLS coed is a bit murky. According to one long-time NOLS instructor, Martha Newbury, in the fall of 1965, after Petzoldt finished a presentation at the Colorado State University Outing Club, she approached him to ask whether there were courses for girls. "No, she recalls him saying, but I don't know why not. You want to come?" As a result, he decided to admit women for 1966. However, it was clear that he had already been thinking of the idea at least since declaring expansion plans to the *Wyoming State Journal* in early August. Dernocoeur, *Worthy Expedition*, 38–39; "26 Youths Isolated"; Stephanie F. Wilson, "Pioneering Women in Outdoor Education: The History of Women at the National Outdoor Leadership School" (MS thesis, Mankato State University, 1998), 16–17, 21.

58. "National Outdoor School Had No Dull Moments," *Wyoming State Journal* (Lander), September 14, 1967, n.p., Newspaper Clipping Scrapbook, NOLS Records; Cockerill and Kelly, "Outdoor Geewhizery"; Raye Price, "Girls Head for Adventure in the High Country," *Salt Lake Tribune* (Salt Lake City, UT), Magazine, May 14, 1967, 4–5,7; Dernocoeur, *Worthy Expedition*, 38–39.

59. Raye Price, "Outdoor Finishing School," *Field & Stream* 72, no. 11 (March 1968): 68–69. Price reportedly attempted to get this article published in women's magazines, none of which were interested. The *Salt Lake Tribune* eventually published one version in 1967, and another appeared the following year in *Field & Stream* with the added opening call to "imagine your little lady." Wilson, "Pioneering Women," 20.

60. Tapley, quoted in Price, "Girls Head for Adventure," 7; Petzoldt, quoted in Cockerill and Kelly, "Outdoor Geewhizery." Photo captions of women students in these earlier years often referenced their physical attractiveness. See multiple clippings in the Newspaper Clipping Scrapbook, NOLS Records, especially, "National Outdoor School Had No Dull Moments"; "Outdoor Leadership School Ends Its 1968 Operations," *Wyoming State Journal* (Lander), September 9, 1968, n.p.; Minnie Woodring, "They'll do to Ride Range With, Journal Writer Tells Graduates," *Wyoming State Journal* (Lander), September 11, 1969, n.p.

61. Wilson, "Pioneering Women," 24–25; Victoria L. Jackson, "Title IX and the Big Time: Women's Intercollegiate Athletics at the University of North Carolina at Chapel Hill, 1950–1992" (PhD diss., Arizona State University, 2015), 7, 18; Susan K. Cahn, *Coming On Strong: Gender and Sexuality in Twentieth-Century Women's Sports* (Cambridge, MA: Harvard University Press, 1998).

62. The letter is undated, written by an unnamed young woman from Muscoda, WI quoted in Keith Melville, *Communes in the Counter Culture: Origins, Theories, Styles of Life* (New York: William Morrow & Company, 1972), 134–35; Yankelovich, *Changing Values on Campus*, 45; Rome, "Give Earth a Chance," 542–44; Timothy Miller, *The Hippies and American Values* (Knoxville: University of Tennessee Press, 1991), 109; Hal K. Rothman, *The Greening of a Nation: Environmentalism in the US Since 1945* (Fort Worth, TX: Harcourt Brace, 1998), 95; Bennett M. Berger, *The Survival of a Counterculture: Ideological Work and Everyday Life among Rural Communards* (Berkeley: University of California Press, 1981), 94; Dona Brown, *Back to the Land: The Enduring Dream of Self-Sufficiency in Modern America* (Madison: University of Wisconsin Press, 2011), 202–26.

63. Felicity D. Scott, *Outlaw Territories: Environments of Insecurity/Architectures of Counterinsurgency* (New York: Zone Books, 2016), 15–16, 73–114.

64. Thomas Frank, *The Conquest of Cool: Business Culture, Counterculture, and the Rise of Hip Consumerism* (Chicago: University of Chicago, 1998), 104–31.

65. Grosbeck quoted in Julie Hwang, "30 Days to Success," *Leader* 21, no. 3 (Summer 2005), http://www.nols.edu/alumni/leader/05summer/30_days_to_success.shtml; Eliza Eddy, "Al Blyth, Remembering Early NOLS," *Leader* 13, no. 2 (Spring 1997), http://www.nols.edu/alumni/leader/97spring/blythal.shtml; Dernocoeur, *Worthy Expedition*, 54; "Michael Wadleigh," Internet Movie Database, https://www.imdb.com/name/nm0905579/ (accessed March 26, 2018); Saunders, *Direct Cinema*, 10.

66. "Thirty Days to Survival." A narrator, well-known New York WABC personality, Dan Ingram, speaks sporadically throughout the film, largely at the beginning to share the history of the school, a brief biography of Petzoldt, and outline the survival test. Direct cinema approaches generally eschewed omniscient narration, and while using this convention, Wadleigh minimized it. Richard Sandomir, "Dan Ingram, 83, New York Disc Jockey Who Spun Hits and Cracked Wise, Dies," *New York Times,* June 26, 2018, A25; Saunders, *Direct Cinema,* 10.

67. Emphasis from the original, Petzoldt and Day, in "Thirty Days to Survival."

68. Petzoldt, in "Thirty Days to Survival."

69. Wadleigh quoted in Saunders, *Direct Cinema,* 99; Wadleigh quoted in *Woodstock: An Inside Look at the Movie that Shook up the World and Defined a Generation,* ed. Dale Bell (Studio City, CA: Michael Wiese Productions, 1999), 11.

70. *Woodstock*; "Thirty Days to Survival"; Saunders, *Direct Cinema,* 116, 124–25. Both of Wadleigh's films also featured the same song: "Swing Low, Sweet Chariot," sung by a line of hiking NOLS students in "Thirty Days to Survival" and Joan Baez,

with a memorable a capella rendition of the folk revival and Civil Rights anthem in *Woodstock*.

71. *New York Daily News* review, quoted in Dernocouer, *Worthy Expedition*, 55; "College Student Special Soon to be Broadcast," *The Guardian* (Wright State University Student Body) 6, no. 13 (January 7, 1970): 3. While most documentaries at the time were more didactic, direct cinema versions meant to serve as provocations, leaving open the possibility of multiple interpretations. Saunders, *Direct Cinema*, 83.

72. Petzoldt, quoted in Dave Knickerbocker, "Paul Petzoldt, 61, Rises to New Height," *Newsday* (New York, NY), January 16, 1970, 41; Minnie Woodring, "Petzoldt Admonishes Tragedy of Conservation Compromise," *Wyoming State Journal* (Lander), January 22, 1970, n.p., Newspaper Clipping Scrapbook, NOLS Records; Hellyer, quoted in Hwang, "30 Days to Success."

73. Minnie Woodring, "NOLS Starts 1970 Season with All Hands Hard at Work," *Wyoming State Journal* (Lander), June 11, 1970, Newspaper Clipping Scrapbook, NOLS Records; Hwang, "30 Days to Success,"; Dernocoeur, *Worthy Expedition*, 57–58. The New England and Tennessee branches closed after two seasons.

74. Day quoted in Hwang, "30 Days to Success"; Petzoldt quoted in John M. Kennedy, "Youth Learn in Wilderness," *St. Paul (MN) Pioneer Press*, April 11, 1971, n.p., Newspaper Clipping Scrapbook, NOLS Records.

75. Petzoldt, quoted in Cockerill and Kelly, "Outdoor Geewhizery."

76. Petzoldt, quoted in Woodring, "Petzoldt Admonishes"; Howard, "Last Mountain Man," 53; Bachert, "The NOLS Experience," 64; Dernocoeur, *Worthy Expedition*, 45–46, 63. For student reminiscences of hunting and killing game (including killing a sheep with a piton hammer because of a lack of a hunting permit), fishing, building bonfires, etc., see Eames Yates, "Graduate Reflections: Back on the Bus," *Leader* 12, no. 4 (Fall 1996), http://www.nols.edu/alumni/leader/96fall/backonbus.shtml; Gary Auxier, "NOLS Then and Now," *Leader* 26, no. 3 (Summer 2011), http://www.scribd.com/doc/63018599/NOLS-Leader-Summer-2011; Tom Reed, "Randy Cerf," *Leader* 16, no. 3 (Summer 2000), http://www.nols.edu/alumni/leader/00summer/35thanniversary/cerfr.shtml.

77. Randy Cerf, quoted in Reed, "Randy Cerf"; Petzoldt, in *High on the Wind Rivers*; Robert Boles, "Eggheads Afield," *Alumnus* 1, no. 2 (May 1971): 4, NOLS Records.

78. Pluma Facinelli, Lander, WY, letter to the editor, *Wyoming State Journal* (Lander), December 1970, quoted in Dernocoeur, *Worthy Expedition*, 92–93; Charles D. Clack, Lander WY, to Petzoldt, October 27, 1970, *Alumnus* 1, no. 2 (May 1971): 2, NOLS Records; Dernocoeur, *Worthy Expedition*, 91–94. For the rift with Wind River Indian Reservation communities, and efforts to mend it, see Dernocoeur, *Worthy Expedition*, 229.

79. "NOLS Limiting Students to 900 during 1971," *Wyoming State Journal* (Lander), February 18, 1971, n.p., Newspaper Clipping Scrapbook, NOLS Records.

80. Paul Petzoldt, "Dear Graduate," *Alumnus* 1, no. 3 (October 1971): 1–2, NOLS Records.

81. Paul Petzoldt "National Outdoor Leadership School, General Information," TS [1968], NOLS Records; National Outdoor Leadership School, *1972 Course Descriptions* [Lander, WY: NOLS, 1972], NOLS Records; National Outdoor Leadership School, *General Course Descriptions, 1972-73* [Lander, WY: NOLS, 1972], NOLS Records.

82. NOLS, *General Course Descriptions, 1972-73*; National Outdoor Leadership School, *The National Outdoor Leadership School: A Field Facility Offering Unusual Educational Opportunity: Summer 1974, Winter 1975*, [Lander, WY: NOLS, 1974], NOLS Records. NOLS efforts mirrored larger shifts away from woodcraft sensibilities and toward minimalist approaches. See James Morton Turner, "From Woodcraft to 'Leave No Trace': Wilderness, Consumerism, and Environmentalism in Twentieth-Century America," *Environmental History* 7, no. 3 (July 2002): 462–84.

83. *Alumnus* 5, no. 4 (December 1975), cover, 1, NOLS Records.

84. Bursts of interest in backpacking accompanied the spikes in camping popularity in the 1920s and 1950s, though it remained a niche pursuit until the 1970s. See, Young, *Heading Out*, 245–65.

85. ORRRC, *National Recreation Survey*, Study Report 19, 33–34, 108; United States, Department of the Interior, National Park Service, *1982-1983 Nationwide Recreation Survey* (Washington, DC: Government Printing Office, 1986), 18. With a US population of 226.5 million in the 1980 census, the estimate of 9 million backpackers and 46 million campers represented approximately 4% and 20% of the total population, respectively.

86. Susan Sands, "Backpacking: 'I Go to the Wilderness to Kick the Man-World Out of Me,'" *New York Times*, May 9, 1971, XX1; Jeffrey L. Marion, "Less Typical Now: A 1970s Retrospective," *Appalachia* 58, no. 1 (Winter/Spring 2007): 18. The National Park System did not begin tracking backcountry overnight camping system-wide until 1979, so earlier figures are illustrative rather than comprehensive. In 1979, backcountry campers numbered 2.4 million. They peaked in 1983 at just under 2.6 million before declining to a low of 1.57 million in 1987. In the following 30 years, backcountry NPS campers have varied between 1.62 and 2.15 million, remaining relatively steady in absolute numbers, while declining as a percentage of the US population (from 0.01% in 1983 to .006% in 2017). US Department of the Interior, National Park Service, "Annual Summary Report, 1904—Last Calendar Year," https://irma.nps.gov/STATS/SSRSReports/National%20Reports/Annual%20Summary%20Report%20(1904%20-%20Last%20Calendar%20Year), (accessed July 15, 2019).

87. Yankelovich, "New Naturalism," 185, 173–76, 185; emphasis from the original, Fletcher, *Romancing the Wild*, 98.

88. *Wilderness Act* of *1964* (16 U.S.C. 1131-1136, 78 Stat. 890), Public Law 88–577 (24 Sep. 1964); Rome, "Give Earth a Chance," 525–54; Turner, *Promise of Wilderness*, 1–13.

89. Colin Fletcher, *The Complete Walker: The Joys and Techniques of Hiking and Backpacking* (New York: Knopf, 1968), 4, 7; Silas Chamberlin, *On the Trail: A History of American Hiking* (New Haven, CT: Yale University Press, 2016), 157–61.

90. Sands, "Backpacking," 7.

91. Diana Sammataro, "Famous Outdoor Leader Teaches Survival is Merely a Matter of Equipment, Training," *Ann Arbor (MI) News*, October 24, 1971, n.p., Newspaper Clipping Scrapbook, NOLS Records; NOLS student, in *High on the Wind Rivers*.

92. Thomas Robertson, *The Malthusian Moment: Global Population Growth and the Birth of American Environmentalism* (New Brunswick, NJ: Rutgers University Press, 2012), 1–4.

93. *Wilderness Act*; Jan Jibben, "'Man Will Commune with Nature," *Wyoming State Journal* (Lander), November 16, 1970, 2, Newspaper Clipping Scrapbook, NOLS Records; Robertson, *Malthusian Moment*, 119–23; Rome, "Give Earth a Chance," 542, 542n48.

94. Paul Erlich, *The Population Bomb* (New York: Sierra Club and Ballantine Books, 1968), 65–66; Robertson, *Malthusian Moment*, 8, 104–19, 143–44; John R. Wilmoth and Patrick Ball, "The Population Debate in American Popular Magazines, 1946-90," *Population and Development Review* 18, no. 4 (December 1992): 649–52. See, for example, the lead photo essay in the same *Life* magazine issue that featured the double-page ad for "Thirty Days to Survival": Ralph Crane, photographer, "Squeezing into the '70s," *Life*, January 9, 1970, 8–15.

95. United States Department of the Interior, Office of the Secretary, *The Race for Inner Space: A Special Report to the Nation* (Washington, DC: n.p., 1964) 5–7, 15, 69. Frustration with crowded parks and fraying social cooperation formed a strong and growing undercurrent in camping publications, a tradition tracing back at least to the radical proposal by conservationist Bernard DeVoto to close the national parks until the federal government provided adequate funding for staff, infrastructure, and ecological protection. Bernard DeVoto, "Let's Close the National Parks," *Harper's Magazine* 207, no. 1241 (October 1953): 49–52.

96. "A Special Issue on Americans at Play," *Life*, September 3, 1971, 8–9. Fear of cultural and generational conflict peaked in response to the so-called Stoneman Meadow Riot at Yosemite, where tensions between youthful campers and park rangers boiled over into violence and led to stricter law enforcement practices in the NPS. Michael Childers, "The Stoneman Meadow Riots and Law Enforcement in Yosemite National Park," *Forest History Today* (Spring 2017): 28–34.

97. Wilbur F. LaPage and Gerald L. Cole, US Forest Service, US Department of Agriculture, Northeastern Forest Experiment Station, *1978 National Camping Market Survey*, Forest Service Research Paper, NE-450, (Broomall, PA: USFS, 1979), 30–31. One-third of those holding negative images of camping mentioned

"inconvenience"; one-quarter of those holding positive images listed "uncrowded" as a positive feature, the least of the twelve choices.

98. *Wilderness Act*; Fletcher, *Complete Walker*, 310, 320.

99. Farrell Grehan, photographer, "Six Wild Havens to Explore," *Life*, September 3, 1971, 52–59; Karen and Derek Craighead, with Sam Abell, photographer, "Yellowstone at 100: A Walk Through the Wilderness," *National Geographic* 141, no. 5 (May 1972): 580, 584, 602.

100. Dill Cole, illustration, in *Wilderness U.S.A.*, ed. Seymour L. Fishbein (Washington, DC: National Geographic Society, 1973), 328; Harvey Manning, "Appendix: A Backpacking Primer," in *Wilderness U.S.A.*, 329.

101. William Kelmsley, "Why Backpacker? A Note from the Publisher," *Backpacker* 1, no. 1 (Spring 1973): 4–5; William Kelmsley Jr., "How the 1970s Backpacking Boom Burst upon Us," *Appalachia* 58, no. 1 (Winter/Spring 2007): 21–28.

102. Emphasis from the original, Kelmsley, "Why Backpacker?" 4.

103. Paul Garguillo, Richmond Hill, NY, and Ronald Jackson, Mt. Vernon, NY, in "Letters," *Backpacker* 1, no. 1 (Spring 1973): 6. For positive endorsements, see Dale Jones, Northwest Coordinator, Friends of the Earth, Seattle, WA; and, John L. Ragle (no address), in "Letters," *Backpacker* 1, no. 1 (Spring 1973): 6.

104. H. B. "Doc" Smith, "People," *Alumnus* 1, no. 1 (February 1971): 2, NOLS Records; Ken Goddard, letter to the editor, *Alumnus* 1, no. 2 (May 1971): 2–3, NOLS Records.

105. Emphasis from the original, Paul Petzoldt, "Commentary," *Alumnus* 3, no. 1 (May 1973): 3, NOLS Records; Molly Absolon, "Paul Tells His Story," *Leader* 11, no. 4 (Fall 1995), http://www.nols.edu/alumni/leader/95fall/paultellshisstory.shtml.

106. Petzoldt, "Commentary," 3–4; Steve Gipe, "Letter to the Editor," *Alumnus* (December 1975): 4–5, NOLS Records.

107. Petzoldt, "Dear Graduate," 1; Petzoldt, "Commentary," 3; "NOLS Conservation Practices," *Outdoor Education Bulletin* (Summer 1975): 4, NOLS Records.

108. NOLS, *General Course Descriptions, 1972–73*; "Publications," *Alumnus* 3, no. 2 (December 1973): 8, NOLS Records.

109. Petzoldt, *Wilderness Handbook*, 13–14, 57, 229.

110. Petzoldt, *Wilderness Handbook*, 107–108.

111. Petzoldt, *Wilderness Handbook*, 108, 227–29.

112. Paul Petzoldt, with Raye Carleson Ringholz, *The New Wilderness Handbook*, revised and updated (New York: Norton, 1984), 21–25.

113. Kelmsley, "Why Backpacker?" 4; Turner, "From Woodcraft," 475.

114. Petzoldt, *Wilderness Handbook*, 229–31, 235–36.

115. Ringholz, *On Belay*, 211; Petzoldt, in *High on the Wind Rivers*; *Outdoor Education Bulletin* (Summer 1975): 1, NOLS Records; Turner, "From Woodcraft," 473. The newsletter returned to the original title *Alumnus* in the next issue, December 1975, continuing until November 1984, when it was renamed *The Leader*.

116. Note from the Editors, *Alumnus* 5, no. 4 (December 1975): 3, NOLS Records; Dernocoeur, *Worthy Expedition,* 104–19.

117. Paul Petzoldt, letter to NOLS Graduates, December 1970, NOLS papers; "NOLS—OLS," *Alumnus* 1, no. 1 (February 1971): 5–6, NOLS Records; Dernocoeur, *Worthy Expedition,* 72–73, 82–83; "NOLS Equipment Timeline," *The Leader* 16, no.3 (Summer 2000), http://www.nols.edu/alumni/leader/ 00summer/35thanniversary/equipmenttimeline.shtml. Petzoldt suggested that one reason he started Outdoor Leadership Supply was to protect NOLS, a non-profit educational institution, from engaging "in the equipment manufacturing and selling business." Petzoldt, letter to NOLS Graduates, December 1970. For details on the financial issues see Dernocoeur, *Worthy Expedition,* 72–83, 106–12; Ringholz, *On Belay,* 200–11.

118. "Paul Petzoldt Wilderness Equipment" Catalog, [1975], 1–2, NOLS Records (hereafter PPWE Catalog); NOLS, "School History," *General Course Descriptions, 1972-73;* Dernocoeur, *Worthy Expedition,* 81–83.

119. Petzoldt, *Wilderness Handbook,* 52–53, 57; Turner, "From Woodcraft," 473–74.

120. Kirk, *Counterculture Green,* 4; Stewart Brand, ed., *The Last Whole Earth Catalog* (Menlo Park, CA and New York: Portola Institute and Random House, 1971), 257.

121. Yvon Chouinard, Tom Frost, and Doug Robinson, *Chouinard Equipment* (Santa Barbara: Sandollar Press, 1972), 2–3; Kirk, *Counterculture Green,* 199–203. Doug Tompkins, founder of North Face in 1966, and Royal Robbins, who founded an outdoor clothing company in 1969, were friends and fellow climbers with Chouinard and Frost.

122. Galen Rowell, review, "*Chouinard Equipment,* by Yvon Chouinard, Tom Frost and Doug Robinson. Santa Barbara, California: Sandollar Press, 1972, 72 pages, $.50," *American Alpine Journal* 18, no. 2, issue 47 (1973): 522–23.

123. Paul Petzoldt, "Dear Friend," PPWE Catalog, 1; Kirk, *Counterculture Green,* 1–5, 29–30.

124. Petzoldt, "Dear Friend," PPWE Catalog, 5, 7. For discussion of 1960s-era counter-intuitive advertising strategies, see Frank, *Conquest of Cool,* 52–73.

125. Brand, *Last Whole Earth,* 2; Kelmsley, "Why Backpacker," 5; "Pick of the Tents: Evaluations," *Backpacker* 1, no. 3 (Autumn 1973): 73; Turner, "From Woodcraft," 475. In cultivating this kind of reader community, *Backpacker* emulated the success of the Rodale Press, which had become a magazine publishing behemoth, with such popular titles as *Organic Gardening* and *Prevention.* See Andrew N. Case, *Organic Profit: Rodale and the Making of Marketplace Environmentalism* (Seattle: University of Washington Press, 2018).

126. "Pick of the Packs," *Backpacker* 1, no. 1 (Spring 1973): 3, 48.

127. Maurice H. Pomeranz, "Backpacking Becomes Big Business," *Backpacker* 2, no. 1 (Spring 1974): 33–36; Stephen Silha, "Focus on Boom in Backpacking," *Christian Science Monitor,* April 27, 1973, 1.

128. Gregory L. Simon and Peter S. Alagona, "Contradictions at the Confluence of Commerce, Consumption and Conservation; or, an REI Shopper Camps in the Forest, Does Anyone Notice?" *Geoforum* 45 (2013): 325–36.

129. John Hart, *Walking Softly in the Wilderness: The Sierra Club Guide to Backpacking* (San Francisco: The Sierra Club, 1977); Laura and Guy Waterman, *Backwoods Ethics: Environmental Concerns for Hikers and Campers* (Washington, DC: Stone Wall Press, 1979). Along with an updated Boy Scout handbook in 1972, the USFS, the NPS, and the Bureau of Land Management also released new informational pamphlets during this era with such titles as *Wilderness Manners, Wilderness Ethics, Minimum Impact Camping,* and *No-Trace Camping.* See Turner, "From Woodcraft," 473–74; Marion, "Less Typical Now," 30; Jeffrey L. Marion and Scott E. Reid, "Development of the U.S. Leave No Trace Program: An Historical Perspective," in *Enjoyment and Understanding of the Natural Heritage,* ed. M. B. Usher (Edinburgh: Her Majesty's Stationery Office, Scottish National Heritage, 2001), 81–92; Dernocoeur, *Worthy Expedition,* 184–86.

130. Hart, *Walking Softly,* 29–31, 33–36. See also Laura and Guy Waterman, "The 'Clean Camping' Crusade," *Appalachia* 42, no. 4 (June 1979): 87–88, 91; Waterman, *Backwoods Ethics,* 3, 51–54.

131. Petzoldt, *New Wilderness Handbook,* 14–15, 267–68; Paul Petzoldt, "Leadership: The Most Dangerous Game," *Backpacker* 9, no. 2 (April/May, 1981): 21–22; Dernocoeur, *Worthy Expedition,* 114–18, 130; Ringholz, *On Belay,* 200–208.

132. Hart, *Walking Softly,* 17; Kelmsley, "How the 1970s," 22; Wilderness Education Association, https://www.weainfo.org/ (accessed December 26, 2018).

133. Hart, *Walking Softly,* 29–31, 33–36, 70, 87; Turner, "From Woodcraft," 473–76; Jennifer Price, *Flight Maps: Adventures with Nature in Modern America* (New York: Basic Books, 1999); Rachel Gross, "From Buckskin to Gore-Tex: Consumption as a Path to Mastery in Twentieth-Century American Wilderness Recreation" (PhD Diss., University of Wisconsin, 2017).

134. Petzoldt, *New Wilderness Handbook,* 147; Ringholz, *On Belay,* 207–13.

135. Elizabeth Royte, "Heigh-Ho, It's Off to the Woods We Go," *Outside Magazine,* Camping Special (April 1997), https://www.outsideonline.com/1840231/heigh-ho-its-woods-we-go; Ringholz, *On Belay,* 219–26; Dernocoeur, *Worthy Expedition,* 261–63.

136. Emphasis from the original, *Leave "No Trace" Land Ethics* (Produced cooperatively by USDA/Forest Service, USDI/National Park Service, USDI/BLM, 1987), 3.

137. Turner, "From Woodcraft," 477–79; Marion and Reid, "Development of the U.S. Leave No Trace," 81–92; David N. Cole, "Leave No Trace: How it Came to Be," (2018), https://leopold.wilderness.net/history-of-wilderness-science/History%20Papers/default.php; "A Short History of Leave No Trace," Leave No Trace Center for Outdoor Ethics, https://lnt.org/blog/short-history-leave-no-trace (accessed September 28, 2018).

138. Simon and Alagona, "Contradictions at the Confluence," 325–36; Jacob Gallagher, "8 Things You've Always Wondered About Fleece Jackets," *Wall Street Journal*, October 31, 2019, https://www.wsj.com/articles/8-things-youve-always-wondered-about-fleece-jackets-11572548462.

139. Kirk, *Counterculture Green*, 203–209; Hilary Greenbaum and Dana Rubinstein, "The Evolution of Fleece, From Scratchy to Snuggie," *New York Times*, November 25, 2011, Magazine, 28; James Morton Turner, "'The Specter of Environmentalism': Wilderness, Environmental Politics, and the Evolution of the New Right," *Journal of American History* 96, no. 1 (June 2009): 123–48.

140. Marianne Bertrand and Emir Kamenica, "Coming Apart? Cultural Distances in the United States Over Time," National Bureau of Economic Research, Working Paper 24771 (June 2018), http://www.nber.org/papers/w24771, 38, A-25-A-26; Richard White, "'Are You an Environmentalist or Do You Work for a Living?': Work and Nature," in Cronon, *Uncommon Ground*, 171–85.

CHAPTER 6

1. Major groups collaborating on the initial Occupy Wall Street protest in New York included U.S. Day of Rage, Anonymous, New Yorkers Against, and the NYC General Assembly. Laura Breeston, "The Ballerina and the Bull: Adbusters Micah White on 'The Last Great Social Movement,'" *The Link,* October 11, 2011, http://thelinknewspaper.ca/article/1951; "Reasons to Love New York 2011: 2. Because It Started Here," *New York Magazine*, December 11, 2011, http://nymag.com/news/articles/reasonstoloveny/2011/occupy-wall-street/; Nathan Schneider, "Occupy Wall Street: FAQ," *The Nation*, September 29, 2011, http://www.thenation.com/article/163719/occupy-wall-street-faq.

2. The Freedom Plaza encampment had been planned by "veteran antiwar activists" long before the Occupy Wall Street campaign. A movement called "October 2001/ Stop the Machine" had applied for a permit to "protest the 10th anniversary of the start of the war in Afghanistan," and began its encampment within a few days of the Occupy DC encampment in McPherson Square, led largely by a younger crowd. "Eventually, the Freedom Plaza group adopted the Occupy moniker" and participated in some joint events, but the two groups were never fully aligned. Meredith Somers, "For D.C. Occupy Camps, It's Divided They Stand," *Washington (DC) Times*, January 20, 2012, A1.

3. Oral argument at 5:57, Clark v. CCNV, 468 U.S. 288 (1982), available at: https://apps.oyez.org/player/#/burger8/oral_argument_audio/19291.

4. Transcript of Record at 4, Quaker Action Group, et. al., and Vietnam Veterans Against the War v. Morton, C.A., No. 688–69 (D.D.C. 1971) (hereafter *VVAW v. Morton I*), in Folder 201748-008-0015, Operation Dewey Canyon III, Vietnam Veterans Against the War Records, 1967-2006, Wisconsin Historical Society, ProQuest History Vault (hereafter VVAW Records); Archie Finagin, quoted in

B. D. Colen, "At Night, Veterans Voice Inner Feelings," *Washington Post,* April 23, 1971, A7.

5. Godfrey E. Rolf, San Jose, CA to President Lyndon Johnson, June 7, 1968, Folder 101120-005-0692, Johnson Administration's Response to Anti-Vietnam War Activities Collection, Part 2: White House Central Files, ProQuest History Vault (hereafter Johnson White House Files); Alfred H. Dorstewitz, President, Village of LaGrange Park, Illinois, to Johnson, May 24, 1968, Folder 101120-005-0281, Johnson White House Files.

6. US Congress, House Subcommittee on Health Care, District of Columbia, Census and the National Archives, *Hearing on McPherson Square: Who Made the Decision to Allow Indefinite Camping in the Park, Focusing on the Impact of the Ongoing 'Occupy' Encampment on Public Health and Public Safety Inside and Outside the Park,* 112th Cong. (January 24, 2012), (questions by Trey Gowdy, R-SC); "Occupy Washington, D.C., McPherson Square Permit Decision," video, C-SPAN, January 24, 2012, https://www.c-span.org/video/?303866-1/occupy-washington-dc-mcpherson-square-permit-decision.

7. "#OCCUPYWALLSTREET: A Shift in Revolutionary Tactics," Adbusters Blog, *Adbusters,* July 13, 2011, http://www.adbusters.org/blogs/adbusters-blog/occupywallstreet.html; Ben Davis, "How a Canadian Culture Magazine Helped Spark Occupy Wall Street," *Artinfo,* October 5, 2011, http://www.artinfo.com/news/story/38786/how-a-canadian-culture-magazine-helped-spark-occupy-wall-street/. Some also cited as inspirations the tent-based protests by youth movements in Spain and Israel that followed that summer. *Adbusters* had pursued other "culture jamming" strategies before, sponsoring events such as an anti-consumerist "Buy Nothing Day" and a "Carnivalesque Rebellion"—neither of which had as much success tapping into American cultural consciousness as Occupy. William Yardley, "The Branding of the Occupy Movement," *New York Times,* November 28, 2011, B1.

8. Schneider, "Occupy Wall Street: FAQ"; Sarah Kunstler, "The Right to Occupy— Occupy Wall Street and the First Amendment," *Fordham Urban Law Journal* 989, 39, no. 4 (2012): 989–93. Regarding the question of demands see, for example, Meredith Hoffman, "Protestors Debate What Demands, if Any, to Make," *New York Times,* October 17, 2011, A19.

9. "#OCCUPYWALLSTREET: Yes We Camp," *Adbusters,* August 16, 2011, http://www.adbusters.org/content/occupywallstreet-yes-we-camp; Daryl Lang, "The Poster Art of Occupy Wall Street," *Breaking Copy,* November 20, 2011, http://www.breakingcopy.com/the-poster-art-of-occupy-wall-street.

10. Tavia Nyong'o, "The Scene of Occupation," *TDR: The Drama Review* 56, no. 4 (Winter 2012): 137–38; Kunstler, "The Right to Occupy," 991n7, 1017n166. Well before Occupy appeared on the scene, Rothman argued that "the battles over private and public space in American society [had] become the terrain on which the national definition is worked and reworked." Hal Rothman, "Gates, Barriers, and the Rise of Affinity: Parsing Public-Private Space in Postindustrial America," in *Public*

Culture: Diversity, Democracy, and Community in the United States, ed. Marguerite S. Shaffer (Philadelphia: University of Pennsylvania Press, 2008), 222.

11. Paul Courson, "Federal Authorities Set to Crack Down on Camping at 'Occupy DC' sites," *Cable News Network*, January 27, 2012, http://www.cnn.com/2012/01/27/us/camping-crackdown/index.html.

12. Joe Richman and Samara Freemark, "The Bonus Army: How A Protest Led To The GI Bill," Radio Diaries, *National Public Radio*, November 11, 2011, http://www.npr.org/2011/11/11/142224795/the-bonus-army-how-a-protest-led-to-the-gi-bill; "The Rachel Maddow Show for October 26, 2011," October 27, 2011, *NBC News*, http://www.nbcnews.com/id/45065858/ns/msnbc-rachel_maddow_show/; Michael Lind, "Protests that Worked," *New York Times*, November 16, 2011, http://www.nytimes.com/roomfordebate/2011/11/16/does-congress-hear-occupy-wall-street/protests-that-worked; Michael Hiltzik, "Occupy Wall Street shifts from protest to policy phase," *Los Angeles Times*, October 12, 2011, B1, B4.

13. US Congress, *Hearing on McPherson Square* (statement of Jonathan B. Jarvis).

14. For a history of the Farmer's Vigil, see John Dinse and William P. Browne, "The Emergence of the American Agriculture Movement, 1977-1979," *Great Plains Quarterly* 5, no. 4 (Fall 1985): 221–35; Sam Brasch, "When Tractors Invaded D.C.," *Modern Farmer*, February 5, 2014, https://modernfarmer.com/2014/02/living-legacy-d-c-tractorcade-35-years-later/; *Tractorcade to D.C.*, Kinsley Public Library, http://kinsleylibrary.info/tractorcade-to-dc/ (accessed March 8, 2019); "History of the American Agriculture Movement," American Agriculture Movement, Inc., http://aaminc.org/history.htm (accessed March 8, 2019).

15. Lucy G. Barber, *Marching on Washington: The Forging of an American Political Tradition* (Berkeley: University of California Press, 2002); Tunney Lee and Lawrence Vale, "Resurrection City: Washington DC, 1968," *Thresholds* 41 (Special Issue: Revolution!), (Spring 2013): 114.

16. John Kelly, "Before Occupy D.C., There was Resurrection City," *Washington Post*, December 4, 2011, C3.

17. Martin Luther King Jr., [statement], December 4, 1967, Atlanta, GA, Folder 001569-028-0168, Records of the Poor People's Campaign, Southern Christian Leadership Conference Collection, 1954-1970, ProQuest History Vault (hereafter PPC Records); Walter Rugaber, "Dr. King Planning to Disrupt Capital in Drive for Jobs," *New York Times*, December 5, 1967, 1, 32; Gordon K. Mantler, *Power to the Poor: Black-Brown Coalition and the Fight for Economic Justice, 1960–1974* (Chapel Hill: University of North Carolina Press, 2013), 94–97, 268n2.

18. "Statement of Purpose: Poor People's Campaign, Washington, DC," ca. March 1968, Folder 001569-028-0540, PPC Records; Anthony R. Henry to Hosea L. Williams, SCLC, March 23, 1968, Folder 001569-026-0592, PPC Records; Bill Wingell, "'If This Campaign Succeeds, All Our Dreams Will Succeed,'" [newspaper clipping], May 5, 1968, Folder 001569-027-1053, PPC Records. Also, see Mantler, *Power to the Poor*, 94–97, 113–19, 121–22, 136. The original name,

"New City of Hope," was scrapped after a hospital in Los Angeles with the same name complained. "Resurrection City" likely emerged in reference to King's death, though the origins of that remain unclear.

19. Mantler, *Power to the Poor*, 127–28, 281n29; Arthur M. Schlesinger Jr., *The Crisis of the Old Order: 1919–1933: The Age of Roosevelt*, (New York: Mariner Books, 2003, c. 1957), 1:257–65; Ben A. Franklin, "U.S. Issues Permit to March of Poor," *New York Times*, May 11, 1968, 33; Lee and Vale, "Resurrection City," 113–14.

20. Josie Williams, Marks, MS, quoted in Faith Berry, "The Anger and Problems and Sickness of the Poor of the Whole Nation Were in This One Shantytown," *New York Times,* July 7, 1968, SM5, 19; "Nation: Plague After Plague," *Time*, May 31, 1968, 16–17; Jill Freedman, "Old News: Resurrection City," JillFreedman.com Blog, October 12, 2015, http://www.jillfreedman.com/blog/2015/10/12/qmr7j9 af7d4pb44dopsyy6nmtm53tn; Press release, April 14, 1968, Folder 001569-028-0168, PPC Records; Damien Cave and Darcy Everleigh, "In 1968, a 'Resurrection City' of Tents, Erected to Fight Poverty," *New York Times,* February 19, 2017, A11.

21. Calvin Trillin, "U.S. Journal: Resurrection City—Metaphors," *New Yorker*, June 15, 1968, 71; Cave and Everleigh, "In 1968"; Mantler, *Power to the Poor*, 122–23, 136.

22. Mantler, *Power to the Poor*, 140, 150–51. Mantler argued that many of the journalists covering Resurrection City did not have experience reporting on recent Civil Rights Movement actions and its loose organizational style and "thus were overly distracted by logistics"—or the lack of them. See Mantler, *Power to the Poor*, 150–58.

23. Ellen C. Wagner, Highland, MD, to Johnson, May 28, 1968, Folder 101120-005-0281, Johnson White House Files; emphasis from the original, Jan Coor-Pender Dodge, Oakland, CA, to Johnson, May 1968, Folder 101120-005-0281, Johnson White House Files.

24. Emphasis from the original, Tommy Taylor, Austin, TX to Johnson, June 1968, Folder 101120-005-0281, Johnson White House Files; Dorstewitz to Johnson, May 24, 1968.

25. Rolf to Johnson, June 7, 1968; "FACT SHEET—CAMPING WHILE VISITING WASHINGTON, D.C.," encl. George B. Hartzog Jr., Director, Department of Interior to Senator Margaret Chase Smith, June 3, 1968, Folder 101120-005-0281, Johnson White House Files. The Fact Sheet also specified that the permit required the PPC to restore the area, that all structures were owned by the SCLC, and that the federal government was not providing any "services or utility facilities" at Resurrection City.

26. Dorstewitz to Johnson, May 24, 1968; Mrs. J.B. Morris, Summerville, SC, to Johnson, April 30, 1968, Folder 101120-003-0503, Johnson White House Files.

27. "Poor Pledge to Step up Pace of Demonstration," [clipping, n.d.], Folder 001569-027-1053, PPC Records; Mantler, *Power to the Poor*, 174–75.

28. Emphasis from the original, Agnes Smith, Santa Ana, CA, to Johnson, June 3, 1968, Folder 101120-005-0281, Johnson White House Files; Masumi Izumi, "Rumors of 'American Concentration Camps': The Emergency Detention Act and the Public

Fear of Political Repression, 1966–1971," *Doshisha Studies in Language and Culture* 4, no. 4 (March, 2002): 737–65.

29. Jesse Jackson, "Resurrection City: The dream. . . The accomplishments," *Ebony* 23, no. 12 (October 1968): 66, 74; Kelly, "Before Occupy"; Mantler, *Power to the Poor*, 221. After leaving Washington, some protestors went on to set up miniature versions of Resurrection City in different sites, from rural Alabama to Olympia, Washington, also later evicted. Mantler, *Power to the Poor*, 182–83.

30. US Congress, *Hearing on McPherson Square* (testimony of Timothy Zick, Cabell Research Professor of Law, William and Mary School of Law).

31. David Thorne and George Butler, eds., *The New Soldier* (New York: Macmillan, 1971), 8–10, 26–31; Barber, *Marching on Washington,* 182–90; John Prados, *Vietnam: The History of an Unwinnable War* (Lawrence: University Press of Kansas, 2009), 1–2.

32. Barber, *Marching on Washington*, 188–90; Prados, *Vietnam*, 2–6, 424–25.

33. Mitchell Melich, Acting Secretary of the Interior, to Michael Phelan, Washington, D.C., April 15, 1971, Folder: 201748-008-0015, VVAW Records.

34. Paul W. Valentine, "Veterans Denied Camp on Mall," *Washington Post*, April 16, 1971, C7; Barber *Marching on Washington*, 190.

35. J. Y. Smith, "U.S. District Judge George L. Hart Jr. Dies at 78," *Washington Post*, May 22, 1984, B6.

36. Barber, *Marching on Washington*, 187–88; Quaker Action Group v. Morton, 460 F.2d 854 (D.C. Cir. 1971), (hereafter *Quaker Action III*), at paragraph 17; Quaker Action Group v. Hickel, Secretary of Interior, 421 F.2d 1111 (D.C. Cir. 1969), (hereafter *Quaker Action I*); Quaker Action Group v. Hickel, 429 F.2d 185 (D.C. Cir. 1970), (hereafter, *Quaker Action II*); Quaker Action Group v. Morton, Secretary of Interior, 516 F.2d 717 (D.C. Cir. 1975), (hereafter *Quaker Action IV*). *Quaker Action III* and *IV* both include a helpful history and summary of the preceding cases. At least one piece of evidence introduced at a later trial suggested that the government may have allowed the 1971 VVAW encampment to proceed specifically "as a means of monitoring" the group and its potential for other "disruptive acts" of protest. Vietnam Veterans Against the War/Winter Soldier Organization v. Morton, Secretary of Interior, 506 F. 2d 53 (D.C. Cir. 1974), note 19 (hereafter *VVAW v. Morton II*).

37. Transcript of Record at 4–5, *VVAW v. Morton I*. Hart had issues with the idea of a "simulated campsite" as well, and worried about any efforts at attempting to reproduce conditions in Vietnam, which the VVAW intended to symbolize rather than recreate in the literal fashion that Hart introduced to absurdist effects.

38. Transcript of Record at 8–9, *VVAW v. Morton I*. Kerry joined the VVAW in 1969, following a brief but consequential service in Vietnam.

39. Transcript of Record at 10, 29–30, *VVAW v. Morton I*. The VVAW lawyer quoted here was Ramsey Clark, who had been Johnson's Attorney General during Resurrection City. He now was a lead counselor in the defense of the veterans'

right of encampment and would become a key advisor to the VVAW leadership throughout the Dewey Canyon protest. For discussion of the VVAW and veterans as citizens with special standing, see Barber, *Marching on Washington,* 184–85.

40. Transcript of Record at 10, 25, *VVAW v. Morton I.*

41. Transcript of Record at 11, 15, 21, 25, *VVAW v. Morton I.*

42. Transcript of Record at 10, 21, 40–41, *VVAW v. Morton I.*

43. Kerry, quoted in Sanford J. Ungar, "Vets' Camping Plea Refused," *Washington Post,* April 17, 1971, B3.

44. Memorandum of Points and Authorities in Support of Motion for Summary Reversal at 2, 13–14, Quaker Action Group v. Morton, No. 71-1276 (D.C. Cir. 19 April 1971); *Quaker Action III,* note 5; Morton v. Quaker Action Group, 402 U.S. 926 (1971); *VVAW v. Morton II,* paragraph 9; Sanford J. Ungar and William L. Claiborne, "Vets' Camp on Mall Banned by Burger," *Washington Post,* April 21, 1971, A1, A12; Paul W. Valentine, "Vets March on Hill, Protest Their War," *Washington Post,* April 20, 1971, A1; Barber, *Marching on Washington,* 190.

45. Henry Aubin, "Vets Defiant Over Ban," *Washington Post,* April 21, 1971, A14; Thorne and Butler, *New Soldier,* 76–87; "Vets Disobey Court Order, Sleep on Mall," *Washington Post,* April 22, 1971, A1; Barber, *Marching on Washington,* 191–93.

46. Marquis Childs, "Veterans' Camp: What They Seek," *Washington Post,* April 23, 1971, A23; Carl Bernstein, "Viet Veterans Camped on Mall Resemble Basic Training Outfit," *Washington Post,* April 22, 1971, A14; Senator Hart quoted in "Vets Disobey Court Order"; Barber, *Marching on Washington,* 193–95.

47. Colen, "At Night"; Finagin, quoted in Colen, "At Night"; Prados, *Vietnam,* 7–9, 425.

48. William L. Claiborne, "Police Move Quickly, Gently In Arresting Protesting Vets," *Washington Post,* April 23, 1971, A6; Barber, *Marching on Washington,* 190; Prados, *Vietnam,* 9.

49. William L. Claiborne and Sanford J. Ungar, "Judge Lifts Ban on Vets, Scolds U.S.," *Washington Post,* April 23, 1971, A1; Ken W. Clawson, "Justice Dept, Admits Misjudgment on Veterans' Camp-Out," *Washington Post,* April 24, 1971, A12; Ivan C. Goldman, "'Good Vibrations' Fill Park As Young Protesters Gather," *Washington Post,* April 24, 1971, A12.

50. Sanford J. Ungar and Carl Bernstein, "Veterans Turn Minor Prelude Into a Major Antiwar Event," *Washington Post,* April 24, 1971, A7.

51. *Quaker Action IV* at paragraphs 724, 725, 729.

52. Complaint, Henke v. Dept. of Interior, Civil Action No. 2011-2155 (D.D.C. 2012), at paragraph 12, National Park Service Documents on Occupy Movement, https:// archive.org/details/NPS-Occupy-FOIA (accessed April 11, 2019) (hereafter NPS Occupy Documents).

53. National Park Service, "Help Us Preserve McPherson Square," McPherson Use Handout, October 26, 2011, NPS Occupy Documents.

54. Complaint, *Henke v. Interior;* Rebecca Schneider, "It Seems As If . . . I Am Dead: Zombie Capitalism and Theatrical Labor," *TDR: The Drama Review* 56, no. 4 (Winter 2012): 153; Nicholas Ridout and Rebecca Schneider, "Precarity and Performance: An Introduction," *TDR: The Drama Review* 56, no. 4 (Winter 2012): 5–6; Lauren Berlant, *Cruel Optimism* (Durham, NC: Duke University Press, 2011), 192.

55. Tyler Kingkade, Hayley Miller, and Saki Knafo, "Occupy Wall Street and Homelessness," *Huffington Post*, November 27, 2011, http://www.huffingtonpost.com/2011/11/27/occupy-wall-street-and-homeless-evictions-cities_n_1111094.html; Tamara Audi, "Protesters, Homeless Share Turf—and Tension," *Wall Street Journal*, November 1, 2011 https://www.wsj.com/articles/SB10001424052970204394804577012293234158470. Henke's complaint indicated that the McPherson Square encampment "averaged approximately 100 participants staying overnight at the tent city, with fewer during the day, since many of the regular participants work and/or attend school during the day." Complaint, *Henke v. Interior* at paragraph 19.

56. US Congress, *Hearing on McPherson Square* (questions by Danny Davis, D-IL, and testimony of Jarvis).

57. Martin Hutchinson, "Rebels Needing a Cause," *Reuters/Breaking Views*, October 12, 2011, http://www.breakingviews.com/occupy-wall-street-may-share-fate-of-coxeys-army/1610689.article; Barber, *Marching on Washington*, 22.

58. One local blogger did link the two: Martin Austermuhle, "Four Months In, Echoes of Reaganville at McPherson Square," *DCist*, February 1, 2012, https://dcist.com/story/12/02/01/at-mcpherson-square-echoes-of-reaga/. Austermuhle's blog was reposted as, "Echoes of Reaganville at McPherson Square," on the online edition of the *Washington Post,* February 1, 2012, https://www.washingtonpost.com/pb/blogs/all-opinions-are-local/post/echoes-of-reaganville-at-mcpherson-square/2011/04/25/gIQAFs9whQ_blog.html.

59. Associated Press, "'Reaganville' Camp Erected to Protest Plight of the Poor," *New York Times*, November 27, 1981, B14; Cynthia J. Bogard, *Seasons Such as These: How Homelessness Took Shape in America* (New York: Walter DeGruyter, 2003), 9–18, 47–48; Kathleen K. Olson, "Homelessness as Political Theater: The Community for Creative Non-Violence and Symbolic Speech," *Free Speech Yearbook* 40, no. 1 (2002): 108–109; Adam Sirgany, "Remembering Mitch Snyder," *National Coalition for the Homeless*, http://www.nationalhomeless.org/news/RememberingMitchSnyder.html (accessed March 25, 2019).

60. Associated Press, "6 Held as Tents Near White House Are Torn Down," *New York Times*, November 28, 1981, 8; UPI, "Protest Group Gets a Permit to Put Tents by White House," *New York Times*, December 1, 1981, A25; Bogard, *Seasons Such as These*, 48–49; CCNV v. Watt, 670 F.2d 1213 (D.C. Cir. 1982), (hereafter *CCNV v. Watt I*).

61. Peter H. Rossi, "The Old Homeless and the New Homeless in Historical Perspective," *American Psychologist* 45, no. 8 (August 1990): 954–56; Todd DePastino, *Citizen*

Hobo: How a Century of Homelessness Shaped America (Chicago: University of Chicago Press, 2003), 220–35; Ronald Tobey, Charles Wetherell, and Jay Brigham, "Moving Out and Settling In: Residential Mobility, Home Owning, and the Public Enframing of Citizenship, 1921–1950," *American Historical Review* 95, no. 5 (December 1990): 1395–422. The definition of transients shifted away from physical lack of housing to living outside family units—a more potent indicator of the era's dominant nuclear family paradigm. The "disaffiliation" of homeless men did provoke some anxiety during the Cold War decades, but it did not tend to appear in recreational camping literature.

62. DePastino, *Citizen Hobo*, 247–72; Bogard, *Seasons Such as These*, 1–4; David Wagner, *Checkerboard Square: Culture and Resistance in a Homeless Community* (New York: Routledge, 1993), 4–5.

63. Anthony Marcus, *Where Have All the Homeless Gone? The Making and Unmaking of a Crisis* (New York: Berghahn Books, 2005); Bogard, *Seasons Such as These*, 1–4; Wagner, *Checkerboard Square*, 4–5; DePastino, *Citizen Hobo*, 247–72. "Street people" in particular tended to reference those homeless who were "mentally disturbed." For discussion of changing terminology, see Bogard, *Seasons Such as These*, 66; DePastino, *Citizen Hobo*, 252, 256. For the trend of "shelterization," see Wagner, *Checkerboard Square*, 31-36, 94-168.

64. For discussions of urban space and design and the homeless, see Mike Davis, *City of Quartz: Excavating the Future in Los Angeles* (New York: Vintage, 1990); Joanne Passaro, *The Unequal Homeless: Men on the Streets, Women in Their Place* (New York: Routledge, 1996); Paul Groth, *Living Downtown: The History of Residential Hotels in the United States* (Berkeley: University of California Press, 1994), 16–17.

65. Reagan, quoted in Marcus, *Where Have All*, 135; Wagner, *Checkerboard Square*, 17–18; Talmadge Wright, *Out of Place: Homeless Mobilizations, Subcities and Contested Landscapes* (Albany: SUNY Press, 1997), 4–7; Bogard, *Seasons Such as These*, 127–28. Joanne Passaro found that many of New York's homeless understood their condition as at least in part an escape from oppressive social roles, or a "haven *from* heartless homes." Emphasis added, Passaro, *Unequal Homeless*, 63, 36.

66. Associated Press, "Sleeping Banned in Tent City," *New York Times*, December 4, 1982, A34.

67. *CCNV v. Watt I*; Olson, "Homelessness as Political Theater," 112.

68. *CCNV v. Watt I* (MacKinnon, Memorandum).

69. *VVAW v. Morton II*, paragraph 6. The matter in *VVAW v. Morton II* centered on a plan for an encampment on the Mall, July 1-4, 1974, to call for "unconditional amnesty" for draft resisters, increased veterans' services and benefits, and a complete termination of "American military presence in Southeast Asia." The Appeals Court chided both the government and the District Court, which had initially allowed the camping, for failing "to defer to" the Supreme Court's clear judgment on the same issue from 1971. The fact that the government failed to enforce Judge

Hart's order, later confirmed by the Supreme Court, made it no less binding as legal precedent. Chief Judge David Bazelon, however, expressed concern about overreliance on the 1971 Supreme Court summary judgment, issued without explanatory opinions. *VVAW v. Morton II* resulted in a clear decision banning the encampment, but left the government in a muddle, as multiple Judges castigated it for "unconstitutionally vague" regulations, a "biased construction of the undefined term 'camping,'" and polices issued without "considered legislative or even administrative judgment." *VVAW v. Morton II*, note 3, paragraph 2.

70. United States v. Abney, 534 F.2d 984 (D.C. Cir. 1976); *CCNV v. Watt I*, note 26. In *U.S. v. Abney*, the D.C. Court of Appeals struck down some NPS camping prohibitions following the multiple arrests of Stacy Abney, a World War II veteran who started a 24-hour vigil to protest being denied benefits by the Veterans Administration. He took up individual action in Lafayette Park, directly across the street from the national VA headquarters, and immediately following his ninth denial. He carried a sign reading: "I will stay here until I get my VA rights." The Appeals court agreed that his sleeping was expressive enough to deserve protection under the First Amendment, but also found his to be "unusual circumstances"—a phrase that probably led to its relative lack of attention in future jurisprudence. Abney was allowed to continue his protest, which he did for more than twenty years, later relocating to the Capitol steps, under which he lived in a cardboard box. Kunstler, "The Right to Occupy," 1000–101.

71. *CCNV v. Watt I* (MacKinnon, Memorandum)

72. "'Reaganville' Folds Up After 4-Month Protest," *New York Times*, March 21, 1982, A33.

73. 47 Fed.Reg.24,299–306 (codified at 36 C.F.R. Secs. 50.10, 50.27, 1982), quoted in CCNV v. Watt, 703 F.2d 586 (D.C. Cir. 1983), note 4 (hereafter *CCNV v. Watt II*); "Sleeping Banned in Tent City"; Robert D. Hershey Jr., Lynn Rosellini, "Briefing: A Right to Sleep?" *New York Times*, December 28, 1982, A20.

74. *CCNV v. Watt II*. The Court also noted that the new 1982 regulations allowed a new set of VVAW protestors to sleep on the Mall without tents and permitted other groups to pitch symbolic tents without sleeping. As such, the new regulations implied that sleeping becomes "impermissible 'camping' when it is done within any temporary structure."

75. *CCNV v. Watt II* (Scalia, dissenting; Ginsberg, concurring); *CCNV v. Watt II*.

76. Oral argument at 35:50, *Clark v. CCNV*.

77. Oral argument at 6:34, *Clark v. CCNV*.

78. *Clark v. CCNV*. In deciding on the fairness of the regulation of camping as expressive conduct the Justices relied on precedent for "reasonable time, place, or manner restrictions" and what was known as the O'Brien test—a multifactor scrutiny meant to ensure that the restriction did not focus on the content, was narrowly tailored, protected a significant government interest, and allowed alternative

channels for communication. *Abney* was not cited in White's majority opinion. *Clark v. CCNV*, note 8; Olson, "Homelessness as Political Theater," 114–16.

79. James B. Putney, "Clark v. Community for Creative Non-Violence: First Amendment Safeguards—Their Sum Is Less Than Their Parts," *University of Miami Law Review* 39, no. 997 (1985): 1003.

80. *Clark v. CCNV* (Burger, concurring); oral argument at 17:21, *Clark v. CCNV*; Putney, "Clark v. Community," 999.

81. *Clark v. CCNV* (Marshall, dissenting); Oral argument at 40:06, *Clark v. CCNV*. The case Marshall obliquely referenced, Brown v. Louisiana, 383 U.S. 131 (1966), was cited in *CCNV v. Watt II*, which compared Reaganville to the "'reproachful presence' of civil rights activists protesting segregation in a silent vigil in a public library" and found the two to be "identical in both concept and purpose." *CCNV v. Watt II*; Kunstler, "The Right to Occupy," 1003, 1006.

82. *Clark v. CCNV* (Marshall, dissenting).

83. *Clark v. CCNV; Clark v. CCNV* (Marshall, dissenting).

84. Oral argument at 9:28, 29:39, 46:06, *Clark v. CCNV*.

85. *Clark v. CCNV* (Burger concurring); *Clark v. CCNV*.

86. Oral argument at 41:46, *Clark v. CCNV*.

87. Nicholas M. May, "Fourth Amendment Challenges to 'Camping' Ordinances: The Government Acquiescence Doctrine as a Legal Strategy to Force Legislative Solutions to Homelessness," *Connecticut Public Interest Law Journal* 8, no. 1 (Fall–Winter 2008): 113–35; Rob Teir, "Restoring Order in Public Spaces," *Texas Review of Law and Politics* 2, no. 2 (Spring 1998): 255–91; Harry Simon, "Towns Without Pity: A Constitutional and Historical Analysis of Official Efforts to Drive Homeless Persons from American Cities," *Tulane Law Review* 66, no. 631 (March 1992): 631-76; "5-6-10 Camping or Lodging on Property Without Consent," The City of Boulder Revised B.R.C. (1981), http://www.colocode.com/boulder2/chapter5-6.htm; Jeremy P. Meyer, "Effect of Camping Bans Debated as Denver Considers Ordinance," *Denver Post*, April 22, 2012, http://www.denverpost.com/politics/ci_20452293/effect-camping-bans-colorado-debated-denver-ordinance.

88. Katharine Q. Seelye, "Sacramento and Its Riverside Tent City," New York Times Blog, *New York Times*, March 11, 2009, http://thelede.blogs.nytimes.com/2009/03/11/tent-city-report/?apage=2;"Tent City in Sacramento, California," *The Guardian*, March 20, 2009, http://www.guardian.co.uk/world/gallery/2009/mar/20/tent-city-homeless-sacramento-california; John D. Sutter, "In a Slump, Camping Comes into Vogue," CNN.com, March 26, 2009, http://www.cnn.com/2009/TRAVEL/03/26/camping.economy.index.html.

89. Erik Devaney, "Occupy Providence Camp Unoccupied at Night? Police Use Infrared Technology to See How Many Protesters Stay Overnight in Tents," *New England Post* (Quincy, MA), November 9, 2011, http://www.newenglandpost.com/2011/11/09/occupy-providence-camp-unoccupied-night-police-infrared-technology-protesters-stay-overnight-tents/; Meyer, "Effect of Camping Bans";

Kunstler, "The Right to Occupy," 1013–16; Erica Meltzer, "Occupy Boulder: Police Violated Constitution By Opening Campers' Tent Flaps," *Boulder (CO) Daily Camera*, January 23, 2012, http://www.dailycamera.com/letters/ci_19801019; John Aguilar, "Denver Initiative 300: Effort to End Camping Ban Fails by a Wide Margin," *Denver Post*, May 7, 2019, https://www.denverpost.com/2019/05/07/camping-ban-denver-homeless-initiative-300/.

90. Eric Verlo, "Occupy Denver Introduces Protest Tent," Not My Tribe blog, October 19, 2011) http://notmytribe.com/2011/pic-occupydenver-introduces-the-protest-tent-828599.html; "#OccupyCal Protesters Circumvent Order Not to Post Tents By Floating Them Above Sproul Hall," *abc7newsBayArea*, Twitter Feed, November 18, 2011, https://twitpic.com/7fmbla.

91. Complaint, *Henke v. Interior;* NPS, "Help Us Preserve"; Henke, et. al. v. Dept. of Interior, 842 F.Supp.2d 54 (D.D.C. 2012); Kunstler, "The Right to Occupy," 1007–18. Precedent did exist for making Fourth Amendment claims for tents, although they had previously been more linked to functional rather than protest camping. See May, "Fourth Amendment Challenges"; Colorado v. Schaefer, No. 97SA142 (Colo. Supreme Court, 1997). For a fuller review of the Colorado case, see Phoebe S. K. Young, "'Bring Tent: The Occupy Movement and the Politics of Public Nature," in *Rendering Nature: Animals, Bodies, Places, Politics*, ed. Marguerite S. Shaffer and Phoebe S. K. Young (Philadelphia: University of Pennsylvania Press, 2015), 303–304.

92. *Henke et. al. v. Interior.* It is clear from a ream of documents released through a Freedom of Information Act request, that NPS officials tried hard to take Occupy and its message quite seriously, as well as consulting pertinent legal decisions and opinions, including those from *Clark v. CCNV*. See NPS Occupy Documents.

93. US Congress, *Hearing on McPherson Square* (questions by Trey Gowdy, R-SC and Darrell Issa, R-CA). Both Gowdy and Issa at different points insinuated that Jarvis was being instructed to ignore the law for political reasons, accusing the Obama administration of giving Occupy unfairly favorable treatment, a conspiracy theory for which there was no evidence, and which Jarvis adamantly denied. Meredith Somers, "Issa Seeks Political Answers on Occupiers; Federal Decisions About Law at Issue," *Washington (DC) Times*, December 14, 2011, A16.

94. US Congress, *Hearing on McPherson Square* (statement of Occupy D.C., read into the record by Danny Davis, D-IL, and statement of Jarvis). As no representative from Occupy was allowed to testify in person, Davis read the group's statement into the record.

95. US Congress, *Hearing on McPherson Square* (statement of Jarvis).; Aubrey Whelan, "Occupy DC Among Last Camps Standing," *Washington (DC) Examiner*, December 21, 2011, 4.

96. US Congress, *Hearing on McPherson Square* (questions by Gowdy and Issa). Gowdy also expressed frustration that Occupy would be allowed to camp where the Boy Scouts could not. He did not seem to be aware that the Boy Scouts had in fact been

allowed to use the Mall for a Jamboree in 1937. Both the VVAW and the CCNV cited the Jamboree as evidence that the government was privileging recreational over protest encampments. That argument did not make much headway in those cases, though it did contribute to the push toward content-neutral restrictions.

97. US Congress, *Hearing on McPherson Square* (questions by Gowdy and testimony by Jarvis); "Occupy Washington, D.C., McPherson Square Permit Decision," video, at 1:36:43.

98. US Congress, *Hearing on McPherson Square* (questions by Gowdy and Issa).

99. US Congress, *Hearing on McPherson Square* (questions by Issa and testimony by Jarvis).

100. US Congress, *Hearing on McPherson Square* (questions by Eleanor Holmes Norton, Congressional Delegate, D-DC); Eleanor Holmes Norton, quoted in, Benjamin Freed, "Congress Tries to Define Camping," *Dcist.com*, January 24, 2012, https://dcist.com/story/12/01/24/congress-tries-to-define-camping-at/.

101. Carter DeWitt to Teresa Chambers, US Park Police Chief, and Bob Vogel, Superintendent National Mall and Memorial Parks, email, November 22, 2011, NPS Occupy Documents; Liz Farmer, "Turf War in McPherson Square," *Washington (DC) Examiner,* October 21, 2011, http://washingtonexaminer.com/article/119538; Freed, "Congress Tries to Define." The city at one point tried to consolidate all the protestors at Freedom Plaza to facilitate the "cleanup and restoration of McPherson Square," but Occupiers from both sites rejected the idea. Somers, "For D.C. Occupy"; Annie Gowen and Jimm Phillips, "District's Two Occupy Camps Headed Toward McPherson Square Merger," *Washington Post,* April 7, 2012, B3.

102. Farmer, "Turf War"; US Congress, *Hearing on McPherson Square* (questions by Issa). Measuring the value of protest in terms of its economic cost-benefit ratio was becoming common in the neoliberal context. Protests against the Iraq War in 2003 came under fire even by ostensible allies for the municipal cost incurred. See "SF Protest Brings Debate on Wage of Din," *New York Times,* June 23, 2003, A14; Wendy Brown, "Neo-liberalism and the End of Liberal Democracy," *Theory & Event* 7, no. 1 (Fall 2003): n.p., doi:10.1353/tae.2003.0020.

103. Emphasis from the original, takomabibelot [Jim Kuhn], [We are not camping], photograph, November 15, 2011, *Flickr.com*, http://www.flickr.com/photos/takomabibelot/6349545090/.

104. Stephen Ewen, Occupy* Posters, owsposters.tumblr.com, November 1, 2011, http://37.media.tumblr.com/tumblr_luosqtjPr31r4k4dho1_r1_1280.png.

105. Monica Hesse and Paul Farhi, "A Protest That's Not in the Bag," *Washington Post,* January 31, 2012, C1.

106. Phillip Kennicott, "A Square Gets Hip: In McPherson Square, Occupy D.C. Creates a Vibrant Brand of Urbanism," *Washington Post*, November 10, 2011, C1; Christopher Hawthorne, "Tents' Time: The Occupy Camps Play into Notions of Civic Space," *Los Angeles Times,* December 18, 2011, E8. For a different architectural

interpretation of Occupy as urban camping, see Charlie Hailey, "Occuper c'est camper/Occupy is Camping," in *Heteropolis*, ed. Marie-Pier Boucher, Jean-Maxime Dufresne, Gema Melgar, and Jean-François Prost (Montreal: Adaptive Actions, 2013), 46–53.

107. John Emerson, "Take Back Wall Street," *Social Design Notes* blog, October 7, 2011, http://backspace.com/notes/2011/10/occupy-wall-street-posters.php; Charles R. Geisst, *Wall Street: A History, from its Beginnings to the Fall of Enron* (New York: Oxford University Press, 1997).

108. Montano, quoted in Adrienne Keene, "Representing the Native Presence in the 'Occupy Wall Street' Narrative," *Native Appropriations*, October 12, 2011, https://nativeappropriations.com/2011/10/representing-the-native-presence-in-the-occupy-wall-street-narrative.html; Ryan Hayes, "(Un)Occupy Canada," *Art & Social Movements*, blog, November 15, 2011, http://www.blog.ryanhay.es/unoccupy-canada/; "Decolonize the 99%" *Ella Baker Center for Human Rights*, November 9, 2011, https://ellabakercenter.org/blog/2011/11/decolonize-the-99; Karen R. Humes, Nicholas A. Jones, and Roberto R. Ramirez, *Overview of Race and Hispanic Origin: 2010* (ser. 2010 Census Briefs), United States Census Bureau, March 2011, C2010BR-02.

109. Whelan, "Occupy DC Among,"; Aubrey Whelan "Occupy DC Vows to Stay Despite Eviction Calls by Mayor, Congressional Scrutiny," *Washington (DC) Examiner,* January 19, 2012, 10.

110. Annie Gowen and Paul Duggan, "Occupy D.C. Deadline Passes Peacefully," *Washington Post,* January 31, 2012, A1; Annie Gowen, "Park Police Clean Up Occupy D.C.'s Encampment at McPherson Square," *Washington Post,* February 5, 2012, A10; Annie Gowen, "After Raid, Occupiers Otherwise Engaged," *Washington Post,* February 28, 2012, B1; Aubrey Whelan, "Occupy DC Skirts Camping Ban," *Washington Examiner,* March 9, 2012, 11; Annie Gowen, "Renovation Underway at Occupy D.C. Protest Site," *Washington Post,* April 27, 2012, B3; Annie Gowen, "Occupy D.C. Protesters Return," *Washington Post,* June 29, 2012, B5.

111. Katrina vanden Heuvel, "Time to Run for Office, 99 Percenters," *Washington Post*, January 31, 2012; Minnesota occupier, quoted in Hesse and Farhi, "A Protest That's Not"; Hesse and Farhi, "A Protest That's Not"; Austermuhle, "Four Months In."

112. Sarah Gaby and Neal Caren, "The Rise of Inequality: How Social Movements Shape Discursive Fields," *Mobilization: An International Quarterly* 21, no. 4 (December 2016): 413–29; Schneider, "It Seems As If," 153; Hesse and Farhi, "A Protest That's Not"; Annie Gowen, "Occupy Protesters Take Over House in Northwest," *Washington Post,* July 20, 2012, B3; "Resist. Insist. Stand Together. Build. Never Surrender," OccupyTheory.org, http://occupytheory.org, (accessed March 30, 2013); Judith Butler, "So What Are The Demands?" *Tidal: Occupy Theory, Occupy Strategy* 2 (March 2012): 9.

113. *Brown v. Louisiana* (Black, dissenting); US Congress, *Hearing on McPherson Square* (questions by Gowdy); Kunstler, "The Right to Occupy," 1018–19.
114. Kunstler, "The Right to Occupy," 1019.

EPILOGUE

1. Emphasis from the original, REI Co-op, "Let's Camp," email to subscribers, May 31, 2017, http://reallygoodemails.com/wp-content/uploads/the-campfire-is-calling.html; REI Co-op, "Camping Is an Instinct," post, May 30, 2017, https://www.facebook.com/REI/videos/10155357077811484/.
2. For orders defining outdoor recreation as an "essential activity," see, for example: Reginald Hardwick, "What is Essential/Prohibited Under IL Stay At Home Order?" *Illinois Newsroom*, March 21, 2020, https://illinoisnewsroom.org/what-is-essential-prohibited-under-il-stay-at-home-order/; "Governor Bullock Issues Stay at Home Directive to Slow the Spread of COVID-19," Montana.gov, March 26, 2020, https://dphhs.mt.gov/aboutus/news/2020/stayathomedirective; Tammy Wells, "Maine IF&W Defines 'Recreation' Under Stay-At-Home Order," *Portland (ME) Press Herald*, April 2, 2020, https://www.pressherald.com/2020/04/02/maine-ifw-defines-recreation-under-stay-at-home-order/; Alicia Lee, "These States Have Implemented Stay-At-Home Orders," *CNN.com*, April 7, 2020, https://www.cnn.com/2020/03/23/us/coronavirus which-states-stay-at-home-order-trnd/index.html.
3. REI, "8 Indoor Camping Tips," Facebook post, April 17, 2020, https://www.facebook.com/REI/posts/10158456438566484; Sarah Grothjan, "8 Tips for Turning Your Living Space Into Your Very Own Campsite," *REI Co-op Journal*, April 3, 2020, https://www.rei.com/blog/camp/indoor-camping-ideas; Christine Ryan, "Making the Most of Staying at Home," *New York Times*, April 3, 2020, https://www.nytimes.com/2020/04/03/travel/staycation-gear.html.
4. Catherine Newman, "Pitch a Tent in Your Own Backyard," *New York Times*, May 15, 2020, D3. See also Kit Dillon, "What to Buy to Create Your Own Backyard Campground," *New York Times*, May 15, 2020, https://www.nytimes.com/2020/05/15/smarter-living/what-to-buy-to-create-your-own-backyard-campground.html and Melanie D.G. Kaplan, "A Guide to Backyard Camping," *Washington Post*, May 21, 2020, https://www.washingtonpost.com/lifestyle/travel/a-guide-to-backyard-camping-turns-out-you-dont-have-to-go-very-far-to-get-away-from-it-all/2020/05/21/9e035822-958a-11ea-91d7-cf4423d47683_story.html.
5. "The 18 New Rules of Camping," *Outside*, June 22, 2020, https://www.outsideonline.com/2414855/new-spirit-camping. See also, Danielle Braff, "Camping, With Fewer People, Becomes a Pandemic Pastime," *Washington Post*, June 5, 2020, https://www.washingtonpost.com/lifestyle/travel/camping-is-back-with-fewer-people-and-activities-and-more-cleaning-and-waiting/2020/06/04/22adce7c-a51c-11ea-b619-3f9133bbb482_story.html; Curtis Tate, "Expert: Camping May be Best Travel

Choice," *USA Today*, June 15, 2020, 4D; Dan England, "Ditch Campgrounds. Here's Your Basic Guide to Dispersed Camping in Colorado," *Boulder (CO) Daily Camera*, June 18, 2020, https://www.dailycamera.com/2020/06/18/ditch-campgrounds-heres-your-basic-guide-to-dispersed-camping-in-colorado/; Jason Blevins, "Coronavirus Has Led to Record Crowds on Colorado's Public Lands," *Colorado Sun*, July 2, 2020, https://coloradosun.com/2020/07/02/coronavirus-record-crowds-on-colorado-public-lands/; Elaine Glusac, "Worried About Social Distancing When Traveling? Join the Crowd and Rent an R.V.," *New York Times*, June 28, 2020, D3; Nellie Bowles, "The #Vanlife is Booming," *New York Times*, July 3, 2020, B1.

6. John D. Sutter, "In a Slump, Camping Comes into Vogue," *CNN.com*, March 26, 2009, http://edition.cnn.com/2009/TRAVEL/03/26/camping.economy/index. html. Federal, state and private campground operators reported drops in visitation in the 1990s and early 2000s, but claims that camping was in permanent decline proved premature as numbers rebounded in the 2010s. Paul Nussbaum, "For Many Vacationers, Lure of Campfire is Dimming," *Philadelphia Inquirer*, August 9, 2004, 1; Christopher Ketcham, "The Death of Backpacking," *High Country News*, July 21, 2014, 38–39; Terence Young, *Heading Out: A History of American Camping* (Ithaca, NY: Cornell University Press, 2017), 300–303.

7. Christopher Elliott, "Everything You Need to Know About the National Park Closures," *National Geographic*, October 4, 2013, https://news.nationalgeographic. com/news/2013/10/131003-national-park-closures-government-shutdown/; Garance Franke-Ruta, "How the National Parks Became the Biggest Battleground in the Shutdown," *Atlantic*, October 11, 2013, https://www.theatlantic.com/poli-tics/archive/2013/10/how-the-national-parks-became-the-biggest-battleground-in-the-shutdown/280439/.

8. John P. Herron, "The Call in the Wild: Nature, Technology and Environmental Politics," in *The Political Culture of the New West*, ed. Jeff Roche (Lawrence: University Press of Kansas, 2008), 310–31; Stephanie Rosenbloom, "Goodbye Pup Tent, Hello Wi-Fi," *New York Times*, August 27, 2017, TR-3; Monica Houghton, "Why Camping Is Rising in Popularity, Especially Among Millennials," *Forbes*, April 16, 2018, https://www.forbes.com/sites/monicahoughton/2018/04/16/why-camping-is-rising-in-popularity-especially-among-millennials/#7f0359f516c0; Helene Stapinski, "The Rise of the Stressed Out Urban Camper," *New York Times*, July 6, 2018, https://www.nytimes.com/2018/07/06/nyregion/the-rise-of-the-stressed-out-urban-camper.html?searchResultPosition=1; Megan Barber, "One Industry Millennials Aren't Killing: Camping," *Curbed*, April 24, 2019, https://www.curbed. com/2019/4/24/18514077/campers-millennials-camping-van-life-glamping.

9. Katie Jackson, "Why You Should Care about the 'Find Your Park' Campaign," *Outside*, April 30, 2015, https://www.outsideonline.com/1969631/why-you-should-care-about-find-your-park-campaign; Lena McDowall, Deputy Director for Management and Administration, NPS, US Department of the Interior,

"National Parks Next Generation," Statement before the Senate Energy & Natural Resources Subcommittee on National Parks, September 27, 2017, https://www. doi.gov/ocl/national-parks-next-generation; Glenn Nelson, "Why Are Our Parks So White?" *New York Times*, July 10, 2015, SR4; Glenn Nelson, "A Backup in the National Parks Jobs Pipeline," *High Country News*, August 22, 2016, 14–18; National Park Service, "National Park Service Comprehensive Survey of the American Public, 2008–2009, Racial and Ethnic Diversity of National Park System Visitors and Non-Visitors," Natural Resource Report NPS/NRSS/SSD/NRR—2011/432, July 2011; Jodi Peterson, "Parks for All?" *High Country News*, May 19, 2014, 10–15.

10. Jarvis quoted in Sam Schipani, "Former Head of National Park Service Talks Conservation's Future," *Sierra*, March 17, 2018, https://www.sierraclub.org/sierra/jonathan-jarvis-national-park-service-the-future-of-conservation.

11. Jessica Bruder, *Nomadland: Surviving America in the Twenty-First Century* (New York: Norton, 2017), 95–114; Jessica Bruder, "Meet the CamperForce, Amazon's Nomadic Retiree Army," *Wired*, September 14, 2017, https://www.wired. com/story/meet-camperforce-amazons-nomadic-retiree-army/; "CamperForce," Amazon.com, https://www.amazondelivers.jobs/about/camperforce/ (accessed July 15, 2019).

12. Bruder, *Nomadland*, 3–28, 46–53; Cally Carswell, "The Privatization of Public Campground Management," *High Country News*, July 18, 2014, https://www.hcn. org/articles/the-privatization-of-public-campground-management; Bret Weber, "The North Dakota Man Camp Project: The Archaeology of Home in the Bakken Oil Fields," *Historical Archaeology* 51, no. 2 (June 2017): 267–87.

13. Kizzy Benedict, "Estimating the Number of Homeless in America," *The Data Face*, January 21, 2018, http://thedataface.com/2018/01/public-health/american-homelessness. Figures for New York homeless populations calculated from "Number of Homeless People in NYC Shelters Each Night," Coalition for the Homeless, https://www.coalitionforthehomeless.org/facts-about-homelessness/ (accessed July 10, 2020). Their database appears to count only shelter populations, not outdoor encampments, but the numbers are suggestive of the broader scope and trend.

14. Jill Cowan, "Homeless Populations Are Surging in Los Angeles. Here's Why," *New York Times*, June 4, 2019, https://www.nytimes.com/2019/06/05/us/los-angeles-homeless-population.html; Ginia Bellafante, "A War on Homelessness, or the Homeless?" *New York Times*, May 31, 2019, MB3; Leanna Garfield, "A Map of America's Homeless Problem Reveals the Best and Worst States for Affordable Housing," *Business Insider*, March 22, 2018, https://www.businessinsider.com/affordable-housing-crisis-homelessness-us-2018-3; Christine Britschgi, "While Homeless Population Balloons, San Francisco Residents Use Environmental Lawsuit to Stop Homeless Shelter," *Reason*, July 15, 2019, https://reason.com/2019/07/15/while-homeless-population-balloons-san-francisco-residents-use-environmental-lawsuit-to-stop-homeless-shelter/.

15. Lee K. Cerveny and Joshua W.R. Baur, "Homelessness and Nonrecreational Camping on National Forests and Grasslands in the United States: Law Enforcement Perspectives and Regional Trends," *Journal of Forestry* 118, no. 2 (March 2020): 139–53; Tracy Ross, "Danger in the Forest," *5280*, January 8, 2018, https://www.5280.com/2018/01/danger-in-the-forest/; John Wildermuth, "Santa Cruz to Test Housing the Homeless at State Parks," *SFGate*, March 29, 1996, https://www.sfgate.com/news/article/Santa-Cruz-to-Test-Housing-the-Homeless-At-State-2988508.php.

16. James B. Stewart, "A Black Friday Campout: As Traditional as Turkey," *New York Times*, November 21, 2014, B1; Jonathan Wolfe, "Campsites in the Heart of New York City," *New York Times*, May 29, 2015, C29; "Family Camping: Queens," New York City Department of Parks & Recreation, https://www.nycgovparks.org/events/2019/07/20/family-camping-queens (accessed July 25, 2019); NYC Parks, Urban Park Rangers, https://www.nycgovparks.org/reg/rangers (accessed July 25, 2019). For more on varieties of urban camping, recreational and otherwise, see Phoebe S. Kropp Young, "Sleeping Outside: The Political Natures of Urban Camping," in *Cities and Nature in the American West*, ed. Char Miller (Reno: University of Nevada Press, 2010), 171–91.

17. "Supreme Court Lets Martin v. Boise Stand: Homeless Persons Cannot Be Punished for Sleeping in Absence of Alternatives," *The National Law Center on Homelessness & Poverty*, December 16, 2019, https://nlchp.org/supreme-court-martin-v-boise/; Martin v. City of Boise, 902 F.3d 1031 (9th Cir. 2018); Sam Lounsberry, "Boulder Officials Defend Urban Camping Ban," *Boulder (CO) Daily Camera*, December 30, 2019, https://www.dailycamera.com/2019/12/30/boulder-officials-defend-urban-camping-ban/.

18. Janie Har and Terence Chea, "San Francisco Sanctions Once-Shunned Homeless Encampments," *AP News*, May 22, 2020, https://apnews.com/a1acce66bedb3310 f39a5c389d849461; "Coronavirus: Here's How Putting California's Homeless in Hotels Actually Works," *San Jose (CA) Mercury News*, April 11, 2020, https://www.mercurynews.com/2020/04/11/coronavirus-heres-how-putting-californias-homeless-in-hotels-actually-works/; Rae Solomon, "Emergency Preventative Housing Begins for Homeless Population in Denver," KUNC, April 16, 2020, https://www.kunc.org/post/emergency-preventative-housing-begins-homeless-population-denver; Annie Nova, "Looming Evictions May Soon Make 28 Million Homeless in U.S., Expert Says," CNBC, July 10, 2020, https://www.cnbc.com/2020/07/10/looming-evictions-may-soon-make-28-million-homeless-expert-says.html.

19. Lizabeth Cohen, "A Market Failure in Affordable Housing," *New York Times*, July 11, 2019, A27.

20. "Sacred Stone Camp History," *Sacred Stone Village*, https://www.sacredstonevillage. net (accessed July 2, 2019); Jack Healy, "Occupying the Prairie: Tensions Rise as Tribes Move to Block a Pipeline," *New York Times*, August 24, 2016, A9; Leah Donnella, "At

the Sacred Stone Camp, Tribes and Activists Join Forces to Protect the Land," *NPR.org*, September 10, 2016, https://www.npr.org/sections/codeswitch/2016/09/10/493110892/at-the-sacred-stone-camp-a-coalition-joins-forces-to-protect-the-land.

21. Allard quoted in Bill McKibben, "A Pipeline Fight and America's Dark Past," *New Yorker*, September 6, 2016. For more on Allard's perspective, the experience in the camp community, and the history and theory of Indigenous resistance in relation to Standing Rock, see Nick Estes, ed. *Standing with Standing Rock: Voices from the #NoDAPL Movement* (Minneapolis: University of Minnesota Press, 2019); Nick Estes, *Our History is the Future: Standing Rock Versus the Dakota Access Pipeline, and the Long Tradition of Indigenous Resistance* (London: Verso, 2019).

22. Alene Tchekmedyian, "Pipeline Protesters Stand their Ground," *Los Angeles Times*, February 23, 2017, A6; Jacey Fortin and Lisa Friedman, "Dakota Pipeline is Ordered Shut Down During Environmental Review," *New York Times*, July 7, 2020, B5.

23. "Sacred Stone Camp Returns," *Sacred Stone Village*, March 19, 2018, https://www.sacredstonevillage.net/latest-news/2018/3/19/sacred-stone-camp-returns; Tracy L. Barnett, "From Encampment to Ecovillage at Standing Rock," *Resilience*, September 5, 2019, https://www.resilience.org/stories/2019-09-05/from-encampment-to-ecovillage-at-standing-rock/; Nick Estes and Jaskiran Dhillon, "The Black Snake, #NoDAPL, and the Rise of a People's Movement," in Estes, *Standing With Standing Rock*, 1–11; Naomi Klein, "The Lesson from Standing Rock: Organizing and Resistance Can Win," *Nation*, December 4, 2016, https://www.thenation.com/article/the-lesson-from-standing-rock-organizing-and-resistance-can-win/.

24. Dakin Andone, Sarah Jorgensen, and Polo Sandoval, "'This Is Our Last Stand.' Protestors on Mauna Kea Dig in Their Heels," *CNN.com*, July 22, 2019, https://www.cnn.com/2019/07/21/us/hawaii-mauna-kea-protests/index.html; Michael Brestovansky, "Protesters, Kim Reach Agreement to Reopen Maunakea Access Road," *Hawaii Tribune-Herald*, December 27, 2019, https://www.westhawaiitoday.com/2019/12/27/hawaii-news/protesters-kim-reach-agreement-to-reopen-maunakea access road/. For connections between Standing Rock and Mauna Kea protests, see David Uahikeaikalei'ohu Maile, "Threats of Violence: Refusing the Thirty Meter Telescope and Dakota Access Pipeline," in Estes, *Standing with Standing Rock*, 328–43.

25. Michael Sainato, "Laid Off and Owed Pay: The Kentucky Miners Blocking Coal Trains," *Guardian*, September 18, 2019, https://www.theguardian.com/us-news/2019/sep/17/harlan-county-coalmine-train-protest; Mihir Zaveri, "Blackjewel Coal Miners to Get Millions in Back Pay After Train Blockade," *New York Times*, October 24, 2019, https://www.nytimes.com/2019/10/24/us/blackjewel-coal-miners.html.

26. Alan Feuer and Juliana Kim, "Occupy City Hall's New Life as Homeless Camp," *New York Times*, July 10, 2020, A22; Juliana Kim, "'Occupy City Hall' Protesters Vow to Stay Until Police Budgets Are Cut," *New York Times*, June 28, 2020,

A18; Shanel Dawson, "'Occupy City Hall' Activists Say Their Movement Isn't Temporary," *NY1*, July 2, 2020, https://www.ny1.com/nyc/all-boroughs/inside-city-hall/2020/07/03/occupy-city-hall-activists-discuss-the-movement-s-future-.

27. Richard Louv, *Last Child in the Woods: Saving Our Children from Nature-Deficit Disorder* (Chapel Hill, NC: Algonquin Books, 2005), 36.

28. Florence Williams, *The Nature Fix: Why Nature Makes Us Happier, Healthier, and More Creative* (New York: Norton, 2017); Gretchen Reynolds, "How Walking in Nature Changes the Brain," New York Times Blog, *New York Times*, July 22, 2015, https://well.blogs.nytimes.com/2015/07/22/how-nature-changes-the-brain/. For an example of a clinically oriented study, see Sara L. Warber, Ashley A. DeHudy, Matthew F. Bialko, Melissa R. Marselle, and Katherine N. Irvine, "Addressing 'Nature-Deficit Disorder': A Mixed Methods Pilot Study of Young Adults Attending a Wilderness Camp," *Evidence-based Complementary and Alternative Medicine* (2015): Article ID 651827, doi:10.1155/2015/651827.

29. "Why Does Wilderness Matter? This Infographic Explains," blog, *The Wilderness Society*, April 22, 2013, https://www.wilderness.org/articles/blog/why-does-wilderness-matter-infographic-explains; Elizabeth Dickinson, "The Misdiagnosis: Rethinking Nature-deficit Disorder," *Environmental Communication*, 7, no. 3 (2013): 315–35. Dickinson notes that many frontline staff, like USFS rangers, were familiar with Louv's book, encouraged her and others to read it, and recited its diagnosis of the problem and suggested remedies.

30. Aaron Reuben, "Special Report: The Nature Cure—Science's Newest Miracle Drug is Free," *Outside*, May 2019, cover, 76–85; Kate Siber, "The National Park Service is Your New HMO," *Outside*, May 2019, https://www.outsideonline.com/2393668/national-park-service-your-new-hmo; Kate Siber, "The Insurers That Pay You for Time Spend Outside," *Outside*, n.d., https://www.outsideonline.com/2393666/we-got-you-covered (accessed July 15, 2019); Christine Yu, "Health Companies Want to Reward You for Going Outside," *Outside*, n.d., https://www.outsideonline.com/2394563/health-companies-want-reward-you-going-outside (accessed July 15, 2019); Scott Rosenfield, "STUDY: The Camping Cure," *Outside*, August 2, 2013, https://www.outsideonline.com/1798571/study-camping-cure.

31. Meg St-Esprit McKivigan, "'Nature Deficit Disorder' Is Really a Thing," *New York Times*, June 23, 2020, https://www.nytimes.com/2020/06/23/parenting/nature-health-benefits-coronavirus-outdoors.html; Louv, quoted in McKivigan, "'Nature Deficit Disorder.'"

32. Sarah Schrank, *Free and Natural: Nudity and the American Cult of the Body* (Philadelphia: University of Pennsylvania Press, 2019).

33. W. E. B. Du Bois, *Darkwater: Voices From Within the Veil* (New York: Harcourt, Brace and Howe, 1920), 30; Anthony William Wood, "The Erosion of the Racial Frontier: Settler Colonialism and the History of Black Montana, 1880–1930, (M.A. Thesis, Montana State University, Bozeman, 2018), 109–11. The Central Park "birdwatching-while-Black" incident provides a revealing contemporary

episode. See Troy Closson, "Amy Cooper's 911 Call, and What's Happened Since," *New York Times*, July 8, 2020, https://www.nytimes.com/2020/07/08/nyregion/amy-cooper-false-report-charge.html.

34. "18 New Rules"; Jenni Gritters, "What's the Ideal Amount of Time to Spend Outside Each week?" REI Co-Op blog, January 13, 2020, https://www.rei.com/blog/news/this-is-the-optimal-amount-of-time-to-spend-outside-each-week; Mathew P. White, Ian Alcock, James Grellier, Benedict W. Wheeler, Terry Hartig, Sara L. Warber, Angie Bone, Michael H. Depledge, and Lora E. Fleming, "Spending At Least 120 Minutes a Week in Nature is Associated with Good Health and Wellbeing," *Nature: Scientific Reports* 9, no. 7730 (June 13, 2019), https://doi.org/10.1038/s41598-019-44097-3; Richard White, "'Are You an Environmentalist or Do You Work for a Living?': Work and Nature," in *Uncommon Ground: Rethinking the Human Place in Nature*, ed. William Cronon (New York: Norton, 1987), 171–85.

35. "Camping is Up in the U.S., Trend Expected to Continue as Millennials Seek the Positive Health Impacts of Time Spent Outdoors" *Business Wire*, March 15, 2017, https://www.businesswire.com/news/home/20170315005391/en/Camping-U.S.-Trend-Expected-Continue-Millennials-Seek; Wes Siler, "For Veterans, Outdoor Therapy Could Become Law," *Outside Magazine*, n.d., https://www.outsideonline.com/2394553/veterans-outdoor-therapy-could-become-law (accessed July 15, 2019).

36. Richard Louv, "EVERY CHILD NEEDS NATURE: 12 Questions About Equity & Capacity," *The Children and Nature Network*, December 9, 2013, https://www.childrenandnature.org/2013/12/09/every-child-needs-nature-12-questions-about-equity-and-capacity/; Amanda Machado, "My Experience on NOLS' First-Ever Leaders of Color Backpacking Trip," *REI Co-op Journal*, February 28, 2020, https://www.rei.com/blog/hike/my-experience-on-nols-first-ever-leaders-of-color-backpacking-trip; Sarah Jacquette Ray, *The Ecological Other: Environmental Exclusion in American Culture* (Tucson: University of Arizona Press, 2013); Robert C. Burns and Alan R. Graefe, "Constraints to Outdoor Recreation: Exploring the Effects of Disabilities on Perceptions and Participation," *Journal of Leisure Research* 39, no. 1 (2007): 156–81.

37. Wendy Brown, "Neo-liberalism and the End of Liberal Democracy," *Theory and Event* 7, no. 1 (2003): n.p.; Kean Birch, "What Exactly Is Neoliberalism?" *The Conversation* (November 2, 2017), https://theconversation.com/what-exactly-is-neoliberalism-84755. For deeper investigations of neoliberalism, see David Harvey, *A Brief History of Neoliberalism* (Oxford: Oxford University Press, 2007); Wendy Brown, *Undoing the Demos: Neoliberalism's Stealth Revolution* (New York: Zone Books, 2015). The economic and political aspects of liberalism did not historically work in lockstep. For example, states might maintain political liberal principles, such as protecting individual freedoms, but lean toward Keynesian or even social-democratic economics, as became the case in the New Deal era.

38. Outdoor Industry Association (OIA) and Southwick Associates, Inc., *The Outdoor Recreation Economy* (Boulder, CO: n.p., 2017), 18. Federal Government estimates ran significantly lower ($373.7 billion or 2% of GDP), but the fact that it was measuring this as an economic sector at all was due to the passage of the Outdoor Recreation Jobs and Economic Impact Act the previous year. Frederick Reimers, "Government Puts Outdoor Industry Size at $373 Billion" *Outside*, February 14, 2018, https://www.outsideonline.com/2281581/government-puts-outdoor-industry-size-673-billion; Jess Bernard, "Outdoor Recreation is 2.2 Percent of the U.S. Economy, New Report Finds," *REI Co-op Journal*, September 21, 2018, https://www.rei.com/blog/news/outdoor-recreation-is-2-2-percent-of-the-u-s-economy-new-report-finds.

39. OIA and Southwick Associates, *Outdoor Recreation Economy*, 3.

40. Stuart Hall, Doreen Massey, and Michael Rustin, "Framing Statement—After Neoliberalism: Analysing the Present," in *After Neoliberalism? The Kilburn Manifesto*, ed. Stuart Hall, Doreen Massey, and Michael Rustin (London: Lawrence & Wishart, 2015): 9–23.

41. Elissa Loughman, "Benefit Corporation Update," *Patagonia.com*, n.d. [ca. 2014], https://www.patagonia.com/stories/benefit-corporation-update-patagonia-passes-b-impact-assessment-improves-score-to-116/story-17871.html (accessed March 20, 2020); "About REI: Who We Are," *REI.com*, n.d. [2020], https://www.rei.com/about-rei (accessed March 20, 2020); Gregory L. Simon and Peter Alagona, "Contradictions at the Confluence of Commerce, Consumption and Conservation; Or, An REI Shopper Camps in the Forest, Does Anyone Notice?" *Geoforum* 45 (March 2013): 325–36.

42. David Kotz, "End of the Neoliberal Era? Crisis and Restructuring in American Capitalism," *New Left Review* 113 (September-October 2018): 29–55; Will Davies, "The Difficulty of 'Neoliberalism,'" Political Economic Research Centre blog, January 1, 2016, http://www.perc.org.uk/project_posts/the-difficulty-of-neoliberalism/; William Davies, *The Limits of Neoliberalism: Authority, Sovereignty and the Logic of Competition*, rev. ed. (London: Sage, 2017).

43. OIA and Southwick Associates, *Outdoor Recreation Economy*, 3.

44. Felicity Scott reflects intriguingly on these connections, drawing upon Hannah Arendt's analysis of the "internment camp" as "the only 'country' the world had to offer the stateless." In my view, the mechanism can also work the other direction: where occupants become effectively "stateless" by residing in such functional or enforced camps. Further, the upbeat version of the biological need argument has its troubling counterpart. Giorgio Agamben, building on Arendt's observation of camps as throwing "people back into a peculiar state of nature," explained camps as embodying a "state of exception" where political "power" can confront "pure biological life without any mediation." Arendt, "The Decline of the Nation State and the End of the Rights of Man," quoted in Scott, *Outlaw Territories: Environments of Insecurity/Architectures of Counterinsurgency* (New York: Zone Books, 2016), 163–64; Scott, *Outlaw Territories*, 163–64, 476n147; Agamben, "What Is a Camp?" in *Means Without End: Notes on Politics* (Minneapolis: University of Minnesota Press, 2000), 38–40.

Index

For the benefit of digital users, indexed terms that span two pages (e.g., 52–53) may, on occasion, appear on only one of those pages.

Figures and tables are indicated by italic *f* and *t*, respectively.